ROMAN CHRISTIANITY AND ROMAN STOICISM

Roman Christianity and Roman Stoicism

A Comparative Study of Ancient Morality

RUNAR M. THORSTEINSSON

OXFORD

UNIVERSITY PRESS

OXFORD
UNIVERSITY PRESS

Great Clarendon Street, Oxford OX2 6DP

Oxford University Press is a department of the University of Oxford.
It furthers the University's objective of excellence in research, scholarship,
and education by publishing worldwide in

Oxford New York

Auckland Cape Town Dar es Salaam Hong Kong Karachi
Kuala Lumpur Madrid Melbourne Mexico City Nairobi
New Delhi Shanghai Taipei Toronto

With offices in

Argentina Austria Brazil Chile Czech Republic France Greece
Guatemala Hungary Italy Japan South Korea Poland Portugal
Singapore Switzerland Thailand Turkey Ukraine Vietnam

Oxford is a registered trade mark of Oxford University Press
in the UK and in certain other countries

Published in the United States
by Oxford University Press Inc., New York

© Runar M. Thorsteinsson 2010

The moral rights of the author have been asserted

Database right Oxford University Press (maker)

Reprinted 2011

ISBN 978-0-19-957864-1

Printed in the United Kingdom by
Lightning Source UK Ltd., Milton Keynes

I dedicate this book to the loving memory of my father

IN MEMORIAM
Þorsteinn Björgvinsson
(1944–1988)

Preface

The immediate background of this study was a larger research project entitled 'Christian Identity—the First 100 Years', which was based at Lund University in Sweden and led by Professor Bengt Holmberg. The project ran roughly from 2003 to 2007, and included several scholars who were all active at Swedish universities at the time, in Lund, Göteborg, Linköping, and Örebro. The project was financed by The Bank of Sweden Tercentenary Foundation (Riksbankens Jubileumsfond). A résumé of some of the project's results can be found in the recently published book, *Exploring Early Christian Identity* (ed. B. Holmberg; WUNT 226; Tübingen: Mohr Siebeck, 2008).

A number of people have lent their hand to improve this study, and I greatly welcome this opportunity to express my gratitude to them in writing. First of all, I wish to thank my colleagues and friends in the 'Identity Project' for many helpful discussions and comments on my work, especially in its early stages. Thank you, Bengt Holmberg, Samuel Byrskog, Dieter Mitternacht, Mikael Tellbe, Fredrik Ivarsson, Rikard Roitto, Håkan Ulfgard, and Bo Brander. I also wish to thank the Senior New Testament Seminar at Lund University for commenting on earlier drafts of Chapters 3 and 4. I am especially grateful to Professor Birger Olsson, who, with his usual generosity, also commented on Chapter 7. Another truly generous scholar, Professor Troels Engberg-Pedersen at the University of Copenhagen, kindly read through the whole of Part III in its penultimate version and made many helpful comments and suggestions. For that I am deeply grateful. I am grateful, too, to Nicholas Meyer, Ph.D. student at McMaster University, who read the entire manuscript (or most of it) and greatly improved its language. Needless to say, any mistakes remain my own.

I wish to express my gratitude to The Bank of Sweden Tercentenary Foundation for the award of a research fellowship from 2003 to 2007 and thus for making this project possible. I am indebted to the Centre for Theology and Religious Studies at Lund University for providing me with the necessary space and tools to work on the project, and I am grateful to the staff at the Centre, especially Ann-Louise Svensson, for seeing to the various practical aspects of the project. Thanks are also due to the Swedish Research Council (Vetenskapsrådet) for a grant to enable the language revision of this book.

I am grateful to Oxford University Press for accepting this work for publication. I wish to thank the competent staff at OUP, as well as the three anonymous readers for OUP who commented on parts of this study and offered valuable advice.

There is a personal level to each scholarly work. I wish to express my deepest gratitude to my family. Thank you, Silla, Sigrún, and Dagur, for your constant love and support!

Runar M. Thorsteinsson
Lund, June 2009

Contents

PART III ROMAN CHRISTIANITY AND ROMAN
STOICISM: A COMPARISON

Abbreviations

Abbreviations of ancient texts follow the guidelines in *The SBL Handbook of Style: For Ancient Near Eastern, Biblical, and Early Christian Studies* (ed. P. H. Alexander et al.; Peabody MA: Hendrickson, 1999). Unless otherwise noted, references to non-biblical texts are from the LCL. As a rule, references to the 'Old Testament' follow the LXX. References to the NT follow NA²⁷. Unless otherwise noted, translations of NT texts are my own (with some aid from the standard English translations, esp. NRSV).

AB	Anchor Bible
AncPhil	*Ancient Philosophy*
ANRW	*Aufstieg und Niedergang der römischen Welt: Geschichte und Kultur Roms im Spiegel der neueren Forschung.* Edited by H. Temporini and W. Haase. Berlin, 1972–
ASV	*American Standard Version* (1901)
BASP	*Bulletin of the American Society of Papyrologists*
BZNW	Beihefte zur Zeitschrift für die neutestamentliche Wissenschaft
CB	*The Classical Bulletin*
CBQ	*Catholic Biblical Quarterly*
CBR	*Currents in Biblical Research*
ConBNT	Coniectanea biblica: New Testament Series
CP	*Classical Philology*
CQ	*The Classical Quarterly*
CurBS	*Currents in Research: Biblical Studies*
EIN	*Einheitsübersetzung* (1980)
ELB	*Revidierte Elberfelder* (1993)
ESCJ	Études sur le christianisme et le judaïsme
FC	Fathers of the Church. Washington, DC, 1947–
FN	*Filología Neotestamentaria*
FRLANT	Forschungen zur Religion und Literatur des Alten und Neuen Testaments
GR	*Greece and Rome*
HNT	Handbuch zum Neuen Testament
HSCP	*Harvard Studies in Classical Philology*
HTR	*Harvard Theological Review*

ICC	International Critical Commentary
JBL	*Journal of Biblical Literature*
JBR	*Journal of Bible and Religion*
JETS	*Journal of the Evangelical Theological Society*
JR	*The Journal of Religion*
JRS	*The Journal of Roman Studies*
JSJSup	Supplements to the Journal for the Study of Judaism
JSNT	*Journal for the Study of the New Testament*
JSNTSup	Journal for the Study of the New Testament: Supplement Series
JSPSup	Journal for the Study of the Pseudepigrapha: Supplement Series
KEK	Kritisch-exegetischer Kommentar über das Neue Testament (Meyer-Kommentar)
L&N	*Greek–English Lexicon of the New Testament: Based on Semantic Domains.* Edited by J. P. Louw and E. A. Nida. 2nd edn. New York, 1989
LCL	Loeb Classical Library
LEC	Library of Early Christianity
LNTS	Library of New Testament Studies
LSJ	Liddell, H. G., R. Scott, H. S. Jones, *A Greek–English Lexicon.* 9th edn. with revised supplement. Oxford, 1996
LXX	Septuagint
MT	Masoretic Text
NA[27]	*Novum Testamentum Graece*, Nestle-Aland, 27th edn.
NEG	*Nouvelle Edition de Genève* (1979)
Neot	*Neotestamentica*
NIV	*New International Version* (1984)
NJahrb	*Neue Jahrbücher für das klassische Altertum*
NovTSup	Novum Testamentum Supplements
NRSV	*New Revised Standard Version* (1989)
NT	New Testament
NTAbh	Neutestamentliche Abhandlungen
NTS	*New Testament Studies*
OSAP	*Oxford Studies in Ancient Philosophy*
OWC	Oxford World's Classics
PL	Patrologia latina. Edited by J.-P. Migne. 217 vols. Paris, 1844–64

SBLDS	Society of Biblical Literature Dissertation Series
SBLMS	Society of Biblical Literature Monograph Series
SNTSMS	Society for New Testament Studies Monograph Series
SVF	*Stoicorum veterum fragmenta.* H. von Arnim. 4 vols. Leipzig, 1903–24
TDNT	*Theological Dictionary of the New Testament.* Edited by G. Kittel and G. Friedrich. Translated by G. W. Bromiley. 10 vols. Grand Rapids, MI, 1964–76
VC	*Vigiliae christianae*
WBC	Word Biblical Commentary
WUNT	Wissenschaftliche Untersuchungen zum Neuen Testament
ZNW	*Zeitschrift für die neutestamentliche Wissenschaft*
ZPE	*Zeitschrift für Papyrologie und Epigraphik*
ZTK	*Zeitschrift für Theologie und Kirche*

Introduction

COMPARISONS OF STOIC AND CHRISTIAN MORALITY

Ancient Christian authors often show awareness of the affinity between Christianity and Stoicism, particularly in terms of morality or ethics. Sometimes we see this awareness hinted at indirectly. Other times we see it expressed quite openly. The latter is the case, for instance, when particular Stoic philosophers, like Musonius Rufus, are expressly praised in writing by such learned authors as Justin Martyr, Clement of Alexandria, and Origen.[1] What these Christians appear to have admired the most with the Stoic teacher was his morality and moral integrity. Origen, for example, could describe Musonius as παράδειγμα τοῦ ἀρίστου βίου ('a model of the highest form of life').[2] Similarly, he observed that while Plato was an aid to the intellectual few, the Stoic Epictetus was accessible to all who sought moral improvement.[3] Another prominent Stoic, the younger Seneca, was held in high esteem, too, by Christians—so much that he soon became subject to a quite unsubtle Christianization. Thus, around 200 CE Tertullian evidently considered Seneca's Stoicism so closely related to Christianity that he referred to him as *Seneca saepe noster* (lit. 'often our Seneca'). Approximately two centuries later Jerome found it fully appropriate to skip the word *saepe* and simply call him *noster Seneca* ('our Seneca').[4] The fact that an anonymous fourth-century Christian author devoted himself to the composition of a fictitious correspondence of fourteen letters between Paul and Seneca, the *Epistulae Senecae et Pauli*,[5] only confirms how

---

[1] See Abraham J. Malherbe, 'Hellenistic Moralists and the New Testament', *ANRW* 26.1: 267–9. See also Chapter 3 below.

[2] *Cels.* 3.66. See further in Chapter 3 on Musonius below.

[3] *Cels.* 6.2. See further John Whittaker, 'Christianity and Morality in the Roman Empire', *VC* 33 (1979): 221–2.

[4] Tertullian, *An.* 20; Jerome, *Jov.* 1.49. I owe these references to Malherbe, 'Hellenistic Moralists', 269.

[5] See Abraham J. Malherbe, '"Seneca" on Paul as Letter Writer', in *The Future of Early Christianity: Essays in Honor of Helmut Koester* (ed. B. A. Pearson; Philadelphia, PA: Fortress, 1991), 414–21. Cf. also the brief discussion in Richard J. Gibson, 'Paul and the Evangelization of

fundamentally close the two systems of thought were considered to be in antiquity.[6]

It was really not until the early nineteenth century that a basically different picture began to emerge.[7] At that time two Göttingen theologians published their dissertations in which they sought to contrast Christian and Stoic ethics, to the unequivocal disadvantage of the latter, and thus initiated the first rush of religiously motivated anti-Stoicism:

Both authors acknowledge that there are some parallels between the two bodies of thought, but quickly move on to their dissimilarities, on which they lavish sustained attention. Both authors, as well, take pains to stress the novelty and uniqueness of biblical ethics and the idea that the New Testament authors breathe a purer air than their pagan contemporaries. Christianity, they urge, offers a teaching and a way of life more profound and inspiring than any philosophy that might be constructed on the basis of reason alone. Both the content of Christian ethics and its source in divine revelation guarantee, for [them], its superiority over Stoic ethics.[8]

This strategy was approved and adopted by many subsequent theologians and biblical scholars. At the close of the century a number of them devoted their attention to Epictetus, and started to develop and defend the view that all the striking similarities between Christian moral teaching and that of Epictetus could be explained by *his* dependence on Christianity. The argument was that,

whether he knew it or not, the philosopher had derived his social ethics from the Bible. Faced with the evidence of Epictetus' magnanimity and moral sensitivity, they reasoned, he must have absorbed those values from the New Testament; otherwise, his ethics would have been cold and formal. Underlying this contention is the assumption, used here as a canon of proof, that Christianity by nature possesses a deeper reservoir of human warmth and social consciousness than paganism, and that a pagan

---

the Stoics', in *The Gospel to the Nations: Perspectives on Paul's Mission* (ed. P. Bolt and M. Thompson; Downers Grove, IL: Intervarsity Press, 2000), 311–12.

[6] As a matter of fact, quite unlike many late classical writers, who criticized Seneca for his political activities and especially his poor literary style, '[i]t was the Christian apologists and Church Fathers, starting in the second century, who gave Seneca a new and more positive appreciation. These authors were less concerned with his biography and his literary style than with his moral philosophy, which they found strikingly compatible with Christian ethics at some points. They concentrated their attention on his ethical works, borrowing heavily from them and occasionally mentioning him by name as a sage' (Marcia L. Colish, *The Stoic Tradition from Antiquity to the Early Middle Ages*. Vol. 1. *Stoicism in Classical Latin Literature* [Studies in the History of Christian Thought 34; Leiden: Brill, 1985], 17).

[7] See the excellent survey in Marcia L. Colish, 'Stoicism and the New Testament: An Essay in Historiography', *ANRW* 26.1: 334–79.

[8] Colish, 'Stoicism', 361.

who manifests these traits in the Christian era must be an *anima naturaliter christiana* ['a naturally Christian soul'] or even a Christian in spite of himself.[9]

At the same time, the old myth that Seneca had been converted to Christianity by Paul still had its proponents, some of whom argued forcefully for the authenticity of the epistolary correspondence between Paul and Seneca.[10]

This brief history of interpretation indicates, if anything, the close relationship between the two systems of thought. It also illustrates how far, from a historically critical point of view, the attempts to explain that relationship have been taken, mainly in order to argue for and defend the idea of the novelty and uniqueness of Christian moral teaching. To be sure, no serious scholar today would claim that either Seneca or Epictetus, or any other Stoic, for that matter, was dependent on Christian writings or ideas.[11] However, some of the underlying assumptions which in the nineteenth century gave rise to a powerful anti-Stoicism can still be seen in scholarly discussions of Stoicism in the field of New Testament and early Christian studies. These assumptions are surprisingly common. Every now and then studies appear in which the 'novelty' and 'uniqueness' of Christian moral teaching is actually professed,[12] or in which it is asserted that, unlike the Christians, the Stoics were primarily concerned with producing lofty schemes without really meaning or practising what they preached.[13] Alternatively, the Stoics, together with other Greek and Roman philosophers, were supposedly egocentric, even in their making of theory, unlike the Christians, whose morality was in every

---

[9] Colish, 'Stoicism', 364. Among the advocates of this opinion was the influential New Testament scholar Theodor Zahn.

[10] See Colish, 'Stoicism', 364–5. The most zealous proponent of this view was the French scholar Amédée Fleury, whose thesis was well received and supported by Ferdinand Christian Baur, the leading figure of the Tübingen school in New Testament studies.

[11] Even though we know that Epictetus was aware of the Christians, whom he in one lecture calls 'Galileans' (*Diss.* 4.7.6) and in another (con)fuses them with Jews (2.9.19–21).

[12] A recent example is Rodney Stark's widely acclaimed study, *The Rise of Christianity: How the Obscure, Marginal Jesus Movement Became the Dominant Religious Force in the Western World in a Few Centuries* (San Francisco, CA: HarperSanFrancisco, 1996). For a critique of Stark's work in this respect, see Runar M. Thorsteinsson, 'The Role of Morality in the Rise of Roman Christianity', in *Exploring Early Christian Identity* (ed. B. Holmberg; WUNT 226; Tübingen: Mohr Siebeck, 2008), 145–57.

[13] See, e.g., J. N. Sevenster, *Paul and Seneca* (NovTSup 4; Leiden: Brill, 1961), *passim*; Wolfgang Schrage, *Die konkreten Einzelgebote in der paulinischen Paränese: Ein Beitrag zur neutestamentlichen Ethik* (Gütersloh: Mohn, 1961), 59 n. 3; Rudolf Schnackenburg, *The Moral Teaching of the New Testament* (trans. J. Holland-Smith and W. J. O'Hara; Tunbridge Wells: Burns & Oates, 1965), 303–6; John Piper, *'Love Your Enemies': Jesus' Love Command in the Synoptic Gospels and in the Early Christian Paraenesis. A History of the Tradition and Interpretation of Its Uses* (Grand Rapids, MI: Baker, 1980), 20–7.

respect other-regarding.[14] Many of these claims gain ground, I think, because the basic assumption that Christian moral teaching *was* indeed or *has to be* something different and unique still lingers on. Common presumptions about the characteristic 'immorality' of the ancient Romans are certainly of no help in changing that belief:

Many of the ancient sources which provide highly coloured descriptions of Roman luxury and vice were written by Christian apologists who had an interest in making pagans appear as 'immoral' as possible (the works of Tertullian and Clement of Alexandria are obvious examples). This early Christian attitude to pagan 'immorality' has been an important, though often unacknowledged, influence on later historians' perceptions of Roman behaviour.[15]

Even today there are scholars who take great pains to prove that all the similarities between Christianity and Stoicism are more apparent than real, and that there really is a fundamental *difference* between the two.[16] More often than not such studies tend to suffer from quite unfair, if not strongly biased, treatment of the Stoic sources, that is, if the sources are actually consulted at all. And yet, some of them gain support and are seconded by others,[17] probably because the soil is still susceptible to the by and large stereotypical ideas they hand down about the Stoics and their philosophy.

Within the field of New Testament and early Christian studies there has long been a considerable lack of information about the Stoics and Stoic philosophy, and a good deal of the information that has circulated is inaccurate, coloured as it often has been by a one-sided treatment of the sources. This has proved very unhelpful for our effort to gain better knowledge of the ancient world. There is an urgent need for a thorough (re)presentation of the Stoic material, and, at the same time, a more balanced approach to the

---

[14] See, e.g., Sevenster, *Paul and Seneca*, 4, 173–85, 215–18, and *passim*; Schrage, *Einzelgebote*, 208–9, 252–3, 260; Piper, 'Love Your Enemies', 24–7; Philip F. Esler, *Conflict and Identity in Romans: The Social Setting of Paul's Letter* (Minneapolis, MN: Fortress, 2003), 315, 325–7.

[15] Catharine Edwards, *The Politics of Immorality in Ancient Rome* (Cambridge: Cambridge University Press, 1993), 33.

[16] e.g. Philip F. Esler, 'Paul and Stoicism: Romans 12 as a Test Case', *NTS* 50 (2004): 106–24. For a critique of Esler's article, see Runar M. Thorsteinsson, 'Paul and Roman Stoicism: Romans 12 and Contemporary Stoic Ethics', *JSNT* 29 (2006): 139–61. Cf. also Troels Engberg-Pedersen, 'The Relationship with Others: Similarities and Differences Between Paul and Stoicism', *ZNW* 96 (2005): 35–60. Further examples of scholarly works in which the difference between Christianity and Stoicism is emphasized are provided in David A. deSilva, 'Paul and the Stoa: A Comparison', *JETS* 38 (1995): 549.

[17] See, e.g., Robert Jewett, *Romans: A Commentary* (Hermeneia; Minneapolis, MN: Fortress, 2007), 772 n. 163, where Jewett discusses Paul's demand of non-retaliation in Rom 12.17, and refers with approval to Esler's 'Paul and Roman Stoicism' (see the previous note) as a source for 'the contrast with Stoic ethics'.

question of the relationship between Christianity and Stoicism, including the question of similarities and differences in terms of ethics or morality.

THE PRESENT APPROACH: FOCUSING ON FIRST-CENTURY ROME

Fortunately, thanks to the unflagging efforts of a handful of scholars, there has been a steadily growing awareness of and interest in this area of research, especially in the last two decades or so.[18] But these efforts need to be continued—and extended. Recent studies of the relationship between Christian and Stoic ethics have mostly looked to the earliest (or earlier) phases of Stoic philosophy.[19] The three main sources for Stoic ethics that have normally been considered include: (a) Book 7 of the *Lives of Eminent Philosophers* by Diogenes Laertius (ca. 200–250 CE), which covers the first leading Stoics, from Zeno (d. 262 BCE) to Chrysippus (d. 206 BCE); (b) the *Epitome of Stoic Ethics* collected by Stobaeus in the early fifth century CE, and attributed to Arius Didymus (late first century BCE), which, according to the author, treats Stoic ethics from Zeno to Panaetius of Rhodes (d. ca. 110 BCE);[20] and (c) Book 3 of Cicero's *On the Ends of Goods and Evils* (*De Finibus*), composed in 45 BCE, the sources for which appear to go back to the mid or late second century BCE.[21] All these texts are of great importance for our knowledge of Stoic ethics and of Stoicism in general.[22] However, it is important to note, first, that they represent individual efforts to epitomize what *other* authors had once written or said about Stoic ethics, and, second, that only one of these authors, Arius (provided that Arius *was* indeed the author of the *Epitome of Stoic Ethics*), was

---

[18] See esp. Troels Engberg-Pedersen, *Paul and the Stoics* (Edinburgh: T&T Clark, 2000).

[19] e.g. Engberg-Pedersen, *Paul*, who bases his study primarily on Cicero's account in *Fin.* 3 (see p. 46). It should be noted, however, that more recently Engberg-Pedersen has devoted considerable attention to the later (Roman) Stoics (cf. the Bibliography below).

[20] Stobaeus, *Ecl.* 2.7.5–12 (ed. Wachsmuth and Hense) = Arius Didymus 7.5–12 (ed. Pomeroy). In addition to Zeno, Cleanthes, and Chrysippus, the work is based on the second-century BCE Stoics Diogenes of Seleucia (Babylon), Antipater of Tarsus, Archedemus of Tarsus, and Panaetius of Rhodes; see further Arthur J. Pomeroy, ed., *Arius Didymus: Epitome of Stoic Ethics* (Atlanta, GA: Society of Biblical Literature, 1999), 10–11 with n. 1.

[21] See Engberg-Pedersen, *Paul*, 46, who finds it most likely that Cicero's main authority here was Antipater of Tarsus (d. ca. 130 BCE). Cf. H. Rackham, 'Introduction', in *Cicero: De finibus bonorum et malorum* (trans. H. Rackham; 2nd edn.; LCL; Cambridge, MA: Harvard University Press, 1931), xvii, who traces Cicero's source back to Diogenes of Babylon (d. 152 BCE).

[22] For comparison of the three writings, see A. A. Long, 'Arius Didymus and the Exposition of Stoic Ethics', in *Stoic Studies* (Berkeley, CA: University of California Press, 1996), 107–33.

a Stoic himself.[23] Whereas Cicero was certainly influenced by and much attracted to Stoicism when it came to ethics, he remained a professed adherent of the (New) Academy.[24] As for Diogenes Laertius, he was not much of a philosopher at all.[25]

There is no doubt that many of the studies that have been based on one or more of these three texts have added much to our knowledge of the relationship between Christian and Stoic ethics. But it needs to be taken into account that they are based on sources for Stoic ethics, which, arguably, are somewhat secondary for the purpose of comparison with Christian writings: none of the sources normally consulted expresses actual thoughts and teachings of Stoics in the Christian era.

While acknowledging the value of the writings of authors like Cicero, Arius Didymus, and Diogenes Laertius for research into ethics in Early (and Middle) Stoicism, I shall take a different approach to the sources in this study: in the following, I shall be comparing early Christian morality with Stoic ethics as the latter was taught by contemporary Stoics. As will be explained more fully in Chapter 1 below, this means that I shall be focusing on the writings of Roman Stoicism in the first (and early second) century CE,[26] that is, the writings and lectures of Seneca, Musonius Rufus, and Epictetus, which are the best sources available for Stoic ethics as it was understood, interpreted, and experienced by the Stoics themselves at the time.

Correspondingly, since every system of thought, like ethics or morality (defined below), may be expressed, understood, and actualized differently in different social settings, the Christian sources that are most properly to be compared with Roman Stoicism are the writings of Roman Christianity. These include Paul's Letter to the Romans, the First Letter of Peter, and the First Letter of Clement, which constitute our earliest and most reliable Christian sources related to first-century Rome (see more fully in Chapter 5 below).

It should be clear, then, that the scope of this study is restricted: it is neither about Stoicism in general nor about Christianity in general, although it may certainly have some significant implications either for Stoicism or Christianity in general, or both. Also, it is not the purpose of this study to define ethical

---

[23] But see Pomeroy, *Arius Didymus*, 3, on Arius' 'considerable philosophical tolerance'.

[24] See, e.g., *Off.* 2.1–8. See also the helpful discussion in Colish, *Stoic Tradition*, 65–79.

[25] According to Tad Brennan, Diogenes was 'merely a nitwit' (*The Stoic Life: Emotions, Duties, and Fate* [Oxford: Clarendon Press, 2005], 19).

[26] A similar approach has recently been taken by Michelle V. Lee, *Paul, the Stoics, and the Body of Christ* (SNTSMS 137; Cambridge: Cambridge University Press, 2006), who focuses specifically on the uses of the 'body' metaphor in Roman Stoicism (including Cicero) and in Paul's First Letter to the Corinthians.

theory in general, either in Stoicism or Christianity, but rather to give some primary examples of how the moral teachings of these systems of thought were understood and taught at a particular time and place. The character of the study is therefore largely descriptive, as it focuses on presenting the ancient material itself.[27] I certainly do not pretend to provide here a comprehensive account of Roman Stoic ethics. But I do claim to have consulted, for present purposes, the most significant sources available for Roman Stoic ethics. The same applies to the Christian material. I shall explain my choice of sources in Chapters 1 and 5, respectively.

What, then, is the purpose of this work? The primary purpose is threefold: first, to give a useful overview of moral teaching in Roman Stoicism as it presents itself in the writings and lectures of Seneca, Musonius, and Epictetus; second, to give a corresponding overview of moral teaching in Roman Christianity as it presents itself in the three texts of Romans, 1 Peter, and 1 Clement; and, finally, to compare the similarities and differences between the two sets of moral teachings.

With this work I hope to increase the interest in the Roman Stoics, particularly in New Testament and early Christian scholarship. I also hope to be able not only to provide some plausible answers to the questions raised by the comparative part of the study, but also to evoke some new questions for further discussion.

METHODOLOGICAL ISSUES AND PROCEDURE OF THE STUDY

Corresponding to its threefold purpose, the study is divided into three main parts, the first part dealing with the Stoic sources, the second with the Christian sources, and the third part devoted to the comparison between the two. Several issues need to be clarified before we turn to the texts.

There are differences between the sources themselves as texts which need to be considered at the outset. As with all writings from antiquity, one

---

[27] Here is a further difference between the present study and that of Engberg-Pedersen (cf. n. 19 above). Not only does Engberg-Pedersen base his study on other sources for Stoic ethics (he includes only three references from Seneca, one from Epictetus, and none from Musonius), but he also puts much less weight on providing examples from the Stoic texts. For instance, unless I am mistaken, there is but a single reference to a Stoic source in his analysis of Romans 12–15 (*Paul*, 261–92; the reference is to Cicero on p. 292). Note, however, that in his study Engberg-Pedersen is primarily concerned with 'the basic structure of Stoic ethics' (p. 46), and that he deals specifically with the Stoic sources earlier in the study (pp. 45–79).

must always take into account the particular settings in which the texts were written, including the question of intended audience. And, like other ancient sources, the texts under discussion differ from each other in that respect. It is not just a question of difference between the Christian sources, on the one hand, and the Stoic ones, on the other. There are differences as well within both sets of writings. As we shall see in the introductory discussions below, the texts attributed to Musonius and Epictetus are primarily classroom lectures, intended for particular groups of people, while Seneca's texts were written for a much wider audience, including even the 124 letters that he wrote to his friend Lucilius. Similarly, while 1 Clement was addressed to a particular group of people with a quite specific purpose, 1 Peter contains mainly general exhortations to several groups of people in several cities. Paul's Letter to the Romans, on the other hand, was written to a particular group of people in one particular city but mostly addressing issues of a general nature. While these differences of settings certainly do not prevent the comparison from being made, it is necessary to have them in mind as we move from one writing to another.

Second, the very form of each writing affects the way in which it is most appropriately read and examined with respect to its moral teaching. Thus each text in the Christian writings includes one (more or less) continuous discourse. However, one of these texts, Paul's Letter to the Romans, differs from the others in that Paul's presentation of his moral teaching is, as it were, compiled or summarized in one particular part of the letter (Romans 12–15), while the moral teachings of the other two letters are scattered throughout the texts. To be sure, this 'scattering' of the moral teaching is not a problem for the analysis of 1 Peter, because the text is simply not that long. But it causes some difficulties for the analysis of 1 Clement, because 1 Clement is an exceedingly long text. Hence, whereas Romans and 1 Peter are best treated (more) 'linearly', i.e. from the beginning onwards, 1 Clement is best treated (more) thematically. This latter procedure is also the one that applies best to the Stoic texts, since they are either too extensive or too diverse in substance to be treated 'linearly'. In the final, comparative, part of the study, on the other hand, a thematic approach will be taken to each and every source.

Third, in this study I have chosen to focus heavily on the primary sources themselves. References to the scholarly discussion and to individual scholars are therefore found mainly in the footnotes. This does not mean that I consider the scholarly discussion unimportant or that I have left it out in the course of the study. Nor does it mean that I have not benefited from other scholars. Quite to the contrary, obvious as it should be to anyone familiar with the subject, I am very much indebted to a number of other scholars and previous scholarly works. The arrangement of referring to the scholarly discussion mainly in the footnotes simply means that I wish to direct the attention of the reader specifically and directly to the primary sources, the presentation of which I intend to give as much space as possible. This focus on the primary sources also means that I shall include as much of the original Greek and Latin texts as space allows.

Fourth, although it may seem superfluous, it is important to point out in plain terms that a comparative study of the ancient sources is always subject to the interests of the scholar who plans and performs it.[28] The present study is no exception: every aspect of the following comparison reflects my own scholarly interests. This book presents *one* way of comparing Christian and Stoic morality in the ancient world.

Fifth, a few words on terminology are in order. While the terms 'morality' and 'ethics' are often used more or less synonymously, there is a certain nuance of difference between them that should be borne in mind. In this study, the term 'ethics' normally refers to conscious, systematic treatments of moral values and rules, while 'morality' normally refers to less conscious and less systematically treated moral values and rules.[29] To recognize this difference is to recognize that the earliest Christian writings do not normally provide us with 'ethics', in the above sense. Thus, at the risk of some over-simplification, one could say that while 'ethics' is more typical of the Stoic material, 'morality' is more typical of the Christian material, and I often use the terms accordingly. However, on some occasions I use the two terms as approximate equivalents, not only for convenience's sake but also because even in some of the earliest Christian writings we do indeed have portions that include 'ethics' in the above sense.[30] As for the uses of the terms 'Christianity', 'Christian', and 'Christians', they will be clarified at a point where it is most appropriate to do so, namely, in Chapter 5, which introduces the analysis of the 'Christian' material in Part II.

---

[28] cf. the fine discussion in Jonathan Z. Smith, *Drudgery Divine: On the Comparison of Early Christianities and the Religions of Late Antiquity* (Chicago, IL: The University of Chicago Press, 1990), esp. 36–53. I am grateful to Troels Engberg-Pedersen for bringing this work to my attention.

[29] cf. Wayne A. Meeks, *The Origins of Christian Morality: The First Two Centuries* (New Haven, CT: Yale University Press, 1993), 4, who describes 'ethics' as 'morality rendered self-conscious'.

[30] cf. David G. Horrell, *Solidarity and Difference: A Contemporary Reading of Paul's Ethics* (London: T&T Clark, 2005), 95–7. Dealing specifically with the letters of Paul, Horrell writes that 'there is, even in Meeks's sense [see the previous note], *ethics* in the Pauline letters. Paul self-consciously addresses a range of "problems" and issues in the communities, grounding his exhortation in the central symbols and stories of the tradition, and giving guidance as to what should and should not be done. Paul's morality is "self-conscious" and reflective, in its community-shaping aims, its articulation of moral norms and practices, and its motivational structure' (pp. 96–7; italics original).

The procedure of the study is as follows: Part I covers Chapters 1 to 4, of which the first chapter gives a general introduction to Roman Stoicism and discusses its main sources. Chapters 2 to 4 provide an overview of the moral teachings of Seneca, Musonius, and Epictetus, respectively. Each of Chapters 2 to 4 begins with a brief introduction to the life and works of the Stoic philosopher concerned.

Part II, then, includes Chapters 5 to 8, of which the fifth chapter offers a general introduction to Roman Christianity and discusses what exactly is meant by the phrase 'Roman Christianity'. In addition, this chapter touches on the question of the social setting of the first believers in Christ in the city of Rome, partly with respect to the local Jewry, but particularly with respect to the Roman Stoics. Chapters 6 to 8 deal with the moral teachings of Romans, 1 Peter, and 1 Clement, respectively. Similar to the procedure in Part I, each of Chapters 6 to 8 starts with an introduction to the historical setting of the text under discussion. In Chapters 7 and 8, i.e. on 1 Peter and 1 Clement, specific sections are also devoted to an assessment of the relationship between these two letters and Paul's Letter to the Romans.

On the basis of Parts I and II, Part III examines the similarities and differences between the moral teachings of Roman Stoicism and Roman Christianity. This part of the study includes two chapters: in Chapter 9, which is the longest chapter of the study, a number of issues and themes from Parts I and II are addressed and compared. The chapter is selective in its interests, divided into the following five sections: (a) 'A Particular Way of Life as Proper Worship'; (b) 'Clothing Oneself with Christ and Seeking to be a Socrates'; (c) 'Mutual Love and Care'; (d) 'Non-Retaliation and "Love of Enemies"'; and (e) 'The Social Dimension'. Since many of these issues and themes were brought up earlier in the study—due to my choice to first give an overview of the moral teachings and then compare the two—some repetition is necessary in this part of the study. However, because we are dealing with quite a large amount of material, some repetition is useful and no doubt often welcomed by the reader. The final chapter of the study, Chapter 10, is devoted to the question of the ethical scope of the Stoic and Christian sources, that is, the question of whether they differ in their inclusion (or exclusion) of people in their moral teachings.

In the Conclusion I bring together some of the main results of the different parts, and draw some conclusions about the similarities and differences between the moral teachings of Roman Christianity and Roman Stoicism.

Part I

Moral Teaching in Roman Stoicism

1

Introduction to Roman Stoicism

ROME AND ROMAN STOICISM

It was Panaetius of Rhodes who in the second century BCE paved the way for the appearance of Stoic philosophy at the centre of the Roman Empire.[1] But it was mostly owing to Cicero's Latinization of the philosophy and his systematic introduction of it to the Romans that the Stoic school became so well established in the city as early as the first century BCE that by the turn of the century it was the most favoured philosophical school in Rome.[2] As it turned out, it was precisely in first- and second-century Rome that Stoicism had its greatest success. This was true in particular among educated, upper-class Romans, but it may be expected that Stoic influences reached lower classes as well, whether directly or indirectly, for Stoic teachers and spokesmen were found not only in the Roman court and public lecture-rooms but also at street corners.[3] As one scholar points out, '[p]hilosophy supplied ethical preconceptions on which moral choices were often based even by those who neither knew nor cared much about the philosophical sects'.[4] In the political arena Stoicism gained wide support, but it is difficult to know the extent to which philosophical doctrines (of any philosophy) influenced particular policies

---

[1] See, e.g., E. Vernon Arnold, *Roman Stoicism* (Cambridge: Cambridge University Press, 1911), 100–4; Max Pohlenz, *Die Stoa: Geschichte einer geistigen Bewegung* (2nd edn.; Göttingen: Vandenhoeck & Ruprecht, 1948), 192–3; Mark Morford, *The Roman Philosophers: From the Time of Cato the Censor to the Death of Marcus Aurelius* (London: Routledge, 2002), 4, 23–8.

[2] On Cicero's Latinization and introduction of Stoic philosophy to the Romans, cf. *Fin.* 3.3–5, 40.

[3] Arnold, *Roman Stoicism*, 111–21, 380–407; F. H. Sandbach, *The Stoics* (2nd edn.; Indianapolis, IN: Hackett, 1989), 16–17. Cf. also Edwards, *Politics of Immorality*, 17–18, on Roman moralists in general and their audience. See also the introduction to Part II below.

[4] Miriam T. Griffin, 'Philosophy, Politics, and Politicians at Rome', in *Philosophia Togata: Essays on Philosophy and Roman Society* (ed. M. Griffin and J. Barnes; Oxford: Clarendon Press, 1989), 37.

and decisions.[5] It may be assumed, though, that a politician's philosophical profession affected at least his frame of reference in the act of forming policies and making political decisions.

A number of Roman senators and political authorities were professed Stoics, which is not surprising considering the fact that, unlike some other philosophical schools in the city (like Cynicism), Stoic teaching encouraged participation in political and public activities.[6] That did not mean that Stoicism urged an uncritical stance and blind submission to governing authorities. Quite to the contrary: during the trying reigns of Nero and the Flavians, virtually the only real critics of the imperial government were Stoics.[7] Some of these critics were politicians by profession; others operated from without, like the influential teacher Musonius Rufus. Among the former were prominent figures like Rubellius Plautus, Barea Soranus, and Thrasea Paetus, all of whom were put to death by Nero, and Thrasea's son-in-law Helvidius Priscus and his friend Paconius Agrippinus, both banished by the emperor.[8] As we shall see, the notable exception to this group of Stoics 'in opposition' was Seneca, at least during his service as imperial counsellor, though in the end even he turned, if not against, then away from the emperor, and subsequently paid the price for doing so. Seneca's nephew, the famous poet Lucan, also a Stoic, lost his life too because of his antagonistic position towards Nero, and so did Lucan's Stoic teacher, Annaeus Cornutus. But, again, the political points of view of these Stoics were not self-evident products of their philosophical adherence. Their criticism did not stem from some idea intrinsic to Stoic philosophy itself. Indeed, Seneca tried to correct rumours of that kind: 'It seems to me erroneous to believe that those who have loyally dedicated themselves to philosophy are stubborn and rebellious, scorners of magistrates or kings or of those who control the administration of public affairs.'[9] A century later, the Roman emperor himself was a devoted Stoic, who was greatly influenced by the teachings of one of a no more august status than an ex-slave (Epictetus). This emperor was Marcus

---

[5] On this difficult question, see the discussion in Griffin, 'Philosophy'. See also Michael Trapp, *Philosophy in the Roman Empire: Ethics, Politics and Society* (Aldershot: Ashgate, 2007), 226–33.

[6] cf. Miriam T. Griffin, *Seneca: A Philosopher in Politics* (Oxford: Clarendon Press, 1976), 340–66.

[7] cf. Ramsay MacMullen, *Enemies of the Roman Order: Treason, Unrest, and Alienation in the Empire* (Cambridge, MA: Harvard University Press, 1966), 46–94; Hans-Josef Klauck, *The Religious Context of Early Christianity: A Guide to Graeco-Roman Religions* (trans. B. McNeil; Minneapolis, MN: Fortress, 2003), 347.

[8] See the discussion in Miriam T. Griffin, *Nero: The End of a Dynasty* (London: Batsford, 1984), 171–7; also eadem, *Seneca*, 362–4. Cf. Arnold, *Roman Stoicism*, 398–402. See also further details below in the introductory sections to each Stoic.

[9] *Ep.* 73.1.

Aurelius, whose death in 180 CE is usually regarded as marking the end—or the beginning of the end—of Stoicism as such.[10]

Stoicism had traditionally divided philosophy into the three realms of logic, physics (the study of nature), and ethics,[11] but by the first century CE the last category had become the primary focus of the discipline. Whereas the Roman Stoics still adhered to this tripartite division of philosophy,[12] they seem to have shown less concern for logic and physics, especially the former.[13] This is not to say that the Stoics of this period were totally uninterested in logic and physics. That would almost certainly be wrong.[14] We know, for instance, of Seneca's engagement in physics through his survey of natural phenomena in *Naturales Quaestiones*. We also know that certain branches of physics, like cosmology and/or theology, were simply basic to the realm of ethics and practically inseparable from it.[15] However, on the whole, it was ethics as such that by far occupied the focus of attention of most first- and second-century Roman Stoics.[16] This goes hand in hand with the prominent position that morality enjoyed in Roman culture and society in general, for the Romans were so deeply concerned with morality that they were almost obsessed with it.[17] The Stoic tenet that only what has moral worth is good

[10] On the 'end' of Stoicism, Klauck remarks: 'The history of the Stoa ends in the second century CE, because—as it has been observed in a joke that is nevertheless not entirely off the mark—by then everyone was a Stoic' (*Religious Context*, 338).

[11] According to Sextus Empiricus, *Math.* 7.19, Posidonius 'preferred to compare philosophy to a living being—physics to the blood and flesh, logic to the bones and sinews, and ethics to the soul'. Translation in A. A. Long and D. N. Sedley, *The Hellenistic Philosophers* (2 vols.; Cambridge: Cambridge University Press, 1987), 1: 159. On the proper order of the three parts in Stoic philosophy, see Julia Annas, 'Ethics in Stoic Philosophy', *Phronesis* 52 (2007): 58–60.

[12] cf. Seneca, *Ep.* 89.9: 'The greatest authors, and the greatest number of authors, have maintained that there are three divisions of philosophy—moral, natural, and rational (*moralem, naturalem, rationalem*).'

[13] cf., e.g., the critique in Seneca, *Ep.* 45; 48; 49; 82; 85; 111; 117; cf. also Epictetus, *Diss.* 2.13.21; 3.24.78–80.

[14] cf. the recent arguments in Trapp, *Philosophy*, 10–13, against the view that philosophy in the Roman Empire was dominated by ethics. However, as Trapp himself notes, '[t]he first and second centuries CE do indeed provide us with a striking array of thinkers whose surviving or attested output is predominantly ethical, and firmly slanted towards the practical application of ethical principle: Seneca, Demetrius, Musonius Rufus, Arrian's Epictetus, Dio Chrysostom, Hierocles, Marcus Aurelius.' It should be noted, first, that all these authors were Stoics, except Demetrius (a Cynic) and Dio Chrysostom (also a Cynic, but whom Trapp actually regards as a Stoic), and, second, that all the Stoic authors considered in the present study are found among those who, according to Trapp, were specifically (though not exclusively) concerned with ethics.

[15] cf. Gretchen Reydams-Schils, *The Roman Stoics: Self, Responsibility, and Affection* (Chicago, IL: University of Chicago Press, 2005), 11–12: 'The Roman Stoics could not write on applied ethics without taking into account a broader theoretical framework that would have included physics' (p. 12).

[16] As early as in Cicero ethics is said to constitute 'the highest branch of philosophy' (*Fin.* 3.6).

[17] See Edwards, *Politics of Immorality*.

thus spoke directly to Roman interests and readily gained ground in the city. And so did many details of the Stoic moral teaching, not least because of the close agreement that existed between these details and traditional Roman virtues.[18]

Most scholars agree that the Roman Stoics were no radical innovators in terms of ethical doctrine compared to earlier Stoics, but rather looked to the earliest phases of the philosophy and were open to reviving its Cynic roots.[19] But it would be wrong to hold that their moral teaching was totally void of new values and perspectives. And though they may not have added much to the theoretical framework, the Roman Stoics refined and broadened certain parts of it, and had their own particular priorities. One such priority was their firm and consistent emphasis on practical application of the ethical demands. In striking contrast to the common opinion that the Stoics were mostly lofty figures who were merely interested in some inner reality of their own with little consequence for society at large, the way in which the philosophical system developed and emerged in the hands of the Roman Stoics was decidedly pragmatic and community-oriented.

A further feature that distinguished Roman Stoicism was the persistent weight lent to universal humanity. The Stoic doctrine of universal humanity taught that since all humans have a share in the divine, all-pervading Reason (λόγος, *ratio*), they have equal value as such. The doctrine was basic to Stoic ethics from the very beginning, but it was Roman Stoicism that first clearly expressed the notion of equality and equal value of all human beings.[20] In principle, the tenet of universal humanity erased all boundaries between people of different origin, race, gender, social status, and so on. 'Parity of natural potentiality is implied by the very definition of Man. Therefore there can be no natural differences between Greek and Barbarian, man and woman, noble and commoner, free man and slave.'[21] As we shall see, time and again the Roman Stoics proclaim precisely this position, sometimes by way of a favourite metaphor of theirs in which humankind as a whole is likened to a

---

[18] cf. Griffin, 'Philosophy', 8.

[19] cf., however, Ludwig Edelstein, *The Meaning of Stoicism* (Martin Classical Lectures 21; Cambridge, MA: Harvard University Press, 1968), referred to in William Klassen, 'Musonius Rufus, Jesus, and Paul: Three First-Century Feminists', in *From Jesus to Paul: Studies in Honour of Francis Wright Beare* (ed. P. Richardson and J. C. Hurd; Waterloo, ON: Wilfrid Laurier University Press, 1984), 192.

[20] cf. Adolf F. Bonhöffer, *The Ethics of the Stoic Epictetus* (trans. W. O. Stephens; New York: Peter Lang, 1996), 141.

[21] Johnny Christensen, 'Equality of Man and Stoic Social Thought', in *Equality and Inequality of Man in Ancient Thought* (ed. I. Kajanto; Helsinki: Societas Scientiarum Fennica, 1984), 46. Cf. Bonhöffer, *Ethics*, 144: 'The cleft between Greeks (or Romans) and barbarians is also eliminated in the Stoa', referring to Seneca, Epictetus, and Marcus Aurelius.

'body'. According to the metaphor, the members of the body are certainly many and dissimilar with different functions, but each member is nonetheless necessary for the whole to function properly. Such is the order of Nature itself, the Stoics taught. Their purpose, it is important to keep in mind, was less to create moral order than to teach people how to recognize and preserve the one already existing in the world.[22]

It is important as well to pay heed to the fact that, somewhat unexpectedly perhaps, the basis of Stoic ethics is not to be found in human psychology but in cosmology or theology,[23] which are basically the same thing in Stoicism (both belong to the realm of physics, the study of the nature of the world).[24] According to Stoic belief, human relations are determined by the very nature of the world. They are determined by man's natural relation to and kinship with the divine. We shall see how clearly this comes to the fore in the sources of Roman Stoicism, especially in Seneca and Epictetus. But it is useful to get a glimpse of some of the basic characteristics of Stoic theology at the outset. Ever since its birth, Stoic theology was a complicated mixture of theism, pantheism, and polytheism, characterized above all by a rather fluid conception of the deity.[25] While some such conceptions are also present in the later Stoics, it is striking how much closer some of them have come to theistic conceptions of the divine, in which God is increasingly described in personal terms as one who cares for and looks after his (usually 'his') creation. Thus eulogizes the early first-century CE Roman Stoic Marcus Manilius:

For I shall sing of God, silent-minded monarch of nature, who, permeating sky and land and sea, controls with uniform compact the mighty structure; how the entire universe is alive in the mutual concord of its elements and is driven by the pulse of reason (*ratio*), since a single spirit dwells in all its parts (*cum spiritus unus per cunctas habitet partes*) and, speeding through all things, nourishes the world and shapes it like a living creature.... In this due order over the whole universe do all things abide, following the guidance of a master (*dominumque sequuntur*). This God and

---

[22] Rightly pointed out by Lee, *Paul*, 74.

[23] Gisela Striker, 'Following Nature: A Study in Stoic Ethics', *OSAP* 9 (1991): 13. Cf. the following statement made by Chrysippus: 'It is not possible to discover any other beginning of justice or any source for it other than that from Zeus and from the universal nature, for thence everything of the kind must have its beginning if we are going to have anything to say about good and evil' (Plutarch, *Stoic. rep.* 1035C). For a different view of the relationship between ethics and cosmology/theology in Stoicism, see Annas, 'Ethics', 66–87.

[24] cf. Long and Sedley, *Hellenistic Philosophers*, 1: 267; David Sedley, 'The Origins of Stoic God', in *Traditions of Theology: Studies in Hellenistic Theology, Its Background and Aftermath* (ed. D. Frede and A. Laks; Leiden: Brill, 2002), 41–2; Michael J. White, 'Stoic Natural Philosophy (Physics and Cosmology)', in *The Cambridge Companion to the Stoics* (ed. B. Inwood; Cambridge: Cambridge University Press, 2003), 124–5; Keimpe Algra, 'Stoic Theology', in ibid., 153.

[25] See, e.g., Bonhöffer, *Ethics*, 302–9; Algra, 'Stoic Theology', 165–70.

all-controlling reason (*deus et ratio, quae cuncta gubernat*), then, derives earthly beings from the signs of heaven.[26]

If pantheistic conceptions are evident, so too is the idea of a certain personal power, a 'single spirit' (*spiritus unus*), that governs all created things and nourishes them. A few decades later Seneca and Musonius Rufus spoke of God/Zeus as a 'father',[27] and Epictetus, a few more decades later, used expressions of God/Zeus that have confused people ever since because of their monotheistic, 'Christian-like' character.[28] For him, the first thing to learn about the divine is 'that there is a God, and that He provides for the universe, and that it is impossible for a man to conceal from Him, not merely his actions, but even his purposes and thoughts'.[29] Epictetus gives a useful overview of different contemporary beliefs and doctrines about the gods (primarily, we may expect, among philosophical circles):

> Concerning gods there are [1] some who say that the divine (τὸ θεῖον) does not so much as exist; and [2] others, that it exists, indeed, but is inactive and indifferent, and takes forethought (προνοεῖν) for nothing; and [3] a third set, that it exists and takes forethought, though only for great and heavenly things and in no case for terrestrial things; and [4] a fourth set, that it also takes forethought for things terrestrial and the affairs of men, but only in a general way, and not for the individual in particular; and [5] a fifth set, to which Odysseus and Socrates belonged, who say 'Nor when I move am I concealed from thee'.[30]

Epictetus himself takes the fifth position, namely, that there is a God and that this God observes and cares for human beings on an individual basis.

This former slave has been described as 'one of the most memorable and influential figures of Graeco-Roman antiquity',[31] and among those known to have been directly influenced by him was none other than the emperor

---

[26] *Astronomica* 2.60–6, 80–3.

[27] Seneca, *Ep.* 110.10; *Prov.* 2.6; *Ben.* 2.29.4; 4.8.1; Musonius Rufus 8.64.14–15; 16.104.31. Cf. also, e.g., Cicero, *Nat. d.* 2.64; Dio Chrysostom, *1 Regn.* 39–40; *2 Regn.* 75; *Borysth.* 35; 60. The Greeks had long referred to God as 'father'; see, e.g., Plato, *Tim.* 28C.

[28] cf. my discussion in Thorsteinsson, 'The Role of Morality'.

[29] *Diss.* 2.14.11: ὅτι ἔστι θεὸς καὶ προνοεῖ τῶν ὅλων καὶ οὐκ ἔστι λαθεῖν αὐτὸν οὐ μόνον ποιοῦντα, ἀλλ' οὐδὲ διανοούμενον ἢ ἐνθυμούμενον.

[30] *Diss.* 1.12.1–3. Epictetus refers here to Homer, *Il.* 10.279–80 (οὐδέ σε λήθω κινύμενος). On Socrates, cf. Xenophon, *Mem.* 1.1.19: 'For, like most men, indeed, he believed that the gods are heedful of mankind, but with an important difference; for whereas they do not believe in the omniscience of the gods, Socrates thought that they know all things, our words and deeds and secret purposes; that they are present everywhere, and grant signs to men of all that concerns man.'

[31] A. A. Long, *Epictetus: A Stoic and Socratic Guide to Life* (Oxford: Oxford University Press, 2002), 8.

himself, Marcus Aurelius,[32] the 'last Stoic'. We see in his *Meditations*, if not the same (mono)theistic tendencies as in Epictetus, then similar convictions about the gods' care for human well-being.[33] We see, too, the same devotion to the service of the deity,[34] and the same position granted to theology/cosmology as the foundation of ethics:

Whosoever does injustice commits sin (ὁ ἀδικῶν ἀσεβεῖ); for Universal Nature having made reasonable creatures for the sake of one another (τῆς γὰρ τῶν ὅλων φύσεως κατεσκευακυίας τὰ λογικὰ ζῷα ἕνεκεν ἀλλήλων), to benefit (ὠφελεῖν) each other according to desert but in no wise to do injury, manifestly he who transgresses her will sins against the most venerable of the gods, because Universal Nature is a nature of what is, and what is is related to all that exists.[35]

Hence, says the emperor, 'Love mankind! Follow God!' (φίλησον τὸ ἀνθρώπινον γένος. ἀκολούθησον θεῷ).[36] The one demand is intimately linked with the other, 'for you will not do any act well which concerns man without referring it to the divine (τὰ θεῖα); and the same is true of your conduct to God'.[37]

It has been stated that in the second-century legislation of the emperors Antoninus Pius and Marcus Aurelius concerning the poor, the sick, the infant, the famine-stricken, and the slave, 'the humane and cosmopolitan principles of Stoic politics at last triumph over Roman conservatism'.[38] Such a connection between politics and ethics would certainly have been in harmony with the latter's moral principles as they are expressed in *Meditations* (which, it should be noted, was not intended for publication by the author himself, but for private use only). One of his convictions was, for instance, that 'we have come into the world to work together (πρὸς συνεργίαν), like feet, like hands, like eyelids, like the rows of upper and lower teeth. To work against one another therefore is to oppose Nature (παρὰ φύσιν)'.[39] And if there was for him, as it were, some specific ethical demand in which others are summarized, it may well have been this: 'Delight in this one thing and take your rest therein—from social act to go on to social act, keeping all your thoughts on

---

[32] See *Med.* 1.7: '...and to make the acquaintance of the *Memoirs of Epictetus* (τοῖς Ἐπικτητείοις ὑπομνήμασιν), which he [i.e. Rusticus] supplied me with out of his own library'. Bertrand Russell even goes so far as to claim that 'Epictetus and Marcus Aurelius are completely at one on all philosophical questions' (*A History of Western Philosophy* [2nd edn.; London: Unwin, 1979], 268).

[33] cf., e.g., *Med.* 2.11; 9.11, 40; 12.5.   [34] See, e.g., *Med.* 2.5, 13; 5.27, 33.

[35] *Med.* 9.1. Trans. Farquharson (OWC). Note that the text (not just the translation) is slightly different in the LCL. Cf. also *Med.* 2.1; 12.26.

[36] *Med.* 7.31.   [37] *Med.* 3.13 (trans. Farquharson, OWC).

[38] Arnold, *Roman Stoicism*, 403; cf. pp. 280–1.

[39] *Med.* 2.1 (trans. Farquharson, OWC). Cf. *Med.* 6.7, 20; 7.13, 22; 8.59; 9.23; 10.6; 11.1, 13; 12.20.

God (τῷ ἀπὸ πράξεως κοινωνικῆς μεταβαίνειν ἐπὶ πρᾶξιν κοινωνικὴν σὺν μνήμῃ θεοῦ).[40] In the following chapters, we shall see how integral this thought was to Roman Stoicism.

'ROMAN STOICISM': DEFINITION AND ASSESSMENT OF PRIMARY SOURCES

Stoicism is conventionally divided into the three phases of Early Stoicism (Zeno, Cleanthes, Chrysippus et al.), Middle Stoicism (esp. Panaetius and Posidonius), and Late or Roman Stoicism[41]—'Roman' because the leading Stoics of the period were Romans or closely related to Rome. The designation 'Roman Stoicism' used in the present work corresponds roughly to the last category, but not entirely: it is more limited (geographically) to the Stoics of Rome itself. More precisely, 'Roman Stoicism' refers here to the Stoic philosophy as it was understood and presented by Stoics who were or had been residents of the city of Rome subsequent to Cicero's introduction of the philosophy in the first century BCE and the Romans' responsive reception of it. Thus 'Roman Stoics' are those authors of extant writings who were professed Stoics in the period from Seneca to Marcus Aurelius.[42]

The main representatives of Roman Stoicism, so defined, are Seneca, Musonius Rufus, Epictetus, and Marcus Aurelius.[43] Cicero, it cannot be denied, is also an important figure to the history of Stoicism in Rome, but although he was definitely influenced by Stoicism, he was not a professed Stoic. Rather, he considered himself and claimed to be an Academic. On the other hand, Cicero's account of Stoicism must continually be considered and compared, for the material he presented as Stoic came largely to be accepted as

---

[40] *Med.* 6.7. Trans. Haines (LCL), with slight modifications.

[41] See, e.g., David Sedley, 'The School, from Zeno to Arius Didymus', in *The Cambridge Companion to the Stoics* (ed. B. Inwood; Cambridge: Cambridge University Press, 2003), 7.

[42] For a similar approach, cf. Reydams-Schils, *Roman Stoics*, 2–3.

[43] Other Stoic authors of the period, whose works we have (fragmentary) access to, include Cornutus (1st century CE) and Hierocles (early 2nd century CE). On Cornutus, see George R. Boys-Stones, *Post-Hellenistic Philosophy: A Study of its Development from the Stoics to Origen* (Oxford: Oxford University Press, 2001), 49–59. On the ethical orientation of Cornutus' work, see idem, '*Fallere sollers*: The Ethical Pedagogy of the Stoic Cornutus', in *Greek and Roman Philosophy 100 BC–200 AD* (ed. R. Sorabji and R. W. Sharples; 2 vols.; Bulletin of the Institute of Classical Studies Supplement 94; London: Institute of Classical Studies, University of London, 2007), 1: 77–88. On Hierocles, see the samples provided in Abraham J. Malherbe, *Moral Exhortation: A Greco-Roman Sourcebook* (LEC 4; Philadelphia, PA: Westminster, 1986), 85–104. A useful overview of the sources of Stoicism is found in Brennan, *Stoic Life*, 10–20.

such by the Romans.[44] Marcus Aurelius, however, who was definitely a professed Stoic, nevertheless falls outside of the scope of this study. His text is simply too late to be of much use for its particular purpose, that is, the comparison with the first-century sources of Roman Christianity. Marcus Aurelius will thus be referred to in passing only and only for further reflection.

Hence the scope of the present study includes Seneca, Musonius Rufus, and Epictetus, who, it is generally recognized, are the three most significant Roman Stoic authors of the period under discussion (i.e. based on the extant sources). Arguably, Epictetus should not be included here because, first, his extant lectures were probably recorded in the beginning of the second century CE rather than in the first century, and, second, they were not delivered in Rome but in Nicopolis (in western Greece). However, to begin with, Epictetus got his philosophical training in Rome and, as we shall see, his connection with the city, even after his departure to Nicopolis, was established enough for us to regard him as a 'genuine' Roman Stoic. Moreover, although his lectures may have been held at the beginning of the second century (ca. 108 CE),[45] the date is close enough to be of relevance for the present study, and the Roman roots of his philosophical teachings are strong and evident enough to be regarded as a useful mirror of late first-century Roman Stoicism.

In what follows, we shall gradually see how consonant the three Stoics were in their moral teaching. Of course there are differences between them as well, for each had his own particular focus of attention, social setting, and audience. Furthermore, whereas Seneca, unlike nearly all philosophers of the time, wrote in Latin, Musonius and Epictetus followed convention and taught in Greek—almost everything attributed to them is written in Greek, too. But even this significant difference of language manages not to conceal the basic agreement between these three major representatives of Roman Stoicism. In the following I shall discuss their moral teaching in chronological order, beginning with the extensive writings of Seneca.

---

[44] cf. Reydams-Schils, *Roman Stoics*, 2.

[45] This is the date most often given for Epictetus' *Discourses*; see, e.g., Fergus Millar, 'Epictetus and the Imperial Court', *JRS* 55 (1965): 142; P. A. Brunt, 'From Epictetus to Arrian', *Athenaeum* 55 (1977): 19; Michele Valerie Ronnick, 'Epictetus', in *Ancient Greek Authors* (ed. W. W. Briggs; Dictionary of Literary Biography 176; Detroit, MI: Gale, 1997), 134. The date is actually rather uncertain. Long estimates that Epictetus' student Arrian, who recorded the *Discourses* (see below), attended Epictetus' school sometime in the period 105–113 CE (*Epictetus*, 38). But there are also those who believe it occurred in 113–117 CE (Chester G. Starr, Jr., 'Epictetus and the Tyrant', *CP* 44 [1949]: 22), or 117–120 CE (Klauck, *Religious Context*, 350), or even as late as around 130 CE (Adolf F. Bonhöffer, *Epiktet und das Neue Testament* [Gießen: Töpelmann, 1911], 82).

2

Lucius Annaeus Seneca

INTRODUCTION: A NOBLE PHILOSOPHER
AND POLITICIAN

Lucius Annaeus Seneca was born at the beginning of the Common Era in Corduba, a town in the southern part of the Roman province of Spain that had a long history of assimilation to Roman culture.[1] A son of an eminent rhetorician, the elder Seneca, he moved to Rome with the Annaei family at an early age and received the customary education of well-to-do Roman citizens.[2] The younger Seneca was the second in a row of three brothers, but his elder brother, Lucius Annaeus Novatus or L. Junius Gallio Annaeanus (Gallio), as he was called after his adoption by the senator Lucius Junius Gallio, was the very same Novatus/Gallio whom the apostle Paul is said to have met in the city of Corinth when the former served as proconsul of the province of Achaea (in 51–52 CE).[3] Seneca's younger brother, Marcus Annaeus Mela, was the father of the famous poet Lucan (Marcus Annaeus Lucanus).

Trained (mainly) in rhetoric, Seneca eventually entered into politics and the Senate, and gained quaestorship in his late thirties. According to Dio Cassius, Seneca was at this time 'superior in wisdom (σοφία) to all the Romans of his day and to many others as well'.[4] Subsequent to the death of emperor Gaius (Caligula) in 41 CE, however, he was banished from Rome by Gaius' successor, Claudius, and sent to the island of Corsica where he dwelt in

---

[1] Corduba is today the city of Córdoba in Andalucía. Besides Seneca's works themselves and the testimonies of the Roman historians, this summary account of Seneca's life benefits much from Griffin, *Seneca*, esp. chs. 2–3.

[2] Among his teachers was Attalus, a Stoic from Alexandria, who probably taught in his native language, Greek (so Paul Veyne, *Seneca: The Life of a Stoic* [trans. D. Sullivan; New York: Routledge, 2003], 4). On Attalus, see Seneca, *Ep.* 9.7; 63.5; 67.15; 72.8; 81.22; 108.3–4, 13–14, 23; 110.14–20. See also the useful discussion of Seneca's philosophical milieu in Brad Inwood, 'Seneca in his Philosophical Milieu', in *Reading Seneca: Stoic Philosophy at Rome* (Oxford: Clarendon Press, 2005).

[3] Acts 18.12–17. [4] *Hist. Rom.* 59.19.7.

exile for no less than eight years.[5] But in the year 49 CE Seneca was recalled from exile mainly through the influence of Claudius' fourth wife, Agrippina, who intended him to serve as a tutor of her son, Nero. A year later, Agrippina also secured Seneca's election to the praetorship.[6] When Nero acceded to the principate in 54 CE Seneca became counsellor to the young emperor.[7] Tacitus observes that Seneca and his associate, the pretorian prefect Sextus Afrianus Burrus, were 'guardians of the imperial youth, and—a rare occurrence where power is held in partnership—both in agreement, they exercised equal influence by contrasted methods' (*hi rectores imperatoriae iuventae et, rarum in societate potentiae, concordes, diversa arte ex aequo pollebant*).[8] Seneca's role and influence as counsellor was in part a moral one. Tacitus, who refers to him as Nero's *amicus* and *magister*, explains thus: 'Burrus, with his soldierly interests and austerity, and Seneca, with his lessons in eloquence and his self-respecting courtliness (*praeceptis eloquentiae et comitate honesta*), aided each other to ensure that the sovereign's years of temptation should, if he were scornful of virtue, be restrained within the bounds of permissible indulgence.'[9] Apparently Seneca was largely successful in this respect, for scholars widely agree that 'the good period' of Nero's reign (the so-called *quinquennium Neronis*) was precisely when the young emperor was still under the personal influence of Seneca and Burrus, especially that of the former.[10] However, after the deaths of Agrippina in 59 CE and, especially, of Burrus in 62 CE, Seneca's power and influence with the emperor waned and, without the latter's approval, he gradually withdrew from court. As a friend of the conspirator C. Calpurnius Piso, Seneca was accused of participation in a conspiracy against Nero in 65 CE (the so-called Pisonian conspiracy),[11] and in the aftermath he was forced to commit suicide.[12]

Seneca's life was in many respects marked by opposites. At one point, his influence with Nero was so great that he was certainly among the most

---

[5] The charge was adultery with Julia Livilla, Gaius' (and Agrippinas') younger sister. What actually caused the sentence is debated; see Griffin, *Seneca*, 59–61.

[6] cf. Tacitus, *Ann.* 12.8.

[7] This was a position that Chrysippus had recommended for the Stoic sage; see Peter Garnsey, 'Introduction: The Hellenistic and Roman Periods', in *The Cambridge History of Greek and Roman Political Thought* (ed. C. Rowe and M. Schofield with S. Harrison and M. Lane; Cambridge: Cambridge University Press, 2000), 404.

[8] *Ann.* 13.2. Cf. also Dio Cassius, *Hist. Rom.* 61.3–4. On the question of the two historians' attitudes to Seneca, see Griffin, *Seneca*, 427–33, 441–4. Generally speaking, whereas Tacitus was mostly—but not always—sympathetic to Seneca, Dio was mostly—but not always—hostile.

[9] *Ann.* 13.2. Cf. also Plutarch, *Mor.* 461F–62A.

[10] cf. Griffin, *Seneca*, 128, 170, 423–7; eadem, *Nero*, 46–8, 64–5, 67–82.

[11] On the 'Pisonian conspiracy' and Seneca's alleged participation in it, see Griffin, *Nero*, 164–77.

[12] See Tacitus, *Ann.* 15.60–3; Suetonius, *Nero* 35.5; Dio Cassius, *Hist. Rom.* 62.24–5.

powerful persons in Rome. At another, he was deprived of his life and everything else by the very person with whom his influence had been so great. Also, being a member of the equestrian Annaei family, Seneca would hardly have experienced anything close to real poverty.[13] In fact, at the height of his political power, Seneca was probably among the wealthiest individuals in Rome. On the other hand, from his youth he suffered from a different kind of poverty, namely, poor physical health caused by various kinds of illnesses, including catarrh, tuberculosis, and angina pectoris (or, perhaps, cardiac asthma).[14] This poor state of health greatly affected his life, even constituting an impetus for his interest in and preference for philosophy.[15] It is an aspect of Seneca's life that is scarcely considered in later reflections on his person, well reflected though it is in his writings. When afflicted time and again by the thought of ending his life because of the illness, it was above all his philosophical studies that kept Seneca alive: 'My studies were my salvation. I place it to the credit of philosophy that I recovered and regained my strength. I owe my life to philosophy.'[16]

Seneca was a dedicated moral philosopher who frequently applied didactic rhetoric of admonition in his writings. As such, he has received his own share of (counter-)criticism throughout history. Modern readers have been very willing indeed to judge him negatively with regard to his own moral integrity, typically seeing in him a kind of a hypocritical aristocrat who said one thing but did another.[17] Naturally, we can have no more certainty that Seneca actually followed his own moral teaching than we can have about any person

---

[13] cf. his notion of the 'simple life' as it is expressed in *Ep.* 87.1–10, where Seneca describes a two days' journey taken by him and one of his friends, a kind of ascetic exercise, on which they took with them 'very few slaves—one carriage-load—and no paraphernalia except what we wore on our persons. The mattress lies on the ground, and I upon the mattress. There are two rugs—one to spread beneath us and one to cover us. Nothing could have been subtracted from our luncheon; it took not more than an hour to prepare' (2–3). Cf. also *Ep.* 123.1–6.

[14] See Griffin, *Seneca*, 42–3. Angina pectoris is a heart condition marked by paroxysms of chest pain due to reduced oxygen to the heart. Seneca describes this condition as *suspirium* (*Ep.* 54), which, according to him, the physicians called 'practising how to die' (*meditationem mortis*). These symptoms might also have been caused by cardiac asthma. On Seneca's catarrh (*destillatio*) and tuberculosis (*phthisis*), see *Ep.* 75.12; 78.1–4. According to *Ep.* 78.2, when he was younger, Seneca often thought of ending his life because of his illness.

[15] For some time against the will of his father who 'detested philosophy' (*Ep.* 108.22) and wanted him to enter politics early on; see Griffin, *Seneca*, 45–6. According to Griffin, 'it was a combination of ill health and the attractions of ascetic preachers that first drew Seneca to philosophy' (*Seneca*, 177).

[16] *Ep.* 78.3: *Studia mihi nostra saluti fuerunt. Philosophiae acceptum fero, quod surrexi, quod convalui. Illi vitam debeo.*

[17] A striking example is Russell, *History*, 260–76. Another is John W. Basore, 'Introduction', in *Seneca: Moral Essays* (trans. J. W. Basore; 3 vols.; LCL; Cambridge, MA: Harvard University Press, 1928), 1: ix.

from antiquity. At best, the sources allow us to extract certain implications for a prominent individual like Seneca. But common opinion about his person seems very much affected, first, by the bare fact that he was a wealthy man, as if that alone would have made him selfish and hypocritical by definition, and, second, by a peculiar fusion of the tutor and counsellor Seneca with the student and emperor Nero, who is best remembered for his bad morality. Here it seems to matter little that our sources suggest that the emperor's 'good period' was in fact precisely when he was under Seneca's influence.

The stereotyped image of Seneca as a pretentious hypocrite is amazingly widespread, often simply found 'as a stock assertion dragged from one second-hand work to another'.[18] To be sure, Seneca himself does imply that there were those in his lifetime who accused him of some kind of hypocrisy, of talking one way and living another,[19] and Tacitus recounts some (political) charges made against him[20]—which is anything but surprising given his political position. And then, of course, we have the hostile remarks of Dio Cassius in the third century.[21] But against these testimonies we should also consider potential evidences to the contrary. Tacitus, for one, does not endorse the accusations against Seneca that he reports, but is instead generally well disposed towards him. 'Seneca's sincerity and good character are stressed to the end ([*Ann.*] 14.52–3) and his continued good repute implied (15.65).'[22] Furthermore, it is well known that Suetonius, in his *Lives of the Caesars*, relished to report whatever unfavourable gossip he had about his subjects.[23] One might therefore expect at least some of this concerning such a man as Seneca. Not only was he prominent, powerful, and moneyed, he also served as the tutor and counsellor of the horribly vicious Nero (as Suetonius portrays him). Yet, of such unfavourable comments there are no traces at all in Suetonius' work. Admittedly, this is an argument from silence. But it is nevertheless worth considering. Moreover, Juvenal, writing in the same period as Suetonius and Tacitus, speaks explicitly of Seneca's generosity as something proverbial and exemplary.[24] So too does Martial.[25] Of course, both Juvenal and Martial are referring to Seneca's generosity towards his friends and clients, not some beggars in the streets. A word of praise for giving to the

---

[18] Villy Sørensen, *Seneca: The Humanist at the Court of Nero* (trans. W. G. Jones; Edinburgh: Canongate, 1984), 319. Cf. Morford's recent criticism of this tendency (*Roman Philosophers*, 166–7). Examples of scholarly discussions based on such stock assertions include Sevenster, *Paul and Seneca*, 173–4, 180–5, and *passim*; Piper, 'Love Your Enemies', 22–5.

[19] *Vit. beat.* 17–28.   [20] *Ann.* 13.42; 14.52.

[21] See the discussion in Griffin, *Seneca*, 427–33.   [22] Griffin, *Seneca*, 443–4.

[23] cf. Catharine Edwards, 'Introduction', in *Suetonius: Lives of the Caesars* (trans. C. Edwards; OWC; Oxford: Oxford University Press, 2000).

[24] *Sat.* 5.108–11. Cf. also Tacitus, *Ann.* 15.62.   [25] *Epigr.* 12.36.5–10.

truly poor is hardly what we should anticipate in this context (or should we? cf. *Ben.* 4.3.1).[26] Nor should we expect Seneca himself to have had any real experience of poverty,[27] or, for that matter, to have been even conscious of that 'lack' of experience when he praised the virtuous life of poverty in his moral writings.[28] But that does not in itself make him a selfish hypocrite. Tacitus tells of Seneca's wish to retire from Nero's service in 62 CE and to return his riches to the emperor,[29] and Suetonius seconds this with the words that 'the old man often pleaded to be allowed to retire and offered to give up his estates'.[30] The wish was not granted. Even Dio Cassius can comment positively on Seneca,[31] despite his hostility towards him and the more famous accusations of hypocrisy.[32]

But why is it that Dio Cassius' third-century version of the story is taken more seriously as a historical source than the other texts referred to above, which are at least a century older? How can the latter (older) testimonies of Seneca be so easily overlooked? Perhaps because, in the end, nobody likes a moralist, least of all a rich one. And yet we must be aware that 'hypocrisy is a convenient charge to hurl at an enemy in any age . . . As long as people profess moral principles, with whatever degree of seriousness, their enemies will quote their words against their deeds.'[33] As Seneca says himself in *De Vita Beata*, 'the same reproach . . . has been made against Plato, against Epicurus, against Zeno; for all these told, not how they themselves were living, but how they ought to live'.[34] And he continues: 'It is of virtue, not of myself, that I am speaking, and my quarrel is against all vices, more especially against my own. When I shall be able, I shall live as I ought.' It is important to have in mind that Seneca always *aimed* to be but never claimed to be a 'wise man'.[35] Against the stock charge that philosophers do not practise what they preach Seneca replies: 'Yet they do practise *much* that they preach, much that their virtuous minds conceive. . . . But if you are a man (*vir*), look up to those who are *attempting* great things (*magna conantis*), even though they fall.'[36] It is the will

---

[26] Seneca, *Ben.* 4.3.1: 'If we made contributions with the expectation of receiving a return, we should give, not to the most worthy, but to the richest, men; as it is (*nunc vero*), we prefer a poor man (*pauperem*) to an importunate rich man.' Cf. the discussion in Chapter 9 below.

[27] cf. *Ep.* 80.6; *Helv.* 12.1.

[28] One useful discussion of the poor in ancient Rome is found in C. R. Whittaker, 'The Poor', in *The Romans* (ed. A. Giardina; trans. L. G. Cochrane; Chicago, IL: University of Chicago Press, 1993), 272–99.

[29] *Ann.* 14.54.　　[30] *Nero* 35.5.

[31] *Hist. Rom.* 59.19.7; 61.3.3; 61.7.5; 62.18.3; 62.24.1.　　[32] See esp. *Hist. Rom.* 61.10.1–6.

[33] Griffin, 'Philosophy', 19.　　[34] *Vit. beat.* 18.1.

[35] cf. *Vit. beat.* 17.3–4; *Helv.* 5.2; *Ep.* 57.3; 116.5; 117.29. The 'wise man' or the sage (ὁ σοφός/φρόνιμος, *sapiens*) was the Stoic term for the ideal philosopher and human being.

[36] *Vit. beat.* 20.1–2.

and effort that counts. With a certain tone of irony Seneca refers to the 'wise man' saying: 'I do not live one way and talk another, but I talk one way and you hear another—only the sound of my words reaches your ears, what they mean you do not inquire.'[37] This is something to consider when we give ear to his moral teaching.

MORAL TEACHING IN SENECA: LOVING EACH AND ALL

Seneca stands out for his choice to practise philosophy in Latin rather than in Greek, which was the predominant philosophical language, even among the Romans.[38] And he succeeded well in doing so, both qualitatively and quantitatively. He appears to have handled most types of literary genres: tragedies,[39] satire(s),[40] scientific works (physics),[41] letters,[42] (epistolary) consolations,[43] philosophical essays,[44] and political works,[45] including the emperor's speeches. Unfortunately, despite the great quantity of his extant works, many are either fragmentary or entirely lost,[46] and their chronology is rather

[37] *Vit. beat.* 25.8.

[38] cf. Inwood, 'Seneca', 11–13. Musonius Rufus, for instance, preferred Greek (cf. below), and so did even (later) the Roman emperor himself, Marcus Aurelius, in his *Meditations* (even if written for private purposes).

[39] *Hercules Furens* (The Madness of Hercules), *Troades* (The Trojan Women), *Phoenissae* (The Phoenician Women), *Medea, Phaedra, Oedipus, Agamemnon, Thyestes.* Tradition also ascribes *Octavia* and *Hercules Oetaeus* (Hercules on Oeta) to Seneca, but these tragedies are probably post-Senecan.

[40] Extant is Seneca's *Apocolocyntosis Divi Claudii* (The Pumpkinification of the Divine Claudius), written after Claudius' death in 54 CE.

[41] *Naturales Quaestiones* (Natural Questions) in seven books, written sometime in 62–64 CE.

[42] Extant are the 124 *Epistulae Morales* (Moral Letters), from the period 62–65 CE.

[43] *Ad Marciam, De Consolatione* (To Marcia, On Consolation), *Ad Polybium, De Consolatione* (To Polybius, On Consolation), *Ad Helviam Matrem, De Consolatione* (To Helvia His Mother, On Consolation), the first one probably written under Gaius (37–41 CE), the latter two during the exile (41–49 CE).

[44] Including *De Ira* (On Anger), *De Brevitate Vitae* (On the Shortness of Life), *De Constantia Sapientis* (On the Firmness of the Sage), *De Tranquillitate Animi* (On Tranquillity of Mind), *De Otio* (On Leisure), *De Vita Beata* (On the Happy Life), *De Beneficiis* (On Benefits), and *De Providentia* (On Providence), composed at various times under the reigns of Claudius and Nero. The political *De Clementia* may also be included as a philosophical work.

[45] *De Clementia* (On Mercy), addressed to Nero in 55–56 CE.

[46] Including *De Lapidum Natura, De Piscium Natura, De Motu Terrarum, De Situ et Sacris Aegyptiorum, De Situ Indiae, De Vita Patris, De Matrimonio, De Remediis Fortuitorum, De Superstitione,* and *Moralis Philosophiae Libri.*

uncertain.[47] Seneca wrote extensively on ethics, both before, during, and after his position as Nero's tutor and counsellor, for besides being a politician Seneca was above all a moral philosopher. Diverse though they are, most of his writings are devoted to moral teaching or ethics, a topic so prominent in Seneca's philosophy that it influences even those of his works whose philosophical substance is secondary at most. This is wholly in line with the increasing weight put on ethics (compared with physics and logic) by the Stoicism of the day.

Seneca expresses well the Stoic belief that morality is rooted in the proper order of Nature itself. As God determined and designed it, it is simply in the nature of each and every human being to love his or her neighbour: 'Nature begot me loving all people' (*natura me amantem omnium genuit*), Seneca declares.[48] According to him and his fellow Stoics, humans received from the very beginning and continue to receive a part of the Reason (*ratio, λόγος*) that pervades the world. The result is a common reason shared by all. And not only is it a common reason but a *divine* common reason, which, in turn, makes the human being sacred as such: *Homo, sacra res homini, . . .* ('Human being, sacred to a human being, . . .').[49] That applies to all humanity.

Seneca underlines that human beings are not intended to dissociate themselves from other human beings but rather to live in accordance with their nature as social creatures, begotten for the common good (*hominem sociale animal communi bono genitum*).[50] The gods have a greater concern for humanity as a whole (*universis*) than for single individuals.[51] There is thus an unbreakable bond between all human beings, devised by the divine Nature itself, which means that 'there is no such thing as good or bad fortune for the individual; we live in common (*in commune vivitur*). And no one can live happily who has regard to himself alone and transforms everything into a question of his own utility.'[52] Instead, one must live for one's neighbour, if one would live for oneself (*alteri vivas oportet, si vis tibi vivere*). Nature produced human beings related to one another (*cognatos*)

---

[47] Griffin provides a helpful table of Seneca's extant prose works and their possible chronology (*Seneca*, 396). But cf. also the discussion in Karlhans Abel, 'Seneca: Leben und Leistung', *ANRW* 32.2: 703–11.

[48] *Ep.* 102.18. My translation. The LCL trans. reads: 'I am naturally born to love all men'. Cf. Cicero, *Fin.* 3.65: 'we are born for society and intercourse, and for a natural partnership with our fellow men'.

[49] *Ep.* 95.33. 'Man, an object of reverence in the eyes of man, . . .' in the LCL trans.

[50] *Clem.* 1.3.2. Cf. *Ben.* 7.1.7: *si [animus] sociale animal et in commune genitus mundum ut unam omnium domum spectat* ('[the soul] that, social creature that it is and born for the common good, views the world as the universal home of mankind').

[51] *Prov.* 3.1. Cf. *Ben.* 7.19.9. Cf. also Cicero, *Fin.* 3.64.   [52] *Ep.* 48.2.

and engendered in them mutual love (*amorem mutuum*), Seneca explains to his friend Lucilius.[53] Hence it can never be right to correct wrongdoing by doing wrong (*non oportet peccata corrigere peccantem*).[54] 'How much more human (*humanius*) to manifest toward wrong-doers (*peccantibus*) a kind and fatherly spirit (*mitem et patrium animum*), not hunting them down but calling them back!' he exclaims.[55] For 'human life is founded on kindness (*beneficiis*) and concord (*concordia*), and is bound into an alliance for common help (*in foedus auxiliumque commune*), not by terror (*terrore*), but by mutual love (*mutuo amore*)'.[56] Every wrongdoing is to be treated with its opposite.[57] In other words, instead of avenging an injury it is by far better to heal one, and it is by far better to treat unkindness with kindness than to match fault with fault.[58] Even enemies should be met with benevolence and care, according to Seneca.[59] He recommends bearing in mind the following maxim: 'You must expect to be treated by others as you yourself have treated them' (*ab alio exspectes, alteri quod feceris*).[60]

Obviously, Seneca's point with the maxim is to urge one to treat other people well. But is its underlying motive 'sincere', or is it *de facto* 'egocentric'? That is, is this a good precept to follow (just) for one's own sake or (also) for the sake of others (is it what some might call a 'passive golden rule')? In one of his letters to Lucilius, Seneca emphasizes that there is a reciprocal relationship between these two facets and ways of benefiting, for when one does good to the other one does good to oneself: 'There is not a man who, when he has benefited his neighbour, has not benefited himself' (*nemo non, cum alteri prodest, sibi profuit*).[61] By this he does not mean that the actual goal of doing good to others is to eventually benefit oneself. It is not for some (material) recompense that one does good to other people. In Seneca's own words: 'I do not mean for the reason that he whom you have aided will desire to aid you, or that he whom you have defended will desire to protect you, or that an example of good conduct returns in a circle to benefit the doer.' His message is rather that 'the reward for all the virtues lies in the virtues themselves'. The wages of every good deed is, in other words, simply to have done it (*recte facti fecisse merces est*). And he continues: 'I am grateful, not in order that my neighbour (*alius*), provoked by the earlier act of kindness, may be more ready to benefit me, but simply in order that I may perform a most pleasant and beautiful act; I feel grateful, not because it profits me, but because it pleases me.'[62]

---

53 *Ep.* 95.52.   54 *Ira* 1.16.1.   55 *Ira* 1.14.3.   56 *Ira* 1.5.3.
57 See, e.g., *Ira* 2.10.6–7; 2.28.4; 2.32.1; 2.34.5; *Ep.* 66.21.   58 *Ira* 3.27.1, 3.
59 *Otio* 1.4. Cf. 8.2; *Vit. beat.* 20.5; *Ep.* 120.10; *Ira* 2.28.4; *Ben.* 7.31.1, 5. Cf. also *Ep.* 66.21.
60 *Ep.* 94.43. Cf. 103.3.   61 *Ep.* 81.19.   62 *Ep.* 81.20.

This is of course wholly in line with the Stoic teaching of virtue as the highest good—indeed the only good, since only what has moral worth is good, according to the Stoics. The good is everyone's end ($\tau \acute{\epsilon} \lambda o s$). To live as a Stoic, then, that is, 'in agreement with Nature',[63] is to have virtue constantly as the ultimate goal. 'Life in accordance with Nature' and 'moral virtue and virtuous acts' amount to the very same thing in Stoicism.[64] According to Seneca, specific virtues include, of course, the four cardinal ones,[65] but in moral terms those of a more subordinate type are imperative as well, like *humanitas*[66] and *clementia*,[67] both of which correspond closely to the Greek $\phi \iota \lambda \alpha \nu \theta \rho \omega \pi \acute{\iota} \alpha$ (*philanthrōpia*).[68] But in order to be able to exercise virtue one needs training in philosophy, for without proper training every human being is in danger of remaining self-centred and indifferent to other people.[69] A prerequisite for proper moral behaviour is thus proper guidance and learning. It is moral education that makes the person conscious of her being in the world and thus of her kinship with other people. For Seneca, it is indeed a primary purpose of philosophy to lead one to and on the virtuous path of unity and mutual care. As he explains in one of his letters to Lucilius, 'the first thing which philosophy undertakes to give is fellow-feeling with all men (*sensum communem*); in other words, sympathy and sociability (*humanitatem et congregationem*)'.[70] Philosophy properly comprehended leads one to the virtue of an 'all-embracing love of the human race even as of oneself' (*humani generis comprendens ut sui amor*).[71]

We have here an echo of the theory of *oikeiōsis* (οἰκείωσις) or 'appropriation',[72] which lies at the heart of Stoic ethics. In simplified

---

[63] On this terminology, see Striker, 'Following Nature', 2–13.

[64] cf. Engberg-Pedersen, *Paul*, 58–9.

[65] i.e. prudence (φρόνησις, *prudentia*), moderation or self-control (σωφροσύνη, *temperantia*), justice (δικαιοσύνη, *iustitia*), and courage (ἀνδρεία, *fortitudo*). Cf. the discussion of Musonius in Chapter 3 below.

[66] *Ep.* 88.29–30; 115.3.   [67] *Clem.* 1.3.2.

[68] However, 'some have suggested that by the late first century AD [*humanitas*] may have conveyed the idea of a warm, human sympathy for the weak and helpless in a measure which *philanthropia* never did' (A. R. Hands, *Charities and Social Aid in Greece and Rome* [Ithaca, NY: Cornell University Press, 1968], 87).

[69] cf. *Ep.* 94.47–8.   [70] *Ep.* 5.4.   [71] *Clem.* 1.11.2.

[72] It is extremely difficult to give an apt translation of *oikeiōsis*, and Nicholas P. White seems to speak for many when he claims that the term is 'impossible to translate into English' ('The Basis of Stoic Ethics', *HSCP* 83 [1979]: 145). 'Appropriation', however, is often used (e.g. Long and Sedley, *Hellenistic Philosophers*, 1: 346–54; Reydams-Schils, *Roman Stoics*, 53, 55). Brad Inwood proposes the translation 'orientation' (*Ethics and Human Action in Early Stoicism* [Oxford: Clarendon Press, 1985], 184–5; he adds, however, that the word is 'ultimately untranslatable'). Julia Annas prefers 'familiarization' (*The Morality of Happiness* [New York: Oxford University Press, 1993], 262), following a suggestion by Jonathan Barnes, and so does Engberg-Pedersen (*Paul*, 54).

terms,[73] the theory teaches that human beings are born with an inclination to preserve and take care of that which 'belongs' to themselves, the Greek root οικ- basically connoting ownership, what belongs to someone or something.[74] This instinctive inclination aims, first, at the individual's own well-being and self-sustaining, but also at his or her concern for humanity as a whole—the so-called 'social *oikeiōsis*'.[75] The theory is fundamentally community-oriented, and in it the distinction between self-interest and altruism is overcome.[76] It holds that human beings are naturally 'programmed' to show affection for other people as well as themselves. It lies in their very nature to be friendly and philanthropic, and to live in organized societies. Philosophical training, on the other hand, is essential. It is moral instruction, including learning of *oikeiōsis*, that calls each individual to an awareness of his or her own identity and nature as a rational human being, and thus to proper conduct. That is precisely what Seneca alludes to above when he explains the role of philosophy, giving specific attention to the second, social aspect of *oikeiōsis*. For Seneca, this aspect is of no less weight than the first. It is rather the other side of the same coin, as is shown by the ideal Stoic sage himself whose good is said to be 'a common good' (*commune bonum est sapientis*)[77] and who 'considers nothing more truly his own than that which he shares in partnership with all mankind (*cum humano genere consortium est*).'[78] In other words, '[t]he Stoic concept of οἰκείωσις connected the Stoic concern to live

---

[73] See further Gisela Striker, 'The Role of *Oikeiosis* in Stoic Ethics', *OSAP* 1 (1983): 145–67; Troels Engberg-Pedersen, 'Discovering the Good: *Oikeiōsis* and *Kathēkonta* in Stoic Ethics', in *The Norms of Nature: Studies in Hellenistic Ethics* (ed. M. Schofield and G. Striker; Cambridge: Cambridge University Press, 1986), 145–83; idem, *The Stoic Theory of Oikeiosis: Moral Development and Social Interaction in Early Stoic Philosophy* (Aarhus: Aarhus University Press, 1990); Gretchen Reydams-Schils, 'Human Bonding and *Oikeiōsis* in Roman Stoicism', *OSAP* 22 (2002): 221–51. For a brief introduction, see Annas, *Morality*, 262–76; Brennan, *Stoic Life*, 154–68.

[74] The opposite to *oikeion* (οἰκεῖον) is *allotrion* (ἀλλότριον), 'what is alien, foreign, strange'. '[I]t is therefore that which "belongs to you", so that you and it go together. *Oikeiōsis* is then the process of making a thing belong, and this is achieved by the recognition that the thing is *oikeion*, that it does belong to you, that it is yours' (Sandbach, *Stoics*, 32).

[75] Brad Inwood, 'Comments on Professor Görgemann's Paper: The Two Forms of *Oikeiōsis* in Arius and the Stoa', in *On Stoic and Peripatetic Ethics: The Work of Arius Didymus* (ed. W. W. Fortenbaugh; New Brunswick, NJ: Transaction Books, 1983), 193. Cf. also idem, *Ethics*, 186; Annas, *Morality*, 265; Reydams-Schils, *Roman Stoics*, 55.

[76] Reydams-Schils, 'Human Bonding', 223, 239–40. Cicero explains well the Stoic point of view that became so prominent in Roman Stoicism: 'It is your duty to consider the interests of your fellow-men and to serve society; you were brought into the world under these conditions and have these inborn principles which you are in duty bound to obey and follow, that your interest shall be the interest of the community and conversely that the interest of the community shall be your interest as well' (*Off.* 3.52).

[77] *Ep.* 85.36.

[78] *Ep.* 73.7. According to Cicero, the sage would in fact die if he were to live in complete isolation from society (*Off.* 1.153). Cf. Diogenes Laertius 7.123: ἀλλὰ μὴν οὐδ' ἐν ἐρημίᾳ, φασί,

according to nature or virtue and the obligation to take care of one's fellow human beings by making the person's identity as part of universal humanity the starting point for social ethics'.[79] Seneca himself provides an excellent summary of the basic thought behind social *oikeiōsis* in an answer to the question, 'How to deal with human beings', and defines it at the same time as a 'rule' (*formula*) for appropriate human behaviour:

I can lay down for mankind a rule, in short compass, for our duties in human relationships (*humani officii*): all that you behold, that which comprises both god and man, is one—we are the parts of one great body (*membra sumus corporis magni*). Nature produced us related to one another (*cognatos*), since she created us from the same source and to the same end. She engendered in us mutual love (*amorem mutuum*), and made us prone to friendships (*sociabiles*). She established fairness and justice (*aequum iustumque*); according to her ruling, it is more wretched to commit than to suffer injury. Through her orders, let our hands be ready for all that needs to be helped. Let this verse be in your heart and on your lips: 'I am a man; and nothing in man's lot do I deem foreign to me' (*'homo sum, humani nihil a me alienum puto'*). Let us possess things in common (*in commune*); for birth is ours in common. Our relations with one another are like a stone arch, which would collapse if the stones did not mutually support each other, and which is upheld in this very way.[80]

Seneca uses here a widely known metaphor to describe the (actual) position of each and every person in the world, and his or her (proper) relation to fellow human beings, namely, *membra sumus corporis magni*. The 'body' metaphor is of great interest for the present study. Highly favoured by the Stoics, it was of course well fit for its purpose because it made use of such a universally familiar and corporeal phenomenon as the body. After all, 'no animal is at loss how to use its body'.[81] The metaphor in Seneca's use above illustrates how each and every individual is naturally related simply through being an integral part of the world itself. There is an invisible but indissoluble interrelation between all human beings, a fundamental, original unity of humankind, the essence of which no one can annul.[82]

βιώσεται ὁ σπουδαῖος [= ὁ σοφός]· κοινωνικὸς γὰρ φύσει καὶ πρακτικός ('Nor yet, they go on to say, will the wise man live in solitude; for he is naturally made for society and action').

[79] Lee, *Paul*, 69.

[80] *Ep.* 95.51–3. The phrase *amorem mutuum* is translated as 'mutual affection' in the LCL. The 'verse' that Seneca quotes here derives from the Roman poet Terence (*Haut.* 77). Cf. also the somewhat different translation of the passage in Brad Inwood, 'Rules and Reasoning in Stoic Ethics', in *Topics in Stoic Philosophy* (ed. K. Ierodiakonou; Oxford: Clarendon Press, 1999), 119; e.g. 'we are limbs of a gigantic body. Nature brought us forth as blood-relatives, for she created us from the same elements and in the same element. It is she who gave us reciprocal love and made us social. . . . Let our possessions be for the general good; we were born for it.'

[81] *Ep.* 121.6.   [82] cf. also Cicero, *Fin.* 3.62–3.

The 'body' metaphor, a very common *topos* in Graeco-Roman antiquity,[83] was frequently used to describe and encourage mutual love, care, and obligation in human relations, whether between relatives, citizens, or human beings in general.[84] It was also utilized in philosophical discourse on the relationship between the whole and its parts. Often it underlined that each and every member of a family, or of an organized community, or indeed of humanity, had some specific function in the whole. It demonstrated logically that the whole is made of and dependent upon different parts, and that all these parts are necessary, if differently positioned, in order for the whole to function properly. Seneca paints this portrait in one of his philosophical writings:

What if the hands should desire to harm the feet, or the eyes the hands? As all the members of the body are in harmony with another because it is to the advantage of the whole that the individual members be unharmed, so mankind should spare the individual man, because all are born for a life of fellowship (*ad coetum*), and society can be kept unharmed only by the mutual protection and love of its parts (*amore partium*).[85]

It is noteworthy that, in this text, Seneca's primary attention is paid, not to the individual member's obligation towards the whole, but vice versa, namely, to society's responsibility towards the individual.[86] His purpose with the metaphor in the passage is to argue that it is always wrong to injure (*nocere*) another human being, for 'if we reverence the whole, the parts are sacred' (*sanctae partes sunt, si universum venerabile est*), and this particular human being, like any human being, is 'your fellow-citizen (*urbe civis*) in the greater commonwealth (*in maiore*)' (ibid.). For Seneca, then, and already before him in Cicero's presentation of Stoicism to the Romans,[87] the 'body' metaphor was a key argument in his call for unity and universal humanity. The associative potentials of the 'body' as an object known to everyone made it

---

[83] A widely celebrated example is the tale of Menenius Agrippa's attempt to restore harmony among Roman citizens (*concordia civium*) by likening the city to a human body. The tale is told in Livy, *Ab urbe cond.* 2.32, and in Dionysius of Halicarnassus, *Ant. rom.* 6.86.

[84] See esp. Lee, *Paul*, 29–58, 83–102. Cf. also John K. McVay, 'The Human Body as Social and Political Metaphor in Stoic Literature and Early Christian Writers', *BASP* 37 (2000): 135–47; Ruth I. Hicks, 'The Body Political and the Body Ecclesiastical', *JBR* 31 (1963): 29–35.

[85] *Ira* 2.31.7.

[86] cf., on the other hand, *Ep.* 33.5, where Seneca accentuates the function of the parts for the whole, and stresses that it is the latter that counts: 'Examine the separate parts (*singula membra*), if you like, provided you examine them as parts of the man himself. She is not a beautiful woman whose ankle or arm is praised, but she whose general appearance (*universa facies*) makes you forget to admire her single attributes (*partibus singulis*).'

[87] See esp. *Fin.* 3.62–3. Cf. also *Nat. d.* 2.86. One may compare Manilius, *Astronomica* 1.247–55; 2.63–8 (written in Latin a few decades before Seneca's works).

a powerful means to illustrate not only the position of human beings in the world and in relation to the divine,[88] but also their relation to one another.

But how far, we may ask, would a well-positioned and wealthy man of the Roman elite such as Seneca have been ready to go with all this in real life? How serious a rule was his own 'rule for our duties in human relationships' (cf. above)? In fact, were not Stoics like him largely self-centred, mostly concerned with themselves as a (potential) group of 'wise men'?[89] I have already addressed the first two questions above,[90] namely, whether Seneca himself practised what he so intensely preached. There I pointed out how strangely and unfairly history seems to have treated him, in part simply due to his wealth, as if that in some automatic and obvious way says something decisive about his morality, but also due to a curious fusion of the tutor–counsellor Seneca and the student–emperor Nero. But the question, again, is extremely difficult, as it is with respect to any figure from antiquity.

As for the third question, it is true that some earlier Stoics, as indeed countless other prominent Greek philosophers, were said to have been rather 'self-centred' and to have distinguished between a certain group of men who were or could be 'wise men' (themselves and their likes) and the rest.[91] But, even if this were the case, the course of history did not simply break off at that point. Stoicism did not cease to develop and change, no more than other major systems of thought. With Roman Stoicism there was a fundamental shift of focus from the (potential) genius of a few men to the potential of all human beings: whereas for (some) earlier Stoics right reason, ὁ ὀρθὸς λόγος, was restricted to the 'wise man', for the Roman Stoics *all* human beings have their share in this universal reason,[92] a thought that we already see in Cicero.[93] The 'community of reason' was in other words taken by the Roman Stoics beyond the bond among the 'wise men' to embrace all those who partake of divine reason.[94] Unfortunately, this development is often overlooked in modern discussions of Stoicism, sometimes largely due to a terribly rigid, even dogmatic, attention to only the earliest stages of the philosophy. But, especially when discussing the Graeco-Roman world of the first two centuries CE, it is necessary (also) to look beyond this earliest of Stoic periods. As we

---

[88] cf. *Ep.* 92.30: *Totum hoc, quo continemur, et unum est et deus; et socii sumus eius et membra* ('All this universe which encompasses us is one, and it is God; we are associates of God; we are his members').

[89] It should be noted that, in antiquity, charges of this kind were made not only against the Stoics, but against philosophers in general. For discussion (and counter-arguments), see Annas, *Morality*, 223–325.

[90] See the introduction to this chapter.

[91] See, e.g., Diogenes Laertius 7.121–5; Stobaeus, *Ecl.* 2.7.5b12; 2.7.11g–s (= Arius Didymus 5b12; 11g–s).

[92] cf. Lee, *Paul*, 62.   [93] *Fin.* 3.62–4.   [94] Reydams-Schils, *Roman Stoics*, 70.

have already seen, Roman Stoic philosophy was anything but self-centred: 'In its relation with fellow human beings, not all of whom endorse the same philosophical ideal, the Stoic self has,... contrary to common opinion, a profoundly altruistic outlook.'[95] Strong support for this assessment comes when in one of his letters Seneca observes that while the (ideal) sage does indeed need friends and friendship like everyone else, he does not make friends in order, for instance, to have someone at his side when he is ill, or to have someone to help him when he is in prison or in want (as Epicurus had explained it, according to Seneca). Rather, he enters into a friendship so 'that he may have someone by whose sick-bed he himself may sit, someone a prisoner in hostile hands whom he himself may set free'.[96] The purpose of making a friend is in Seneca's opinion 'to have someone for whom I may die, whom I may follow into exile, against whose death I may stake my own life, and pay the pledge, too'.[97] Instead of the commonly alleged 'self-centred' philosophy, we see here a decidedly altruistic one. That is also why Seneca can claim:

I am aware that among the ill-informed the Stoic school is unpopular on the ground that it is excessively harsh... But the fact is, no school is more kindly and gentle (*benignior leniorque*), none more full of love to man (*amantior hominum*) and more concerned for the common good (*communis boni attentior*), so that it is its avowed object to be of service and assistance, and to regard not merely self-interest, but the interest of each and all (*universis singulisque*).[98]

In their adaptation of an originally Greek philosophical ideal, the Roman Stoics applied it to their own society and everyday life in a way that reveals a distinctive pattern of underlining social responsibility.[99] Characteristic of this Roman development of Stoicism was not only its call for priority of ethics over logic and physics, but also the strong emphasis on practical application of the former—ethics in action.[100] Telling perhaps is the fact that we know of no theoretical composition authored by the great Stoic teacher Musonius Rufus, nor indeed by his student Epictetus.[101] Like Socrates, their prime model, they do not seem to have written anything of that sort—unfortunately for later generations, of course. But even an effective and skilful wordsmith like Seneca stressed the importance of practical application and learning.[102]

---

[95] Reydams-Schils, *Roman Stoics*, 51.   [96] *Ep.* 9.8.   [97] *Ep.* 9.10.

[98] *Clem.* 2.5.2–3.   [99] Reydams-Schils, *Roman Stoics*, 1, 3.

[100] cf. Christopher Gill, 'The School in the Roman Imperial Period', in *The Cambridge Companion to the Stoics* (ed. B. Inwood; Cambridge: Cambridge University Press, 2003), 40–4; Reydams-Schils, *Roman Stoics*, 1–13; Sandbach, *Stoics*, 19.

[101] See further below.

[102] cf. Arnold, *Roman Stoicism*, 115: Seneca's works 'admirably illustrate for us Stoicism in its practical application to daily life'.

For instance, in a letter to Lucilius he informs his friend that he intends to send him some books from which to learn certain things. Then he adds: 'Of course, however, the living voice and the intimacy of a common life will help you more than the written word. You must go to the scene of action' (*plus tamen tibi et viva vox et convictus quam oratio proderit. In rem praesentem venias oportet*).[103] Despite his own extensive theoretical work, Seneca refers approvingly to the opinion of Demetrius the Cynic that a few philosophical maxims continually put into practice are of much more worth than piles of knowledge never used.[104]

This is not to say that Seneca wished to derogate the value of (theoretical) knowledge. There is little doubt that he adhered to the Stoic doctrine of knowledge as prerequisite to anything else (see esp. *Ep.* 95). Rather, he sometimes downplays the role of the theoretical in order to underline the practical, that is, in order to stress that 'philosophy teaches us to act, not to speak' (*facere docet philosophia, non dicere*).[105] Hence Seneca's advice to Lucilius: 'Choose as a guide one whom you will admire more when you see him act than when you hear him speak' (*eum elige adiutorem, quem magis admireris, cum videris quam cum audieris*).[106] Seneca also clearly held to the Stoic view that one should endeavour to serve one's fellow human beings in practice by engaging public affairs.[107]

The doctrine that human beings have equal share in divine reason, and that they thus have moral obligations towards each other that transcend all structures of society, gives Stoic ethics 'an inescapable social dimension'.[108] Seneca confirms this time and again: because people are naturally related to one another, and are thus by nature social and mutually loving, they ought to give aid to one another in all possible ways. They even obliged to help as many people as they can.[109] Due to common origin, 'the human race have certain rights in common' (*aliquod esse commune ius generis humani*).[110] Should one, then, stretch forth the hand to the shipwrecked sailor, or point out the way to the wanderer, or share a crust with the starving?[111] Yes, says Seneca. Should one care as much for one's neighbour as for oneself?[112] Yes, says Seneca. What about slaves? Does all this count for them as well? Naturally, Seneca states. Social status is of no consequence in this regard: 'Nature bids me do good to all mankind—whether slaves or freemen, freeborn

---

[103] *Ep.* 6.5.   [104] *Ben.* 7.1.3.

[105] *Ep.* 20.2. Cf. 16.3; 20.1; 24.15; 34.4; 89.14–15; *Vit. beat.* 27.4, 6.

[106] *Ep.* 52.8. Cf. Sørensen, *Seneca*, 307: 'Seneca always took issue with those philosophers who were less concerned with reality than with their language.'

[107] e.g. *Otio* 3.5. Cf. *Tranq.* 3.1.   [108] Colish, *Stoic Tradition*, 38.

[109] *Otio* 3.5. Cf. Cicero, *Fin.* 3.65.   [110] *Ep.* 48.3 (*sic* LCL trans.).

[111] *Ep.* 95.51.   [112] *Ep.* 90.40.

or freed-men, whether the laws gave them freedom or a grant in the presence of friends—what difference does it make? Wherever there is a human being there is the opportunity for a kindness.'[113]

In terms of moral obligation, of course, the ideal sage enjoys no exceptions, but is rather the ultimate example of helping others and serving the common good.[114] The sage embodies social virtues such as *humanitas* ('kindliness'), a virtue that 'forbids you to be over-bearing towards your associates (*socios*), and it forbids you to be grasping. In words and in deeds and in feelings it shows itself gentle and courteous to all men. It counts no evil as another's solely.'[115] Seneca lists here *humanitas* along with *fides* (= πίστις) and the two cardinal virtues *fortitudo* (= ἀνδρεία) and *temperantia* (= σωφροσύνη). Subsequently, he also adds the virtue *clementia*, which 'spares a neighbour's life as if it were one's own and knows that it is not for man to make wasteful use of his fellow-man'.[116] This notion agrees with Seneca's abhorrence of such savage spectacles as gladiatorial shows and slaughter of criminals in the arena.[117]

This concern for the less fortunate is a direct consequence of the Stoic doctrine of universal humanity, the consistent endorsement of which we have seen many times above. The human race *as a whole* is the object of love and care, not just some portion of it.[118] And the world itself is 'the universal home of mankind'.[119] Social effects of the Stoic tenet are inevitable. One such effect comes to expression in Seneca's *De Beneficiis*, where he discusses, among other things, the question of whether it is possible for a slave to give benefit to his master (*Ben.* 3.18–28). According to Seneca, there is nothing in principle to

---

[113] *Vit. beat.* 24.3: *Hominibus prodesse natura me iubet. Servi liberine sint hi, ingenui an libertini, iustae libertatis an inter amicos datae, quid refert? Ubicumque homo est, ibi benefici locus est.* Cf. *Ben.* 3.18–28. The question of slaves and slavery will be discussed further in Chapter 9 below.

[114] *Clem.* 2.6.2–3.

[115] *Ep.* 88.30: *Humanitas vetat superbum esse adversus socios, vetat avarum. Verbis, rebus, adfectibus comem se facilemque omnibus praestat. Nullum alienum malum putat.* On *humanitas* in Seneca, see Griffin, *Seneca*, 178–81.

[116] *Ep.* 88.30. For a discussion of *clementia* as a Roman virtue, see David Konstan, 'Clemency as a Virtue', *CP* 100 (2005): 337–46.

[117] *Ep.* 7.2–4; 80.2–3; 90.45; 95.33.

[118] e.g. *Ep.* 88.30; 95.52–3; 102.18; *Vit. beat.* 24.3. Cf. also Cicero, *Off.* 3.28: 'For that is an absurd position which is taken by some people, who say that they will not rob a parent or a brother for their own gain, but that their relation to the rest of their fellow-citizens is quite another thing. Such people contend in essence that they are bound to their fellow-citizens by no mutual obligations, social ties, or common interests. This attitude demolishes the whole structure of civil society. Others again who say that regard should be had for the rights of fellow-citizens (*civium*), but not of foreigners (*externorum*), would destroy the universal brotherhood of mankind (*communem humani generis societatem*).'

[119] *Ben.* 7.1.7.

prevent this,[120] for what counts is not the status of the person concerned but his or her *intention* with the benefit.[121] Indeed, everyone is capable of virtuous deeds: 'Virtue closes the door to no man; it is open to all, admits all, invites all, the freeborn and the freedman, the slave and the king, and the exile.'[122] It is important to note that people are here grouped, neither in philosophical nor religious terms, but in terms of social position. As Seneca continues, 'neither family nor fortune determines its choice [i.e. virtue's choice]—it is satisfied with the naked human being.'[123] Hence, when a benefit is offered by a slave to a master it is actually from a human being to a human being (*homo ab homine*).[124] Their social status is certainly different, and remains so, but their 'source' as human beings and their 'parent' as such is one and the same:

We all spring from the same source (*principia*), have the same origin (*origo*); no man is more noble than another (*nemo altero nobilior*) except in so far as the nature of one man is more upright and more capable of good actions. Those who display ancestral busts in their halls, and place in the entrance of their houses the names of their family, arranged in a long row and entwined in the multiple ramifications of a genealogical tree—are these not notable rather than noble (*non noti magis quam nobiles sunt*)? Heaven is the one parent of us all (*unus omnium parens mundus est*), whether from his earliest origin each one arrives at his present degree by an illustrious or obscure line of ancestors.[125]

Elsewhere Seneca expresses his opinion that if there is any good in philosophy, it is its indifference to pedigree: 'Philosophy neither rejects nor selects anyone; its light shines for all', he says,[126] and then explains that virtuous individuals like Socrates, Plato, and Cleanthes were certainly no aristocrats.[127] The truly upright, good, and great soul (*animus rectus, bonus, magnus*) 'may descend into a Roman knight just as well as into a freedman's son or a slave. For what is a Roman knight, or a freedman's son, or a slave? They are mere titles, born

---

[120] Seneca says that 'a slave can sometimes (*aliquando*) give a benefit to his master' (*Ben.* 3.18.2), presumably having in mind occasions when the slave has the opportunity or means to do so.

[121] *Ben.* 3.18.2. Cf. 1.6.1–3; 2.17.4.

[122] *Ben.* 3.18.2: *Nulli praeclusa virtus est; omnibus patet, omnes admittit, omnes invitat, et ingenuos et libertinos et servos et reges et exules.*

[123] *Ben.* 3.18.2: *non eligit domum nec censum, nudo homine contenta est.*

[124] *Ben.* 3.22.4.

[125] *Ben.* 3.28.1–2. Note that the word *mundus* is usually translated as 'world' or 'universe', but the LCL prefers to translate it here as 'heaven'.

[126] *Ep.* 44.2: *Nec reicit quemquam philosophia nec eligit; omnibus lucet.*

[127] *Ep.* 44.3–5: 'Socrates was no aristocrat (*patricius*). Cleanthes worked at a well and served as a hired man watering a garden. Philosophy did not find Plato already a nobleman; it made him one.... A hall full of smoke-begrimed busts does not make the nobleman.'

of ambition or of wrong. One may leap to heaven from the very slums (*subsilire in caelum ex angulo licet*).'[128]

We can easily imagine how shocking these statements may have sounded to many Romans, particularly the noble ones, because of the enormous import-ance of the ancestral tradition and lines of nobility in Roman society. Himself a son of a prominent writer and *rhetor* of good means,[129] and, indeed, one of the wealthiest men in all of Rome and an owner of a countless number of slaves, this Roman knight makes no attempt to argue for his own nobility in those terms. Instead, as a 'naked human being', he sees another kind of nobility belonging to himself—and to the rest of humankind:

Do not despise any man, even if he belongs with those whose names are forgotten, and have had too little favour from Fortune. Whether your line before you holds freedmen or slaves or persons of foreign extraction, boldly lift up your head, and leap over the obscure names in your pedigree; great nobility awaits you at its source (*expectat vos in summo magna nobilitas*).[130]

The source, of course, is none other than the divine itself.[131] The Stoic doctrine of universal humanity has, in other words, theology and/or cosmol-ogy as its very point of departure. And it is precisely because of its under-standing of the divine and of human relationship with the divine that Seneca can claim with confidence that it is the 'avowed object' (*propositum*) of Stoicism 'to regard the interest of each and all' (*universis singulisque consulere*).[132]

---

[128] *Ep.* 31.11.
[129] Whose biography the younger Seneca wrote: *De Vita Patris*. Unfortunately, it is lost.
[130] *Ben.* 3.28.3.
[131] cf. *Ep.* 44.1: *Omnes, si ad originem primam revocantur, a dis sunt* ('All men, if traced back to their original source, spring from the gods').
[132] *Clem.* 2.5.3.

3

Gaius Musonius Rufus

INTRODUCTION: A SOCIAL AND POLITICAL
PROVOCATEUR

It is one of the great losses of history that we do not possess more and better sources on the life and teaching of Musonius Rufus, this key figure in Roman Stoicism. The sources that we have are rather limited, and all are secondary as well.[1] For, as with some other key figures in history, Musonius does not seem to have written anything himself.[2] Instead, records of his life and teaching were preserved and furthered, first, by his students and followers, and, then, by Roman historians. These are the two main groups which contribute most to our knowledge of Musonius Rufus.

But even if the sources on Musonius are somewhat limited, there is no denying that he has yet to receive the attention he deserves in scholarly discussions—even in classical studies, not to mention New Testament scholarship.[3] This can only be grieved. It is in proportion neither to the (lack of) sources on him nor his importance in history. Even if fragmentary, we actually

---

[1] The texts attributed to Musonius are conveniently collected (with English translations) in Cora E. Lutz, 'Musonius Rufus: "The Roman Socrates"', Yale Classical Studies 10 (1947): 32–147. A brief, recent survey of modern research on Musonius is found in J. T. Dillon, *Musonius Rufus and Education in the Good Life: A Model of Teaching and Living Virtue* (Dallas, TX: University Press of America, 2004), vii–viii.

[2] cf. A. C. van Geytenbeek, *Musonius Rufus and Greek Diatribe* (Assen: Van Gorcum, 1963), 7–9.

[3] Klassen's criticism and complaint in this regard more than twenty years ago is (sadly) still appropriate ('Musonius Rufus', 188–9, 191–2). Nussbaum points out the startling fact that the comprehensive and widely used collection of texts by Long and Sedley, *Hellenistic Philosophers* (1987), 'includes neither any text from Musonius nor any mention of him, even in the section dealing with Stoic views on the political equality of women [a topic to which Musonius' views are undeniably of major importance]' (Martha C. Nussbaum, 'The Incomplete Feminism of Musonius Rufus, Platonist, Stoic, and Roman', in *The Sleep of Reason: Erotic Experience and Sexual Ethics in Ancient Greece and Rome* [ed. M. C. Nussbaum and J. Sihvola; Chicago, IL: The University of Chicago Press, 2002], 283). Telling is also the fact that Lutz's 1947 collection and English translation of the Musonian works (as a whole) still appears to be the only one of its kind. Lutz's text follows the 1905 edition of O. Hense, which is the sole modern edition (*C. Musonii Rufi reliquiae* [Leipzig: Teubner]).

do have some sources on this 'Roman Socrates',[4] whose life and philosophy were far too important in the ancient world to be ignored or referred to in passing only.

According to our sources, Gaius Musonius Rufus was born into an Etruscan family in the city of Volsinii[5] early in the first century CE, probably sometime in 20–30 CE.[6] He was thus some twenty to thirty years younger than his fellow Stoic Seneca. Musonius was a member of the equestrian order and a prominent teacher of philosophy who had several followers of high reputation in Roman society.[7] He associated with a group of distinguished Stoics in Rome who actively opposed the emperor, including such prominent men as Rubellius Plautus (exiled by Nero in 60 CE and executed in 62 CE), Barea Soranus (proconsul in Asia, condemned to death by Nero in 66 CE), and Thrasea Paetus (a senator of considerable influence, also condemned to death by Nero in 66 CE).[8] The historian Tacitus so revered the character of these men that he stated that with the death sentences of the latter two Nero killed 'virtue herself'.[9] Musonius, the sources suggest, was specifically concerned with social affairs and seems to have been quite active in advocating his ideas for reform. That may also have been one of the main reasons for which Nero exiled him to Gyara in 65 CE, a desolate island in the Cyclades, south-east of the mainland of Greece, often used as a place of banishment in early imperial times.[10] This was subsequent to the Pisonian conspiracy and the death of Lucius Annaeus Seneca that same year, but it is unlikely that Musonius was ever involved in the conspiracy. According to Tacitus, the real ground for Musonius' expulsion was simply

---

[4] As Rudolf Hirzel called him in *Der Dialog* (1895); cf. Lutz, 'Musonius Rufus', 4.

[5] The approximate location is the modern city of Bolsena, about 130 km north of Rome.

[6] On the life of Musonius, see esp. the important work of Lutz, 'Musonius Rufus', 14–30. See also Geytenbeek, *Musonius*, 3–7.

[7] See Lutz, 'Musonius Rufus', 18–20, according to whom Fronto noted that the students/ followers of Musonius included Euphrates of Tyre, Timocrates of Heracleia, Minucius Fundanus, Athenodotus (Fronto's own teacher), and Dio Cocceianus of Prusa (later called 'Chrysostom'). From Pliny's letters we learn that Pliny himself was a great admirer of Musonius (though scarcely one of his students), and that he enjoyed the friendship of Musonius' son-in-law, Artemidorus (*Ep.* 3.11). And then we have, of course, Musonius' most famous student, Epictetus (specifically treated below). Whereas the early second-century Stoic Hierocles did not belong to Musonius' closest circle, he effectively passed on his teachings within Stoicism (several examples from Hierocles may be found in Malherbe, *Moral Exhortation*, 85–104).

[8] On the so-called 'philosophical opposition' and Nero's persecution of the Stoics, see Griffin, *Seneca*, 100–3; eadem, *Nero*, 171–7. Cf. also MacMullen, *Enemies*, 46–94 (ch. 2); Jürgen Malitz, 'Philosophie und Politik im frühen Prinzipat', in *Antikes Denken—Moderne Schule: Beiträge zu den antiken Grundlagen unseres Denkens* (ed. H. W. Schmidt and P. Wülfing; Heidelberg: Carl Winter Universitätsverlag, 1988), 164–76.

[9] *Ann.* 16.21. As for Tacitus' (favourable) view of Rubellius Plautus, see *Ann.* 14.22.

[10] See, e.g., Epictetus, *Diss.* 1.25.20; 2.6.22.

his prominence and influence as a teacher of philosophy.[11] Sociopolitical concerns may well have been involved as well. The notion that philosophy was responsible for political opposition does not appear to have flourished in Rome except for a period of some forty years under Nero and the Flavian dynasty,[12] and the only serious local critics of the Roman government in the second half of the first century CE were Stoic philosophers.[13]

After the death of Nero in 68 CE Musonius returned to Rome. He seems to have been on good terms with emperor Vespasian, since he was the only philosopher we know of who was exempted when the emperor banished all philosophers from Rome in 71 CE. However, for reasons unknown, a few years later Musonius too was banished from the city. It was probably during this second exile that Pliny the Younger met him in Syria.[14] But when Titus, an old friend of his, acceded to the principate (79–81 CE), Musonius went back to Rome and (presumably) resumed his lectures on philosophy. The year of his death is uncertain, but scholars agree that it must have been at the very end of the first century, perhaps as late as 100 CE.[15]

There is no evidence of any direct relationship between Musonius and Seneca. Each belonged to a circle of his own, whose contact with the other seems to have been rather limited. The senator Thrasea Paetus, for example, was a close friend of Musonius and at least loosely acquainted with Seneca. But the political stances of Seneca and the senator differed enough to create a certain distance between them.[16] It is nevertheless clear that, in addition to Stoicism itself, Musonius and Seneca had several things in common. Both belonged to the high ranks of Roman society, and both philosophers focused on issues of morality in particular. Also, precisely as Seneca, Musonius reached the height of his influence under Nero, although the nature and extent of his influence differed somewhat from Seneca's. Furthermore, both affected the politics of their day, each in his own way. Their political stances differed widely, to be sure: whereas Seneca operated (mostly) from 'within', as a professional politician and imperial counsellor, Musonius worked actively

---

[11] *Ann.* 15.71: 'To Verginius Flavus and Musonius Rufus expulsion was brought by the lustre of their names (*claritudo nominis*); for Verginius fostered the studies of youth by his eloquence, Musonius by the precepts of philosophy (*praeceptis sapientiae*).' (Verginius Flavus was a rhetorician and tutor of the satirist Persius.)

[12] cf. Griffin, 'Philosophy', 21–2. Cf. the comments of Seneca in *Ep.* 73.1.

[13] cf. Klauck, *Religious Context*, 347.

[14] See *Ep.* 3.11. According to Musonius 8.60.4–5, he was actually once visited by a certain 'king from Syria'.

[15] The reference to Musonius in Pliny's *Ep.* 3.11, probably written in 101 CE, suggests that the former was already dead by then.

[16] See Griffin, *Seneca*, 100–3.

though (mostly)[17] indirectly from the 'outside', through his socially reformist lectures and thus in some ways in opposition to governing authorities.[18] But in the end, both paid the price for defying the will of Nero.

MORAL TEACHING IN MUSONIUS: THE WELFARE OF THE NEIGHBOUR

Most of what has been preserved of Musonius' teachings is found in the anthologies of Stobaeus: twenty-one treatises, written by Musonius' student Lucius, and nineteen fragments of sayings. An additional thirteen sayings have also been transmitted by Epictetus (through Arrian), Plutarch, Aulus Gellius (in Latin), and Aelius Aristides.[19] Some of the sayings may derive from Annius Pollio, the son-in-law of Barea Soranus.[20] While the sources are fragmentary, together they give a general idea of Musonius' philosophical points of view, several of which are expressed in detail. A number of the longer and more detailed discourses deal with practical issues and concrete ethical problems. (The following references are made from Lutz's collection of the texts attributed to Musonius [referred to by number of discourse, page number(s), line(s); e.g. 1.32.5].[21])

Musonius Rufus downplays the role of physics and logic in philosophy, and defines ethics as the primary part of the discipline. According to him, 'philosophy is training in nobility of character and nothing else' (φιλοσοφία καλοκἀγαθίας ἐστὶν ἐπιτήδευσις καὶ οὐδὲν ἕτερον).[22] Musonius aligns himself with other Stoics in distinguishing four cardinal virtues, i.e. prudence (φρόνησις, *prudentia*), moderation or self-control (σωφροσύνη, *temperantia*),

---

[17] Tacitus relates how Musonius once participated directly in the politics of his day by engaging in a diplomatic mission on behalf of the emperor Vitellius in 69 CE (*Hist.* 3.81).

[18] Christopher Gill notes that Musonius' 'principled political involvement may have played a significant role in making him a widely influential Stoic teacher' ('Stoic Writers of the Imperial Era', in *The Cambridge History of Greek and Roman Political Thought* [ed. C. Rowe and M. Schofield with S. Harrison and M. Lane; Cambridge: Cambridge University Press, 2000], 601).

[19] See Lutz, 'Musonius Rufus', 6–13, 146–7; Geytenbeek, *Musonius*, 8–12. On Epictetus and Arrian, see below.

[20] So Lutz, 'Musonius Rufus', 9–13. Differently Geytenbeek, *Musonius*, 8–9.

[21] Ever since it was published in 1947, Lutz's collection has been the standard work on Musonius in which English translation is included. As for the Greek (and Latin) text, it has already been noted above that Lutz follows Hense's edition (except in a few instances), and so do I in the present study.

[22] Musonius 4.48.25–6. Cf. 3.40.5–6; 8.66.1.

justice (δικαιοσύνη, *iustitia*), and courage (ἀνδρεία, *fortitudo*),[23] but shows at the same time a remarkable and quite unusual consistency in building his arguments precisely on these virtues.[24] The more typical Stoic fashion was to subdivide or add to the four, as we see, for instance, in Seneca.[25] Musonius' systematic treatment of the cardinal virtues, on the other hand, suggests that he considered them to constitute an adequate basis for his moral theory.[26] Occasionally he appears to depart from this pattern, as when he contrasts virtue (ἀρετή) with evil (κακία), the latter of which 'consists in injustice and cruelty and indifference to a neighbor's trouble' (ἀδικία τε καὶ ἀγριότης καὶ τὸ τοῦ πλησίον πράττοντος κακῶς ἀφροντιστεῖν), and describes virtue as 'brotherly love and goodness and justice and beneficence and concern for the welfare of one's neighbor' (φιλανθρωπία καὶ χρηστότης καὶ δικαιοσύνη ἐστὶ καὶ τὸ εὐεργετικὸν εἶναι καὶ τὸ κηδεμονικὸν εἶναι τοῦ πέλας).[27]

But, as a rule, it is the four cardinal virtues that form the basis for the presence of other virtues and for every virtuous thought or act. A good example is when the disposition of being 'high-minded, beneficent, and kindly' (μεγαλόφρων καὶ εὐεργετικὸς καὶ φιλάνθρωπος), which in fact matches closely the description of virtue above, is clearly understood as a consequence of the four cardinal virtues.[28] It is important to note, however, that 'when characterizing virtue as φιλανθρωπία καὶ χρηστότης καὶ δικαιοσύνη, which are nearer qualified by the εὐεργετικὸν εἶναι and κηδεμονικὸν τοῦ πέλας, [Musonius] gives quite an interesting proof of how much in those days, also in the Stoic circle, virtue was felt to be essentially the love of, and active care for, one's fellow man'.[29]

Musonius is optimistic about human capacity to live virtuously. He believes that human beings are born with an inclination towards virtue, and that they are good by nature.[30] This conviction follows quite naturally from the Stoic belief of the divine origin of humankind and of the kinship between

---

[23] See, e.g., Seneca, *Ep.* 85.2; 90.46; 120.11; Plutarch, *Stoic. rep.* 1034C; *Virt. mor.* 440E–41D; Stobaeus, *Ecl.* 2.7.5a–5b7 (= Arius Didymus 5a–5b7); 2.31.123; 2.59.4–60.24; 2.63.6–24; *Flor.* 1178.

[24] cf. 3.40.17–42.9; 4.44.10–35; 4.46.9–10; 4.48.1–14; 6.52.15–23; 8.60.8–64.9; 9.74.24–6; 17.108.10–11.

[25] e.g. *Ep.* 92.19; *Ben.* 2.31.1; 4.8.3. Cf. also Stobaeus, *Ecl.* 2.59.4–60.24; 2.7.5b–5b7 (= Arius Didymus 5b–5b7); Cicero, *Fin.* 3.11.

[26] cf. Lutz, 'Musonius Rufus', 27 n. 113.   [27] Musonius 14.92.29–33.

[28] Musonius 17.108.14. It is actually God who is μεγαλόφρων καὶ εὐεργετικὸς καὶ φιλάνθρωπος, but Musonius adds that so also is the human being as the image of God (οὕτω καὶ τὸ ἐκείνου μίμημα τὸν ἄνθρωπον ἡγητέον). According to Musonius, God has these qualities through the possession of the four cardinal virtues (διὰ τὴν παρουσίαν τούτων τῶν ἀρετῶν) (lines 10–16).

[29] Geytenbeek, *Musonius*, 28.   [30] Musonius 2.38.1–3.

gods and human beings. As Musonius formulates it, the supreme being, Zeus, is the common 'father' of all human beings and gods (κοινὸς ἁπάντων πατὴρ ἀνθρώπων τε καὶ θεῶν).[31] Of all the earthly creatures the human being alone is in the image of God (μίμημα θεοῦ) and has the same virtues that God has, from which it follows of course that provided they live in accordance with nature (ὅταν ἔχῃ κατὰ φύσιν), human beings should be regarded as being like God, i.e. in moral excellence.[32] There is, in other words, an 'innate inclination (φυσικὴν ὑποβολήν) of the human soul toward goodness and nobleness (καλοκἀγαθίαν)', and there are 'seeds of virtue (σπέρμα ἀρετῆς) in each one of us'.[33]

The opinion that human beings by nature are good was a traditional Stoic doctrine.[34] It did not mean that every human being, as it were, automatically possessed virtue itself, but rather that every human being possessed a natural *disposition* to virtue. Evil, the morally bad, on the other hand, was believed by Stoics like Musonius to be external to man, something that comes from without and infects the human soul from the very beginning. The result is moral illness, against which the study of philosophy is the sole remedy: one must search out and examine how to lead a good life.[35] It is philosophy alone that teaches one how to live in harmony with one's true nature as an originally good creation of God.[36]

The philosophical education is twofold: theoretical and practical (ἡ ἀρετή, ἔφη, ἐπιστήμη ἐστὶν οὐ θεωρητικὴ μόνον, ἀλλὰ καὶ πρακτική).[37] While there is no question that Musonius considered the theoretical part to be decisive as a foundation on which to build one's way of living,[38] he put more weight on the practical side, arguing that 'in effectiveness, practice takes precedence over theory as being more influential in leading men to action' (δυνάμει μέντοι τὸ ἔθος προτερεῖ τοῦ λόγου, ὅτι ἐστὶ κυριώτερον ἐπὶ τὰς πράξεις ἄγειν τὸν ἄνθρωπον ἤπερ ὁ λόγος).[39] That is, if one wants to influence others towards a particular behaviour or way of life, one's deeds are of much more importance than words. Indeed, according to one of his students, Musonius himself was 'always earnestly urging those who were associated with him to make practical application of his teachings' (παρώμα δὲ πρὸς ἄσκησιν τοὺς συνόντας ἐντεταμένως ἀεὶ τοιοῖσδέ τισι λόγοις χρώμενος).[40] Without conduct added to the teaching, the Stoic teacher professed, philosophical education is of no

---

[31] Musonius 16.104.31. [32] Musonius 17.108.8–18.
[33] Musonius 2.38.12–14. [34] See the discussion in Geytenbeek, *Musonius*, 28–33.
[35] Musonius 3.40.5–6.
[36] cf. Musonius 3.38.26–40.6; 14.92.6–8; 16.104.30–7; 17.108.1–4.
[37] Musonius 6.52.8–9. [38] cf. Musonius 5.52.1–2.
[39] Musonius 5.52.2–4. On the translation of ἔθος as 'practice', see Lutz, 'Musonius Rufus', 49 n.
[40] Musonius 6.52.7–8; cf. 11.82.22–84.27; 17.110.14–15.

use.[41] The human being is after all neither soul nor body alone, but a synthesis of the two.[42]

With his firm emphasis on praxis, Musonius is in good harmony with Stoic philosophy. But the Cynic tendencies in his teaching are quite clear. Such traits are wholly in line with the Stoicism of the day, of which his student, Epictetus, represents but one example (cf. below). Musonius, however, went further with his Cynic-like preaching than most of his contemporaries who, like himself, belonged to the upper socioeconomic class of Roman society. In matters of clothing, for instance, he commended moderation: 'Wearing one chiton is preferable to needing two, and wearing none but only a cloak is preferable to wearing one.'[43] Clothes were for covering the body, not for display. Also, in matters of housing and furnishings Musonius strongly spoke against any extravagance, arguing that bare necessities should suffice for all alike. Consider the following comments on expensive abodes and decorations:

Are not all these things superfluous and unnecessary, without which it is possible not only to live but also to be healthy? Are they not the source of constant trouble, and do they not cost great sums of money from which many people (πολλοὺς ἀνθρώπους) might have benefited by public and private charity (καὶ δημοσίᾳ καὶ ἰδίᾳ)? How much more commendable than living a life of luxury it is to help many people (τὸ πολλοὺς εὐεργετεῖν). How much nobler than spending money for sticks and stones to spend it on men (ἀνθρώπους).... What would one gain from a large and beautiful house comparable to what he would gain by conferring the benefits of his wealth (χαρίζεσθαι) upon the city and his fellow-citizens?[44]

At times one can sense a certain idealization of material poverty,[45] the kind of unrealistic idealization that, I dare to say, can come only from a person who has never experienced real poverty.[46] Nevertheless, for a man of his means and status, Musonius seems to have been quite radical in terms of practical ethics. The (ostensibly) faithful application of his ethics is also the aspect for which he was best known by the ancients. Our sources show very clearly that in antiquity he was generally praised for his character, wisdom, and moral integrity.[47] Moreover, 'unlike some

---

[41] Musonius 1.36.10–12. Cf. 14.96.6–7.   [42] Musonius 6.54.2–4.

[43] Musonius 19.122.3–4. His fellow Stoic Seneca had a more balanced opinion of this: 'Do not wear too fine, nor yet too frowzy, a toga. One needs no silver plate, encrusted and embossed in solid gold; but we should not believe the lack of silver and gold to be proof of the simple life' (*Ep.* 5.3).

[44] Musonius 19.122.22–32. Cf. 20.124.4–7.

[45] Musonius 15.98.17–100.16; 18B.118.36–120.5.

[46] This goes for Seneca, too; cf. the discussion in Chapter 2 above.

[47] See Geytenbeek, *Musonius*, 14–15.

philosophers, Musonius was no *doctor umbraticus*, but was rather a public figure, a conspicuous participant in civic affairs'.[48] It is surely illustrative that so many of the extant texts attributed to him concern civic and social affairs, and that so many of them are concerned with concrete practical aspects of such affairs.

If anything, it is probably Musonius' views on the status of women that are most familiar to the modern reader. But these are parts of a broader subject relating to questions of the family and relations within the family. Marriage is one such topic,[49] having children another,[50] and having parents still another.[51] The discourses indicate that, for Musonius, the family is the very cornerstone of society, whereas marriage is the foundation on which the familial structure is built. Few things are more manifestly 'in accord with Nature' than marriage, and few conform closer to the will and purpose of God as the creator of humankind.[52] Destroy marriage and you destroy not only the family itself, but the whole city as well and eventually also the entire human race.[53] This is because procreation of children should, according to Musonius, occur only within marriage. And so should sexual intercourse, which, even in marriage, should never be mere pleasure-seeking but conducted for begetting children only.[54] As for marriage itself, what is particularly noteworthy in these first-century discourses is Musonius' view of the reciprocal roles and mutual affection of the partners, both husband and wife: '[I]n marriage there must be above all perfect companionship and mutual love ($\kappa\eta\delta\epsilon\mu o\nu\iota\alpha$) of husband and wife, both in health and in sickness and under all conditions, since it was with desire for this as well as for having children that both entered upon marriage.'[55] The basic thought here is that of union and balanced partnership, which, together with the concept of $\dot{o}\mu\dot{o}\nu o\iota a$ (concord or 'sympathy of mind'),[56] runs through all the discourses on marriage and the family. One is tempted even to see in Musonius a champion of equal roles for the

---

[48] Lutz, 'Musonius Rufus', 24. (*Doctor umbraticus* [lit. 'private tutor'] is a rather cloistered figure who has little or no practical solidity in his teaching.)

[49] Musonius 13A.88 (under the title: 'What is the Chief End of Marriage?'); 13B.90 (same title); 14.90–6 ('Is Marriage a Handicap for the Pursuit of Philosophy?').

[50] Musonius 15.96–100 ('Should Every Child that is Born be Raised?').

[51] Musonius 16.100–6 ('Must One Obey One's Parents under All Circumstances?').

[52] Musonius 14.92.9–17. One may add that Musonius disapproves of same-sex sexual relations (he mentions only males in this respect), which he finds 'a monstrous thing and contrary to nature' ($\pi\alpha\rho\dot{a}\ \phi\dot{v}\sigma\iota\nu\ \tau\dot{o}\ \tau\dot{o}\lambda\eta\mu\alpha$, 12.86.10).

[53] Musonius 14.92.35–6.

[54] Musonius 12.86.4–8. Cf. also Musonius' rejection of abortion, child exposure, and infanticide in Disc. 15. Note his sharp criticism of wealthy people in particular who practise any of these things, although they 'do not even have poverty as an excuse' (15.98.28–9).

[55] Musonius 13A.88.17–20. [56] Musonius 13B.90.4, 13–20.

spouses.[57] To him, this balanced state of the marriage is so imperative that the marriage is doomed to disaster if it so happens that 'each looks only to his own interests and neglects the other'. When sincere mutuality is undermined, 'eventually they separate entirely or they remain together and suffer what is worse than loneliness'.[58] Given the social importance of marriage, the consequences for society as a whole are equally disastrous. According to Musonius, 'one could find no other association (κοινωνία) more necessary nor more pleasant than that of men and women'. After all, 'to whom is everything judged to be common, body, soul, and possessions, except man and wife? For these reasons all men consider the love of man and wife to be the highest form of love (φιλία)'.[59] In this way the bond between husband and wife has become an expression of the virtuous life, an extension of the concept of friendship in philosophical discourse that typically applied to the bond among the sages.[60]

In striking contrast to conventional thinking of his day, Musonius underlines that outward things such as material possessions and social status—or looks, for that matter—should not determine whom one is to marry:

Therefore those who contemplate marriage ought to have regard neither for family (γένος), whether either one be of high-born parents, nor for wealth, whether on either side there be great possessions, nor for physical traits, whether one or the other have beauty. For neither wealth nor beauty nor high birth (εὐγένεια) is effective in promoting partnership of interest (κοινωνία) or sympathy (ὁμόνοια), nor again are they significant for producing children.[61]

But, as for character, one should expect both partners to be naturally disposed to virtue, in particular to self-control (σωφροσύνη) and justice (δικαιοσύνη).[62] It is telling that while Musonius himself could easily have found a well-born and wealthy son-in-law from his own ranks, he favoured the philosopher Artemidorus, despite the fact that the man was a foreigner and famous for his simple lifestyle. Correspondingly, then, when confronted with the question of whether marriage is a handicap for the pursuit of philosophy, Musonius' answer was unreservedly negative. According to him, it is entirely fitting for the philosopher to marry and a good thing for him to have children.[63] This view runs counter to the ideas of some other prominent philosophers,

---

[57] cf., however, Musonius 3.42.5–11, a passage that reminds us of the necessity to read his discourses in their own historical context.

[58] Musonius 13A.88.24, 27–9.   [59] Musonius 14.94.2–3, 8–11.

[60] cf. Reydams-Schils, 'Human Bonding', 245–7. Referring also to Hierocles, she rightly states: 'The Roman Stoic stance is firm: there will be no community unless we start with the one close to home' (246).

[61] Musonius 13B.90.4–8.   [62] Musonius 13B.90.12–13.   [63] Musonius 14.96.2–4.

e.g. Cicero,[64] and to common opinion of the Stoics in general, who have typically, but mistakenly, been seen as emotionally indifferent and rather isolated characters. However, as one scholar rightly points out, Musonius Rufus even 'considers affection and *eros* to be as important as the care for offspring and social duty—so much for the stereotypical image of the Stoics as being cold and detached'.[65] In his praising of marriage and the mutual love of the married couple, Musonius does not fail to emphasize the more emotional and affectionate side of the union: compared to that of husband and wife, he asks, whose presence would do more to 'lighten grief (λύπη) or increase joy (χαρά) or remedy misfortune?'[66] Recall that, according to Stoic theory, both λύπη and χαρά belong to the passions, τὰ πάθη, and were thus normally understood by the Stoics as something negative.[67] Evidently, Musonius did not share this view entirely.

One related question addressed by the Stoic teacher was if women should study philosophy as well as men.[68] Given his opinion of the reciprocal roles of men and women in marriage, it is not surprising to see Musonius' positive answer to the question. The same goes for his response to the question of whether daughters should receive the same education as sons.[69] There is some debate among scholars about Musonius' views of women and their roles in society, particularly as to whether he can be considered a full-scale 'feminist'.[70] The debate strikes me as unnecessary at best, coloured as it is by an unwarranted value judgement. It can hardly be justified to impose upon this first-century figure modern values and concepts such as 'feminism' and make a judgement of his discussion in that light, as we see, for instance, in the recent complaints of his 'incomplete feminism'.[71] A scale of more or less 'feminism' is simply irrelevant in this case and, even worse, potentially misleading. As with all other figures of his time, the views of Musonius must be seen in the

---

[64] In a fragment of his lost *De Matrimonio*, Seneca states that Cicero refrained from remarrying because 'he could not possibly devote himself to a wife and to philosophy'; see Reydams-Schils, *Roman Stoics*, 148. One may also compare Cicero's standpoint with Paul's, expressed in 1 Corinthians 7 (esp. vv. 8, 32–4, 38–40).

[65] Reydams-Schils, *Roman Stoics*, 150.   [66] Musonius 14.94.5–8.

[67] Although χαρά, it should be noted, is an εὐπάθεια (a 'good feeling') in Stoic theory; see, e.g., Tad Brennan, 'The Old Stoic Theory of Emotions', in *The Emotions in Hellenistic Philosophy* (ed. J. Sihvola and T. Engberg-Pedersen; The New Synthese Historical Library 46; Dordrecht: Kluwer, 1998), esp. 34–6.

[68] Musonius 3.38–42 (under the title 'That Women Too Should Study Philosophy').

[69] Musonius 4.42–8 (under the title 'Should Daughters Receive the Same Education as Sons?').

[70] See, e.g., David M. Engel, 'The Gender Egalitarianism of Musonius Rufus', *AncPhil* 20 (2000): 377–91; Nussbaum, 'Incomplete Feminism'; Klassen, 'Musonius Rufus'.

[71] Nussbaum, 'Incomplete Feminism'.

context of the ancient Graeco-Roman world of thought, and their potential variations assessed in that light. Only thus can we reach a historically sound judgement of his contribution to ancient discussions of women and their positions in society.

Seen in that light, there is little doubt that for many in his audience, who, we should keep in mind, were probably all male students,[72] Musonius' statements in this regard were quite radical, if not shocking. According to him, there is no difference at all between men and women with respect to inclination towards virtue and the capacity for acquiring it. Unlike Plato, who argued that women were weaker than men in every respect, the Stoic philosopher makes emphatic in his teaching that both genders have equal moral value and philosophical ability.[73] Due to physical differences, however, some tasks are better suited for the one than the other, although this is not an absolute rule:

> For all human tasks, I am inclined to believe, are a common obligation and are common for men and women, and none is necessarily appointed for either one exclusively (πάντα μὲν γὰρ ἴσως ἐν κοινῷ κεῖται τὰ ἀνθρώπεια ἔργα καὶ ἔστι κοινὰ ἀνδρῶν καὶ γυναικῶν, καὶ οὐδὲν ἀποτακτὸν ἐξ ἀνάγκης τῷ ἑτέρῳ), but some pursuits are more suited to the nature of one, some to the other, and for this reason some are called men's work (ἀνδρεῖα) and some women's (γυναικεῖα). But whatever things have reference to virtue, these one would properly say are equally appropriate to the nature of both (ὀρθῶς ἐπ' ἴσον ἑκατέρᾳ προσήκειν φύσει), inasmuch as we agree that virtues are in no respect more fitting for the one than the other.[74]

To be sure, it so turns out that Musonius speaks much in favour of the 'traditional' order when he assigns to (most) women typical tasks relating to the household, and some typical physical outdoor tasks to (most) men. But it is important to observe that there is no indication whatsoever that he considered the former to be less meaningful than the latter. Why then should we presume (as some do) that he thought so? The sources certainly give no support to such assumptions. Recall that Musonius considered the family and household to be the very foundation of society. Moreover, by professing the equality of men and women with respect to the possession and capability of virtue, Musonius was in fact simply following the Stoic theory of universal humanity in which no distinction is made between the sexes: all humans have received a part of the divine reason and all are born with an inclination towards virtue. To speak of equality of women and men in this respect proceeds naturally from this doctrine. And this must also apply to the study

---

[72] See the discussion in Dillon, *Musonius Rufus*, 49–57.

[73] See esp. the discussion in Reydams-Schils, *Roman Stoics*, 153–63, which argues that Musonius' standpoint is essentially a response to Plato's views in the *Republic*.

[74] Musonius 4.46.27–34.

of philosophy: 'If then men and women are born with the same virtues, the same type of training (τροφή) and education (παιδεία) must, of necessity, befit both men and women.'[75] Musonius was not the first Stoic to recognize this,[76] but he was certainly among those who were most true to this self-evident but neglected aspect of the doctrine.

A particularly interesting case comes to the fore in Discourse 12, where Musonius lectures on sexual indulgence (Περὶ ἀφροδισίων). The discussion still involves issues of gender, now with the main focus aimed at male dominance. Discussing adultery, inter alia, which for him is a lucid manifestation of a lack of self-control, the Stoic teacher censures the (married) man who has sexual relations with his maid-servant.[77] The occasion of the censure would not have been all that obvious to everyone, because such conduct, as Musonius clarifies, was widely considered legitimate, if not fully natural, due to the master's absolute domination over his slaves. In a harsh and ironic tone, the philosopher turns the scene on its head and asks: what would this same man say if his wife had sexual relations with a male slave? Wouldn't he consider it completely intolerable? Of course he would! And yet, Musonius declares, it is the very same thing! It is easy to imagine several jaws dropping in the audience. Even more so when he proceeds to challenge the prevailing notion that it is acceptable or even appropriate for unmarried men to have relations with slaves, whereas it is considered outrageous for unmarried women to do so. According to Musonius, this kind of behaviour should of course be considered disgraceful for women and men alike. He concludes the discourse by setting up a sort of rhetorical trap for his male audience through ironical remarks about men's claimed superiority.[78] We can only speculate as to whether he actually caught some students in his trap, but perhaps Epictetus' description of his mentor's teaching methods and their effects are suggestive: 'He spoke in such a way that each of us as we sat there fancied someone had gone to Rufus and told him of our faults; so effective was his grasp of what men actually do, so vividly did he set before each man's eyes his particular weaknesses (κακά).'[79]

While Musonius' primary concern in Discourse 12 is to condemn sexual relations that involve adultery, his rebuke of the master's abuse of the slave-maid goes hand in hand with his general understanding of virtue and its duties, which, in turn, is rooted in the Stoic theory of universal humanity. The

---

[75] Musonius 4.44.35–46.2.
[76] See Klassen, 'Musonius Rufus', 194–6; Bonhöffer, *Ethics*, 125–7; Reydams-Schils, 'Human Bonding', 245–7; Gill, 'School', 46–7.
[77] Musonius 12.86.29–38.
[78] Musonius 12.86.38–88.6. Cf. also Reydams-Schils, *Roman Stoics*, 157.
[79] Epictetus, *Diss.* 3.23.29.

cardinal virtue 'justice' (δικαιοσύνη) is of particular importance here. Musonius underlines that the serious student of philosophy knows that it is God's own law that bids the human being to be just.[80] The student has also learned that 'to shun selfishness and to have high regard for fairness and, being a human being, to wish to help and to be unwilling to harm one's fellow men is the noblest lesson, and it makes those who learn it just (δικαίους)'.[81] If, on the other hand, the student holds that each one should have concern for his or her own interests alone, she or he represents man as no different from wild creatures, which have no share of any notion of justice.[82] Such indifference to the interests of the neighbour is nothing but evil, whereas concern for the neighbour's welfare is virtue.

But who is the 'neighbour' in the teaching of Musonius? How comprehensive, really, is the sense of the concept of neighbour in his discussion? The discourses suggest that we should take it in truly wide terms, referring, at least, to friends, family, strangers, and even enemies. Thus one discourse claims that it is not only a sin against Zeus, the god of friendship (τὸν φίλιον [Δία]), to be unjust (ἄδικος) to one's friends (φίλους), and it is not only a sin against Zeus, the guardian of the family (τὸν ὁμόγνιον Δία), to be unjust to one's own family (γένος), but it is also a sin against Zeus, the god of hospitality (τὸν ξένιον Δία), to be unjust to strangers (ξένους).[83] In another discourse, Musonius insists that it is not enough simply to refrain from harming one's enemies, but that one must be ready to offer them help as well.[84] Discussing the question of how wrongdoers should be met by 'the philosopher' (i.e. the ideal sage), Musonius strongly objects to any form of retaliation. Such behaviour, he underlines, is the mark of anything but proper human behaviour: 'For to scheme how to bite back the biter (ἀντιδήξεταί τις τὸν δακόντα) and to return evil for evil (ἀντιποιήσει κακῶς τὸν ὑπάρξαντα) is the act not of a human being but of a wild beast.'[85] What is expected of the properly thinking and genuinely rational person is forgiveness (συγγνώμη).[86] Musonius adopts the Socratic principle that it is better to suffer injury than to cause one.[87] Any harm done to a fellow being, even as payback for some

---

[80] Musonius 16.104.32–3: πρόσταγμά τε γὰρ ἐκείνου καὶ νόμος ἐστὶ τὸν ἄνθρωπον εἶναι δίκαιον...

[81] Musonius 4.48.9–12: πλεονεξίαν μὲν φεύγειν, ἰσότητα δὲ τιμᾶν, καὶ εὖ ποιεῖν μὲν θέλειν, κακοποιεῖν δὲ μὴ θέλειν ἄνθρωπον ὄντα ἀνθρώπους, ἔστι μὲν δίδαγμα κάλλιστον καὶ δικαίους ἐπιτελεῖ τοὺς μανθάνοντας. Cf. 7.58.1–2.

[82] Musonius 14.92.20–5.   [83] Musonius 15.96.28–98.1.

[84] See esp. Musonius 41.136. Cf. Epictetus, frg. 7.

[85] Musonius 10.78.27–8.   [86] Musonius 10.78.33–80.3.

[87] See Musonius 10.78.4–5. Cf. also Seneca, *Ep.* 95.52. On the Socratic principle and Musonius' adoption of it, see Geytenbeek, *Musonius*, 134–42. For a Christian version of this principle, see 1 Pet 3.17.

other wrongdoing, is an act of ignorance, for the person who harms another does so only because she or he does not know any better. The person who, on the other hand, acts out of knowledge shows forgiveness and benevolence, for 'to accept injury not in a spirit of savage resentment and to show ourselves not implacable toward those who wrong us, but rather to be a source of good hope to them is characteristic of a benevolent and civilized way of life' (τὸ δὲ δέχεσθαι τὰς ἁμαρτίας μὴ ἀγρίως, μηδὲ ἀνήκεστον εἶναι τοῖς πλημμελήσασιν, ἀλλ᾽ αἴτιον εἶναι αὐτοῖς ἐλπίδος χρηστῆς, ἡμέρου τρόπου καὶ φιλανθρώπου ἐστίν).[88] Put differently, according to Musonius, one should not only forgive evildoers but also endeavour to bring about a change in their disposition by leading them towards a better understanding. Such was indeed the case, says the Stoic teacher, when Lycurgus the Lacedaemonian was blinded in one eye by the hand of a fellow citizen, a young man, whom he later received as prisoner and could treat in whatever way he wanted. Lycurgus, to everyone's amazement, chose not to harm the man, but 'trained him instead and made a good man of him', eventually returning the young man to the Lacedaemonians with the words: 'This man I received from you an insolent and violent creature; I return him to you a reasonable man and a good citizen.'[89] Musonius' admiration for this story is not difficult to understand, particularly if one takes into further account that he was said to have been a vigorous antagonist of such violent events as gladiatorial games.[90]

According to one scholar, Musonius' 'high idealism, combined with the noble humanitarianism of his teachings, represents the greatest height Stoicism ever reached'.[91] Considering his great influence and reputation throughout the ancient world, this rather bold statement is probably not wide of the mark. It is true that some scholars have identified in Musonius' teaching a certain lack of originality in terms of philosophical theory, including ethics.[92] However, as others continue to note,[93] Musonius preferred applied ethics to theory, and there seems to be no lack of 'originality' in his various efforts to develop earlier philosophical doctrines to that end, nor in his apparently unmatched manner of

---

[88] Musonius 10.78.31–3.   [89] Musonius 39.136.15–16.

[90] Dio Chrysostom, *Rhod.* 121–2 (= *Or.* 31.121–2). See also Lutz, 'Musonius Rufus', 17 with n. 60.

[91] Lutz, 'Musonius Rufus', 30.

[92] Esp. Geytenbeek, *Musonius* (conclusion on pp. 159–63). A century ago, Arnold observed, on the other hand, that because of his great influence Musonius should be regarded as 'a third founder of the philosophy' (*Roman Stoicism*, 117), presumably in addition to Zeno (p. 71) and Panaetius (p. 101).

[93] See, e.g., Klassen, 'Musonius Rufus', 188; Morford, *Roman Philosophers*, 207–8; Gill, 'School', 47. Klassen rightly points out that one has to ask what exactly is meant by 'originality' in this context. Cf. also Reydams-Schils, *Roman Stoics*, 147–8, 166.

successfully embodying his own moral teaching. Musonius Rufus, it appears, effectively practised what he preached. Thus the church father Origen testifies:

There are found in every philosophical sect, and in the word of God, persons who are related to have undergone so great a change that they may be proposed as a model of excellence of life. Among the names of the heroic age some mention Hercules and Odysseus, among those of later times, Socrates, and of those who have lived very recently, Musonius.[94]

---

[94] *Cels.* 3.66: εἰσὶ γὰρ καὶ κατὰ πᾶσαν φιλοσοφίας αἵρεσιν καὶ κατὰ τὸν θεῖον λόγον οἱ τοσοῦτον μεταβεβληκέναι ἱστορούμενοι, ὥστε αὐτοὺς ἐκκεῖσθαι παράδειγμα τοῦ ἀρίστου βίου. καὶ φέρουσί τινες ἡρώων μὲν τὸν Ἡρακλέα καὶ τὸν Ὀδυσσέα, τῶν δ' ὕστερον τὸν Σωκράτην, τῶν δὲ χθὲς καὶ πρώην γεγονότων τὸν Μουσώνιον (trans. from FC). Similarly, Justin comments (*2 Apol.* 8.1–2): 'And those of the Stoic school—since, so far as their moral teaching went, they were admirable [...]—were, we know, hated and put to death,—Heraclitus for instance, and, among those of our own time, Musonius and others. For, as we intimated, the devils have always effected, that all those who anyhow live a reasonable and earnest life, and shun vice, be hated' (trans. from FC). Cf. also the favourable comments in Dio Chrysostom, *Rhod.* 122 (= *Or.* 31.122); Pliny, *Ep.* 3.11; Philostratus, *Vit. Apoll.* 4.46.

4

Epictetus

INTRODUCTION: A LEARNED EX-SLAVE

Many details of Epictetus' life are unknown.[1] He was born ca. 55 CE at the city of Hierapolis in Phrygia, Asia Minor.[2] Much unlike the two equestrian Stoics discussed above, he was a slave, and presumably so by birth or from a very early stage in his life.[3] Perhaps when still a teenager, Epictetus moved to Rome when he was acquired by a Roman called Epaphroditus, himself an ex-slave.[4] Though formerly a slave, Epaphroditus was rich and well distinguished as emperor Nero's administrative secretary (*a libellis*),[5] a post that he lost at Nero's death in 68 CE but may have resumed under Domitian (who acceded to the principate in 81 CE). Hence it is possible that early on in his life Epictetus had direct experience of the imperial court, even if he first came to Rome after 68 CE.[6] Epictetus was still a slave when his master granted him permission to attend lectures by none other than Musonius Rufus. Soon thereafter, it seems, Epaphroditus freed him from his service as a slave. Epictetus now followed in the footsteps of his academic master, Musonius, under whose patronage he began his own teaching career in Rome. We may take it as evidence of

---

[1] A brief introduction to Epictetus' life can be found in Long, *Epictetus*, 10–12. On pp. 34–5 Long includes a useful list of ancient testimonies to the life of Epictetus.

[2] i.e. in present-day Denizli Province in south-western Turkey. In antiquity, a Roman road connected Hierapolis with the great city of Ephesus.

[3] cf. Klauck, *Religious Context*, 346–7, who notes that the name 'Epictetus' (᾽Επίκτητος) derives from ἐπικτᾶσθαι, which means literally 'obtained in addition' or 'purchased addition-ally', pointing to his slavish origin.

[4] See *Diss.* 1.1.20; 1.19.19–22; 1.26.11–12.

[5] According to Tacitus, Epaphroditus played a major role in the exposure of the Pisonian conspiracy (*Ann.* 15.55). Suetonius credits him with having assisted Nero to commit suicide (*Nero* 49.3; *Dom.* 14.4).

[6] cf. Long, *Epictetus*, 10. Millar, however, finds it unlikely that Epaphroditus resumed his secretarial post under Domitian, who, according to some sources, executed the former in the year 95 CE ('Epictetus', 141). P. R. C. Weaver, who argues forcefully against the view that Epaphroditus held the post again under Domitian, even doubts that Epictetus' master was the same individual as the secretary of Nero ('Epaphroditus, Josephus, and Epictetus', *CQ* 44 [1994]: 468–79).

Epictetus' established position as such when sometime in 89–95 CE Domitian banished him, along with all other philosophers, from Italy.[7] Epictetus then moved to the city of Nicopolis in the Epirus region of Greece where he opened a school and earned his living by teaching philosophy to groups of young students. Nicopolis was located at the coast of the Ionian Sea in an almost direct line between Athens and Rome.[8] It enjoyed a metropolitan status and functioned as the political and economic centre for Roman rule in western Greece. As such it was an excellent place for a philosophical academy, and Epictetus' school seems indeed to have been both well attended and well regarded.[9] A number of prominent figures visited the school,[10] including perhaps even emperor Hadrian (117–138 CE), with whom Epictetus may have been personally acquainted. Having a school located at the main route between the two great cities, Epictetus could easily follow happenings in Rome.[11] But, as far as we know, he never returned to the city, but spent most of his remaining days devoted to his teaching activity in Nicopolis. He died around 135 CE.

It is very unlikely that Epictetus ever met Seneca. On the other hand, it is equally unlikely that Epictetus was unaware of this famous politician and Stoic philosopher. Curiously, though, there is not a single mention of Seneca in the extant works attributed to Epictetus.[12] While we cannot rule out the possibility that this is simply due to a coincidence caused by our (lack of) sources, it may also point to a certain distance between the two Stoics. A social distance seems fairly obvious at least, namely, between a wealthy Roman senator who also served as tutor and counsellor of the emperor himself, on the one hand, and a foreign (ex-)slave—indeed, initially a slave of an ex-slave—on the other. Of course, we should not overstate the case: the two Stoics hardly count as polar opposites in Roman society. Epictetus was a

---

[7] The exact date of the banishment is disputed: on the date 89 CE, see, e.g., Gill, 'Stoic Writers', 607; David Noy, *Foreigners at Rome: Citizens and Strangers* (London: Duckworth, 2000), 44–5; on the date 95 CE, see, e.g., Starr, 'Epictetus', 20–1; Long, *Epictetus*, 10. W. A. Oldfather gives the dates 89 or 92 CE ('Introduction', in *Epictetus* [2 vols.; LCL; Cambridge, MA: Harvard University Press, 1925], 1:xi), and Millar ('Epictetus', 142) follows A. N. Sherwin-White in dating the event to 92–93 CE ('Pliny's Praetorship Again', *JRS* 47 [1957]: 126–7).

[8] The remains of Nicopolis lie some 5 km north of the Greek town Préveza.

[9] cf. Oldfather, 'Introduction', xi; Long, *Epictetus*, 10–11.

[10] cf. *Diss.* 1.10; 2.14; 3.4; 3.7; 3.9. Cf. also the discussion in Brunt, 'Epictetus', 19–22.

[11] *Diss.* 1.24 suggests that Epictetus may in fact have sent 'spies' to Rome to enquire about the current situation.

[12] Needless to say, that does not mean that Epictetus never mentioned Seneca in his lectures or otherwise. It simply means that Seneca is never mentioned *in these particular writings*, which in itself is curious enough. The sources themselves are discussed below.

slave, to be sure, but nevertheless a relatively well-off slave who was educated at the feet of a distinguished Roman philosopher, and presumably had some connection with the imperial court as well through his master, Epaphroditus. It has already been noted that even after Epictetus' departure from Rome to Nicopolis, many upper-class Romans continued to seek him for advice. Nevertheless, there is no denying that Seneca and Epictetus were quite differently positioned socially. However, so were Epictetus and such well-to-do Roman politicians as Thrasea Paetus, Helvidius Priscus, and Paconius Agrippinus, who, like Seneca, were all Stoics but, unlike Seneca, are mentioned in Epictetus' lectures.[13] That suggests that Epictetus' silence concerning Seneca may (also) have been caused by ideological/political differences between the two, rather than social distinctions alone. We have already seen that Senator Thrasea Paetus was a close friend of Musonius, Epictetus' teacher and patron, and that Seneca does not seem to have sympathized with that particular group of Stoics. These previous circumstances may to some extent explain Epictetus' silence about Seneca.[14]

Another possible explanation is the fact that Seneca chose to write in Latin instead of Greek, the former of which was widely considered to be not only unnecessary but also unworthy as a philosophical language, even among the Romans themselves.[15] All serious philosophers wrote and taught in Greek, the opinion went. And so too may have been Epictetus' opinion: he taught in Greek and, as it appears, totally ignored Latin literature in his lessons. Hence, Epictetus' somewhat unexpected passing over of Seneca was probably grounded in a combination of different factors.

But despite all differences between the two, social, political, or otherwise, Epictetus and Seneca also had a significant thing in common in their everyday lives: both suffered from chronic ill health; Epictetus, it seems, from some

---

[13] *Diss.* 1.1.26–30; 1.2.12–24; 4.1.123; frs. 21–2.

[14] The issue is extremely complicated. Personal relations within and between these 'groups' of Stoics are far from easy to trace. Thrasea Paetus, for instance, was married to a woman called Arria, who was a relative of the satirist Persius (34–62 CE), who, in turn, was a student (and friend) of the Stoic Lucius Annaeus Cornutus, but Cornutus was, as the name indicates, a freedman of the Annaei family (Seneca's family). Another student of Cornutus and a close friend of Persius was the epic poet Lucan (Marcus Annaeus Lucanus; 39–65 CE), Seneca's nephew (son of his younger brother, Marcus Annaeus Mela). See J. M. K. Martin, 'Persius—Poet of the Stoics', *GR* 8 (1939): 172–82; Morford, *Roman Philosophers*, 192–6; Susanna Morton Braund, 'Introduction', in *Juvenal and Persius* (ed. and trans. S. M. Braund; LCL; Cambridge, MA: Harvard University Press, 2004), 14–15. One may also add that Cornutus was banished by Nero to the island of Gyara along with Musonius (cf. the introduction to Chapter 3 above).

[15] See Cicero, *Fin.* 1.1, 4–10. Cf. also Griffin, *Seneca*, 7–8.

kind of lameness (cf. *Diss.* 1.16.20: γέρων χωλός). And both Stoics express it in their works.[16]

As for the relationship between Epictetus and Musonius Rufus, there can be little doubt that the student was strongly influenced by the teacher, whose legacy the former carried on far beyond the city walls of Rome.[17] That, in turn, attests to the first-century Roman roots of Epictetus' teaching. Again, the social difference between the two may have been considerable, but, as we shall see, their ethical doctrines went very much hand in hand.

MORAL TEACHING IN EPICTETUS: LOVE
WITHOUT LIMITS

Precisely as his mentor Musonius and his ideal philosopher Socrates, Epictetus did not write anything for publication.[18] At least, no work authored by Epictetus himself has been preserved, and there is no evidence that there ever was such a work. The main sources we have are instead the works of his student Arrian (Lucius Flavius Arrianus Xenophon; ca. 86–150 CE), who put together two distinct bodies of sources on Epictetus' teaching. The first one is known to us as the *Discourses* or Διατριβαί (*Dissertationes*), originally in eight books but of which only four are extant. The second is the *Manual* or *Handbook* (᾿Εγχειρίδιον), a brief compilation made by Arrian from the *Discourses*. The *Discourses* are far more valuable as a source of Epictetus' teaching, particularly because most of them appear to express

---

[16] On Epictetus' ill health, see the discussion in Oldfather, 'Introduction', ix–x, with n. 5.

[17] cf. the following comments of Oldfather: 'the system of thought in the pupil is little more than an echo, with changes of emphasis due to the personal equation, of that of the master' ('Introduction', ix n. 4). Whereas Oldfather overstates the case a bit, his words rightly point to the Roman setting of Epictetus' philosophy.

[18] It is true that Epictetus himself once remarks, quite surprisingly, that Socrates actually 'wrote' a great deal: τί οὖν; Σωκράτης οὐκ ἔγραφεν; —καὶ τίς τοσαῦτα; ('What then? Did not Socrates write?—Yes, who wrote as much as he?' *Diss.* 2.1.32). However, it should be noted that Epictetus is here primarily concerned with the *practice* of philosophy as an act of 'writing'. The question is *how* Socrates wrote, i.e. in what way he conducted his 'writing': 'But how (ἀλλὰ πῶς)? Since he could not have always at hand someone to test his judgements, or to be tested by him in turn, he was in the habit of testing and examining himself (ἑαυτὸν ἤλεγχεν καὶ ἐξήταζεν), and was always in a practical way trying out some particular primary conception. That is what a philosopher writes (ταῦτα γράφει φιλόσοφος); but trifling phrases, and "said he", "said I" he leaves to others...' (32–3). On Socrates' 'writing' as an exercise in self-examination, cf. also 2.6.26–7.

words of his own through his pupil.[19] The *Manual* owes more to the latter.[20]

As we recall, Stoic tradition had divided philosophy into the three parts of physics, ethics, and logic. Epictetus, however, differed somewhat from his predecessors in this respect by teaching his students a tripartite version of his own. According to him, philosophy is divided into three stages or fields of study (τόποι): (1) the first one has to do with desires and aversions (ὁ περὶ τὰς ὀρέξεις καὶ τὰς ἐκκλίσεις); (2) the second with cases of choice and refusal (ὁ περὶ τὰς ὁρμὰς καὶ ἀφορμάς), and with what is appropriate (τὸ καθῆκον); (3) and the third deals with the avoidance of error and rashness in judgement (ὁ περὶ τὴν ἀνεξαπατησίαν καὶ ἀνεικαιότητα), and with cases of assent (συγκαταθέσεις).[21] At first sight, this division may appear overloaded with tangled terminology, but, more concisely, the three fields can be said to differentiate between stages of desire, volition or action, and judgement (ὄρεξις, ὁρμή, συγκατάθεσις).[22] Admittedly, these correspond roughly to the classic division into physics, ethics, and logic, especially the latter two, but Epictetus' definition is nevertheless quite original. It is also basic to his teaching: each and every individual who expects to make any moral progress must be trained in the three fields of study.[23] The first field is of particular importance, training in which is regarded as a prerequisite for all further progress in philosophy—not the erudite and bookish kind of philosophy but philosophy as 'the art of living' (ἡ περὶ βίον τέχνη).[24] Why is the first field so essential? Because it deals with the individual self and its desire towards all things, good or bad, within or beyond one's grasp. It deals in essence with

---

[19] See esp. Karl Hartmann's classic study 'Arrian und Epiktet', *NJahrb* 15 (1905): 248–75. Cf. Arrian's own words in his (epistolary) introduction to the *Discourses*: 'I have not composed these *Words of Epictetus* (τοὺς 'Επικτήτου λόγους) as one might be said to "compose" books of this kind, nor have I of my own act published them to the world; indeed, I acknowledge that I have not "composed" (συγγράψαι) them at all. But whatever I heard him say I used to write down, word for word, as best I could, endeavouring to preserve it as a memorial (ὑπομνήματα), for my own future use, of his way of thinking and the frankness of his speech' (see the LCL edn.). While one should probably not take Arrian's claim too literally of having added *nothing* of his own to the text, there is enough evidence, both external and internal, to take the *Discourses* in effect as Epictetus' own words; see Oldfather, 'Introduction', xiii–xiv; Long, *Epictetus*, 38–43. For different opinions, see the brief overview in Jackson Hershbell, 'The Stoicism of Epictetus: Twentieth Century Perspectives', *ANRW* 36.3: 2152–3.

[20] cf. W. A. Oldfather, 'The *Encheiridion*, or *Manual*', in *Epictetus* (2 vols.; LCL; Cambridge, MA: Harvard University Press, 1928), 2: 479.

[21] *Diss.* 3.2.1–5; cf. 2.17.15–16. The three fields of study are thoroughly treated in Bonhöffer, *Ethics*, 30–165 (= *Ethik* [1894], 16–127), especially in relation to ethics. An excellent summary discussion is found in Long, *Epictetus*, 112–18. On Epictetus' use of the terms ὄρεξις and ὁρμή, esp. compared to their usage in Early Stoicism, see Inwood, *Ethics*, 115–26.

[22] cf. Bonhöffer, *Ethics*, 32.   [23] *Diss.* 3.2.1.   [24] *Diss.* 1.15.2.

human nature as such (hence the relation to 'physics', in the ancient sense).[25] The training aims at an understanding of the desires and, eventually, the individual's restriction of them solely to things good and within grasp. The untrained student, however, must not expose himself to any kind of desire until he is able to recognize the difference between good and bad, and has full control over the desires.[26] Only those who have reached that stage are truly equipped for proper social relations, the main subject of the second field of study.[27] While the first field may perhaps be described as 'introverted', concerned as it is with freeing oneself from false conceptions of one's own nature and being, the second field is largely other-directed or 'outward'-looking. It is an Epictetan tenet that one has to deal with and care for one's individual self in order to be capable of doing the appropriate thing for others.[28] In this regard also, Epictetus gives full force to the Stoic principle that there are things that are under our control and things that are not: 'Under our control are moral purpose (προαίρεσις)[29] and all the acts of moral purpose; but not under our control are the body, the parts of the body, possessions, parents, brothers, children, country—in a word, all that with which we associate', i.e. external things.[30] To the 'diseased' students in his 'hospital' (ἰατρεῖον),[31] Epictetus offers this prescription: 'Distinguish matters and weigh them one against another, and say to yourself, "Externals (τὰ ἔξω) are not under my control; moral choice (προαίρεσις) is under my control. Where am I to look for the good and the evil? Within me (ἔσω), in that which is my own (ἐν τοῖς ἐμοῖς)".'[32] The 'healing' begins with the awareness of one's own weakness and ignorance concerning things of real consequence in life,[33] and the willingness to change one's life accordingly.[34]

---

[25] i.e. physics as the study of the cosmos and its nature, including the nature of human beings as a part of that cosmos.

[26] cf. *Diss.* 1.4.   [27] cf. *Diss.* 2.17.29–33.

[28] cf. Long, *Epictetus*, 115–16. For similar thought in Seneca, see *Tranq.* 6.1.

[29] It is difficult to translate the word προαίρεσις, of which several translations are in use in scholarly works, e.g. 'moral purpose' and 'moral choice'. Literally the word means 'pre-choice' (προ-αίρεσις). See the discussion in Long, *Epictetus*, 207–20, who proposes the translation 'volition', and Reydams-Schils, 'Human Bonding', 250, who explains προαίρεσις (in passing only but nonetheless quite helpfully) as 'our moral character as governed by reason'. See also the helpful discussion in Troels Engberg-Pedersen, 'Self-sufficiency and Power: Divine and Human Agency in Epictetus and Paul', in *Divine and Human Agency in Paul and His Cultural Environment* (ed. J. M. G. Barclay and S. J. Gathercole; LNTS 335; London: T&T Clark, 2007), 120–1.

[30] *Diss.* 1.22.10.

[31] *Diss.* 3.23.30: 'Men, the lecture-room of the philosopher is a hospital (ἰατρεῖόν ἐστιν, ἄνδρες, τὸ τοῦ φιλοσόφου σχολεῖον); you ought not to walk out of it in pleasure, but in pain. For you are not well when you come...'

[32] *Diss.* 2.5.4–5.   [33] cf. *Diss.* 2.11.1; 2.14.14–22; 3.1.25.

[34] e.g. *Diss.* 3.15.12–13; 3.22.13.

Musonius Rufus had based much of his teaching on the four cardinal virtues. Therefore it is a bit surprising that his student pays virtually no attention to the traditional virtues. At times he gives a list of certain virtues and virtuous attributes,[35] but he hardly mentions the cardinal virtues at all and makes no categorical use of them as his teacher had done.[36] Nevertheless, it is probably correct to assume that *in substance* they are more or less present in Epictetus' lectures as well.[37] The same applies to the principal Stoic theory of *oikeiōsis* (see the chapter on Seneca above). Epictetus was well aware of its key position in Stoic ethics,[38] even though he does not explicitly accredit the theory with a major role in the structure of his philosophical reasoning.[39] He clearly expresses and verifies, on the other hand, the beliefs of his fellow Roman Stoics that human beings are 'by nature social beings' (φύσει κοινωνικοί)[40] and that it lies in human nature to do good and to benefit others.[41] Human beings are, in other words, not born morally neutral. That does not mean that they can be 'sinless' (ἀναμάρτητον), i.e. without fault altogether. No, that is not possible, says the philosopher, 'but it is possible ever to be intent upon avoiding faults',[42] a characteristic Stoic stance (cf. Seneca above). It is the will and intention that count.

This natural goodness of human beings emanates, of course, from their divine origin, according to Epictetus.[43] It is a straightforward result of them being λογικοί, rational beings, as sharers of the divine λόγος, Reason.[44] Thus, precisely as we saw in Seneca above, the very foundational principle in the moral teaching of Epictetus is universal humanity, which, in turn, is based on the belief that all human beings are equal partakers of the λόγος. This is classic Stoicism. But one of the things that characterizes Epictetus' teaching the most is precisely his strong emphasis on the theological foundation of ethics. To this subject he devotes considerably more space than his fellow Stoics, including even Seneca. In fact, except for the name Socrates,[45] no proper name occurs more frequently in the *Discourses* than Zeus. Taken together with the designation 'God' (in the singular alone), it surpasses

---

[35] e.g. *Diss.* 2.8.23; 4.1.109; 4.3.7.

[36] Instances where (some of) the cardinal virtues actually do occur include 3.26.32 (δικαιοσύνη); 4.1.109 (ἀνδρεία); cf. 4.9.17 (σώφρων).

[37] cf. Bonhöffer, *Ethics*, 31.   [38] See *Diss.* 1.19.11–15.

[39] cf. Long, *Epictetus*, 184, 197–8.

[40] *Diss.* 1.23.1. Cf. also 1.19.12–13; 2.20.6; 3.13.5; 3.24.12; 4.7.8; 4.11.1.

[41] See, e.g., *Diss.* 2.10.23.

[42] *Diss.* 4.12.19: τί οὖν; δυνατὸν ἀναμάρτητον ἤδη εἶναι; ἀμήχανον, ἀλλ' ἐκεῖνο δυνατὸν πρὸς τὸ μὴ ἁμαρτάνειν τετάσθαι διενεκῶς.

[43] e.g. *Diss.* 1.1.12; 1.3.1; 1.9.4–5, 13; 1.13.3–4; 1.14.6; 2.8.11–14.

[44] cf. *Diss.* 1.3.3; 1.16.18–20.

[45] Long observes that in the lectures of Epictetus we have 'the most creative appropriation of Socrates subsequent to the works of Plato and Xenophon' (*Epictetus*, 94).

even Socrates by far. Readers of Epictetus have also long noticed how personal his portrayal of the deity is, whether it be called Zeus, God, or gods: God/Zeus is the father of human beings,[46] their guardian,[47] and their guide.[48] God the 'father' is omnipresent, continually observing the ways of his children,[49] not only their conduct but also their purposes and thoughts.[50] People's passions and vices are in fact only dealt with through God's help. There is no other way: 'These things you cannot cast out in any other way than by looking to God alone, being specially devoted to Him only, and consecrated to His commands.'[51] God is helpful too, Epictetus says,[52] especially in hours of darkness and despair: 'Remember God; call upon Him to help you and stand by your side, just as voyagers, in a storm, call upon the Dioscuri.'[53] And 'when you close your doors and make darkness within, remember never to say that you are alone, for you are not alone; nay, God is within (ὁ θεὸς ἔνδον ἐστί)'.[54] Personal expressions of such depth concerning the deity are quite rare in earlier Stoic writings, with the notable exception of Cleanthes' famous *Hymn to Zeus* (third century BCE),[55] a much-celebrated text in antiquity.

It is true, as noted earlier,[56] that Stoic theology was from its very beginning a complex combination of theism and pantheism (and polytheism). But scholars have rightly noted that although it is probably fruitless to attempt to fit his theology into boxes of 'either/or' categories, Epictetus' conception of the deity comes regularly much closer to theism than to

---

[46] *Diss.* 1.3.1; 1.6.40; 1.9.6–7; 1.19.9, 12; 3.22.82; 3.24.3, 15–16. Cf. Seneca, *Ep.* 110.10; *Prov.* 2.6; *Ben.* 2.29.4; 4.8.1; Musonius 8.64.14–15; 16.104.31.

[47] *Diss.* 1.9.7; 1.14.12–14. Cf. Seneca, *Ep.* 41.2.

[48] *Diss.* 2.7.11; 3.22.53. Cf. also 3.21.18–19.

[49] *Diss.* 1.14.1, 9; 1.30.1; 3.26.28. Cf. also the quotation of Homer, *Il.* 10.279–80 in *Diss.* 1.12.3 (cited in Chapter 1 above).

[50] *Diss.* 2.14.11. Cf. Seneca, *Ep.* 83.1.

[51] *Diss.* 2.16.46: ταῦτα δ' οὐκ ἔστιν ἄλλως ἐκβαλεῖν, εἰ μὴ πρὸς μόνον τὸν θεὸν ἀποβλέποντα, ἐκείνῳ μόνῳ προσπεπονθότα, τοῖς ἐκείνου προστάγμασι καθωσιωμένον. Cf. Seneca, *Ep.* 41.2.

[52] *Diss.* 2.8.1. Cf. 3.26.37. Cf. also Seneca, *Ep.* 95.47–9.

[53] *Diss.* 2.18.29: τοῦ θεοῦ μέμνησο, ἐκεῖνον ἐπικαλοῦ βοηθὸν καὶ παραστάτην ὡς τοὺς Διοσκόρους ἐν χειμῶνι οἱ πλέοντες. In Greek mythology the Dioscuri (*Dioskouroi*, Διόσκουροι) were the twins Castor and Polydeuces (Pollux in Latin), sons of Zeus (*Dios kouroi*). Initially they were mostly associated with warfare, but eventually they became even more celebrated as saviours and rescuers from personal distress, particularly from perils at sea. See further Walter Burkert, *Greek Religion: Archaic and Classical* (trans. J. Raffan; Oxford: Blackwell, 1985), 212–13.

[54] *Diss.* 1.14.13–14. Cf. 2.8.11–14. Cf. also Seneca, *Ep.* 41; 73.16.

[55] Preserved in Stobaeus, *Ecl.* 1.1.12 [= *SVF* 1.537]. For a recent introduction to Cleanthes' *Hymn*, see Johan C. Thom, 'Cleanthes' *Hymn to Zeus* and Early Christian Literature', in *Antiquity and Humanity: Essays on Ancient Religion and Philosophy. Presented to Hans Dieter Betz on His 70th Birthday* (ed. A. Y. Collins and M. M. Mitchell; Tübingen: Mohr Siebeck, 2001), 477–99.

[56] See the introduction to Part I above.

pantheism.[57] As one scholar puts it, 'theist rather than pantheist, personalist rather than impersonal, ethical rather than physical—these are distinct tendencies in Epictetus' theological language and emphasis'.[58] All this is important for the present discussion because it cannot be emphasized enough how basic theology is to Epictetus' moral teaching. The foundations of his ethics are to be sought, not in human psychology, as might have been expected of a Hellenistic moralist, but in theology (or cosmology, which, as we have seen, is practically the same thing in Stoicism).[59] Epictetus is truly 'a theologically centred philosopher'.[60]

This theologically centred philosopher has much to say, not merely about the nature of the deity itself, but also about the ways in which people should worship their god. For him, proper worship consists in part in praising God with hymns and songs: 'If we had sense ($\nu o\hat{v}s$), ought we to be doing anything else, publicly and privately, than hymning and praising the Deity, and rehearsing His benefits? Ought we not, as we dig and plough and eat, to sing the hymn of praise to God?' As an example of such praise, he recites the following: 'Great is God, that He hath furnished us these instruments wherewith we shall till the earth. Great is God, that He hath given us hands, and power to swallow, and a belly, and power to grow unconsciously, and to breathe while asleep.'[61] According to Epictetus,

this is what we ought to sing on every occasion, and above all to sing the greatest and divinest hymn, that God has given us the faculty to comprehend these things and to follow the path of reason.... What else can I, a lame old man, do but sing hymns to God? If, indeed, I were a nightingale, I should be singing as a nightingale; if a swan, as a swan. But as it is, I am a rational being ($\lambda o\gamma\iota\kappa\acute{o}s$ $\epsilon\acute{\iota}\mu\iota$), therefore I must be singing hymns of praise to God. This is my task; I do it, and will not desert this post, as long as it may be given me to fill it; and I exhort ($\pi a\rho a\kappa a\lambda\hat{\omega}$) you to joint me in this same song.[62]

The importance of giving thanks to God ($\epsilon\mathring{v}\chi a\rho\iota\sigma\tau\epsilon\hat{\iota}\nu$ $\tau\hat{\omega}$ $\theta\epsilon\hat{\omega}$, etc.) is repeatedly stressed in the *Discourses*,[63] and praying is also affirmed in this communication

---

[57] cf. Bonhöffer, *Epiktet*, 341–5, 359–60; idem, *Ethics*, 112–20; Long, *Epictetus*, 142–56.

[58] Long, *Epictetus*, 156.

[59] To be sure, this is probably true of Stoic ethics in general (cf. Striker, 'Following Nature', 13), but the theological (and/or cosmological) foundations rarely receive so much and so vivid attention as they do in Epictetus.

[60] Long, *Epictetus*, 193. Long also observes that while 'the early Stoics favoured a "bottom-up" rather than "top-down" procedure for showing that their distinctive ethical principles... are ingrained in human nature' (p. 182), Epictetus opted for the latter: 'Epictetus' difference from his Stoic authorities can be broadly summed up by saying that he proceeds *from* rather than *to* God' (p. 184).

[61] *Diss.* 1.16.15–17.   [62] *Diss.* 1.16.18–21. Cf. 3.26.29–30.

[63] cf. *Diss.* 1.4.32; 1.10.3; 1.12.32; 1.19.25; 2.23.5; 4.1.105; 4.4.7, 18; 4.5.35; 4.7.9.

with God.[64] One such prayer is a hymn by Cleanthes that begins with the words 'Lead thou me on, O Zeus, and Destiny, to that goal long ago to me assigned. I'll follow and not falter; if my will prove weak and craven, still I'll follow on.'[65] These are the verses which, according to Epictetus, one should be ready to say 'upon every occasion',[66] 'always',[67] and 'at any time' with one's 'whole heart' (ἐξ ὅλης ψυχῆς).[68] Moreover, to a potentially willing student of his, the Stoic teacher gives the following instruction about praying:

Lift up your neck at last like a man escaped from bondage, be bold to look towards God and say, 'Use me henceforward for whatever Thou wilt; I am of one mind with Thee (ὁμογνωμονῶ σοι); I am Thine; I crave exemption from nothing that seems good in Thy sight; where Thou wilt, lead me; in what raiment Thou wilt, clothe me. Wouldst Thou have me to hold office, or remain in private life; to remain here or go into exile; to be poor or be rich? I will defend all these Thy acts before men; I will show what the true nature of each thing is.'[69]

Like many Greeks and Romans of his time,[70] Epictetus himself kept household gods,[71] and, somewhat unlike his fellow Stoic Seneca,[72] he does not seem to have been negatively disposed towards traditional cultic service to the deity,[73] although he sometimes appears to downplay its real value.[74] Nevertheless, there can be no doubt that for Epictetus the essential service to God is to seek and pursue the morally good; it is to be a 'good and excellent man' (καλὸς καὶ ἀγαθός).[75] Such is the primary assignment given to God's 'servant' (διάκονος/ὑπηρέτης),[76] whoever that person may be. The ultimate service is continually to strive and struggle to 'follow' God,[77] a following that is properly carried out by an act of imitation:

We must learn what the gods are like; for whatever their character is discovered to be, the man who is going to please and obey them must endeavour as best he can to resemble (ἐξομοιοῦσθαι) them. If the deity is faithful (πιστόν), he also must be faithful;

---

[64] *Diss.* 3.21.14. Contrast Seneca, *Ep.* 31.5, 8; 41.1; 60.1.

[65] Epictetus, *Ench.* 53: ἄγου δέ μ᾽, ὦ Ζεῦ, καὶ σύ γ᾽ ἡ Πεπρωμένη, ὅποι ποθ᾽ ὑμῖν εἰμὶ διατεταγμένος· ὡς ἕψομαί γ᾽ ἄοκνος· ἢν δέ γε μὴ θέλω, κακὸς γενόμενος, οὐδὲν ἧττον ἕψομαι (cf. *SVF* 1.527). Cf. also Seneca's Latin rendering of the hymn in *Ep.* 107.11 (Seneca adds one verse: *Ducunt volentem fata, nolentem trahunt* ['Aye, the willing soul Fate leads, but the unwilling drags along']). Curiously, Augustine of Hippo assigned this hymn to Seneca himself (*Civ.* 5.8)— 'if I am not mistaken' (*nisi fallor*).

[66] *Ench.* 53: ἐπὶ παντός.　　　[67] *Diss.* 3.22.95: πανταχοῦ (lit. 'everywhere').

[68] *Diss.* 2.23.42; 4.1.131; cf. 4.4.34.

[69] *Diss.* 2.16.41–3 (the LCL has 'things' instead of 'thing' in §43). Cf. 1.6.37.

[70] cf. Klauck, *Religious Context*, 59–60.　　　[71] *Diss.* 1.18.15.

[72] See *Ep.* 95.47–50; 115.5; *Ben.* 1.6.3; 4.25.1.

[73] *Diss.* 1.19.24–5; 3.21.12–16; *Ench.* 31.5. Cf. Musonius 20.126.26–30.

[74] *Diss.* 2.18.19–21. Cf. also the similar contexts in 1.4.31–2; 1.6.23–4; 1.22.15–16; 2.7.9–14; 2.8.15–20.

[75] *Diss.* 3.24.95. Cf. 3.24.110.

[76] cf. *Diss.* 3.22.56, 69, 82, 95; 3.24.65, 95–102; 3.26.28; 4.7.20; 4.8.32.

[77] *Diss.* 1.30.5. Cf. 1.12.5; 3.26.29; 4.7.20. Cf. also Seneca, *Ep.* 16.5; 96.2; *Vit. beat.* 15.5; Cicero, *Fin.* 3.22.

if free (ἐλεύθερον), he also must be free; if beneficent (εὐεργετικόν), he also must be beneficent; if high-minded (μεγαλόφρον), he also must be high-minded, and so forth; therefore, in everything he says and does, he must act as an imitator of God (θεοῦ ζηλωτήν).[78]

The faithful follower and imitator of God truly lives 'according to Nature' and thus fulfils 'the profession of being human' (ἡ τοῦ ἀνθρώπου ἐπαγγελία).[79] Proper service to God consists of living up to the divine principles which have been given to humankind, viz. the law of God which is 'most good and most just' (ὁ τοῦ θεοῦ νόμος κράτιστός ἐστι καὶ δικαιότατος).[80] Traditional, ritual worship of the deity is not exactly worthless, but much more important to God is the way in which human beings live as such, including the way they treat one another.[81] That is the decisive thing for the rational creature, the human being, in God's creation.

God has so fashioned human nature that no man can actually benefit from his own goods unless he makes some contribution to the common interest (τὸ κοινὸν ὠφέλιμον).[82] This means that self-interest, if properly construed, *embraces* social duties.[83] For human beings have a natural sense of fidelity (φύσει πιστόν), a natural sense of affection (φύσει στερκτικόν), a natural sense of helpfulness (φύσει ὠφελητικόν), and a natural sense of tolerance towards one another (ἀλλήλων φύσει ἀνεκτικόν).[84] All this is ordained by Nature itself (= God = λόγος). Every individual is from the very beginning well disposed towards other individuals and finds joy in associating with them (ἡδέως συναναστρέφεσθαι ἀνθρώποις), simply because the human being as such is a social and affectionate being (φύσει κοινωνικὸς καὶ φιλάλληλος).[85] It lies in the nature of humans to do good (εὖ ποιεῖν), to work together (συνεργεῖν), and to pray for each other's well-being (ἐπεύχεσθαι).[86] Indeed, in Epictetus' mind, a work that is ἀνθρωπικόν, that is, a work that befits a human being, should be something beneficent (εὐεργετικόν), something of common utility (κοινωφελές), something noble (γενναῖον).[87]

Like Seneca, though less frequently, Epictetus applies the Stoics' favourite metaphor to describe the essence of this universal humanity and its implications for individual human beings: precisely as each and every member is an integral

---

[78] *Diss.* 2.14.12–13. Cf. 2.17.23–5; 2.19.26–7; 4.1.98–9. Cf. also Musonius 8.64.14 (ζηλωτὴς τοῦ Διός).

[79] *Diss.* 2.9.1, 7. Cf. 2.10.4.

[80] *Diss.* 1.29.13. Cf. 1.13.5; 1.25.3–6; 1.29.4; 2.16.27–8; 3.24.42; 4.3.12; 4.7.17. Cf. also Musonius 16.104.32–6: 'His [i.e. Zeus'] command and law (πρόσταγμά τε καὶ νόμος) is that man be just and honest, beneficent, temperate, high-minded, superior to pain, superior to pleasure, free of all envy and all malice; to put it briefly, the law of Zeus bids man be good (ἀγαθὸν εἶναι κελεύει τὸν ἄνθρωπον ὁ νόμος ὁ τοῦ Διός).'

[81] See *Diss.* 1.13; 3.21.12–19.   [82] *Diss.* 1.19.13.

[83] cf. Reydams-Schils, 'Human Bonding', 204.   [84] *Diss.* 2.10.23.

[85] *Diss.* 3.13.5.   [86] *Diss.* 4.1.122.   [87] *Diss.* 4.10.12.

part of the body, every human being is an integral part of humanity as a whole. If a foot is detached from the body, of which it is an integral part, it loses its function as a foot and is indeed no longer a foot as such. So also with human beings. If detached from society, the human being no longer functions as such and is no longer a human being.[88] Such a person would be unable to fulfil the 'profession' (ἐπαγγελία) that every 'citizen of the world' (πολίτης τοῦ κόσμου) has, namely,

to treat nothing as a matter of private profit, not to plan about anything as though he were a detached unit, but to act like the foot or the hand, which, if they had the faculty of reason (λογισμός) and understood the constitution of nature, would never exercise choice or desire in any other way but by reference to the whole.[89]

But why do some persons act erroneously and weigh only, it seems, their own private profit, even to the extent of harming others? Why do these particular members of humanity behave as if detached from the whole? To answer these difficult questions Epictetus follows in the footsteps of Socrates and the Socratic heritage: all sins and errors are due to sheer ignorance and false opinion. No one really wishes to live in error. The man who does wrong is doing what he in truth does not want to do. In Epictetus' words, 'there is no bad man who lives as he wills'.[90] If the bad man is to change his disposition and way of life, it needs to be pointed out to him how contradictory his conduct really is,[91] namely, that 'he is not doing what he wishes, and is doing what he does not wish' (ὃ θέλει οὐ ποιεῖ καὶ ὃ μὴ θέλει ποιεῖ).[92] For virtue results from knowledge and correct opinion. It follows that the responsibility lies partly with other people to bring the man to his senses, for 'as soon as anyone shows a man this, he will of his own accord abandon what he is doing'.[93] Blame yourself, Epictetus adds, if you bypass this responsibility towards a fellow human being.

Because people sin merely out of ignorance, there is no valid reason, according to Epictetus, to pay them back for their wrongdoings, to render evil for evil. Retaliation has no place in Stoic ethics.[94] Forgiving, on the other hand, does.[95] Hence if a person keeps in mind that the person who treats her badly does so basically out of ignorance, she will meet badness with

---

[88] *Diss.* 2.5.24–6.   [89] *Diss.* 2.10.4.

[90] *Diss.* 4.1.3: οὐδεὶς ἄρα τῶν φαύλων ζῇ ὡς βούλεται. Cf. 2.22.1–3; 2.26; *Ench.* 42.

[91] *Diss.* 1.18.3–4.

[92] *Diss.* 2.26.4–5. Cf. the interesting parallel in Rom 7.15–20. Cf. also Seneca, *Ep.* 21.1; 61.3; 94.26.

[93] *Diss.* 2.26.5.   [94] cf. *Diss.* 4.1.122, 167; *Ench.* 43.

[95] *Diss.* 2.22.36. Referring also to similar viewpoints expressed by Seneca and Musonius Rufus, Bonhöffer states: 'All this proves...not just that the reproach of inhuman harshness which is often raised against the Stoa is completely unfounded, but also that in these questions

goodness.[96] No one embodies this principle more clearly and exquisitely than the (ideal) sage, who, if genuine, must *love* (φιλεῖν) those who wrong him, even if it involves some terrible torture.[97] He must, as it were, love those whose conduct would normally make them well worth hating, and he must love them as if he were their 'father or brother', which is precisely why 'the power to love belongs to the wise man and to him alone' (τοῦ φρονίμου τοίνυν ἐστὶ μόνου τὸ φιλεῖν).[98] In other words, it is not in the power of everyone to truly love in such paradoxical terms, only in the power of the 'wise man'. To be sure, real 'wise men' are as rare as white ravens,[99] but it is the continuing task of each and every person to have the sage's mindset and pattern of life as the ultimate goal.[100] This is at the same time the very reason for which God has sent the sage into the world, namely, to serve as an example, to show people the proper way of living.[101] And the example must be shown in practice. Otherwise it is quite pointless.

Epictetus places himself wholly in line with other Roman Stoics, with his strong and consistent emphasis on praxis or applied ethics. While for him the task of philosophy is certainly 'to examine and to establish the standards' (τοὺς κανόνας) according to which one lives, he underlines that 'to go ahead and *use* (χρῆσθαι) them after they have become known is the task of the good and excellent man'.[102] There is no question that theoretical knowledge is good and prerequisite to any progress, but it is first in real life where its significance is truly tested and the actual learning of the student is tried.[103] Epictetus explains this further with an analogy of a builder of a house: the builder does not come forward with the purpose of delivering a speech on the art of building. No, his purpose is to build a house, which is exactly what he carries out, and proves thereby his possession of the art.[104] Urging each of his students accordingly, Epictetus continues:

Do something of the same sort yourself too; eat as a man (ἄνθρωπος), drink as a man, adorn yourself, marry, get children, be active as a citizen; endure revilings, bear with an unreasonable brother, father, son, neighbour, fellow-traveller. Show us that you can

the Stoics developed an outlook which ran far ahead of their time and must really be taken to heart nowadays as well' (*Ethics*, 151).

[96] *Ench.* 42.

[97] *Diss.* 3.22.54. Typically, the sage is here represented by Epictetus' ideal 'Cynic'. Cf. also 3.24.64–5.

[98] *Diss.* 2.22.3.

[99] cf., e.g., Seneca, *Ep.* 20.2; *Const.* 7.1; *Ira* 2.10.6; Alexander of Aphrodisias, *Fat.* 199.14–22 (ed. Bruns) [= *SVF* 3.658]; Sextus Empiricus, *Math.* 9.133. The Stoic sage or 'wise man' was more of an ideal type than a designation of a real person (Socrates being the main exception). None of the Roman Stoics ever claimed that he was a 'wise man', least of all Seneca (cf. *Vit. beat.* 17.3–4). See further in Chapter 9 below.

[100] cf. *Ench.* 51.3.   [101] *Diss.* 3.22.23, 46, 56, 87; 4.8.30–1.

[102] *Diss.* 2.11.24–5.   [103] *Diss.* 1.26.3.   [104] *Diss.* 3.21.4.

do these things, for us to see that in all truth you have learned something of the philosophers.[105]

The student of philosophy (= every human being) should not be content with merely learning the conceptual basics in the abstract, but should add practice to learning, together with continuous training ($\check{\alpha}\sigma\kappa\eta\sigma\iota\varsigma$).[106] It does not do simply to forget or brush off the principles of philosophy the moment one leaves the lecture room and enters into everyday life.[107] Philosophy is 'the art of living',[108] bearing upon all aspects of life, every hour.

As observed above, for nearly half his life Epictetus served as a slave. Therefore his reticence to speak of things concrete, material, and social may come as a surprise—even if we grant that he was certainly not among the most unfortunate slaves of Rome. For instance, he seems quite uninterested in criticizing or denouncing riches as such,[109] in spite of all his Cynic tendencies.[110] His focus stays instead on the *attitude* towards riches and possessions. As any genuine Stoic would have done, he aims his criticism at people's dependence on material things. Furthermore, Epictetus rarely discusses issues of slaves and slavery,[111] despite his earlier life in servitude and subjection. In fact, nowhere does he question the social structure of his society, including the institution of slavery,[112] but underlines instead that every person should accept and remain in the position in which she or he is called to serve, whatever its nature.

I do not wish to maintain that there is no attention whatsoever paid to concrete social affairs in Epictetus' teaching. We can see, for instance, that he

---

[105] *Diss.* 3.21.5–6. Cf. 2.1.29–31.

[106] *Diss.* 2.9.13. On the concept of $\check{\alpha}\sigma\kappa\eta\sigma\iota\varsigma$ in Epictetus, see esp. Benjamin L. Hijmans, Jr, *ΑΣΚΗΣΙΣ: Notes on Epictetus' Educational System* (Assen: Van Gorcum, 1959), 64–91. See also John Sellars, 'Stoic Practical Philosophy in the Imperial Period', in *Greek and Roman Philosophy 100 BC–200 AD* (ed. R. Sorabji and R. W. Sharples; 2 vols.; Bulletin of the Institute of Classical Studies Supplement 94; London: Institute of Classical Studies, University of London, 2007), 1: 115–40.

[107] *Diss.* 3.20.18.   [108] *Diss.* 1.15.2: $\acute{\eta}\ \pi\epsilon\rho\grave{\iota}\ \beta\acute{\iota}o\nu\ \tau\acute{\epsilon}\chi\nu\eta$.

[109] cf., however, *Diss.* 1.18.11–14; 3.6.6; 4.1.144; *Ench.* 44. It is clear from *Diss.* 1.1.10 that Epictetus himself had a 'small estate' ($\kappa\tau\eta\sigma\acute{\iota}\delta\iota o\nu$); cf. also 1.2.37.

[110] It is telling in this respect that, next to Socrates, Diogenes (the 'father' of Cynicism) is the philosopher who is most often mentioned in the *Discourses*. Long observes that this is a mark of Epictetus' 'entirely correct recognition that the principal influences on Zeno's Stoicism were Socratic and Cynic. In canonizing Socrates, Diogenes, and Zeno, Epictetus looks back to the founder of Stoicism and to the two great figures whom later Stoics regarded as the closest approximations to their ideal sage' (*Epictetus*, 58).

[111] cf., however, *Diss.* 1.9.8; 1.13; 3.26.1; 4.1.33–40, 144–50. To be sure, 'freedom' ($\grave{\epsilon}\lambda\epsilon\upsilon\theta\epsilon\rho\acute{\iota}\alpha$) is a key concept in Epictetus, but not in the concrete, physical/social sense.

[112] cf., e.g., *Diss.* 2.23.24–5; 4.1.33–40. I seriously doubt, however, that the statement in *Ench.* 33.7 gives us a trustworthy picture of Epictetus' own perspective (rather than Arrian's), where a person's 'bare (bodily) needs' are said to include food, drink, clothing, shelter, and *household slaves* ($o\grave{\iota}\kappa\epsilon\tau\acute{\iota}\alpha$)!

followed in the footsteps of Seneca and Musonius in speaking unfavourably of public shows such as gladiatorial games.[113] We can also see that he shared his mentor's (negative) view on adultery,[114] whereas the positions of the two Stoics as to the question of women's status in society appear poles apart.[115] And then there is Epictetus' discourse on family affection and parenthood.[116] But, all in all, given his background, it seems odd that Epictetus does not pay more attention to social issues of this sort. However, it is important to remember that the texts we are dealing with were class-room lectures, not general essays intended for publication. And in these lectures Epictetus was not addressing people in general but quite specific people, namely, young male students of well-to-do families and, occasionally, some passers-by (also well-to-do and male).[117] The identity of the audience is crucial to the content of the lectures,[118] and can to a large extent explain Epictetus' silence on concrete social issues.

Having said that, it is necessary to pay due attention to the fact that in his (rather scant) discussion of slaves, Epictetus nevertheless holds that they are equal to their masters *as human beings*. Slaves have and will continue to have an inferior position in society, he maintains, but they have the same divine origin as other humans and enjoy the same worth as such. A slave is 'your own brother, who has Zeus as his progenitor and is, as it were, a son born of the same seed as yourself and of the same sowing from above'.[119] Regardless of social status, slaves are kinsmen (συγγενεῖς), brothers by nature (ἀδελφοὶ φύσει), and the offspring of Zeus (τοῦ Διὸς ἀπόγονοι), Epictetus lectures his students.[120] This view is nothing but a direct result of the Stoic principle of universal humanity, which Epictetus elsewhere labels 'the natural fellowship of men with one another' (ἡ φυσικὴ κοινωνία ἀνθρώποις πρὸς ἀλλήλοις).[121] It is not a question of relationships between specific individuals only or of relationships between particular groups of people, the kind of in- or

---

[113] *Ench.* 33.2, 10.   [114] *Diss.* 2.4; 2.10.18; 3.7.16, 21.

[115] cf. *Diss.* 2.4.8–11: τί οὖν; οὐκ εἰσὶν αἱ γυναῖκες κοιναὶ φύσει; κἀγὼ λέγω ('What then, you say; are not women by nature common property? I agree'); 3.7.20: πονηρά ἐστι τὰ δόγματα, ... οὐδὲ γυναιξὶ πρέποντα ('Your doctrines are bad, ... not even fit for women'). Cf., however, the more positive implications in 3.22.76; 3.24.22; 4.11.35.

[116] *Diss.* 1.11.   [117] cf. Brunt, 'Epictetus', 19–30.

[118] This is well pointed out by Long, *Epictetus*, 4, 43.

[119] *Diss.* 1.13.3: [οὐκ ἀνέξῃ] τοῦ ἀδελφοῦ τοῦ σαυτοῦ, ὃς ἔχει τὸν Δία πρόγονον, ὥσπερ υἱὸς ἐκ τῶν αὐτῶν σπερμάτων γέγονεν καὶ τῆς αὐτῆς ἄνωθεν καταβολῆς ...

[120] *Diss.* 1.13.4. But, again, contrast the striking claims in 2.23.24: 'There is some use in an ass, but not as much as there is in an ox; there is use also in a dog, but not as much as there is in a slave (οἰκέτης); there is use also in a slave, but not as much as there is in your fellow-citizens; there is use also in these, but not as much as there is in the magistrates.'

[121] *Diss.* 2.20.6.

out-group relations that are subject to ever-shifting interests. Neither is it a question of specific relations between people of common nationality or race. Rather, it is a question of a constant, inherent fellowship among *all* people as an integral part of human existence.[122] It is a fellowship beyond and above any nationalism and patriotism.[123] This might be phrased as follows: 'We are asked to regard the relationships in which we stand to other people not as external states of affairs but as constituents of our personal identity and hence as falling within the realm of our essential self or our volition [= προαίρεσις].'[124] Or as Epictetus himself chooses to express it: 'If I am where my moral purpose (προαίρεσις) is, then, and then only, will I be the friend and son and the father that I should be.'[125]

Again, according to Epictetus, it is the Stoic sage who embodies this principle for others to follow, for 'he has made all mankind his children (πάντας ἀνθρώπους πεπαιδοποίηται); the men among them he has as sons, the women as daughters (τοὺς ἄνδρας υἱοὺς ἔχει, τὰς γυναῖκας θυγατέρας); in that spirit he approaches them all and cares for them all (πᾶσιν οὕτως προσέρχεται, οὕτως πάντων κήδεται)'.[126] The sage is a universal philanthropist.[127] As the perfect human being, but mere human being nonetheless, he does not, however, follow this through without an example himself: 'It is as a father he does it, as a brother, and as a servant of Zeus, who is Father of us all' (ὡς πατὴρ αὐτὸ ποιεῖ, ὡς ἀδελφὸς καὶ τοῦ κοινοῦ πατρὸς ὑπηρέτης Διός).[128] The Stoic sage is a divinely guided, universal philanthropist.

---

[122] cf. *Diss.* 3.13.5.　　　[123] cf. Bonhöffer, *Ethics*, 135. Cf. also Cicero, *Off.* 3.28.
[124] Long, *Epictetus*, 236–7.　　　[125] *Diss.* 2.22.20.
[126] *Diss.* 3.22.81.　　　[127] cf. Long, *Epictetus*, 60.　　　[128] *Diss.* 3.22.82.

Part II

Moral Teaching in Roman Christianity

5

Introduction to Roman Christianity

FIRST-CENTURY ROMAN CHRISTIANITY

The origins of Roman Christianity are unknown. It is likely that the first accounts of Jesus of Nazareth as the promised Messiah were told in (some of) the Jewish synagogues, and that the synagogue was thus the initial setting for the Christian narrative in the city.[1] But for how long the followers of Jesus continued to be a part of the Roman Jewry we do not know. Much is also obscure regarding the structure and practice of the Jewish communities in Rome in the first century CE. There are indications of at least eleven synagogues in the city in antiquity, five of which may date from the first century CE, but the evidence is relatively late and little is known about the foundation of these synagogues.[2] While the question is still debated, an increasing

---

[1] cf. Peter Lampe, *From Paul to Valentinus: Christians at Rome in the First Two Centuries* (trans. M. Steinhauser; Minneapolis, MN: Fortress, 2003), 7–10, 69–79; idem, 'Early Christians in the City of Rome: Topographical and Social Historical Aspects of the First Three Centuries', in *Christians as a Religious Minority in a Multicultural City: Modes of Interaction and Identity Formation in Early Imperial Rome* (ed. J. Zangenberg and M. Labahn; JSNTSup 243; London: T&T Clark, 2004), 20–2; Rudolf Brändle and Ekkehard W. Stegemann, 'The Formation of the First "Christian Congregations" in Rome in the Context of the Jewish Congregations', in *Judaism and Christianity in First-Century Rome* (ed. K. P. Donfried and P. Richardson; Grand Rapids, MI: Eerdmans, 1998), 117–27; James C. Walters, 'Romans, Jews, and Christians: The Impact of the Romans on Jewish/Christian Relations in First-Century Rome', in ibid., 175–95; William L. Lane, 'Social Perspectives on Roman Christianity during the Formative Years from Nero to Nerva: Romans, Hebrews, *1 Clement*', in ibid., 202–3; Mark D. Nanos, 'The Jewish Context of the Gentile Audience Addressed in Paul's Letter to the Romans', *CBQ* 61 (1999): 283–304; James D. G. Dunn, *Romans* (2 vols.; WBC 38; Dallas, TX: Word Books, 1988), 1: xlvi–l.

[2] See George La Piana, 'Foreign Groups in Rome during the First Centuries of the Empire', *HTR* 20 (1927): 341–71; Harry J. Leon, *The Jews of Ancient Rome* (updated edn.; Peabody, MA: Hendrickson, 1995), 139–66; Romano Penna, 'Les Juifs à Rome au temps de l'apôtre Paul', *NTS* 28 (1982): 326–8; Irina Levinskaya, *The Book of Acts in Its Diaspora Setting* (vol. 5 of *The Book of Acts in Its First Century Setting*; ed. B. W. Winter; Grand Rapids, MI: Eerdmans, 1996), 182–5; Peter Richardson, 'Augustan-Era Synagogues in Rome', in *Judaism and Christianity in First-Century Rome* (ed. K. P. Donfried and P. Richardson; Grand Rapids, MI: Eerdmans, 1998), 17–29.

number of scholars are of the opinion that the synagogues must have operated quite independently, without any major centralized coordination or organizational head.[3]

According to the Acts of the Apostles, the apostle Paul met Christ-believers (ἀδελφοί) in Puteoli and Rome when he arrived in Italy,[4] sometime around 60 CE. These locations fit well with our evidence of Jewish settlements along the Puteoli–Rome trade route, and with the fact that in the first half of the first century CE it was the harbour of Puteoli (rather than that of Ostia) that served as the main gateway of Rome to the East.[5] The author of Acts, Luke, gives no further information about the 'brothers' in these places but reports merely that Paul and his travelling companions stayed with the ἀδελφοί in Puteoli for seven days, and then went to the city of Rome where they met other ἀδελφοί who, when they heard of their coming, 'came as far as the Forum of Appius and Three Taverns' to meet them. Paul thanked God and 'took courage' when he saw these fellow believers, Luke adds. But instead of telling us more about the Roman ἀδελφοί, Acts (typically) turns the attention to the Jewish residents and relates how Paul, three days later, summoned 'the leaders of the Jews' (τοὺς ὄντας τῶν Ἰουδαίων πρώτους) in order to account for his mission and coming to Rome.[6] According to Acts, the Jewish leaders informed Paul that they had received no news whatsoever of him or his mission, but that they were nonetheless acquainted with the 'sect' (αἵρεσις) of Christ-believers and were eager to hear more of it from Paul, 'for with regard to this sect we know that everywhere it is spoken against.'[7] In this case, Luke makes no mention of any invitation to Paul on the part of his fellow Jews to

---

[3] Heikki Solin, 'Juden und Syrer im westlichen Teil der römischen Welt: Eine ethnisch-demographische Studie mit besonderer Berücksichtigung der sprachlichen Zustände', *ANRW* 29.2: 696–8; Wolfgang Wiefel, 'The Jewish Community in Ancient Rome and the Origins of Roman Christianity', in *The Romans Debate* (rev. and exp. edn.; ed. K. P. Donfried; Peabody, MA: Hendrickson, 1991), 89–92; Margaret H. Williams, 'The Structure of Roman Jewry Re-Considered: Were the Synagogues of Ancient Rome Entirely Homogenous?' *ZPE* 104 (1994): 129–41; Leon, *Jews*, 167–70; Levinskaya, *Acts*, 185–93; Noy, *Foreigners*, 264–6; Silvia Cappelletti, *The Jewish Community of Rome: From the Second Century* B.C. *to the Third Century* C.E. (JSJSup 113; Leiden: Brill, 2006), 3–30.

[4] Acts 28.13–15. Puteoli is known in modern times as Pozzuoli, located at the northern end of the Gulf of Naples (Napoli). East of Puteoli were the famous cities of Herculaneum and Pompeii, and just west of it was the popular bathing place Baiae, particularly favoured by the Roman elite (cf., e.g., Seneca, *Ep.* 51; Suetonius, *Cal.* 19; *Nero* 34.2).

[5] Lampe, *From Paul*, 9–10. Lampe observes that 'Jews had lived in Puteoli since Augustan times (Josephus, *Bell.* 2.104; *Ant.* 17.328)' and that 'Rome (e.g., Philo, *Leg. ad Gaium* 155), perhaps Aquileia in the north (*CIL* 1²: 3422), and Puteoli accommodated the only pre-Christian Jewish settlements in Italy known to us' (p. 9).

[6] Acts 28.17–20.

[7] Acts 28.22: περὶ μὲν γὰρ τῆς αἱρέσεως ταύτης γνωστὸν ἡμῖν ἐστιν ὅτι πανταχοῦ ἀντιλέγεται.

speak in the synagogues,[8] but tells instead that on a pre-arranged day, 'many' ($\pi\lambda\epsilon\acute{\iota}o\nu\epsilon s$) came to Paul's own 'lodging' ($\xi\epsilon\nu\acute{\iota}a$) in the city, where he began to teach them about Jesus as the promised Messiah, of the truth of which some became convinced, while others did not.[9]

Interesting as this tradition may be for the question of the origins of Roman Christianity, it is very difficult to assess its historical value. Acts was penned as late as in the last quarter of the first century (ca. 80–100 CE),[10] at a time when Christianity had already made the first steps towards establishing itself as a religion of its own wholly distinct from Judaism. There is little doubt that Luke's account is influenced by the new religion's awareness of itself as such and its relation to and criticism of the mother religion. That explains Luke's preoccupation with delivering Paul's apologetic speech to the local Jewry and with showing the latter's failure to acknowledge the divine legitimacy of Paul's teaching about Jesus Christ. Of the Christ-believers in Rome, on the other hand, Luke tells almost nothing, except of course of their very presence in the city. However, the implication that the 'Jewish leaders' knew the 'sect' mostly by reputation may suggest that, according to the sources and/or judgement of Luke, the number and prominence of the Roman Christ-believers was relatively insignificant at this point. Moreover, the fact that the Jewish leaders refer to the movement as a 'sect' ($a\H{\iota}\rho\epsilon\sigma\iota s$)[11] indicates a context of an *inner*-Jewish discussion.

It is Paul's Letter to the Romans that is our earliest source for the presence of Christ-believers in Rome, and it is also the earliest document related to the city that speaks of Jesus Christ. When Paul wrote the letter in the 50s he was clearly writing to people who were already acquainted with the 'good news' about Jesus Christ and (some of) their wider implications. But how well informed they actually were, and how well informed Paul believed them to be, is much less clear. Pauline scholars commonly take for granted that the letter's recipients were full-blown 'Christians', but such a point of departure is both anachronistic and in contradiction to the bare fact that the apostle wrote such an extensive letter to Rome in which he gave such a comprehensive account of the 'good news'.[12] That strongly suggests

---

[8] cf. Acts 9.20; 13.5, 14–43; 14.1; 17.1–2, 10, 17; 18.4, 19; 19.8.   [9] Acts 28.23–4.

[10] For this date of Acts, see, e.g., Hans Conzelmann, *Acts of the Apostles* (trans. J. Limburg, A. T. Kraabel, and D. H. Juel; Hermeneia; Philadelphia, PA: Fortress, 1987), xxxiii.

[11] cf. also Acts 5.17: 'the sect ($a\H{\iota}\rho\epsilon\sigma\iota s$) of the Sadducees'; 15.5: 'some believers who belonged to the sect ($a\H{\iota}\rho\acute{\epsilon}\sigma\epsilon\omega s$) of the Pharisees'; 24.5: 'a ringleader of the sect ($a\H{\iota}\rho\acute{\epsilon}\sigma\epsilon\omega s$) of the Nazarenes'; 24.14: 'according to the Way, which they call a sect ($a\H{\iota}\rho\epsilon\sigma\iota\nu$)'; 26.5: 'I have belonged to the strictest sect ($a\H{\iota}\rho\epsilon\sigma\iota\nu$) of our religion and lived as a Pharisee' (trans. NRSV).

[12] cf. Rom 1.14b–15: $\dot{o}\phi\epsilon\iota\lambda\acute{\epsilon}\tau\eta s$ $\epsilon\dot{\iota}\mu\acute{\iota}$ ... $\kappa a\grave{\iota}$ $\dot{\upsilon}\mu\hat{\iota}\nu$ $\tauo\hat{\iota}s$ $\dot{\epsilon}\nu$ $'P\acute{\omega}\mu\eta$ $\epsilon\dot{\upsilon}a\gamma\gamma\epsilon\lambda\acute{\iota}\sigma a\sigma\theta a\iota$ ('I am bound...to announce the gospel to you also who are in Rome'). On this reading of the text,

that Paul, at least, considered his Roman addressees to be in need of knowing more fully about (his version of) the 'good news'. In other words, the Christ-movement in Rome was probably much less developed and established as 'Christianity' at this point in time than commonly thought. Needless to say, Paul himself nowhere applies terms such as 'Christian(s)' and 'Christianity', terms that in all likelihood were alien to him. As a self-designation, the label 'Christian' ($X\rho\iota\sigma\tau\iota\alpha\nu\acute{o}s$) first occurs in writing at the close of the century,[13] i.e. some ten to twenty years after the pivotal 70 CE and long after Paul's death, whereas the term 'Christianity' ($X\rho\iota\sigma\tau\iota\alpha\nu\iota\sigma\mu\acute{o}s$) does not appear until the early second century.[14] We may safely postulate that Paul did not establish the community or communities of Christ-believers in Rome, but there is no way of knowing who did—if anyone in particular.[15] Nor do we know if (some of) these believers in Christ were still operating within the synagogues, within which the movement initially grew, or if they gathered in 'house churches',[16] and, if the latter, whether they did so under the auspices of (some of) the synagogues. Scholars often tend to view these two possibilities as mutually exclusive, but that is surely a mistake. According to the description of Ambrosiaster (ca. 375 CE), the original ties with Judaism were (unusually) strong in Roman Christianity:

It is established that there were Jews living in Rome in the time of the apostles and that those Jews who had believed [in Christ] passed on to the Romans the tradition that they ought to profess Christ but keep the Law (*Christum profitentes, Legem servarent*).... One ought not to condemn the Romans [i.e. the Roman

---

see Runar M. Thorsteinsson, 'Paul's Missionary Duty Towards Gentiles in Rome: A Note on the Punctuation and Syntax of Rom 1.13–15', *NTS* 48 (2002): 531–47.

[13] Acts 11.26; 26.28; 1 Pet 4.16.   [14] Ignatius, *Magn.* 10.1, 3; *Phld.* 6.1; *Rom.* 3.3.

[15] Paul's reference to his reluctance to 'build on someone else's foundation' (Rom 15.20) may suggest that he did not know of any particular person (apostle) who had founded the Roman community/-ies, i.e. that it lacked a proper apostolic foundation (cf. Günter Klein, 'Paul's Purpose in Writing the Epistle to the Romans', in *The Romans Debate* [rev. and exp. edn.; ed. K. P. Donfried; Peabody, MA: Hendrickson, 1991], 29–43). Some have suggested that the Roman visitors to Jerusalem referred to in Acts 2.10–11 (οἱ ἐπιδημοῦντες ῾Ρωμαῖοι) brought the 'good news' with them back to Rome. There is also the (much later) legend that the apostle Peter was the founder of Roman Christianity (e.g. Eusebius, *Hist. eccl.* 2.14.6; 2.17.1; Jerome, *Vir. ill.* 1). Ignatius speaks of Peter's presence in Rome together with Paul (*Rom.* 4.3), and 1 Clement 5 alludes to their martyrdom in the city, but neither source says anything about them being founders of the movement.

[16] On the so-called 'house churches' in Rome in the first century, see Peter Lampe, 'The Roman Christians of Romans 16', in *The Romans Debate* (rev. and exp. edn.; ed. K. P. Donfried; Peabody, MA: Hendrickson, 1991), 222–30; idem, *From Paul*, 359–65, 373–80; Roger W. Gehring, *House Church and Mission: The Importance of Household Structures in Early Christianity* (Peabody, MA: Hendrickson, 2004), 144–51, with further references.

Christ-believers], but to praise their faith, because without seeing any of the signs or miracles, and without seeing any of the apostles, they nevertheless accepted faith in Christ, although in a Jewish manner (*ritu licet Iudaico*).[17]

To be sure, Ambrosiaster's description is rather late. But one should take into account that Roman Christian writings from the first century onwards do not disaffirm such a context of the earliest Christ-believing community/-ies.[18] Neither does the ease with which Roman writers could (con)fuse the Christ-movement with Judaism, even as late as the second century CE.[19] It is also likely that the first Romans of non-Jewish descent who heard the message about the new 'sect' were 'god-fearing' gentiles who were interested in or in some way linked to the Jewish religion and attended synagogue meetings. This is probably the group of people that the apostle Paul had in mind when he wrote his letter to the Romans. 'Already open to a new and different religion, but unwilling to go the whole way and become proselytes [through circumcision] . . ., they would be all the more open to a form of Judaism which did not require circumcision and which was less tied to Jewish ethnic identity.'[20] Hence, to proclaim the 'good news' in synagogues would have been an excellent way to reach and attract such individuals, who would not only have some basic knowledge of Judaism and the Jewish Law but would also have understood the Christ-movement, not as a new religion, but precisely as an integral part of the Jewish religion.

In his story of the Roman emperors, Suetonius relates that when Claudius expelled Jews from Rome, perhaps in the year 49 CE (i.e. some five to ten years before Paul wrote his letter to the Romans), it was on account of certain disturbances made by (the) Jews 'at the instigation of Chrestus' (*impulsore Chresto*).[21] Many scholars believe that by 'Chrestus' Suetonius was actually referring to 'Christus', that is, Jesus Christ, and that the turmoil was caused by disagreements about him and his message.[22] Others remain sceptical,

---

[17] Ambrosiaster, *In ep. ad Romanos* (PL 17, cols. 45A–46A). English trans. in Lane, 'Social Perspectives', 203.

[18] cf. Raymond E. Brown and John P. Meier, *Antioch and Rome: New Testament Cradles of Catholic Christianity* (New York: Paulist Press, 1983), 159–83, 203–4; F. F. Bruce, 'The Romans Debate—Continued', in *The Romans Debate* (rev. and exp. edn.; ed. K. P. Donfried; Peabody, MA: Hendrickson, 1991), 178; Lampe, *From Paul*, 75–9, 217; Lane, 'Social Perspectives', 203.

[19] Epictetus, *Diss.* 2.9.20–1; Galen (see Robert Louis Wilken, *The Christians as the Romans Saw Them* [2nd edn.; New Haven, CT: Yale University Press, 2003], 72–3).

[20] Dunn, *Rom*, 1: xlviii.

[21] *Claud.* 25.4: *Iudaeos impulsore Chresto assidue tumultuantis Roma expulit* ('Since the Jews constantly made disturbances at the instigation of Chrestus, he [i.e. Claudius] expelled them from Rome'). Cf. Acts 18.2.

[22] See the discussion in Helga Botermann, *Das Judenedikt des Kaisers Claudius: Römischer Staat und Christiani im 1. Jahrhundert* (Hermes 71; Stuttgart: Franz Steiner, 1996);

including me.[23] But even if 'Chrestus' does allude to Jesus Christ and the dispute concerned the legitimacy of the 'Christian' message, this tells us merely, first, that there was indeed a significant presence of Christ-believers in Rome already before the year 50 CE (cf. Acts above), and, second, that the movement still found itself and/or was seen by others as an integral part of the Jewish community, since the debate was clearly regarded as an inner-Jewish debate. Thus, if Suetonius' reference to 'Chrestus' tells us anything at all about the earliest stages of the Christ-movement in Rome, it reinforces the hypothesis above, that its roots were in the synagogue, that it grew and developed within that context, as a Jewish αἵρεσις, and that it was still seen as such in the middle of the first century.

Tacitus' famous account of emperor Nero's persecution of 'Christians' (*Christiani*) in 64 CE[24] need not presuppose any more than this, despite the widespread scholarly willingness—or should I say enthusiasm?—to take that account as the ultimate evidence of a first-century Roman recognition of Christianity as a new and distinct religion.[25] Scholars often overlook the fact that when Tacitus wrote about these events, no fewer than fifty years had passed since they occurred. Since Christians were clearly known as such to the Romans by that time,[26] Tacitus' account says probably more about Roman attitudes towards Christians in the early second century than about the latter group's identity as *Christiani* in 64 CE.[27] Moreover, and more to the point for the present discussion, even if Tacitus' use of the label *Christiani* does reflect

---

David Alvarez Cineira, *Die Religionspolitik des Kaisers Claudius und die paulinische Mission* (Herders biblische Studien 19; Freiburg: Herder, 1999), 194–214.

[23] See Thorsteinsson, *Paul's Interlocutor*, 92–7, with references to both sides of the debate.

[24] *Ann.* 15.44: *Ergo abolendo rumori Nero subdidit reos et quaesitissimis poenis adfecit, quos per flagitia invisos vulgus Christianos appellabat* ('Therefore, to scotch the rumour [that he had started the fire], Nero substituted as culprits, and punished with the utmost refinements of cruelty, a class of men, loathed for their vices, whom the crowd styled Christians').

[25] To take but one recent example out of many, cf. Margaret H. Williams, 'The Shaping of the Identity of the Jewish Community in Rome in Antiquity', in *Christians as a Religious Minority in a Multicultural City: Modes of Interaction and Identity Formation in Early Imperial Rome* (ed. J. Zangenberg and M. Labahn; JSNTSup 243; London: T&T Clark, 2004), 41: 'Mutual forbearance was no answer to the problems facing the [Jewish] community, for it now contained people whose identities were not only different but irreconcilable. The end result we know. Before Nero's reign was out (68 CE), the gulf between observant Jews and converts to Christianity… had become so wide that even the Roman authorities had no difficulty distinguishing between the two groups. Their targeting of the Christian sect in the aftermath of the Great Fire of 64 CE… is a clear indication that by then significant numbers of Jews and Christians must have had distinct identities.'

[26] cf. Pliny, *Ep.* 10.96–7; Suetonius, *Nero* 16.2.

[27] cf. Wilken, *Christians*, 49, who rightly warns against reading too much into Tacitus' story: 'On the basis of Tacitus's account of the burning of Christians, later Christian tradition created a fantastic picture of persecution after the burning of Rome; but his account was written sixty

first-century usage, nothing in his account contradicts the suggestion that in the time of Nero Christ-believers were still a subgroup of Judaism. In fact, there are indications in Tacitus' writings that even he took *Christiani* to be a Jewish sect.[28]

Be that as it may. These are all difficult questions; far too difficult and wide-ranging to be touched on anything more than briefly here. The bottom line is that the earliest Christ-movement in Rome originated and grew within the synagogue, and that we do not know for how long it remained a more or less integral part of the Jewish community, but that it may well have been longer than commonly presumed.

Recent research into the socio-economic status of the earliest Christ-believers in Rome suggests a broad social spectrum with most members found at the lower levels of society and a small but significant minority at a higher social level.[29] Roman Christianity thus reflects the general social strata of Roman society, in which only a small minority belonged to the ruling upper classes (the equestrian and senatorial orders), while most people were of lower classes, with means varying from fair to very poor.[30] It is unlikely that many of the first Christ-believers in Rome came from the upper classes, but the number of such individuals seems to have increased gradually as more and more people joined the movement. At the close of the first century some members of the Christ-movement may even have been of senatorial rank, although most members probably still belonged to lower classes. Such gradual movement up the social ladder coincides with the

---

years later, and the sparsity of detail in the text should caution one from making too much of the event. Tacitus's account tells us more about Roman attitudes in his own time, the early second century, than it does about the misfortunes of Christians during Nero's reign.'

[28] See Stephen Benko, 'Pagan Criticism of Christianity During the First Two Centuries A.D.', *ANRW* 23.2: 1062–8. Cf. also idem, *Pagan Rome and the Early Christians* (Bloomington, IN: Indiana University Press, 1984), 14–20.

[29] See Lampe, *From Paul*, 65–6, 71–2, 80, 86, 89, 90–2, 138–50, 184–6, 198–205, 234–6, 351–5; idem, 'Early Christians', 23–6; James S. Jeffers, *Conflict at Rome: Social Order and Hierarchy in Early Christianity* (Minneapolis, MN: Fortress, 1991), 35, 97–105, 115–20, 121–44. Cf. also idem, 'Jewish and Christian Families in First-Century Rome', in *Judaism and Christianity in First-Century Rome* (ed. K. P. Donfried and P. Richardson; Grand Rapids, MI: Eerdmans, 1998), 128–50.

[30] On class structure in Roman society, see Ramsay MacMullen, *Roman Social Relations: 50 B.C. to A.D. 284* (New Haven, CT: Yale University Press, 1974), esp. 88–120; Valerie Hope, 'Status and Identity in the Roman World', in *Experiencing Rome: Culture, Identity and Power in the Roman Empire* (ed. J. Huskinson; London: Routledge, 2000), 125–52. A brief overview can be found in Jo-Ann Shelton, *As the Romans Did: A Sourcebook in Roman Social History* (2nd edn.; New York: Oxford University Press, 1998), 4–11. As Shelton informs us, three major factors determined the Roman class structure, namely, (1) wealth (or lack of it), (2) freedom (or lack of it), and (3) Roman citizenship (or lack of it).

increasing interest shown in Judaism by the Roman elite in the first century.[31] Some of the non-Jewish sympathizers of Judaism, or 'god-fearers',
who heard the initial proclamation of the 'good news' in the synagogues,
may therefore have belonged to the upper classes. There is evidence that a
significant number of these persons were women.[32]

It may thus be expected that a small but potentially powerful portion of
Roman Christianity consisted of quite well-off individuals with relatively high
education. Persons with sufficient means were important to the movement's
activities and continuing existence, especially as it gradually grew away from its
Jewish matrix, socially and economically. The well-to-do were needed to
(eventually) house meetings[33] and to provide for members whose circumstances were poorer and whose number was largest within the movement. It is not
difficult to see why characteristic Roman patron–client relationships developed out of such settings, as we witness for instance in the First Letter of
Clement (discussed below).[34] It may also be expected that the few better-off
and educated members of the Christ-movement, at least those who were
gentile, were largely moulded by traditional Graeco-Roman culture, and
were well acquainted with conventional Roman customs and principles, as
well as the most prominent philosophical schools and teachings in the city,
including Stoicism. The social and ideological influence of these individuals
on the poor majority of the movement would have been more or less in
proportion to their relatively strong socio-economic and educational position.

The overwhelming majority of Christ-believers belonged, on the other
hand, to the lower classes. That, however, does not rule out the possibility
that this same majority were to some extent familiar with current Roman
values, whether or not they were aware of the primary sources of such things.
Morality would be counted among such values, with which, we have seen, the
Romans were almost obsessed.[35] This is not to say that the poorer members of
the Christ-movement would have had the prerequisites or the opportunities,

---

[31] See Michele Murray, *Playing a Jewish Game: Gentile Christian Judaizing in the First and
Second Centuries CE* (ESCJ 13; Waterloo, ON: Wilfrid Laurier University Press, 2004), 15–21. Cf.
also Lampe, *From Paul*, 71–2.

[32] In addition to Murray (cited above), see Shelly Matthews, *First Converts: Rich Pagan
Women and the Rhetoric of Mission in Early Judaism and Christianity* (Stanford, CA: Stanford
University Press, 2001); Lampe, *From Paul*, 146–8, 352.

[33] cf. Lampe, *From Paul*, 366–72.

[34] On Roman patron–client relations, see Richard P. Saller, *Personal Patronage under the Early
Empire* (Cambridge: Cambridge University Press, 1982); Andrew Wallace-Hadrill, ed., *Patronage in Ancient Society* (London: Routledge, 1989). A brief discussion with primary examples can
be found in Shelton, *Romans*, 11–15. On patron–client relationships in early Christianity, see the
discussion in Peter Lampe, 'Paul, Patrons, and Clients', in *Paul in the Greco-Roman World: A
Handbook* (ed. J. P. Sampley; Harrisburg, PA: Trinity Press, 2003), 488–523.

[35] cf. the introduction to Roman Stoicism in Chapter 1 above.

as it were, to wander the city streets philosophizing about proper morality. Rather, it is to point out and underline the often neglected fact that, physically, Roman society, with its great gulf between the privileged and the poor, was largely structured vertically. That is, instead of being spread or divided horizontally, as tends to be the case with modern cities with more or less separate neighbourhoods depending on the degree of material wealth, the homes of the rich and poor in ancient Rome were widely interwoven. Large areas of the city were populated, not by either rich or poor inhabitants, but by most or all social groups simultaneously. Because of Rome's great population density,[36] rich and poor typically lived together in multistoried apartment buildings (*insulae*) that marked out socio-economic status by the vertical placement of residences in the building: as living quarters became smaller and simpler as one climbed higher, the higher your quarters, the lower your status.[37] A rich family could thus live in a spacious apartment (*cenaculum*) near street level, while poor families lived in cheap, cramped rooms (*cellae*) perhaps on the fourth or fifth floor, usually in unpleasant conditions.

All this suggests a strong social mixture in the city. Unfortunately, scholarly discussions of social relations in ancient Rome seem to be somewhat skewed by retrojections of modern circumstances.[38] Different social classes had probably more to do with each other, directly or indirectly, than scholars often presume, precisely because of this characteristic vertical structure of Roman society. Of course certain areas in the city were reserved for the most privileged, like the Palatine hill for the imperial palaces, and some areas were primarily inhabited by the lowest classes, like Trastevere (Transtiberim) in

[36] cf. Walter Scheidel, 'Germs for Rome', in *Rome the Cosmopolis* (ed. C. Edwards and G. Woolf; Cambridge: Cambridge University Press, 2003), 175, who notes that 'the ancient city may well have grown by some 60 per cent within seventy years. If the metropolitan population had numbered 150,000 in 200 BCE and steadily grown at that rate [i.e. 60 per cent per 70 years], Rome would have been home to 600,000 people at the beginning of the Christian era and to a million by the time of the Flavians'! See also Noy, *Foreigners*, 15–17.

[37] See, e.g., Alex Scobie, 'Slums, Sanitation, and Mortality in the Roman World', *Klio* 68 (1986): esp. 401–7; Christiane Kunst, 'Wohnen in der antiken Grosstadt: Zur sozialen Topographie Roms in der frühen Kaiserzeit', in *Christians as a Religious Minority in a Multicultural City: Modes of Interaction and Identity Formation in Early Imperial Rome* (ed. J. Zangenberg and M. Labahn; JSNTSup 243; London: T&T Clark, 2004), 2–19. Cf. also Whittaker, 'Poor', 283.

[38] cf. Andrew Wallace-Hadrill, '*Domus* and *Insulae* in Rome: Families and Housefuls', in *Early Christian Families in Context: An Interdisciplinary Dialogue* (ed. D. L. Balch and C. Osiek; Grand Rapids, MI: Eerdmans, 2003), 13–14: 'This perception of the fabric of the ancient city as profoundly mixed, which I first commented on for Pompeii, and am no less struck by in Rome, makes me unhappy with the conventional wisdom that the rich and poor lived apart in imperial Rome, the rich in large airy houses on the hills, the poor crowded in unsanitary apartment blocks in the valleys. That seems a retrojection of modern conditions.' Cf. also David L. Balch, 'Paul, Families, and Households', in *Paul in the Greco-Roman World: A Handbook* (ed. J. P. Sampley; Harrisburg, PA: Trinity Press, 2003), 259.

which many Jews and Christ-believers lived.[39] But, on the whole, 'the houses of the rich and poor were jumbled together in considerable confusion'.[40] The Roman poet Martial (ca. 40–104 CE), for instance, who belonged to the equestrian class, lived on the west side of the Quirinal, a somewhat mixed neighbourhood, in an apartment on the third floor of an *insula*.[41] He describes his housing conditions as follows: 'I live in a little cell (*cella*), with a window that won't even close, in which Boreas himself [i.e. the North wind] would not want to live.'[42] Long before Martial, Cicero's famous friend, Atticus, also lived on the Quirinal.[43] Even Seneca himself, highly privileged as he was, lived from time to time on the first floor of an *insula* near the 'Trickling Fountain' (*Meta Sudans*) in the valley between the Palatine and the Caelian hills.[44] His complaints about his neighbours are not only amusing but indicative as well, and worth citing at some length:

I have lodgings right over a bathing establishment (*supra ipsum balneum habito*). So picture to yourself the assortment of sounds, which are strong enough to make me hate my very powers of hearing! When your strenuous gentleman, for example, is exercising himself by flourishing leaden weights; when he is working hard, or else pretends to be working hard, I can hear him grunt; and whenever he releases his imprisoned breath, I can hear him panting in wheezy and high-pitched tones.... Add to this the arresting of an occasional roysterer or pickpocket, the racket of the man who always likes to hear his own voice in the bathroom (*in balineo*), or the enthusiast who plunges into the swimming-tank (*in piscinam*) with unconscionable noise and splashing. Besides all those whose voices, if nothing else, are good, imagine the hair-plucker with his penetrating, shrill voice,—for purposes of advertisement,—continually giving it vent and never holding his tongue except when he is plucking the armpits and making his victim yell instead. Then the cakeseller[45] with his varied cries, the

[39] See Lampe, *From Paul*, 19–47.

[40] Ramsay MacMullen, 'The Unromanized in Rome', in *Diasporas in Antiquity* (ed. S. J. D. Cohen and E. S. Frerichs; BJS 288; Atlanta, GA: Scholars Press, 1993), 49.

[41] Martial, *Epigr.* 1.108.3; 1.117.6–7. See further discussion in Kunst, 'Wohnen', 9–12.

[42] *Epigr.* 8.14.5–6: *At mihi cella datur, non tota clusa fenestra, in qua nec Boreas ipse manere velit.*

[43] Nepos, *Att.* 13. Atticus was of the equestrian rank like Martial, but, unlike the latter, he lived in a villa (*domus*).

[44] Note that some scholars believe that the *insula* was actually located in Baiae (in Campania, just west of Puteoli) rather than Rome, since Seneca seems to be staying in Baiae at the time of writing, cf. *Ep.* 49.1; 51.1; 53.1; 55.1–2, 6–11; 57.1 (cf., however, the reference to Rome in 50.3). But that does not necessarily call for Baiae as the place alluded to, and the reference to *Meta Sudans* strongly suggests a location in the city of Rome. For Rome, see Kunst, 'Wohnen', 10; James M. May, 'Seneca's Neighbour, the Organ Tuner', *CQ* 37 (1987): 240–3; Raymond L. DenAdel, 'Seneca the Younger and the Meta Sudans', *CB* 60 (1984): 1–4; Gustav Hermansen, *Ostia: Aspects of Roman City Life* (Edmonton, AB: University of Alberta, 1981), 45–6. For Baiae: e.g. Hellfried Dahlmann, 'Über den Lärm', *Gymnasium* 85 (1978): 220–7.

[45] The text has *libari* (from *libum* = '[consecrated] cake'). But some MSS read *biberari*; still other read *liberarii*.

sausageman, the confectioner, and all the vendors of food hawking their wares, each with his own distinctive intonation.... Among the sounds that din round me without distracting, I include passing carriages (*esseda transcurrentes*), a machinist in the same block (*faber inquilinus*), a saw-sharpener near by (*serrarius vicinus*), or some fellow who is demonstrating with little pipes and flutes at the Trickling Fountain, shouting rather than singing.[46]

It is certainly telling that all these classes of people had one of the wealthiest individuals of Rome as a neighbour. We must also observe that not all Christ-believers lived in neighbourhoods as base as Trastevere or the like, although most probably did. Some even lived on the Aventine hill, which in imperial times was a much-preferred residential area by the Roman aristocracy,[47] where the social variety appears to have been particularly great: 'everyone was represented, from consul to slave'.[48] We should expect at least some form of communication between the different classes in settings like these.

But even if the poor majority of Roman residents actually had little or no real contact with those of the upper classes, we must not forget that they were constantly exposed to the latter through public proclamations, shows, political speeches, and buildings and statues that often served some public-relations function.[49] The great public monument and centre of the empire, the *Forum Romanum* itself, stood open to anyone, whether he or she was rich or poor, a Roman citizen or a foreigner. 'There were slaves in Rome, and there were desperately poor people, but even they seem to have been able to move through the city with very few restrictions. There was nothing like the laws in Greek cities which allowed no one but citizens into the marketplace. Public areas in the Roman city were open to all'.[50] The same was true of the public baths. 'Socially the baths were important meeting— and mixing—places... A veteran soldier might be addressed by the man next to him in the sweat chamber, and find himself talking to the

---

[46] Seneca, *Ep.* 56.1–4. Cf. also 83.7. On the constant noise and generally unpleasant living conditions in the city of Rome, cf. Martial, *Epigr.* 12.57; Juvenal, *Sat.* 3.190–314.

[47] Lampe, *From Paul*, 58–61; idem, 'Early Christians', 22; Noy, *Foreigners*, 152.

[48] Lampe, *From Paul*, 65.

[49] cf. O. F. Robinson, *Ancient Rome: City Planning and Administration* (London: Routledge, 1992), 56–8, 77–9, 160–72; Janet Huskinson, 'Élite Culture and the Identity of Empire', in *Experiencing Rome: Culture, Identity and Power in the Roman Empire* (ed. J. Huskinson; London: Routledge, 2000), 95–123; Susan Walker, 'The Moral Museum: Augustus and the City of Rome', in *Ancient Rome: The Archaeology of the Eternal City* (ed. J. Coulston and H. Dodge; Oxford: Oxford University School of Archaeology, 2000), 61–75; Kathleen Coleman, 'Entertaining Rome', in ibid., 210–58.

[50] John E. Stambaugh, *The Ancient Roman City* (Baltimore, MD: Johns Hopkins University Press, 1988), 240. Cf. pp. 93, 139–41.

Emperor.'[51] Moreover, the Romans tended to conduct their activities out-doors, whether that be parades, plays, funerals, trials, or political meetings, and privacy was a luxury unheard of by most people.

Despite all the class differences and privileges of the few, then, daily life in the city involved a great cross-section of all groups in Roman society:

The various social classes came in contact the moment the appointed slave went to wake the master, and again at the formal *salutatio*, when clients waited outside, were admitted to the house by one slave, identified by another slave, and received— individually or in groups, depending on their importance—by the paterfamilias. Often the clients were dismissed with some kind of handout (*sportula*), which might be a basket of food or a small number of coins. When the patron, attended by slaves and clients, set off to the Forum, he was able to show the world how large and devoted his *familia* was.[52]

Many Christ-believers in Rome were slaves and freedmen (ex-slaves).[53] Some served or had served upper-class people like the patron described above. Others, no doubt, were imperial slaves or freedmen, a number of whom enjoyed a relatively high status in slave-born society, as members of the large and powerful *Familia Caesaris*.[54] One was Claudius Ephebus, of whom it is said in 1 Clement that he had been a Christ-believer 'from youth to old age' (ἀπὸ νεότητος ... ἕως γήρους).[55] His Greek cognomen (᾿Εφηβος) reveals his background as a slave, and the Latin *gentilicia* (Claudius) indicates that he

---

[51] J. P. V. D. Balsdon, *Life and Leisure in Ancient Rome* (London: Phoenix, 1969), 28. But note that Balsdon adds: 'Yet it is obvious that not all the bathing of the rich was done in public baths. The large town house had its own baths, and so had every luxurious villa.'

[52] Stambaugh, *Roman City*, 159. Cf. also the description in Jérôme Carcopino, *Daily Life in Ancient Rome: The People and the City at the Height of the Empire* (ed. H. T. Rowell; trans. E. O. Lorimer; 2nd edn.; New Haven, CT: Yale University Press, 2003), 171–3.

[53] cf. Rom 16.10b: ἀσπάσασθε τοὺς ἐκ τῶν Ἀριστοβούλου ('Greet those who belong to the family of Aristobulus'); 16.11b: ἀσπάσασθε τοὺς ἐκ τῶν Ναρκίσσου ('Greet those who belong to the family of Narcissus'). Both Aristobulus and Narcissus were probably non-Christians; see further Wayne A. Meeks, *The First Urban Christians: The Social World of the Apostle Paul* (2nd edn.; New Haven, CT: Yale University Press, 2003), 75–6. On the (continued) close relationship between slaves and ex-slaves, see Beryl Rawson, 'Family Life among the Lower Classes at Rome in the First Two Centuries of the Empire', *CP* 61 (1966): 72.

[54] cf. P. R. C. Weaver, *Familia Caesaris: A Social Study of the Emperor's Freedmen and Slaves* (Cambridge: Cambridge University Press, 1972), 1–8. Weaver concludes: 'The literary sources show clearly that the Familia Caesaris in general was an élite among the slave and freedman classes of Imperial society. But it is also clear that this was not equally true for all its members, nor for all periods. A detailed examination of the voluminous inscriptional material reveals a considerable degree of social differentiation *within* the Familia Caesaris' (p. 295; italics original).

[55] 1 Clem. 63.3; 65.1. Cf. also Phil 4.22, possibly written in Rome: 'All the saints greet you, especially those of the emperor's household' (ἀσπάζονται ὑμᾶς πάντες οἱ ἅγιοι, μάλιστα δὲ οἱ ἐκ τῆς Καίσαρος οἰκίας).

was a freedman of the Claudian family.[56] Some scholars believe that the author of 1 Clement himself belonged to the group of imperial freedmen, and that he had first-hand knowledge of the ruling elite, with whom he shows more affinity than with the lower classes.[57] Slaves normally lived in the home of their masters, and sometimes even so after they had been set free, for freedmen often continued to serve or work for their former masters.[58] A number of the first Christ-believers in Rome thus served and/or were raised in a traditional Roman milieu permeated with Graeco-Roman culture:

These Christians [here: 'Clement' and those Christians close to him] probably were imperial freedmen and slaves or the freedmen and slaves of the great houses of Rome. Clement's attitudes toward the various social classes confirm this notion. He demonstrates an intimate knowledge of the ruling elite's values. He understood that they valued honor over wealth. He agreed with their high estimation of education. Although he shows a personal dislike of slavery and poverty, he also reflects the elite's attitudes toward slaves and the poor. The slave's submission to his master was for Clement a symbol of the peace and concord that comes when Christians submit to God. Clement showed a genuine concern for those in momentary need, but, like the upper classes, he had little to say about the perpetually poor.[59]

In light of all this, it seems reasonable to infer that many, if not most, first-century members of the Christ-movement would have been familiar with basic moral values of Roman society. Whether they were conscious of it or not, the moral teaching of Roman Stoicism would thus have had its place in their frames of reference as the most prominent philosophical teaching of the city, a teaching that coincided so well with traditional Roman morality. The common assumption that the lower classes were almost totally isolated from the upper classes, physically and otherwise, rests largely on retrojections of modern conditions that neglect the characteristic vertical dimension of Roman society. In other words, whether they knew it or not, many Christ-believers of the lower classes would have been exposed to Stoic moral teaching in one way or another. In addition, a small but powerful minority would probably have been informed and educated enough to recognize the Stoic teaching as such, and that influential minority may well have carried its knowledge of Stoicism further to fellow believers, including those of the lower classes. This is important to have in mind as we move on to discuss

---

[56] cf. Lampe, *From Paul*, 184–6.

[57] Jeffers, *Conflict*, 32–5, 97–105; followed, e.g., by Odd M. Bakke, *'Concord and Peace': A Rhetorical Analysis of the First Letter of Clement with an Emphasis on the Language of Unity and Sedition* (WUNT 2.143; Tübingen: Mohr [Siebeck], 2001), 6–8. Cf. also Kirsopp Lake, '[Introduction to] The First Epistle of Clement to the Corinthians', in *The Apostolic Fathers* (trans. K. Lake; 2 vols.; LCL; Cambridge, MA: Harvard University Press, 1912), 1: 4.

[58] cf. Jeffers, 'Families', 132–3.   [59] Jeffers, *Conflict*, 105.

moral teaching in Roman Christianity. The two systems of thought—the Christian and the Stoic—belonged indeed to the same physical world.

'ROMAN CHRISTIANITY': DEFINITION AND ASSESSMENT OF PRIMARY SOURCES

So far I have referred to 'Roman Christianity' without providing a specific definition of the phrase. Here I wish to explain more plainly what I mean by this phrase. I also want to clarify which sources I consider most revealing and representative of this particular component of 'Christianity'.

By 'Roman Christianity' I mean the religious movement that eventually became known as Christianity as it emerged and evolved in the city of Rome from its beginnings in the first century CE onward—it is mainly the first century CE that is our focus of attention here. The modifier 'Roman' is here not intended to denote a specific 'type' of Christianity, but rather to denote a certain location, in line with current scholarly discussion.[60]

Admittedly, I have used the phrase 'Roman Christianity' rather sparingly so far in this study, and while I shall use it more frequently in the following chapters, I shall still try to do so within certain limits. The reason is that the term 'Christianity' is partly anachronistic for the period under discussion and potentially misleading as such, for one can at times be led by the term to read later developments relating to the Christian Church backwards into the first century CE. Any historical interpretation that wants to take the linear (and only possible) development of history seriously must be aware of this danger and must intend to minimize the extent of that danger, among other things, by careful use of terminology. In the previous section we saw that the cognate term 'Christian' ($X\rho\iota\sigma\tau\iota\alpha\nu\delta\varsigma$) does not occur in writing until the late first century, and that 'Christianity' or, perhaps more properly, 'Christianism' ($X\rho\iota\sigma\tau\iota\alpha\nu\iota\sigma\mu\delta\varsigma$) appears first in the early second century. Hence my preference above for phrases such as 'the Christ-movement' or 'Christ-believers' and so on.

However, it should be plain from the very title of this study, if nothing else, that I nevertheless make use of the phrase 'Roman Christianity'. And it should be clear that I do so entirely deliberately. This is mostly done for convenience's sake when referring to the Christ-movement in Rome as a whole, especially in

---

[60] cf., e.g., the various essays in Karl P. Donfried and Peter Richardson, eds., *Judaism and Christianity in First-Century Rome* (Grand Rapids, MI: Eerdmans, 1998); Lampe, *From Paul*, *passim*.

relation to previous and current scholarly discussion of the subject, where the phrase is regularly applied. I use it, on the other hand, to a somewhat limited extent. Sometimes I use the term 'Christian(s)' as well—a use practically impossible to avoid in a study such as this—but I do so mostly in connection with actual uses of the term in the ancient sources, as in 1 Peter, which is the one of only two writings in the New Testament collection that contains the word 'Christian'.[61] But, again, in the following discussion I shall normally use phrases such as 'the Christ-movement', 'Christ-believers', etc., in order to signify and emphasize that we are in this case not (yet) dealing with Christianity as a full-grown religion of its own, a separate entity neither Jewish nor 'pagan'.

The texts that I have judged to be the most revealing sources for the moral teaching of the earliest Christ-movement in Rome are three, all of the epistolary genre: Paul's Letter to the Romans, the First Letter of Peter, and the First Letter of Clement. The letters cover approximately forty years in the history of the movement (ca. 55–95 CE), that is, from the beginning of the reign of Nero (54 CE) to the end of the Flavian dynasty (96 CE). The first letter was written and despatched *to* Rome (probably from Corinth), whereas the other two were written *from* Rome (to fellow believers in Asia Minor and Corinth, respectively). In this regard Romans differs quite essentially from the other two writings, but it is my conviction, for which I shall give arguments below, that Paul's letter was essential to the formation of the moral teaching that became established and actualized among the earliest Christ-believers in this capital of the Roman empire.

It should be clear that my choice of primary sources presents no substantial challenge to New Testament and early Christian scholarship. Most scholars who concentrate on the literary sources for first-century Roman Christianity base their research on Romans and 1 Clement, and some add 1 Peter to the list. By choosing these three main sources for the present purpose I am therefore in basic agreement with prevailing scholarly opinion.

To be sure, there are other sources that have sometimes been associated with the city of Rome, like Hebrews,[62] but the case for the Roman provenance of that writing is, in my view, much too weak to be safely included in the study.[63] The same holds true for the Gospel of Mark. The hypothesis that

---

[61] The other being Acts (see the previous section). Note, on the other hand, that I do not use the term 'Christian(s)' when dealing specifically with Paul's Letter to the Romans below (dated ca. 55–58 CE).

[62] See, e.g., Lane, 'Social Perspectives', 214–24.

[63] The case rests much on the final greeting in the 'epistolary' closing of the text, Heb 13.24: ἀσπάζονται ὑμᾶς οἱ ἀπὸ τῆς Ἰταλίας ('Those from Italy send you greetings'). However, first, the text does not actually mention the city of Rome but, more generally, Italy. Second, and more

Mark was written in Rome is (yet) too weak and too disputed in order for that text to be of any positive help here.[64] Paul's Letter to the Philippians, on the other hand, may have been despatched from Rome,[65] and might therefore be included in the present study as a potential reflection of a Roman setting. But the letter does not seem to add much to the question of Paul's moral teaching (as the teaching was received in Rome) in addition to his letter to the Romans.[66] And then, of course, we have texts like the *Shepherd of Hermas* and the *Gospel of Truth*, both of which betray interesting aspects of Roman Christianity, but these writings bring us closer to the middle of the second century CE and beyond the scope of this study.

Hence the primary texts that will be analysed below are Romans, 1 Peter, and 1 Clement. The relation of these texts to the city of Rome and their relevance to the subject will be explained in the introductory discussion to each text.

Let us begin with the earliest extant evidence for the presence of Christ-believers in Rome, Paul's Letter to the Romans.

---

importantly, the unmistakably Pauline style of the closing and the reference to 'our brother Timothy' in particular in 13.23 strongly suggest that this part of Hebrews was later added to the text, in order to make it more like a letter and more like a Pauline letter (it was probably neither). On the other hand, the argument that Hebrews was first known and used in Rome (as far as we know), and that the author of 1 Clement may have been acquainted with it, is a stronger argument, but not strong enough. The fact that 1 Clement knew and cited Paul's First Letter to the Corinthians (1 Clem. 47.1–4) does not make 1 Corinthians a 'Roman' letter.

[64] For discussion of that debate, see, e.g., Adela Yarbro Collins, *Mark: A Commentary* (Hermeneia; Minneapolis, MN: Fortress, 2007), 7–10, with further references.

[65] See discussions in the standard commentaries, e.g. Gerald F. Hawthorne and Ralph P. Martin, *Philippians* (rev. and exp. edn.; WBC 43; Nashville, TN: Nelson, 2004), xxxiv–l (Hawthorne and Martin themselves lean towards an Ephesian provenance).

[66] But cf. esp. Phil 1.9–10; 2.1–4.

6

Paul's Letter to the Romans

INTRODUCTION: PROCLAIMING THE TEACHING IN ROME

It is probably no overstatement to claim that Paul's Letter to the Romans can be counted among the most influential letters in the history of humankind. The present study also concerns its influence, not on humankind as a whole, but on the formation of Christian identity and morality in first-century Rome. Even within these limited parameters, this intricate and fascinating letter remains a demanding object of study.

Paul wrote his letter to the Romans in the mid or late 50s (ca. 55–58 CE),[1] i.e. in the early reign of Nero (54–68 CE), most probably from Corinth.[2] There is some dispute among scholars as to the letter's intended audience, that is to say, whether Paul's intended audience was of gentile and Jewish origin, or of gentile origin only. The former view is the traditional one, followed by the scholarly majority, but the number of scholars who argue for the latter reading, including myself,[3] is steadily growing. Since the question of Paul's intended audience in Romans does have some bearing on the present study, it should be clear from the outset that I shall presume that in Romans Paul is (primarily) addressing people of gentile origin. This, I think, should not be a matter of much debate with respect to Romans 12–15.

---

[1] These are the dates which are accepted by most Pauline scholars. For a brief overview, see Joseph A. Fitzmyer, *Romans: A New Translation with Introduction and Commentary* (AB 33; New York: Doubleday, 1993), 87.

[2] This is already stated in the subscript of the MSS B[1] and D[1] ($\pi\rho o\varsigma$ $P\omega\mu\alpha\iota o\upsilon\varsigma$ $\epsilon\gamma\rho\alpha\phi\eta$ $\alpha\pi o$ $Ko\rho\iota\nu\theta o\upsilon$). Cf. Rom 16.1, where Paul commends Phoebe to the Romans, stating that she is a 'deacon of the congregation in Cenchreae', one of the seaports of Corinth. Also, according to 16.23, Paul's host at the time of writing is a certain Gaius, probably to be identified with the Gaius of 1 Cor 1.14.

[3] I have addressed this question in detail in Runar M. Thorsteinsson, *Paul's Interlocutor in Romans 2: Function and Identity in the Context of Ancient Epistolography* (ConBNT 40; Stockholm: Almqvist & Wiksell, 2003), 87–122. It is important to note that this latter and more recent view does not claim, as is sometimes held, that (Christ-believing) Jews were absent when the letter was received and read in Rome, nor indeed that Paul himself had envisioned it so. Rather, the claim is that the people whom Paul *addressed* in the letter were of gentile origin only, whether or not the actual audience was a mixed group of (Christ-believing) Jews and gentiles.

The question of the occasion and purpose of Romans is no less debated than that of its audience.[4] According to the letter itself, the immediate occasion for Paul's writing was his long delay in coming to Rome[5] due to his assignment among 'the rest of the gentiles, Greeks as well as barbarians, wise as well as ignorant',[6] that is, gentiles in the eastern part of his missionary province.[7] But as the letter would soon verify,[8] Paul does not intend to visit Rome at present either. He has more work to do in the East before he can come and do his duty in the city of Rome as well. Hence he writes a letter. And in this letter he does what he wished he had done already but did not have the opportunity to do: he proclaims his εὐαγγέλιον, his 'good news', to the Roman recipients. His apostolic duty tells him to 'proclaim the good news' (εὐαγγελίσασθαι) also to those who are in Rome (καὶ ὑμῖν τοῖς ἐν ῾Ρώμῃ).[9]

Many scholars have been rather reluctant to take Paul's statements in Romans 1.8–15 at face value, mostly because they find it contradictory on his part to proclaim the εὐαγγέλιον to people who, according to these scholars, are already 'Christians'. I would suggest that Paul's statements should be taken exactly as they stand. Whatever the exact 'Christian' identity of the recipients, and whatever Paul's own knowledge and opinion of their identity as 'Christians', both his words in 1.8–15 and the lengthy text that follows suggest that he does precisely what he would have done had he been present himself: he proclaims the εὐαγγέλιον to the Romans.[10] And that is also the main purpose of the letter. The letter functions as a surrogate for Paul's apostolic presence and his announcement and exposition of the 'good news' until the eventual arrival in person.[11] This function of Paul's letter also

---

[4] The 'classic' work is Karl P. Donfried, ed., *The Romans Debate: Revised and Expanded Edition* (Peabody, MA: Hendrickson, 1991). An updated overview is available in James C. Miller, 'The Romans Debate: 1991–2001', *CurBS* 9 (2001): 306–49; Angelika Reichert, *Der Römerbrief als Gratwanderung: Eine Untersuchung zur Abfassungsproblematik* (FRLANT 194; Göttingen: Vandenhoeck & Ruprecht, 2001), 13–75; and, most recently, A. Andrew Das, *Solving the Romans Debate* (Minneapolis, MN: Fortress, 2007).

[5] Rom 1.10–12.

[6] Rom 1.13–14a: πολλάκις προεθέμην ἐλθεῖν πρὸς ὑμᾶς, καὶ ἐκωλύθην ἄχρι τοῦ δεῦρο, ἵνα τινὰ καρπὸν σχῶ καὶ ἐν ὑμῖν καθὼς καὶ ἐν τοῖς λοιποῖς ἔθνεσιν, ῞Ελλησίν τε καὶ βαρβάροις, σοφοῖς τε καὶ ἀνοήτοις. On this reading of Rom 1.13–14a, see Thorsteinsson, 'Paul's Missionary Duty'.

[7] On Paul's missionary province, see esp. Gal 2.7–9 (cf. also 1.16; 2.2; Rom 1.5–6; 15.15–16, 18).

[8] i.e., in Rom 15.25–32.   [9] Rom 1.15.

[10] It should be noted, again, that we are speaking of 'Christians' before Christianity, i.e. before Christianity as 'the idea of the third race neither Jewish nor pagan' (Stanley K. Stowers, *A Rereading of Romans: Justice, Jews, and Gentiles* [New Haven, CT: Yale University Press, 1994], 23).

[11] According to Paul himself (2 Cor 10.10–11), some people were of the opinion that he succeeded much better when absent (and writing letters) than when present (and giving speeches): ' "His letters", they say, "are weighty and powerful, but his bodily presence is weak and his speech contemptible" ' (αἱ ἐπιστολαὶ μέν, φησίν, βαρεῖαι καὶ ἰσχυραί, ἡ δὲ παρουσία τοῦ

explains why it has so many characteristics of typical official correspondence from Graeco-Roman antiquity, such as letters of diplomatic, royal, and administrative provenance.[12] The Paul who presents himself and addresses his audience in Romans is primarily Paul in the 'official' role as one who has been 'called to be an apostle, set apart for God's good news'[13] with a mission to proclaim the εὐαγγέλιον also to those in Rome.

An important aspect of Paul's εὐαγγέλιον in Romans is the letter's moral teaching. The teaching is found mainly in chapters 12–15, where it receives its most extensive and clearly defined presentation. We have no extant evidence of any corresponding 'Christian' teaching in the city of Rome prior to Romans. Nor do we know anything about the immediate response to Paul's letter. It follows that we cannot know if and to what extent Paul's moral teaching reflects an already established teaching among Roman Christ-believers. We can only study the teaching itself as it is found in Romans and then try to estimate its potential place in 'Roman Christianity' by assessing its influence on later Roman writers, such as the authors of 1 Peter and 1 Clement. This, among other things, is my aim in the following chapters.

It should be noted at this point that I do not share the view of those scholars who hold that in Romans 14–15 Paul is addressing some dispute or tension between 'Jewish Christians' and 'gentile Christians' in Rome, represented, it is claimed, by Paul's 'weak' and the 'strong' respectively.[14] While this view has become quite popular among Pauline scholars, Paul himself nowhere identifies the 'weak' and the 'strong' as such, and there is actually not much, if anything, in his text that points in that direction. The different attitudes described in chapter 14 towards eating, drinking, and judging days are no reliable marks of Jewish versus gentile dispositions.[15] Rather, what Paul refers

σώματος ἀσθενὴς καὶ ὁ λόγος ἐξουθενημένος). Paul's answer to such assertions was that 'what we say by letter when absent, we will also do when present'.

[12] On these characteristics in Romans, see Thorsteinsson, *Paul's Interlocutor*, esp. 31–85. On the official character of Paul's other letters, see M. Luther Stirewalt, Jr., *Paul, the Letter Writer* (Grand Rapids, MI: Eerdmans, 2003).

[13] Rom 1.1: κλητὸς ἀπόστολος ἀφωρισμένος εἰς εὐαγγέλιον θεοῦ.

[14] Rom 14.1: τὸν δὲ ἀσθενοῦντα τῇ πίστει προσλαμβάνεσθε ('welcome the weak in faith'); 15.1: ὀφείλομεν δὲ ἡμεῖς οἱ δυνατοὶ τὰ ἀσθενήματα τῶν ἀδυνάτων βαστάζειν (lit. 'we who are strong are obliged to bear the weaknesses of those without strength'). A recent sketch of the scholarly discussion is found in Mark Reasoner, *The Strong and the Weak: Romans 14.1–15.13 in Context* (SNTSMS 103; Cambridge: Cambridge University Press, 1999), 1–22.

[15] See, e.g., Reichert, *Römerbrief*, 271–333, esp. 323–5. Also Clarence E. Glad, *Paul and Philodemus: Adaptability in Epicurean and Early Christian Psychagogy* (NovTSup 81; Leiden: Brill, 1995), 330–1. The identification of the 'weak' and the 'strong' as 'Jewish Christians' and 'gentile Christians' is largely based on the hypothesis that Claudius' banishment of Jews from the city of Rome some years earlier had created tensions between Christ-believing Jews, on the one hand, and Christ-believing gentiles, on the other. But the basis for this hypothesis is very weak; see my discussion in Thorsteinsson, *Paul's Interlocutor*, 92–7, with further references.

to with these designations are different *types* of persons and dispositions: '[W]hen Paul addresses the "weak," "strong" or "wise," he does not wish to accentuate the ethnic identity of his addressees but rather their psychological disposition or character type.'[16] They represent characteristic roles with which the recipients can either identify or sympathize. In other words, the 'weak' and the 'strong' are *typical* characters and characteristics that constitute a part of Paul's general moral teaching of mutual love, respect, and adaptability, and serve as a rhetorical means by which to argue successfully for that teaching.

MORAL TEACHING IN ROMANS: MUTUAL LOVE, RESPECT, AND ADAPTABILITY

Scholars have often described chapters 12–15 in Romans as the letter's 'imperative' part.[17] The description is fully appropriate with respect to the distinctive hortatory character of these chapters within the letter as a whole. Paul's earlier discourse in chapters 3–11 had been characterized by a dialogical style, and largely structured according to recurring exchanges of questions and answers typical of that style (often labelled 'diatribe'),[18] but from 12.1 the form of the text changes radically: the exchanges of questions and answers disappear entirely,[19] and are supplanted predominantly by the imperative, with frequent uses of the second person plural. In substance, these latter chapters are also almost exclusively concerned with questions of morality or ethics. Moral issues are certainly addressed elsewhere in the letter as well, especially in chapters 1–2 and 6–7, but it is in chapters 12–15 (more precisely 12.1–15.14)[20] that Paul provides specific moral instructions to the Romans

---

[16] Glad, *Paul*, 331 (cf. pp. 213–35 on Rom 14–15). See also Stanley K. Stowers, 'Paul on the Use and Abuse of Reason', *Greeks, Romans, and Christians: Essays in Honor of Abraham J. Malherbe* (ed. D. L. Balch, E. Ferguson, and W. A. Meeks; Minneapolis, MN: Fortress, 1990), 281–6.

[17] A useful survey of previous approaches to Pauline ethics, including in Romans 12–15, is found in Horrell, *Solidarity*, 7–46.

[18] Rom 3.1–9; 3.27–4.1; 6.1–2, 15; 7.7, 13; 8.31; 9.14, 19–20, 30–2; 10.18–19; 11.1, 7, 11. On the dialogical ('diatribal') style in Romans, compared with analogous features in other letters from Graeco-Roman antiquity, see Thorsteinsson, *Paul's Interlocutor*, 123–50.

[19] Although uses of the second person singular still occur now and then (Rom 12.21; 13.3–4; 14.4, 10, 15, 20–2).

[20] Many scholars would say 15.13 instead of 15.14 (influenced, perhaps, by the traditional division of the text in modern editions, e.g. NA²⁷). But there is a stronger connection between v. 14 and the foregoing than between v. 14 and the following. Verse 14 still concerns the recipients' mutual concern for each other, including their ability to instruct or admonish (νουθετεῖν) one another, whereas in v. 15 Paul turns to questions of his own writing and relation to the audience. Cf. also Glad, *Paul*, 213–35 (esp. 217, 232–3).

within a clearly defined framework. It is in these chapters that he focuses entirely on his community-forming ethic. Perhaps one ought to speak of Paul's *sketch* of such an ethic, for Romans 12–15 scarcely contain a full, systematic treatise on ethics like those of the philosophers. No doubt he planned to explain and supplement his moral instructions, either at his future arrival in Rome or by way of further correspondence (as, for example, in 1 Corinthians).

Paul opens his moral teaching in Romans 12–15 with a well-known epistolary formula of request, παρακαλῶ οὖν ὑμᾶς, ἀδελφοί, etc., which he applies in a typical 'official' fashion:

I urge you therefore, brothers (παρακαλῶ οὖν ὑμᾶς, ἀδελφοί), through the mercies of God, to present your bodies as a living sacrifice (παραστῆσαι τὰ σώματα ὑμῶν θυσίαν ζῶσαν), holy and acceptable to God (ἁγίαν εὐάρεστον τῷ θεῷ), which is your reasonable worship (τὴν λογικὴν λατρείαν ὑμῶν). Do not be conformed to this world, but be transformed (μεταμορφοῦσθε) by the renewing of the mind (τῇ ἀνακαινώσει τοῦ νοός), so that you may discern (δοκιμάζειν) what is the will of God, what is good, acceptable, and perfect (τὸ ἀγαθὸν καὶ εὐάρεστον καὶ τέλειον).[21]

This request, which also functions as the letter's very centre in terms of its epistolary structure, is based on the previous discourse as a whole (implied, among other things, by the inferential conjunction οὖν, 'therefore'), and has a programmatic, expository function for the subsequent moral teaching.[22] It sets the stage for the entire text of Romans 12–15 by providing, as it were, a synoptic account of what Paul has to say in these chapters. It is important to note that Paul's moral teaching is not merely a formal 'parenetic' closing of the letter, nor simply an obligatory part of 'the Pauline way of writing letters'.[23] Rather, it is an integral aspect of his 'good news'—the other side of the same coin, so to speak. Based on what he has proclaimed so far in his εὐαγγέλιον, Paul speaks here of the way in which his readers are to offer their bodies as a 'living sacrifice', which is also their 'reasonable worship'. Moreover, according to Paul, the addressees are to 'be transformed by the renewing of the mind' so that they may recognize the will of God, 'what is good, acceptable, and perfect'. In other words, their 'sacrifice' involves, not death (in the literal sense), but an embodiment of the 'reasonable' service to God, which is in the very physical form of leading their life in accordance with God's good will and directions. Paul speaks here both of the recipients' *proper way of living* and their *proper way of thinking*. These aspects of their identity as Christ-believers are intertwined in the subsequent discourse.

---

[21] Rom 12.1–2.   [22] See further Thorsteinsson, *Paul's Interlocutor*, 47–54.

[23] cf. William G. Doty, *Letters in Primitive Christianity* (Philadelphia, PA: Fortress, 1973), 27. See further my discussion in Thorsteinsson, *Paul's Interlocutor*, 24–30.

It is clear that Paul does not intend to leave it entirely up to the readers to discern what is the will of God, but proceeds precisely by explaining what is 'good, acceptable, and perfect' in the eyes of God. But before presenting and expounding his moral teaching in more detail, Paul (re)turns to his 'official' role towards the audience by noting that what he is about to say is in fact uttered 'by the grace given to me [by God]'.[24] By so doing he provides the addressees with an assurance of the legitimacy of his teaching, and affirms at the same time his own proper authority to speak to them in the way he does, namely, 'rather boldly'.[25] To begin with, the apostle urges the audience 'not to think highly' (μὴ ὑπερφρονεῖν) of themselves 'beyond what [they] ought to think' (παρ' ὃ δεῖ φρονεῖν), but to 'think' (φρονεῖν) 'so as to mind a proper moderation' (εἰς τὸ σωφρονεῖν).[26] Paul's playing with the root φρον-, as in the cardinal virtue φρόνησις, would scarcely have been missed by the Roman audience, but, in that case, the reference to σωφροσύνη, another cardinal virtue, would almost certainly have sufficed to direct their thoughts towards the traditional virtues of Greek philosophy and Graeco-Roman society. In Paul's treatment, the virtue and act of σωφροσύνη becomes the social antithesis of ὑπερφρονεῖν.[27] According to him, no one in the audience should think too highly of him- or herself, regardless of position or status. For, as he continues to explain, although there may be and certainly are different roles and gifts (χαρίσματα) among Christ-believers,[28] everything is purposed for the benefit of the whole. It is not the individual believer him- or herself who benefits from the particular position or 'gift' which he or she enjoys but the community of believers as a whole, of which the individual is a member. Paul demonstrates this community-oriented aspect by way of a metaphor:

For as in one body (ἐν ἑνὶ σώματι) we have many members (πολλὰ μέλη), and not all the members have the same function (τὰ δὲ μέλη πάντα οὐ τὴν αὐτὴν ἔχει πρᾶξιν), so we, who are many, are one body in Christ (ἐν σῶμα ἐσμεν ἐν Χριστῷ), and individually we are members one of another (τὸ δὲ καθ' εἷς ἀλλήλων μέλη).[29]

---

[24] Rom 12.3. Cf. 1.5–6; 15.15–16.   [25] Rom 15.15.

[26] Rom 12.3. The rsv and nrsv translate φρονεῖν εἰς τὸ σωφρονεῖν as 'to think with sober judgment'. Similarly niv and Fitzmyer (_Romans_, 16, 644). Dunn translates: 'observe proper moderation' (_Romans_, 2: 719). Ernst Käsemann, _An die Römer_ (3rd edn.; HNT 8a; Tübingen: Mohr [Siebeck], 1974), 319: 'auf Besonnenheit bedacht zu sein'; cf. Hans Lietzmann, _Einführung in die Textgeschichte der Paulusbriefe: An die Römer_ (5th edn.; HNT 8; Tübingen: Mohr [Siebeck], 1971), 108: 'nach Besonnenheit zu streben'.

[27] cf. also Halvor Moxnes, 'The Quest for Honor and the Unity of the Community in Romans 12 and in the Orations of Dio Chrysostom', in _Paul in His Hellenistic Context_ (ed. T. Engberg-Pedersen; Edinburgh: T&T Clark, 1994), 219–23.

[28] Rom 12.6–8.   [29] Rom 12.4–5 (trans. nrsv).

That is, those who are 'in Christ' are also one 'body' in him, and precisely as the human body has many members with different functions, so must individual members of the group of believers have different positions and tasks within the whole—the 'one body in Christ'. Paul is here calling for a certain 'social moderation'. According to the apostle, it is the duty of each and every member to regard his or her own position with proper moderation (σωφρονεῖν). All roles within the community are interconnected, and one function cannot do without the other, however insignificant that function may seem. In this way the plural becomes embodied in the singular: it is precisely through such community-oriented thought, volition, and conduct that the addressees are able to present their 'bodies' (plural) as a 'sacrifice' (singular) to God, which is also their 'reasonable' worship (12.1). The purpose of Romans 12.3 and the following text is to spell out some essential ways in which this may be carried out in practice.

One may compare Paul's more detailed account in 1 Corinthians 12 with Romans 12.3–8, the former of which in all likelihood serves as the basis for the latter. Although the discourse in 1 Corinthians shows signs of being adapted specifically to the situation in Corinth, the underlying thought is the same: while there are varieties of gifts (χαρίσματα), services (διακονίαι), and activities (ἐνεργήματα) accorded to different individuals within the Christ-believing community, there is one spirit (πνεῦμα), one lord (κύριος), and one god (θεός). The divine spirit who allots these things to individual believers does so not just for the benefit of these particular persons but above all for the common good (πρὸς τὸ συμφέρον).[30] Precisely as in Romans, Paul presents the 'body' and its members as the illustrative proof:

Indeed, the body does not consist of one member but of many. If the foot would say, 'Because I am not a hand, I do not belong to the body,' that would not make it any less a part of the body. And if the ear would say, 'Because I am not an eye, I do not belong to the body,' that would not make it any less a part of the body. If the whole body were an eye, where would the hearing be? If the whole body were hearing, where would the sense of smell be? But as it is, God arranged the members in the body, each one of them, as he chose. If all were a single member, where would the body be? As it is, there are many members, yet one body.[31]

Furthermore, Paul warns his readers that things are not always what they seem. Those members of the Christ-believing community who may seem to have less honourable positions and functions than others are not necessarily less important within the function of the whole:

---

[30] 1 Cor 12.4–11.   [31] 1 Cor 12.14–20 (trans. NRSV).

The eye cannot say to the hand, 'I have no need of you,' nor again the head to the feet, 'I have no need of you.' On the contrary, the members of the body that seem to be weaker (ἀσθενέστερα) are indispensable, and those members of the body that we think less honorable we clothe with greater honor, and our less respectable (ἀτιμότερα) members are treated with greater respect; whereas our more respectable members do not need this. But God has so arranged the body, giving the greater honor to the inferior member, that there may be no dissension within the body, but the members may have the same care for one another. If one member suffers, all suffer together with it; if one member is honored, all rejoice together with it.[32]

Paul then proceeds by bringing the audience's attention to the concept and virtue of 'love' (ἀγάπη), which he considers fundamental to the forming and maintenance of the community ethic (1 Cor 13).

It is probably no coincidence that this is also the structure of Paul's discourse in Romans 12, albeit on a much smaller scale. For immediately following the discussion in 12.3–8 of the 'body' and different 'gifts' within the whole, Paul refers to ἀγάπη, stating that it is (or should be) 'unhypocritical' (ἀνυπόκριτος). In 1 Corinthians 12–13 the same move was made from the 'body' and so on to the concept of ἀγάπη. However, with respect to Paul's addressees in Rome, it would not be wise to make too much out of this structural parallel with 1 Corinthians 12–13. The reference to ἀγάπη in Romans 12.9a is actually quite peripheral, especially compared to 1 Corinthians 13, and it cannot be assumed that the Roman readers had any knowledge of Paul's account in the latter text at this point of time. The importance of ἀγάπη will become clear to the Roman audience later on in Paul's letter, in 13.8–10, but at this point in the text, in 12.9a, it is not that clear at all. Some scholars have claimed that the reference to ἀγάπη in v. 9a is so discernibly underlined that it serves as an 'introductory heading' to the subsequent exhortations.[33] This is hardly the case.[34] Instead, it functions as a bridge between the discourse in vv. 3–8 and the following text. Thus, corresponding to Paul's design in 1 Corinthians 12–13, the concept of ἀγάπη in Romans 12.9a is firmly tied to the foregoing discussion of mutual respect and so on in vv. 3–8, but it is not 'introductory' in any clear and sensible way.[35] It is, on the other hand, one component of many in the series of exhortations in vv. 9–21, most of which appear to be singled out rather randomly by the apostle

---

[32] 1 Cor 12.21–6 (trans. NRSV).

[33] Victor P. Furnish, *The Love Command in the New Testament* (Nashville, TN: Abingdon, 1972), 103. Cf. also Walter T. Wilson, *Love without Pretense: Romans 12.9–21 and Hellenistic-Jewish Wisdom Literature* (WUNT 2.46; Tübingen: Mohr [Siebeck], 1991), 150; Thomas Söding, *Das Liebesgebot bei Paulus: Die Mahnung zur Agape im Rahmen der paulinischen Ethik* (NTAbh 26; Münster: Aschendorff, 1995), 241–50; Jewett, *Romans*, 756, 758.

[34] See Thorsteinsson, 'Paul and Roman Stoicism', 144–6.

[35] So also Käsemann, *Römer*, 331.

without any thoroughly calculated pattern. Indeed, the heavy use of asyndeta in this passage (cf. also v. 8) gives the impression that it mostly contains a jumble of rather loosely related maxims. The statement ἡ ἀγάπη ἀνυπόκριτος in v. 9a is one such maxim,[36] which primarily relates to the foregoing text and is, if anything, a direct continuation of Paul's exhortation to his addressees 'not to think (too) highly' of themselves (μὴ ὑπερφρονεῖν) with respect to one another. The term ἀγάπη does not occur again until 13.8.

In 12.9b–13 Paul continues to discuss the addressees' proper attitude and behaviour towards each other and towards other Christ-believers. In principle, they are to stick to what is good (τὸ ἀγαθόν) and avoid evil (τὸ πονηρόν).[37] Paul urges them to devote themselves to mutual 'brotherly love' (τῇ φιλαδελφίᾳ εἰς ἀλλήλους φιλόστοργοι), and to treat one another with respect and honour (τῇ τιμῇ ἀλλήλους προηγούμενοι), as he had already implied in vv. 3–8. Also, in their zeal for proper service to God the addressees should have compassion and concern for each other.[38] They are obliged to contribute to the needs of 'the holy' (οἱ ἅγιοι)—presumably the (Jewish) Christ-believers in Jerusalem[39]—and to practice hospitality.[40] In addition, Paul exhorts the audience to 'rejoice with those who rejoice' and 'weep with those who weep', and, once again, not to be overly prideful towards others, but to live in harmony.[41] In short, among the traits that should dominate all relations within the community of Christ-believers are mutual love, respect, sympathy, and care.

Paul's discourse in 12.14–21 is somewhat entangled by his rather unsystematic procedure of speaking interchangeably of in-group and out-group relations. While vv. 15–16 refer to the in-group,[42] v. 14 and vv. 17–21 include or refer exclusively to outsiders. In v. 14 Paul sets forth the rather radical demand, 'Bless [or: speak well of] those who persecute you' (εὐλογεῖτε τοὺς διώκοντας ὑμᾶς),[43] and in vv. 17–18 he exhorts the audience never to repay evil for evil, but to take thought for what is noble (καλά) in the sight of all men, and, if possible, to live at peace with everyone.[44] Clearly, all people are considered in these latter verses (cf. πάντες ἄνθρωποι), whereas we may safely assume that the 'persecutors' in v. 14 belong to the outside group. In vv. 19–20

---

[36] cf. 2 Cor 6.6 in which the phrase ἀγάπη ἀνυπόκριτος occurs among a number of other, randomly listed traits.

[37] Rom 12.9b.   [38] Rom 12.11–12.   [39] cf. 15.25–7, 31b.

[40] Rom 12.13. We shall return to the concept of 'hospitality' in Chapter 7 on 1 Peter below.

[41] Rom 12.15–16.   [42] This is definitely true of v. 16, and probably of v. 15.

[43] This is followed in v. 14b by εὐλογεῖτε καὶ μὴ καταρᾶσθε ('bless and do not curse [them]'). Note that some important MSS omit ὑμᾶς in v. 14a (as well as εὐλογεῖτε in v. 14b). But the omission of ὑμᾶς may probably be seen as an attempt to generalize Paul's message by removing the specific address to the Roman community.

[44] Rom 12.17–18.

Paul iterates the command of non-retaliation (cf. v. 17) but now adds that the addressees are to 'give opportunity' ($\delta\acute{o}\tau\epsilon$ $\tau\acute{o}\pi o\nu$) for God's wrath and revenge on such people as their enemies. It is God who takes care of vengeance, if necessary. The task of the addressees, on the other hand, is to show charity to their enemies so that the latter may be driven to repentance.[45] Christ-believers must take care not to be overcome by evil ($\mu\grave{\eta}$ $\nu\iota\kappa\hat{\omega}$ $\acute{v}\pi\grave{o}$ $\tau o\hat{v}$ $\kappa\alpha\kappa o\hat{v}$), Paul sums up in v. 21. Instead, they should overcome evil with good ($\grave{a}\lambda\lambda\grave{a}$ $\nu\acute{\iota}\kappa\alpha$ $\grave{\epsilon}\nu$ $\tau\hat{\omega}$ $\grave{a}\gamma\alpha\theta\hat{\omega}$ $\tau\grave{o}$ $\kappa\alpha\kappa\acute{o}\nu$).[46]

This last thought in chapter 12 is something that Paul develops further in 13.1–7, now with the focus aimed specifically at proper attitude and behaviour towards a particular group of outsiders, namely, governing authorities. According to him, Christ-believers should show full obedience ($\acute{v}\pi o\tau\acute{a}\sigma\sigma\epsilon\sigma\theta\alpha\iota$) to the Roman emperor and his agents,[47] since the authorities in charge, even among the gentiles, can only be so because they are 'under' ($\acute{v}\pi\acute{o}$) God, instituted by God.[48] And as such they are God's instruments. They serve God's purpose by punishing those who do wrong and praising those who do good. Thus, according to Paul's vision, those who do good have nothing to fear at all from the Roman authorities. Only evildoers have reason to fear.[49] Paul actually implies here that God and the Roman authorities have corresponding views of what counts as 'good', $\tau\grave{o}$ $\grave{a}\gamma\alpha\theta\acute{o}\nu$, and what counts as 'bad', $\tau\grave{o}$ $\kappa\alpha\kappa\acute{o}\nu$.

It is hard to believe that Paul would have insisted unwaveringly on every detail of his sweeping statements in Romans 13.1–7 about such total submission to civic authorities if faced with actual complications in this respect. It is therefore probably better not to take his words too literally, but to read them as a hyperbolic attempt to persuade his audience to abide by his moral instructions to choose 'good' before 'evil'—as defined by the apostle himself. His main point relates to what he stated in the previous chapter about proper behaviour towards outsiders in general: on the one hand, to 'take thought for what is noble in the sight of all',[50] and, on the other, to 'live at peace with all'.[51]

---

[45] Rom 12.19–20. Paul's point in 12.20, where he quotes Prov. 25.21–2 (LXX), is disputed among scholars. The reading above is followed by many, e.g. Dunn, *Romans*, 2: 750–1; Fitzmyer, *Romans*, 657–8 (both commentators provide helpful overviews of other possible readings). A similar point is made in 1 Pet 2.12; 3.16.

[46] cf. the reference to 'good' and 'evil' in 12.9b.

[47] Paul does not speak explicitly about the 'emperor' here, but I take his references to the governing authorities in this passage to express the same thing. Note that while the overwhelming majority of scholars take 13.1–7 to concern civic authorities, Mark D. Nanos has suggested that it concerns Christian obedience to synagogue authority (*The Mystery of Romans: The Jewish Context of Paul's Letter* [Minneapolis, MN: Fortress, 1996], 289–336).

[48] Rom 13.1–2.   [49] Rom 13.3–4.

[50] Rom 12.17: $\pi\rho o\nu o o\acute{v}\mu\epsilon\nu o\iota$ $\kappa\alpha\lambda\grave{a}$ $\grave{\epsilon}\nu\acute{\omega}\pi\iota o\nu$ $\pi\acute{a}\nu\tau\omega\nu$ $\grave{a}\nu\theta\rho\acute{\omega}\pi\omega\nu$.

[51] Rom 12.18: $\mu\epsilon\tau\grave{a}$ $\pi\acute{a}\nu\tau\omega\nu$ $\grave{a}\nu\theta\rho\acute{\omega}\pi\omega\nu$ $\epsilon\grave{\iota}\rho\eta\nu\epsilon\acute{v}o\nu\tau\epsilon\varsigma$.

The passage in 13.1–7 explains that these general rules also apply when it comes to such specific groups of outsiders as the Roman authorities. In Paul's opinion, it is important that the Christ-believers in Rome avoid drawing unnecessary attention to themselves on behalf of the civic authorities, but try instead to fit into the surrounding Roman society as much as possible—εἰ δυνατὸν τὸ ἐξ ὑμῶν.[52] Romans 13.1–7 is therefore partly about the need for the Roman Christ-believers to be tactful and wise in their dealings with civic authorities and Roman society at large.

After his collection of (mostly) general exhortations and instructions in Romans 12.3–13.7, and before he turns to the more specific issues of chapters 14–15, Paul presents the principle upon which he bases his moral teaching for the Christ-believing community. This principle is the one single virtue by which all relations within the group are determined, namely, ἀγάπη.[53] Paul had referred to ἀγάπη mostly in passing in 12.9a, but now, in 13.8–10, his purpose is more pointed. The primary position of ἀγάπη in Paul's moral teaching finally comes to the fore, and does so in absolute, downright terms:

Owe no one anything (μηδενὶ μηδὲν ὀφείλετε), except to love one another (εἰ μὴ τὸ ἀλλήλους ἀγαπᾶν). For the one who loves the other has fulfilled the Law (ὁ γὰρ ἀγαπῶν τὸν ἕτερον νόμον πεπλήρωκεν). The commandments, 'You shall not commit adultery', 'You shall not kill', 'You shall not steal', 'You shall not covet', and any other command-ment, are summed up (ἀνακεφαλαιοῦται) in this word: 'You shall love your neighbour as yourself' (ἀγαπήσεις τὸν πλησίον σου ὡς σεαυτόν). Love does no wrong to the neighbour (ἡ ἀγάπη τῷ πλησίον κακὸν οὐκ ἐργάζεται). Therefore, the fulfilment of the Law is love (πλήρωμα οὖν νόμου ἡ ἀγάπη).[54]

The main question raised in the passage is how the (non-Jewish) addressees may fulfil the (Jewish) Law. Previously Paul had taken great pains to make clear that the letter's addressees should not, and indeed cannot, follow the 'works of the Law'.[55] But now he tells them that they can nonetheless 'fulfil' the Law properly:[56] it is simply by 'loving one another'. For 'the one who loves the other has fulfilled the Law'. Every other commandment of the Law is in fact summed up in this one (from Lev 19.18): 'Love your neighbour as yourself.' It is as simple as that. Moreover, according to Paul, the person whose life is continually led by ἀγάπη will never wrong her or his neighbour, since 'love does no wrong to the neighbour'. Hence, for the gentile audience, love is the very fulfilment of the Law (πλήρωμα οὖν νόμου ἡ ἀγάπη). This is in

---

[52] Rom 12.18 ('if possible for your part').
[53] We shall discuss the 'ethical scope' of the Pauline ἀγάπη in Chapter 10 below.
[54] Rom 13.8–10.   [55] cf. Rom 3.20, 27–8.
[56] cf. Rom 2.26: ἐὰν οὖν ἡ ἀκροβυστία τὰ δικαιώματα τοῦ νόμου φυλάσσῃ...('So, if the uncircumcised keeps the requirements of the law...').

fact the first time Paul mentions the Law since 10.4–5, and the statement in
13.10 about ἀγάπη being the 'fulfilment of the Law' is the last thing that Paul
has to say about the Law as such in his letter to the Romans.[57]

Concluding chapter 13 in metaphorical terms of 'light' and 'darkness', Paul
then urges the Roman addressees to lay aside 'the works of darkness' (τὰ ἔργα
τοῦ σκότους, cf. μὴ συσχηματίζεσθε τῷ αἰῶνι τούτῳ in 12.2) and to 'put on the
armour of light' instead (ἐνδυσώμεθα τὰ ὅπλα τοῦ φωτός), and thus to 'live
honourably as in the day' (ὡς ἐν ἡμέρᾳ εὐσχημόνως περιπατήσωμεν).[58] Paul
informs his audience that by so doing they will 'put on (ἐνδύεσθαι) the lord
Jesus Christ',[59] that is, imitate his person and way of life.

In Romans 14.1–15.14 Paul lists some of the principal ways in which the
letter's recipients can and should actualize the community-oriented ethic of
Christ-believers and their 'love' of one another. Compared to the moral
teaching in chapters 12–13 on which it is built, this subsequent discourse is
more pragmatic and focused, with several potential examples given of proper
and improper dispositions, personalities, and social conduct—and with further exhortations in each case. As noted above, scholars often claim that in
Romans 14–15 Paul refers to two specific (socio-religious) groups of people in
Rome, represented by the 'weak' and the 'strong'. But the text itself gives little
occasion for that reading. In fact, it takes no small deal of unwarranted
'eisegesis' in order to fit Paul's text into such a scheme. What he speaks of
here are not specific, identifiable groups of people in the city of Rome but a
spectrum of dispositions, each end of which is represented by the 'weak' and
the 'strong' respectively. As one scholar explains, 'Paul's description of people
as "weak" and "strong" is an attempt at character portrayal, where typical
characteristics of certain dispositions and character types are given voice and
dramatized. Paul stresses the interacting obligations of different types of
people as he focuses on the behavior of the personified characters of these
encoded readers.'[60] Paul is still concerned with presenting his general moral
teaching to Christ-believers, now in the form of potential, even likely,
examples.

He begins with the 'weak' (14.1)—he does not mention the 'strong' until
15.1. It is important to observe, first, that Paul does not speak in the plural
here (in 14.1). He does not say 'the weak ones',[61] as if he were referring to a

---

[57] The Law (νόμος) is a major issue in Romans 2–11 (2.12–15[9 ×], 17–27[10 ×]; 3.19–21
[6 ×], 27–31[5 ×]; 4.13–16[5 ×]; 5.13[2 ×], 20; 6.14–15; 7.1–6[8 ×], 7–25[15 ×]; 8.2–7
[5 ×]; 9.31[2 ×]; 10.4–5), but outside chs. 2–11 it occurs only here in 13.8–10.
[58] Rom 13.12–13. Cf. 1 Thess 4.12.   [59] Rom 13.14.   [60] Glad, *Paul*, 329.
[61] cf. the NRSV translation: 'Welcome *those who are* weak in faith'. So also, e.g., Ben Witherington with Darlene Hyatt, *Paul's Letter to the Romans: A Socio-Rhetorical Commentary*
(Grand Rapids, MI: Eerdmans, 2004), 328.

specific group of people, but 'the weak one' (ὁ ἀσθενῶν).[62] Of course this phrasing does not rule out the possibility that he has a specific group of people in mind, but it is more suggestive of a specific *type* of person and behaviour, that is, an imaginary individual who represents the character in question. This is also the reason why the whole of chapter 14 is characterized by such frequent uses of the singular form, both in second and third persons, when bringing up certain types of disposition.

Second, in 14.1 Paul may appear to include all the addressees in his appeal to 'welcome' (προσλαμβάνεσθε, second person plural) the one who is weak in faith, as if the latter were not addressed at all in this passage. However, this is probably not the case. In 15.7 he uses this same verb, προσλαμβάνεσθαι, and there he clearly speaks to his audience as a whole, whether 'weak' or 'strong': 'Welcome one another', he says (προσλαμβάνεσθε ἀλλήλους). This suggests that, instead of addressing any 'weak' persons directly, Paul wishes to speak to his addressees *as if* they are all 'strong' in order not to affront and 'judge' anyone openly (cf. 14.13: μηκέτι οὖν ἀλλήλους κρίνωμεν), and in order not to be an example himself of such judging. To say in 15.1 that *we the strong* (ἡμεῖς οἱ δυνατοί) are obliged to bear the weaknesses of those without strength (τὰ ἀσθενήματα τῶν ἀδυνάτων)[63] is Paul's rhetorical means to lead (some of) the addressees towards an imitation of himself as 'strong',[64] especially those among the audience who (yet) are 'weak' in one way or another, but may eventually become (more) 'strong'. Paul's moral teaching and the recipients' own mutual guidance based on it[65] will help them on their way to that goal.

But what is it that makes 'the weak one' weak, according to Paul's reasoning? First of all, the discussion concerns persons who are 'weak in faith' (ἀσθενῶν τῇ πίστει), i.e. in the practice of their faith. Some are driven by quite rigid attitudes towards issues of food, for instance, by insisting on eating vegetables only.[66] Others are engaged in the practice of 'judging days',[67] while still others may wish to abstain from drinking wine.[68] These are, in other words, things that involve ascetic tendencies towards certain practical aspects of the Christ-believer's religious observance and everyday life.[69] To be sure, in

---

[62] cf. v. 2: ὁ δὲ ἀσθενῶν λάχανα ἐσθίει.   [63] Or: 'the weaknesses of the powerless'.

[64] cf. Rom 14.14: 'I (myself) know and am convinced (οἶδα καὶ πέπεισμαι) in the lord Jesus that nothing is unclean in itself'.

[65] cf. Rom 15.14: δυνάμενοι καὶ ἀλλήλους νουθετεῖν ('being able also to admonish/instruct one another').

[66] Rom 14.2–3.   [67] Rom 14.5–6 (ἡμέραν κρίνειν).   [68] Rom 14.17, 21.

[69] Note, again, that the different attitudes towards eating, drinking, and judging days are no sure indicators of Jewish versus non-Jewish dispositions, as sometimes held. On the contrary, all of these issues are known to have been dealt with by non-Jews in Graeco-Roman antiquity, and both the vegetarianism alluded to in Rom 14.2 and the abstention from wine (vv. 14, 17) fit quite badly with Jewish practices; see further Wayne A. Meeks, 'Judgment and the Brother: Romans

Paul's own view, the attitudes listed are quite unnecessary at best.[70] But his main point is something else. It does not revolve around these particular issues per se, which are merely *examples* of dispositions that may certainly be inessential but are a reality nonetheless. Paul's main point is rather that, whatever the dispositions, all members of the community are to be treated with care and respect. While this exhortation certainly applies to the 'weak one' too,[71] the question is particularly how the 'weak' members are treated by others within the group. Instead of being ridiculed and judged for their attitude towards some practical aspect of their faith, 'weak' members should be met with proper respect. The emphasis is put on the responsibility of the more 'powerful' individuals within the community, the 'strong'. That is also why Paul chooses to address the audience as if he is only or primarily addressing the 'strong'. According to him, some members of the group may indeed have certain (excessive) leanings towards this or that, but it is decisive for all that those who are 'strong' bear with these leanings (or 'weaknesses') and adapt to the need of the 'weak' brother or sister. For, in the end, it is *God* who judges,[72] not the Christ-believers themselves. 'Let us therefore no longer pass judgement on one another (μηκέτι οὖν ἀλλήλους κρίνωμεν),' Paul exhorts, 'but resolve instead never to put a stumbling block or an obstacle in the way of your brother.'[73] Otherwise, he explains, 'you are no longer walking in love' (οὐκέτι κατὰ ἀγάπην περιπατεῖς).[74] Love thus expresses itself here as thoughtfulness and adaptability to the needs of others. Issues of food and drink and so on are not important enough to be the causes for another's offence and fall.[75] What is essential is what makes for peace and for mutual upbuilding, τὰ τῆς εἰρήνης καὶ τὰ τῆς οἰκοδομῆς τῆς εἰς ἀλλήλους.[76] Paul underlines that it is the duty of each and every one to please (ἀρέσκειν) his or her neighbour for the purpose of the good (εἰς τὸ ἀγαθόν), which aims at nothing but building up (πρὸς οἰκοδομήν).[77] He even expresses his wish that 'the God of endurance and encouragement' (ὁ θεὸς τῆς ὑπομονῆς καὶ τῆς παρακλήσεως) may grant the addressees to 'live in mutual harmony' (τὸ αὐτὸ φρονεῖν ἐν ἀλλήλοις),[78] in accordance with Christ Jesus.[79] His hope is that they may 'with one mind and one voice' (ὁμοθυμαδὸν ἐν ἑνὶ στόματι) glorify God, precisely as God has planned.[80] Therefore he addresses them all directly and

---

14:1–15:13', in *Tradition and Interpretation in the New Testament: Essays in Honor of E. Earle Ellis for His 60th Birthday* (ed. G. F. Hawthorne with O. Betz; Grand Rapids, MI: Eerdmans, 1987), 291–3; Stowers, 'Paul', 281–6; Reichert, *Römerbrief*, 323–5.

[70] cf. the comments in 14.14, 17, 20.   [71] See Rom 14.3, 10.   [72] Rom 14.4, 7–12.
[73] Rom 14.13.   [74] Rom 14.15.   [75] Rom 14.15, 17, 20–1; 15.3.
[76] Rom 14.19.   [77] Rom 15.2.
[78] Or, more literally, 'to be of the same mind one with another' (asv).
[79] Rom 15.5.   [80] Rom 15.6, 9.

urges them to 'welcome one another' (προσλαμβάνεσθε ἀλλήλους),[81] whether they are 'strong' or 'weak'. The apostle closes his moral teaching by declaring his trust in the recipients' ability to instruct and admonish one another (ἀλλήλους νουθετεῖν),[82] and thus to heed his words.

In short, the 'strong' represent the ideal type or role, with which Paul himself identifies.[83] He wants the recipients to identify with the 'strong' as well, implying what everyone should at least *strive* to be. But he also wants his addressees to understand that there can be various kinds of 'weak' dispositions and personalities within the community, with whom they must sympathize and to whose needs they must adapt themselves whenever necessary. Hence the 'strong' should show thought for and support the 'weak', even if they have to disregard their own beliefs and convictions (*pro tempore*), giving precedence instead to the 'weak' dispositions of the latter. By doing so they will indeed 'walk in love' (κατὰ ἀγάπην περιπατεῖν). This is the main point of the passage. Romans 14–15 exemplifies how Christ-believers can and should 'put on' Christ himself,[84] that is, how they, in Paul's view, should imitate Jesus Christ and his love of others in practice—the very ἀγάπη spoken of in 13.8–10. For Paul, the purpose must always be the mutual upbuilding and unity of the community as a whole.[85]

Paul rounds off his moral teaching by alluding to its opening words, thus further linking the more general exhortations of chapters 12–13 to the subsequent exemplifying text in chapters 14–15. First he expresses his wish that the addressees will τὸ αὐτὸ φρονεῖν ἐν ἀλλήλοις (15.5), recalling his playing with the root φρον- in 12.3: μὴ ὑπερφρονεῖν παρ' ὃ δεῖ φρονεῖν ἀλλὰ φρονεῖν εἰς τὸ σωφρονεῖν (cf. 12.16: τὸ αὐτὸ εἰς ἀλλήλους φρονοῦντες, etc.), and that they may thereby praise God in absolute unity, 'with one mind and one voice' (15.6), i.e. as 'one body in Christ' (12.5). Then, at its very closing (15.14), Paul marks the formal *inclusio* of his moral teaching as a whole by way of a widely used and well-known epistolary form in Graeco-Roman antiquity in which the author of the letter expressed his or her confidence in the addressees. As a rule, such confidence-expressions related to the purpose of the letter, often by alluding to some specific request made in it; the expression functioned so as to 'undergird the letter's requests or admonitions by creating a sense of obligation through praise'.[86] In Romans such a request is put forth in the letter's very centre in terms of its epistolary

---

[81] Rom 15.7.   [82] Rom 15.14.   [83] cf. Rom 15.1: ἡμεῖς οἱ δυνατοί ('we the strong').
[84] cf. Rom 13.14; 15.3, 5, 7.   [85] cf. 1 Cor 8.1: ἡ ἀγάπη οἰκοδομεῖ ('love builds up').
[86] Stanley N. Olson, 'Pauline Expressions of Confidence in His Addressees', *CBQ* 47 (1985): 289. Note that I disagree with Olson's sub-categorizing of Rom 15.14 in this respect (Olson divides the confidence-expressions into four sub-types); see further Thorsteinsson, *Paul's Interlocutor*, 54–5.

structure, i.e. the key verses of 12.1–2. Thus, when Paul expresses his confidence in the addressees (πέπεισμαι δέ, ἀδελφοί μου, etc.) that they are 'full of goodness, filled with all knowledge, and capable of admonishing one another' (15.14), his concern is not simply and only to let them know that he has faith in them but also to urge them to act in accordance with the request made in 12.1–2. Paul wants them to understand that by following the request as elaborated upon in 12.3–15.13, the addressees can show that they have indeed been 'transformed by the renewing of the mind' and thus that they can discern what the will of God is, 'the good, acceptable, and perfect' (12.2). Paul wants them to understand that their 'reasonable worship' (v. 1) embodies the moral principles presented in chapters 12–15. To abide by these principles *is* their 'living sacrifice'. Their reasonable worship is in essence a moral one.

7

The First Letter of Peter

INTRODUCTION: AN ENCYCLICAL LETTER WITH GENERAL EXHORTATIONS

Most scholars agree that Rome was the place of composition of 1 Peter. It is true that the only explicit statement in the letter itself of its geographical origin is the reference to 'Babylon' in 5.13,[1] but this location is most likely used figuratively for the city of Rome.[2] The letter was probably written sometime between 70 CE and 95 CE,[3] i.e. during the reign of the Flavian dynasty (69–96 CE) and subsequent to the destruction of the Jewish temple in Jerusalem. A more precise date is very difficult to determine, but there is reason to doubt that the letter was penned in the earlier part of this period.[4] The author presents himself as no less a figure than 'Peter, the apostle of Jesus Christ',[5] a 'witness of the sufferings of Christ' who is now an 'elder' (πρεσβύτερος).[6] In that name the author claims to have the proper authority

---

[1] 1 Pet 5.13: ἀσπάζεται ὑμᾶς ἡ ἐν Βαβυλῶνι συνεκλεκτὴ καὶ Μᾶρκος ὁ υἱός μου ('Your sister congregation [lit. "the one who is also chosen"] in Babylon greets you, and so does my son Mark').

[2] See, e.g., Leonhard Goppelt, *Der Erste Petrusbrief* (KEK 12; Göttingen: Vandenhoeck & Ruprecht, 1978), 66; Paul J. Achtemeier, *1 Peter* (Hermeneia; Minneapolis, MN: Fortress, 1996), 63–4; John H. Elliott, *1 Peter: A New Translation with Introduction and Commentary* (AB 37B; New York: Doubleday, 2000), 131–4; David G. Horrell, 'The Product of a Petrine Circle? A Reassessment of the Origin and Character of 1 Peter', *JSNT* 86 (2002): 31.

[3] The scholarly majority appears to opt for this date of 1 Peter (cf. Raymond E. Brown, *An Introduction to the New Testament* [Anchor Bible Reference Library; New York: Doubleday, 1997], 721–2). Elliott narrows the date to 73–92 CE (*1 Peter*, 134–8). Achtemeier favours the dating 80–100 CE, but 'most likely in the earlier years of that range' (*1 Peter*, 50). For an overview of the scholarly discussion of the issues of date, authorship, and historical setting of 1 Peter, see Mark Dubis, 'Research on 1 Peter: A Survey of Scholarly Literature Since 1985', *CBR* 4 (2006): 200–4.

[4] If, as Tacitus tells us (*Ann.* 15.44) and most scholars believe, the 'Christians' in Rome were severely abused and tortured by emperor Nero in 64 CE, it seems unlikely that merely a few years have passed before the Roman author of 1 Peter urged his readers not only to submit to the emperor and his governors, who (rightly) 'punish those who do wrong', but also to *honour* him (2.13–17). To be sure, this emperor would not have been of the same dynasty as Nero (viz. the Julio-Claudian), but he was nevertheless the Roman emperor.

[5] 1 Pet 1.1.   [6] 1 Pet 5.1: ὁ συμπρεσβύτερος καὶ μάρτυς τῶν τοῦ Χριστοῦ παθημάτων.

to despatch an encyclical letter with general exhortations to Christ-believers who are scattered throughout almost the whole of Asia Minor.[7] But the letter is in all likelihood pseudepigraphical and we know little about the author's identity.

First Peter shows some resemblance to typical Graeco-Roman letters of request (cf. the παρακαλεῖν-constructions in 2.11 and 5.1), in a way strikingly similar to, though more concise than, Paul's Letter to the Romans.[8] Also similar is the strong element of exhortation ('parenesis'). At the closing of 1 Peter, the author looks back and sums up the main purpose of his 'short' letter (δι' ὀλίγων ἔγραψα): it is to exhort (παρακαλεῖν) his readers and to testify (ἐπιμαρτυρεῖν) to what 'the true grace of God' is in which they should stand firm.[9] Accordingly, the text includes large amounts of hortatory material. In terms of function, the letter as a whole may even be described as a hortatory or 'parenetic' letter.[10] As with many such letters, moral teaching plays a significant role in 1 Peter. The letter's moral teaching is mostly of a general kind, that is, it is not specifically aimed at particular circumstances at the other end of the epistolary communication,[11] though it may occasionally relate to the addressees' background as gentiles.[12]

The letter's rather general character makes it most relevant to an investigation of the identity of the Christ-believers in Rome. For such a letter reflects a *shared* identity—not necessarily an actual one, but an identity which *to these Roman Christians* should be shared by fellow believers elsewhere. In other words, even if the intended audience is outside Rome, the letter offers important clues to local perceptions and experiences and, particularly, how (some) Christ-believers in Rome construed their own identity as 'Christians'.[13]

---

[7] The letter is addressed to 'the exiles of the Dispersion in Pontus, Galatia, Cappadocia, Asia, and Bithynia' (ἐκλεκτοῖς παρεπιδήμοις διασπορᾶς Πόντου, Γαλατίας, Καππαδοκίας, Ἀσίας καὶ Βιθυνίας, 1.1; trans. NRSV).

[8] See Thorsteinsson, *Paul's Interlocutor*, 47–60. Cf. the discussion of Rom 12.1–2 in Chapter 6 above.

[9] 1 Pet 5.12.

[10] So Stanley K. Stowers, *Letter Writing in Greco-Roman Antiquity* (LEC 5; Philadelphia, PA: Westminster, 1986), 96–7; David E. Aune, *The New Testament in Its Literary Environment* (LEC 8; Philadelphia, PA: Westminster, 1987), 221–2; Troy W. Martin, *Metaphor and Composition in 1 Peter* (SBLDS 131; Atlanta, GA: Scholars, 1992), 85–103; Karl Olav Sandnes, 'Revised Conventions in Early Christian Paraenesis: "Working Good" in 1 Peter as an Example', in *Early Christian Paraenesis in Context* (ed. J. Starr and T. Engberg-Pedersen; BZNW 125; Berlin: de Gruyter, 2004), 374–81; cf. Elliott, *1 Peter*, 11–12.

[11] With some possible exceptions: cf. 1 Pet 1.6; 4.12.

[12] cf. 1 Pet 1.14 (cf. Rom 12.2), 18; 2.10; 4.3–4.

[13] Recall that 1 Peter is the one of only two NT writings in which the term 'Christian' (Χριστιανός) occurs (cf. Chapter 5 above).

Due to its general character 1 Peter gives us limited information about the recipients' socioeconomic status, but it leaves some clues about the author's own position in that respect. To begin with, the letter was evidently written by a highly literate Greek-speaking person who was intimately familiar with the LXX (the Greek translation of the Hebrew Bible). Compared to other early Christian writings, the quality of the Greek is excellent, which, along with the uses of rhetorical devices, suggests an authorship with relatively good education.[14] That, in turn, is clearly not in favour of a poor social standing. Also, in 3.3–4 the author urges the Christ-believing women to be content with the 'inner being' as their adornment, instead of the outward appearance: 'Do not adorn yourselves outwardly by braiding your hair, and by wearing gold ornaments (περιθέσεως χρυσίων) or fine clothing (ἱματίων κόσμος).' The very thought of the possibility of such adornment by these women points to the presence of some relatively well-off individuals in the Christ-movement. While it is possible that the author has some of his addressees in Asia Minor in mind, the reference may also be rooted in his own socio-economic setting. He may well be thinking of or alluding to (some particular) women who belong to the Christ-movement in Rome, and who have the means to adorn themselves in this way. This possibility speaks against the common assumption that the letter's authorship must have come from the poorest classes of society, and should suffice as a warning against making premature assumptions about the letter's social context. To be sure, we should hardly expect the author to have been of the upper crust of Roman society, but neither should we simply assume the opposite.

In this chapter, I shall first identify and briefly discuss the passages in 1 Peter that are most to the point for the present study, and then compare and assess the relationship between the moral teaching in 1 Peter and Paul's moral teaching in Romans.

MORAL TEACHING IN 1 PETER: LOVE AS THE PRIMARY VIRTUE

Subsequent to his introductory discourse in 1.3–12,[15] the author of 1 Peter launches his lesson. He urges the addressees not to be conformed (μὴ συσχηματιζόμενοι) to their former life of ignorance and desire but to be

---

[14] See the discussion in Achtemeier, *1 Peter*, 2–6, with further references.

[15] This part of the letter includes an important theme in 1 Peter, the theme of 'suffering' (πάθημα, 1.11; cf. 4.1, 13; 5.1, 9, 10). But since this theme does not belong directly to the letter's moral teaching proper, it is beyond the immediate scope of the present study.

holy in all their conduct (ἐν πάσῃ ἀναστροφῇ),[16] like their holy father 'who judges everyone impartially according to their deeds' (τὸν ἀπροσωπολήμπτως κρίνοντα κατὰ τὸ ἑκάστου ἔργον).[17]

In 1.22–3, then, the author presents his ethic of mutual love:

Now that you have purified your souls (τὰς ψυχὰς ὑμῶν ἡγνικότες) by your obedience to the truth (ἐν τῇ ὑπακοῇ τῆς ἀληθείας) so that you have sincere brotherly love (εἰς φιλαδελφίαν ἀνυπόκριτον), love one another fervently from a pure heart (ἐκ καθαρᾶς καρδίας ἀλλήλους ἀγαπήσατε ἐκτενῶς), having been born again (ἀναγεγεννημένοι), not of perishable but of imperishable seed, through the living and abiding word of God.

The text implies that the very act of purifying one's soul (through 'rebirth')[18] in 'obedience to the truth' leads to 'sincere brotherly love' (φιλαδελφίαν ἀνυπόκριτον). This means that right conduct is rooted in true learning, in 'the truth'. According to the author, his addressees in the East have indeed already purified their souls (note the perfect tense of ἡγνικότες) but he exhorts them nevertheless to 'love one another fervently from a pure heart'.[19] In other words, right conduct is certainly rooted in true learning, but it must be restated and reinforced.[20]

The key terms here are φιλαδελφία ('brotherly love') and ἀγαπᾶν (to 'love'). The former will occur again in 3.8 in the cognate form φιλάδελφοι, but it is the concept of 'love', ἀγάπη, that shows itself to carry special weight in the letter's moral teaching. The exhortation to love one another 'runs like a red thread through the entire letter. Paul sometimes closes his letters with "a holy kiss". 1 Peter concludes with "a kiss of love".'[21] As for φιλαδελφία, we can see from 1.22 that for the author of 1 Peter 'sincere brotherly love' is actually tantamount to 'loving one another fervently from a pure heart'. The two are basically the same thing. On the other hand, unless 1.22 is to some extent exemplified by the subsequent exhortation in 2.1 to rid oneself of all

---

[16] The word ἀναστροφή ('a mode of life', 'behaviour', 'conduct') is highly favoured by this author (1.15, 18; 2.12; 3.1, 2, 16); it is used six times in 1 Peter, but only seven times elsewhere in the NT (Gal 1.13 is a much-discussed example).

[17] 1 Pet 1.14–17. Cf. Rom 2.6, 11.

[18] cf. ἀναγεγεννημένοι in 1.23, which, in turn, points back to ἀναγεννήσας in 1.3. That this 'rebirth' is to a large extent seen as moral is evident by the statements in, e.g., 1.14, 17–18; 2.1–2; 3.9, 21; 4.3–4.

[19] Some manuscripts omit the word καθαρᾶς (here 'pure').

[20] Corresponding to the 'parenetical' function: '[P]araenesis is more of a reminder of what one ought or ought not to do than an introduction to new rules of conduct' (Martin, *Metaphor*, 115). Cf. also Aune, *New Testament*, 191. On the term 'parenesis', see more fully the discussion in James Starr and Troels Engberg-Pedersen, eds., *Early Christian Paraenesis in Context* (BZNW 125; Berlin: de Gruyter, 2004).

[21] Birger Olsson, *Första Petrusbrevet* (Kommentar till Nya testamentet 17; Stockholm: EFS-förlaget, 1982), 62–3 (my translation).

'wickedness', 'deceit', 'hypocrisy', 'envy', and 'slander', at this point the author does not specify more precisely what such φιλαδελφία and ἀγάπη imply in concrete, social terms.

In 2.11 the direct address ἀγαπητοί ('beloved') followed by the epistolary formula παρακαλῶ with the infinitive (ἀπέχεσθαι) marks a major turning point in the letter. This well-known epistolary expression initiates a lengthy passage that closes with the word ἀμήν in 4.11.[22] What characterizes the passage in 2.11–4.11 are various forms of moral teachings and exhortations, loosely divided into several sub-sections.[23] The author opens the passage by exhorting his 'beloved' to abstain from 'the desires of the flesh' (τῶν σαρκικῶν ἐπιθυμιῶν), thus echoing his earlier remark in 1.14 about their former life as gentiles. 'Peter' reminds them that they should conduct themselves honourably in the larger society (τὴν ἀναστροφὴν ὑμῶν ἐν τοῖς ἔθνεσιν ἔχοντες καλήν), that is to say, in everyday life. As a part of that ἀναστροφὴ καλή, they should submit (ὑποτάσσεσθαι) to the authority of the Roman emperor and his governors.[24] Whether by God or by the civic authorities, those who do good (ἀγαθοποιοί)[25] will be rewarded and those who do evil (κακοποιοί) will be punished. To do good is the proper way as well, says the author, to win over those who are still unbelievers.

In 2.17, then, 'Peter' provides a certain rundown of the letter's moral teaching so far: while the addressees are to 'fear' (φοβεῖσθαι) God and 'honour' (τιμᾶν) the emperor, they should 'love the brotherhood' (τὴν ἀδελφότητα ἀγαπᾶν), that is, the brotherhood of Christians: 'Honour everyone. Love the brotherhood. Fear God. Honour the emperor.'[26]

Similar language of fear and submission is found in the advice that the author gives in 2.18–3.6 to specific groups of people within the Christ-movement, household slaves (οἰκέται) and (house)wives (γυναῖκες). Wholly in line with the preceding words on total submission to governing authorities, the Christ-believing slaves are urged to submit (ὑποτάσσεσθαι) to their masters 'in all fear' (ἐν παντὶ φόβῳ). Not only are they to submit to those masters who are good and considerate, but to the mean ones as well.[27] For it is

---

[22] So also Achtemeier, *1 Peter*, 73; Olsson, *Petrusbrevet*, 201. Differently Elliott, *1 Peter*, viii–ix; Martin, *Metaphor*, 78–9.

[23] Approximately 2.11–17; 2.18–3.7 (2.18–25; 3.1–6; 3.7); 3.8–22; 4.1–6 (or 7a?); 4.7(7b?)–11. The way in which scholars divide the passage varies considerably.

[24] 1 Pet 2.13–14.

[25] The use of the word ἀγαθοποιεῖν and cognates is characteristic of 1 Peter (2.14, 15, 20; 3.6, 17; 4.19); it occurs six times in 1 Peter, but only five times elsewhere in the NT.

[26] The word ἀδελφότης ('brotherhood') does not occur outside 1 Peter in the NT (also in 1 Pet 5.9). But cf. 1 Clem. 2.4; Herm. *Mand.* 8.10 (38.10). On πάντας τιμήσατε ('honour everyone') in 1 Pet 2.17, see Chapter 10 below.

[27] 1 Pet 2.18.

indeed a credit to the slave if he or she endures pain while suffering unjustly, the author explains. The ultimate example for this is Christ himself: when one suffers unjustly and well endures the suffering, one is following in the footsteps of Jesus. The fact that the first-century author of 1 Peter makes no attempt to question the existence or legitimacy of slavery is hardly surprising. He is, like other people of his time, intimately bound to his historical context in which society without slavery was not an option, even in theory.[28]

The subsequent advice in 3.1–6 to married women in the Christ-movement is marked by a similar language of submission: wives are to be submissive ($\dot{v}\pi o\tau\acute{a}\sigma\sigma\epsilon\sigma\theta a\iota$) to their husbands.[29] Their duty is to imitate Sarah who 'obeyed Abraham and called him lord' ($\dot{v}\pi\acute{\eta}\kappa o v\sigma\epsilon v$ $\tau\hat{\omega}$ 'Aβρα \grave{a}μ κύριον αὐτὸν καλοῦσα). According to the author of 1 Peter, it is of no consequence in this respect if husbands themselves are 'disobedient to the word' ($\dot{a}\pi\epsilon\iota\theta o\hat{v}\sigma\iota v$ $\tau\hat{\omega}$ λόγῳ). In that case, it is even more important that the wives' conduct be marked by chastity and fear ($\tau\grave{\eta}v$ $\dot{\epsilon}v$ $\phi\acute{o}\beta\omega$ $\dot{a}\gamma v\grave{\eta}v$ $\dot{a}v a\sigma\tau\rho o\phi\acute{\eta}v$). They are not to adorn themselves outwardly with fine and expensive things, but to let the character of their 'inner being' ($\dot{o}$ $\kappa\rho v\pi\tau\grave{o}s$ $\tau\hat{\eta}s$ $\kappa a\rho\delta\acute{\iota}as$ $\check{a}v\theta\rho\omega\pi os$) be their true adornment. For so it was with the god-fearing 'holy women' of old who, like Sarah, 'adorned' themselves by submitting to their husbands.[30] Submission was their true adornment.[31]

Compared to the rather detailed directions to slaves and wives, the advice in 3.7 to husbands ($\check{a}v\delta\rho\epsilon s$) is quite brief. They are urged to live with their wives in an understanding manner ($\kappa a\tau\grave{a}$ $\gamma v\hat{\omega}\sigma\iota v$), because the latter are the 'weaker vessel' ($\dot{a}\sigma\theta\epsilon v\acute{\epsilon}\sigma\tau\epsilon\rho o v$ $\sigma\kappa\epsilon\hat{v}os$), and to show them respect ($\tau\iota\mu\acute{\eta}v$), since they too are heirs to the grace of life.

Following these directions to specific groups of people, the author turns to the letter's recipients as a whole and exhorts them to be of one mind ($\dot{o}\mu\acute{o}\phi\rho o v\epsilon s$), to have sympathy ($\sigma v\mu\pi a\theta\epsilon\hat{\iota}s$) and brotherly love ($\phi\iota\lambda\acute{a}\delta\epsilon\lambda\phi o\iota$), and to be kind-hearted ($\epsilon\check{v}\sigma\pi\lambda a\gamma\chi v o\iota$) and humble-minded ($\tau a\pi\epsilon\iota v\acute{o}\phi\rho o v\epsilon s$). They should not render evil for evil ($\mu\grave{\eta}$ $\dot{a}\pi o\delta\iota\delta\acute{o}v\tau\epsilon s$ $\kappa a\kappa\grave{o}v$ $\dot{a}v\tau\grave{\iota}$ $\kappa a\kappa o\hat{v}$) but rather repay evil with a blessing ($\epsilon\dot{v}\lambda o\gamma o\hat{v}v\tau\epsilon s$).[32] Under no circumstances

---

[28] I cannot agree with Glancy that '1 Peter offers grounds for condemning the system of slavery by inviting comparisons between the abuse of slaves and the passion of Jesus' (Jennifer A. Glancy, *Slavery in Early Christianity* [New York: Oxford University Press, 2002], 150). To be sure, the text does include such comparisons, but not for the purpose of 'condemning the system of slavery'.

[29] 1 Pet 3.1.   [30] 1 Pet 3.5.

[31] Discussing the use of 1 Peter in the context of domestic violence, Kathleen E. Corley states: 'Of all Christian Testament texts, the message of 1 Peter is the most harmful in the context of women's lives' ('1 Peter', in *Searching the Scriptures*. Vol. 2. *A Feminist Commentary* [ed. E. Schüssler Fiorenza; London: SCM, 1994], 355).

[32] 1 Pet 3.8–9.

must evil (τὸ κακόν) be preferred over good (τὸ ἀγαθόν), even in the face of abuse and suffering.[33] The 'good conduct in Christ' (ἡ ἀγαθὴ ἐν Χριστῷ ἀναστροφή) must be followed at all costs.[34]

Having again alluded to the addressees' former way of life, i.e. living, as gentiles do, in licentiousness, desire, drunkenness, revels, carousing, and abominable idolatry,[35] the author reminds them that 'the end of all things' (πάντων δὲ τὸ τέλος) is at hand. According to him, it is therefore crucial to show proper moderation (σωφρονεῖν) and to be disciplined (νήφειν).[36] But most important of all, they must sincerely love one another:

Above all (πρὸ πάντων), maintain fervent love for one another (τὴν εἰς ἑαυτοὺς ἀγάπην ἐκτενῆ ἔχοντες), for love covers a multitude of sins (ἀγάπη καλύπτει πλῆθος ἁμαρτιῶν). Be hospitable to one another without grumbling (φιλόξενοι εἰς ἀλλήλους ἄνευ γογγυσμοῦ). Like good stewards of the manifold grace of God, serve one another (εἰς ἑαυτοὺς διακονοῦντες) with whatever gift (χάρισμα) each of you has received.[37]

Again, ἀγάπη presents itself as central to the moral teaching of 1 Peter. Moreover, whereas in 1.22 and 2.17 it seems to be assumed that the readers will realize what it actually means to 'love one another' and to 'love the brotherhood',[38] since in neither case is it defined in more detailed terms, in 4.8–11 we appear to have a few examples of how this 'love' may be expressed in actual life. The first example is when the author explains the demand of mutual love by citing Proverbs 10.12 (the explanatory function is marked by ὅτι): 'for love covers a multitude of sins' (ὅτι ἀγάπη καλύπτει πλῆθος ἁμαρτιῶν). Unfortunately, the point of this citation in 1 Peter 4.8 is not entirely clear,[39] that is, whether the sins covered belong to the one who loves or to the one who is loved. But given the present context of mutuality (vv. 8–10: ... εἰς ἑαυτούς ... εἰς ἀλλήλους ... εἰς ἑαυτούς ...), the issue under discussion must involve mutual forgiveness.[40] The sins are 'covered' when

---

[33] 1 Pet 3.10–17.　　[34] 1 Pet 3.16. Cf. also 1.6–7; 2.13–16, 19–21; 4.14–19; 5.9–10.

[35] 1 Pet 4.3–4.

[36] 1 Pet 4.7. On σωφρονεῖν, cf. Rom 12.3 (discussed above). On νήφειν, cf. 1 Thess 5.6, 8.

[37] 1 Pet 4.7–10.

[38] It is also presupposed that the readers are familiar with the 'kiss of love' at the closing of the letter (5.14). The greeting in 5.14 (ἀσπάσασθε ἀλλήλους ἐν φιλήματι ἀγάπης) is almost identical to the typical Pauline greeting ἀσπάσασθε ἀλλήλους ἐν φιλήματι ἁγίῳ and the like (Rom 16.16; 1 Cor 16.20; 2 Cor 13.12; 1 Thess 5.26).

[39] The source of the citation is not clear either. As a rule 1 Peter cites from the LXX, but in this case the Hebrew text comes much closer ('love ['ahavah] covers all transgressions [pesha'im]'). The LXX is so different (πάντας δὲ τοὺς μὴ φιλονεικοῦντας καλύπτει φιλία) that it was unlikely to be the source of 1 Pet 4.8b.

[40] So Achtemeier, *1 Peter*, 295–6; Elliott, *1 Peter*, 750–1.

they are forgiven.[41] The point is thus that if the addressees' love for one another is genuine and 'fervent' (ἐκτενῆ), they must be ready to forgive each others' misdeeds, even if it concerns a 'multitude of sins'. Forgiveness constitutes therefore one aspect of ἀγάπη in 1 Peter.

Another aspect comes to the fore in v. 9: 'Be hospitable to one another without grumbling.' Hospitality (φιλοξενία) was widely valued as a virtue in the Graeco-Roman world, whether the soil was Greek, Roman, or Jewish. Hospitality constituted a sacred duty that responded to the physical, social, and spiritual needs of the stranger.[42] The author of 1 Peter embraces this virtue of his surroundings, and seems to give it equal import by presenting it as one expression of ἀγάπη. The fact that he adds the words 'without grumbling' may suggest that he had some knowledge or experience of such 'grumbling',[43] or that he understood φιλοξενία to be so worn-out a concept that it needed to be supplemented and reinforced in this way. In any case, according to the author of 1 Peter, the Christian brotherhood should take great care to honour the old virtue of hospitality and receive well the 'stranger' (ξένος) among them, physically, socially, and otherwise.[44] Mutual hospitality was of course vital to the advance of the new movement,[45] and it seems likely that the author of 1 Peter is here primarily referring to 'strangers' who are fellow Christians.

The ensuing verses emphasize that, 'like good stewards (καλοὶ οἰκονόμοι) of the manifold grace of God', the addressees should serve (διακονεῖν) one another with whatever gift (χάρισμα) they may have received. These gifts must be used for the benefit of the whole. What we see here is an ethic of

---

[41] cf. Ps 31.1 (MT 32.1): 'Blessed are those whose transgressions (ἀνομίαι) are forgiven (ἀφέθησαν) and whose sins (ἁμαρτίαι) are covered (ἐπεκαλύφθησαν).' 84.3 (MT 85.2): 'You [i.e. God] have forgiven (ἀφῆκας) the people their transgressions (ἀνομίας); you have covered (ἐκάλυψας) all their sins (ἁμαρτίας).'

[42] See Amy G. Oden, ed., *And You Welcomed Me: A Sourcebook on Hospitality in Early Christianity* (Nashville, TN: Abingdon, 2001), 13–18, with further references.

[43] cf. 3 John 9–10 where Diotrephes' inhospitality (and grumbling?) is spoken of in very disdainful terms.

[44] Elliott observes that '[b]etween "be hospitable" (*philoxenoi*) and "brotherly love" (*philadelphia*, 1:22), both terms from the root *phil-*, there is a social as well as linguistic relationship' (*1 Peter*, 751). Commenting on the subject of 'brotherly love' in 1 Thess 4.9–10, Abraham J. Malherbe observes that 'Paul does not say how the Thessalonians exhibited their love, but their hospitality to travelers was one likely expression of love' (*The Letters to the Thessalonians: A New Translation with Introduction and Commentary* [AB 32B; New York: Doubleday, 2000], 245).

[45] *Did.* 11–13 is an example of an early Christian text in which the issue of hospitality is discussed, not least in order to set certain safeguards against its potential misuse. The discussion itself indicates how important hospitality was to the spread and growth of the movement in its earliest phases. Elliott notes that Adolf von Harnack once attributed 'the rapid rise of the Roman Church to supremacy in Western Christendom, not simply to its geographical position at the capital of the Empire or to its location as a seat of apostolic activity, but also to its generous hospitality and support of communities abroad' (*1 Peter*, 753).

mutual aid and giving, the aim of which is not so much to wipe out all social differences as to promote each and everyone's use of whatever position or 'gift' they may enjoy for the benefit of the others. At the same time the letter demands mutual respect, something that the author wishes to exhibit himself. For even though he claims the authoritative persona of the apostle Peter himself, he occasionally uses fraternal expressions of uniformity[46] and calls the addressees 'beloved' (ἀγαπητοί).[47] Being a spiritual leader, he speaks to them not only as a fatherly figure[48] but also as a loving fellow believer.

The description in 4.8–11 of what it means to 'love one another' is as concrete as it gets in 1 Peter—if indeed it is right to take vv. 9–11 as a further explanation of v. 8.[49] It implies that expressions of ἀγάπη, as understood by the Roman author of 1 Peter, include forgiveness, hospitality, and mutual aid and respect. Even though they are somewhat vaguely formulated, the author seems to have regarded these aspects of ἀγάπη to be particularly important components of Christian morality and identity.

FROM PAUL TO 'PETER': A CONTINUITY OF MORAL TEACHINGS

The relationship between 1 Peter and the letters of Paul is a matter of some debate. What is debated is whether 1 Peter was the product of the Pauline tradition, of a 'Petrine school' (in Rome), or perhaps of a synthesizing Roman Christianity.[50] The present discussion will focus primarily on the relationship of the moral teaching in Paul's Letter to the Romans and in 1 Peter.

It should be clear at the outset that there are, of course, significant differences between Romans and 1 Peter.[51] But the similarities between the two letters are too many and too close to deny some form of dependence, whether literary or something less direct.[52] The parallels found in the moral teachings

---

[46] cf. 1 Pet 5.1, 12–13.   [47] 1 Pet 2.11; 4.12. Cf. Martin, *Metaphor*, 105.

[48] e.g. 1 Pet 1.14: ὡς τέκνα ὑπακοῆς ... 2.2: ὡς ἀρτιγέννητα βρέφη ...

[49] According to J. J. Janse van Rensburg's analysis of particles and asyndeton in 1 Peter, the asyndeta in 4.8–11 serve as markers of subordinate intersentence relations ('The Use of Intersentence Relational Particles and Asyndeton in First Peter', *Neot* 24 [1990]: 292), which supports the reading above that vv. 9–11 may be understood as a further description of v. 8.

[50] See the fine discussion in Horrell, 'Product of a Petrine Circle?', who argues for the last mentioned. See also the general survey in Dubis, 'Research on 1 Peter', 209–10.

[51] See, e.g., the discussion in Elliott, *1 Peter*, 37–40.

[52] It is telling that even Elliott, who has long sought to release 1 Peter from its 'Pauline bondage', has to acknowledge this; cf. Elliott, *1 Peter*, 37: 'It is possible, if not probable, that the Petrine author was familiar with one or more of Paul's letters (esp. Romans).'

of these two letters are particularly striking, both in general as well as in many details.

The author of 1 Peter initiates his moral lesson by urging his addressees 'not to be conformed' (μὴ συσχηματιζόμενοι) to their former (pagan) way of life. As we saw in Chapter 6, Paul begins his moral teaching in Romans 12 by using exactly this same verb when he exhorts his audience 'not to be conformed to this world' (μὴ συσχηματίζεσθε τῷ αἰῶνι τούτῳ).[53] This is the only time Paul uses the verb συσχηματίζειν in his letters, and 1 Peter 1.14 is the only other occurrence of the verb in the entire New Testament. Moreover, according to Paul, his Roman addressees are to offer themselves as a 'living sacrifice' (θυσίαν ζῶσαν), a sacrifice that is 'holy and acceptable to God' (ἁγίαν εὐάρεστον τῷ θεῷ) and their 'reasonable worship' (τὴν λογικὴν λατρείαν).[54] Such worship and 'sacrifice' by his gentile audience would indeed fulfil the purpose of Paul's own priestly service (ἱερουργῶν) of God's good news, namely, to bring about 'the offering of the gentiles' (ἡ προσφορὰ τῶν ἐθνῶν) as 'acceptable, sanctified by the holy spirit' (εὐπρόσδεκτος, ἡγιασμένη ἐν πνεύματι ἁγίῳ).[55] Correspondingly, the author of 1 Peter wants his addressees to let themselves be 'built into a spiritual house' (οἰκοδομεῖσθε οἶκος πνευματικός) like 'living stones' (λίθοι ζῶντες), and to be a 'holy priesthood' (ἱεράτευμα ἅγιον) that offers 'spiritual sacrifices acceptable to God' (πνευματικὰς θυσίας εὐπροσδέκτους τῷ θεῷ).[56] The verbal parallels are striking. Also, in both cases the 'sacrifices' of the gentile Christ-believers are largely thought to be offered through proper moral conduct. Sacrifice is embodied in their way of living.

There is a close conformity, too, between Romans and 1 Peter concerning what counts as proper moral conduct. As we have seen, the virtue of ἀγάπη is central to the teachings of these letters. But both authors emphasize other moral aspects as well, many of which reveal remarkable resemblance. Examples include the more socially oriented exhortations that the readers are to be 'hospitable' (φιλόξενοι, 1 Pet 4.9; τὴν φιλοξενίαν διώκοντες, Rom 12.13), and 'of one mind' (ὁμόφρονες, 1 Pet 3.8; τὸ αὐτὸ ... φρονοῦντες, Rom 12.16; τὸ αὐτὸ φρονεῖν, 15.5), and that it is their duty to serve one another with whatever 'gift' (χάρισμα) each of them has received (1 Pet 4.10–11; Rom 12.3–8). So also the exhortation to be sympathetic (1 Pet 3.8; Rom 12.15) and 'not to render evil for evil' (μὴ ἀποδιδόντες κακὸν ἀντὶ κακοῦ, 1 Pet 3.9; μηδενὶ κακὸν ἀντὶ κακοῦ ἀποδιδόντες, Rom 12.17).[57] For both authors it is imperative as well to be humble-minded, not overbearing in one's dealings with others (ταπεινόφρονες, 1 Pet 3.8; cf. 5.5–6; μὴ τὰ ὑψηλὰ φρονοῦντες ἀλλὰ τοῖς

---

[53] Rom 12.2.　　[54] Rom 12.1.　　[55] Rom 15.16.　　[56] 1 Pet 2.5.
[57] cf. also 1 Thess 5.15: ὁρᾶτε μή τις κακὸν ἀντὶ κακοῦ τινι ἀποδῷ.

ταπεινοῖς συναπαγόμενοι, Rom 12.16), towards whom it is imperative to
show proper moderation (σωφρονήσατε, 1 Pet 4.7; σωφρονεῖν, Rom 12.3).
Especially noteworthy is the rather unusual but nevertheless shared conception that one is to 'bless' one's abusers or persecutors (εὐλογοῦντες, 1 Pet 3.9;
εὐλογεῖτε, Rom 12.14). But even more striking are the passages in which the
recipients of the letters are urged to submit to civic authorities (Rom 13.1–7; 1
Pet 2.13–17), where both authors make use of similar *moral* arguments to
substantiate such submission, namely, that one has only to do 'good' in order
to enjoy the goodwill of the authorities, because these (merely) punish those
who do 'evil' (τὸ κακόν, ἡ κακία) and give 'praise' (ἔπαινον) to those who do
'good' (τὸ ἀγαθόν, τὸ καλόν). Here we must keep in mind that 1 Peter was
despatched from the very place to which Paul only few decades earlier had
addressed his own unique exhortation to submit to civic authorities.[58] Paul
concluded those instructions to his Roman readers by urging them to render
to all what is due them, including 'fear' (φόβος) to whom fear is due and
'honour' (τιμή) to whom honour is due. Similarly, the Roman author of 1
Peter concludes his analogous discussion by telling his addressees to 'fear'
(φοβεῖσθαι) God and 'honour' (τιμᾶν) the emperor. It is also worth considering that in this same verse the readers are told to 'love the brotherhood' of
fellow believers, τὴν ἀδελφότητα ἀγαπᾶτε, but, as we have seen, Paul continues
his discussion in Romans 13.8 precisely by speaking of this same sort of love:
μηδενὶ μηδὲν ὀφείλετε εἰ μὴ τὸ ἀλλήλους ἀγαπᾶν ('owe no one anything,
except to love one another')!

It seems to me that these and other correspondences between Romans and
1 Peter suggest not only a continuity between the two letters but also the
latter's dependence on the former.[59] That does not necessarily mean that the
author of 1 Peter had his own copy of Romans—a possibility that I do not
find unlikely at all—but it implies that 'Peter' was at least very familiar with
Paul's letter. In fact, I detect no real discrepancies between the moral teachings
of these two writings. What I find somewhat surprising, on the other hand, is
the fact that 1 Peter does not ignore or make any basic adjustments to Paul's
urging of submission to the Roman authorities, nor disregard the demand to
'bless' one's persecutors, given that emperor Nero persecuted Christ-believers
in Rome only ten to thirty years earlier (in 64 CE), that is, if we are to trust
Tacitus on that point.[60] It is very difficult, however, to assess what implications this may have for our knowledge of the (reported) incident itself, of the

---

[58] This exhortation is not found in Paul's other (extant) letters, but it is echoed in the post-
Pauline Tit 3.1.
[59] For more examples and discussion of such correspondences, see Horrell, 'Product of a
Petrine Circle?', 32–8, with further references.
[60] *Ann.* 15.44. Cf. the introduction to Part II above.

date of 1 Peter (pointing towards the latter part of 70–95 CE), or of the standpoint or rhetorical strategy of the author.

But one thing is clear at least: the discussion in this chapter has shown that, precisely as in Romans, the primary virtue in 1 Peter is ἀγάπη. Just as Paul's audience is to 'owe no one anything, except to love one another' (13.8), the addressees in 1 Peter are 'above all' to have 'love for one another' (4.8). And just as Paul sees reason to stress that love must be 'sincere' (ἡ ἀγάπη ἀνυπόκριτος, 12.9), the author of 1 Peter does the same with respect to 'brotherly love' (φιλαδελφίαν ἀνυπόκριτον, 1.22), which, as we have seen, is tantamount to 'loving one another fervently from a pure heart'. Moreover, it is also evident that the author of 1 Peter has underlined even more firmly than Paul that ἀγάπη stands at the core of Christian moral teaching and conduct.[61]

But what did ἀγάπη really mean in these writings? Was it expressed in any concrete terms or did it present itself more abstractly as a matter of proper disposition? The information we gathered from the texts themselves appeared to call for both alternatives. In Romans we saw that ἀγάπη was the very principle on which Paul based his moral teaching for the community of Christ-believers, but we also saw that the virtue of ἀγάπη was being expressed in quite concrete terms. As the apostle envisioned it, particularly important aspects of love were mutual respect and adaptability to the needs of others. The 'stronger' members of the Christ-movement were obliged to show respect and thoughtfulness to the 'weaker' members, and to adapt to their needs if necessary. The moral teaching of 1 Peter is expressed in more abstract terms, and the discussion is not nearly as detailed as in Paul's letter, although we saw that particular expressions of ἀγάπη in 1 Peter could include features such as forgiveness, hospitality, and mutual aid and respect. But, on the whole, ἀγάπη in 1 Peter is primarily presented as the underlying moral principle for the Christian brotherhood. It is presented as *the* proper disposition that almost automatically leads to the right moral conduct towards fellow believers in Christ. That, in turn, is a basic thought in Romans as well, which again indicates the close continuity between the moral teachings of Paul and 'Peter'.

---

[61] We will address the question of the 'ethical scope' of this primary Christian virtue in the final chapter of the study.

8

The First Letter of Clement

INTRODUCTION: AN EPISTOLARY REQUEST FOR UNITY

Even compared to Paul's Letter to the Romans, the First Letter of Clement[1] is an exceedingly long letter. And yet it is a real letter that, unlike 1 Peter, deals mainly with specific issues and incidents at the other end of the epistolary communication. As the prescript clearly states, the letter's recipients were Christ-believing residents in Corinth, and its place of origin was the city of Rome (ἡ ἐκκλησία τοῦ θεοῦ ἡ παροικοῦσα ‘Ρώμην).[2] Tradition has ascribed the letter to a certain 'Clement', but we really do not know who wrote the letter. No Clement is actually mentioned in it. In fact, its specified sender is not an individual at all but the Roman ἐκκλησία ('congregation') as a whole, and the first person plural is used consistently throughout the text.[3] (In the following, I shall interchangeably refer to the 'author' of the letter, its 'senders', or the 'Roman ἐκκλησία'.) There is some dispute among scholars over the date of the letter, but most agree that it was probably written in the mid-90s, around the closing years of the reign of emperor Domitian (96 CE).[4]

The immediate occasion of 1 Clement was strife within the Corinthian ἐκκλησία caused by a power struggle in which the senders of the letter wished to intervene,[5] possibly on request from Corinth.[6] The purpose was to bring

---

[1] Unless otherwise noted, translations of 1 Clement are from the most recent LCL edition (Ehrman). I do not italicize the title 'First Letter of Clement / 1 Clement' in this study.

[2] 'The church of God that temporarily resides in Rome', as Ehrman translates it (LCL). Lake's earlier LCL translation reads, 'The Church of God which sojourns in Rome'.

[3] Most scholars assume nonetheless that the letter was composed by a single author. However, Lampe rightly observes that 'although written by one individual', 1 Clement reveals itself 'as a genuinely communal work' (*From Paul*, 217).

[4] See Jeffers, *Conflict*, 90–4; Bart D. Ehrman, 'Introduction [to First Clement]', in *The Apostolic Fathers* (ed. & trans. B. D. Ehrman; 2 vols.; LCL; Cambridge, MA: Harvard University Press, 2003), 1: 23–5. Other suggestions of date range from ca. 70 to 140 CE; cf. Andrew Gregory, 'Disturbing Trajectories: *1 Clement*, the *Shepherd of Hermas* and the Development of Early Roman Christianity', in *Rome in the Bible and the Early Church* (ed. P. Oakes; Carlisle: Paternoster, 2002), 142–66.

[5] 1 Clem. 1.1; 3; 44; 46.5–9; 47; 57.1–2; 63; 65.1.

[6] See 1 Clem. 1.1; 44.6; 47.6–7. Cf. also Lane, 'Social Perspectives', 226–7, 230.

about 'peace and harmony' (εἰρήνη καὶ ὁμόνοια)[7] in this ἐκκλησία, mainly by persuading the 'few' or 'one or two' troublemakers[8] to (re)submit to the properly appointed presbyters.[9] As a whole, 1 Clement is thus well described as a 'request... for peace and harmony' in the Corinthian ἐκκλησία.[10] However, in spite of this occasion and purpose, details about the precise situation in Corinth are surprisingly scanty. To argue their case, the senders focus much on aspects which they consider general principles for Christ-believers and applicable as such to the Corinthian strife.

In this light, it seems reasonable to assume, as many scholars do,[11] that 1 Clement can also provide us with valuable information about its Roman context. The senders of the letter hint at this themselves early on in the text (7.1): 'We are writing these things, loved ones, not only to admonish you but also to remind ourselves (ἑαυτοὺς ὑπομιμνήσκοντες). For we are in the same arena (ἐν γὰρ τῷ αὐτῷ ἐσμὲν σκάμματι) and the same contest is set before us (ὁ αὐτὸς ἡμῖν ἀγὼν ἐπίκειται).' The senders then immediately refer to the 'famous and venerable rule of our tradition',[12] which indicates a tradition common to both sides of the correspondence. In other words, the text of 1 Clement partly reflects the senders' (or author's) conception of a shared identity of Christ-believers, and thus their own as well. This includes their understanding of the proper way of life, namely, 'living according to what is appropriate in Christ' (πολιτεύεσθαι κατὰ τὸ καθῆκον τῷ Χριστῷ).[13] A general acceptance of a moral ideal is clearly presupposed in the text.

What can be known of the letter's social setting? First, several features in the text indicate an educated authorship. Apart from verbal and rhetorical traits in the letter,[14] which all point in this direction, the senders explicitly express

---

[7] 1 Clem. 20.10, 11; 60.4; 63.2; 65.1. For detailed discussion of εἰρήνη καὶ ὁμόνοια and related terms in 1 Clement, see Bakke, 'Concord', 63–203.

[8] 1 Clem. 1.1 (ὀλίγα πρόσωπα); 47.6 (ἐν ᾗ ἢ δύο πρόσωπα).

[9] See 1 Clem. 1.3; 14.1–2; 21.6; 44.3–6; 47.6; 57.1–2.

[10] 1 Clem. 63.2: ... κατὰ τὴν ἔντευξιν, ἣν ἐποιησάμεθα περὶ εἰρήνης καὶ ὁμονοίας ἐν τῇδε τῇ ἐπιστολῇ ('... in accordance with the request, we have made in this letter for your peace and harmony'). Cf. Andreas Lindemann, *Die Clemensbriefe* (HNT 17; Tübingen: Mohr [Siebeck], 1992), 13: 'Näher liegt für die Gattungsbestimmung die Aussage des Vf in 63,2, er habe den Adressaten eine briefliche ἔντευξις περὶ εἰρήνης καὶ ὁμονοίας gegeben'. See also Ehrman, 'Introduction', 18.

[11] e.g. Barbara E. Bowe, *A Church in Crisis: Ecclesiology and Paraenesis in Clement of Rome* (Harvard Dissertations in Religion 23; Minneapolis, MN: Fortress, 1988), 22–3, 119–20, 157; Walters, 'Romans, Jews, and Christians', 190–1; Lane, 'Social Perspectives', 231; Jeffers, *Conflict*, 97, 105.

[12] 1 Clem. 7.2: τὸν εὐκλεῆ καὶ σεμνὸν τῆς παραδόσεως ἡμῶν κανόνα.

[13] 1 Clem. 3.4; cf. 1.2; 21.8; 47.6; 49.1.

[14] See Bowe, *Church*, 58–74; Horacio E. Lona, *Der erste Clemensbrief* (Kommentar zu den Apostolischen Vätern 2; Göttingen: Vandenhoeck & Ruprecht, 1998), 30–40, 72–3; Bakke, 'Concord', 33–62. Cf. also Jeffers, *Conflict*, 31–2; Ehrman, 'Introduction', 19–20.

their contempt for the 'uneducated' (ἀπαίδευτοι).[15] Second, some observations in the letter suggest that we are dealing with authorship of some means. For example, when the senders of the letter exhort the wealthy among Christ-believers in Corinth to provide for the poor, the latter are urged to 'offer thanks to God, since he has given him [i.e. the poor fellow] someone to supply his need'.[16] In agreement with traditions from the Jewish scriptures, 1 Clement holds that rich people are made so by God, but also that poor people are made poor by God.[17] The letter makes no evident attempt to challenge existing social order by criticizing the low status of the poor in society. On the contrary, 1 Clement appears to accept it as it is.[18] As we shall see, the author assumes the traditional Roman social system of patronage. Indicative also is the letter's notion of total obedience to the Roman authorities, which is referred to in the very same moment as human obedience to God (60.4–61.1). No signs of oppressive relations or negative attitudes to the authorities are visible in the text. The Roman army is even referred to as the model on which to base the structure of authority in the Christ-movement, and the Roman generals are spoken of as 'our' generals.[19] All this suggests an author who enjoys a fairly well-off position in society.

This is not to say that the person who authored the text belonged to the upper classes, the Roman aristocracy. Rather, whereas the author of 1 Clement was almost certainly of the lower classes of Rome, he appears to have been relatively fortunate socially.[20] It was noted earlier that some scholars have suggested that the author was an imperial freedman, which seems reasonable. Many ex-slaves of the *Familia Caesaris* were quite well positioned in Roman society.[21]

Corresponding to the procedure in the previous chapter, I shall first determine and discuss briefly the relevant passages in 1 Clement. Then I

---

[15] 1 Clem. 39.1: ἄφρονες καὶ ἀσύνετοι καὶ μωροὶ καὶ ἀπαίδευτοι ('ignorant, unlearned, foolish, and uneducated'). Cf. also 3.3; 21.5.

[16] 1 Clem. 38.2: ὁ πλούσιος ἐπιχορηγείτω τῷ πτωχῷ, ὁ δὲ πτωχὸς εὐχαριστείτω τῷ θεῷ, ὅτι ἔδωκεν αὐτῷ, δι' οὗ ἀναπληρωθῇ αὐτοῦ τὸ ὑστέρημα. Note that in 13.1, the author does not denounce material wealth as such, but declares it irrelevant; it is an *adiaphoron* (in Stoic terms): 'the one who is wealthy [should not boast] about his wealth; instead the one who boasts should boast about the Lord' (from Jer 9.22–3 [MT: 9.23–4]; cf. 1 Cor 1.31; 2 Cor 10.17).

[17] 1 Clem. 59.3: God is ὁ πλουτίζων καὶ πτωχίζων, i.e. not only the one who enriches but also the one who impoverishes. Cf. 1 Kgdms 2.7 (MT: 1 Sam 2.7).

[18] cf. Jeffers, *Conflict*, 104.

[19] 1 Clem. 37.1–4 (v. 2: κατανοήσωμεν τοὺς στρατευομένους τοῖς ἡγουμένοις ἡμῶν).

[20] cf. Jeffers, *Conflict*, 97–105; Lane, 'Social Perspectives', 241–2; Martin Meiser, 'Das Christentum in Rom im Spiegel des ersten Clemensbriefes', *Christians as a Religious Minority in a Multicultural City: Modes of Interaction and Identity Formation in Early Imperial Rome* (ed. J. Zangenberg and M. Labahn; JSNTSup 243; London: T&T Clark, 2004), 143–6.

[21] See the discussion and references in Chapter 5 above.

shall assess the relationship between the moral teaching in 1 Clement and
Paul's moral teaching in Romans.

MORAL TEACHING IN 1 CLEMENT: UNITY, LOVE, AND SOCIAL OBLIGATION

First Clement is in many respects a reminder of the proper moral life 'in
Christ'. As such, the letter has been described as 'an extended piece of ethical
paraenesis'.[22] In dealing with the dispute in Corinth, the Roman ἐκκλησία
makes much use of moral reasoning—and naturally so, since the issue at stake
concerns interpersonal relations within the Christ-movement. At the closing
of the letter, the senders provide a kind of summary of its content:

> We have now written to you, brethren, sufficiently touching the things which befit our
> worship, and are most helpful for a virtuous life (εἰς ἐνάρετον βίον) to those who wish
> to guide their steps in piety and righteousness (εὐσεβῶς καὶ δικαίως). For we have
> touched on every aspect (πάντα τόπον) of faith and repentance and true love and self-
> control and sobriety and patience (πίστεως καὶ μετανοίας καὶ γνησίας ἀγάπης καὶ
> ἐγκρατείας καὶ σωφροσύνης καὶ ὑπομονῆς), and reminded you that you are bound to
> please almighty God with holiness in righteousness and truth and long-suffering, and
> to live in concord (ὁμονοοῦντας), bearing no malice, in love and peace with eager
> gentleness (ἐν ἀγάπῃ καὶ εἰρήνῃ μετὰ ἐκτενοῦς ἐπιεικείας), even as our fathers... were
> well-pleasing in their humility (εὐηρέστησαν ταπεινοφρονοῦντες) towards God, the
> Father and Creator, and towards all men ([πρὸς] πάντας ἀνθρώπους).[23]

The summary implies that in its moral teaching 1 Clement is concerned not only
with the Corinthian ἐκκλησία but also with the Christ-movement as a whole.
The 'virtuous life' (ἐνάρετος βίος) detailed in the letter constitutes an identity
marker for all Christ-believers. What this ἐνάρετος βίος embodies is here divided
into several categories, such as love (ἀγάπη), self-control (ἐγκρατεία), sobriety
or moderation (σωφροσύνη), and patience (ὑπομονή). This division should not
be taken too literally, however, because the categories referred to are not
systematically treated as if in a philosophical treatise on ethics. Nor should we
make too much of the senders' claim to have discussed 'every aspect' (πάντα
τόπον) of these categories in the letter. While some of them receive recurring and
somewhat lengthy discussion (e.g. ἀγάπη), others are merely mentioned in
passing. For instance, although the senders assert in 62.2 (cited above) that

---

[22] Donald A. Hagner, *The Use of the Old and New Testaments in Clement of Rome* (NovTSup
34; Leiden: Brill, 1973), 7.
[23] 1 Clem. 62.1–2 (trans. Lake).

earlier in their letter they have given full thought to concepts like σωφροσύνη, this term does not actually occur in previous chapters, only later.[24]

Nevertheless, there is little reason to question the senders' claim and/or belief of having more or less expressed their own understanding of 'what is most helpful for a virtuous life'. At the same time, it is important to keep in mind that in any (real) letter, like 1 Clement, both the choice and weight of specific topics are contingent upon its occasion, purpose, and intended audience. In 1 Clement the moral teaching is largely guided by the purpose of the letter as a plea for unity in Corinth. Prominent virtues advocated in this 'request for peace and harmony' include therefore those that above all are thought to promote and uphold unity. Most importantly, these are virtues like humility (ταπεινοφροσύνη),[25] submission (ὑποταγή),[26] and obedience (ὑπακοή).[27] Indeed, it has been claimed that, for the senders of 1 Clement, ταπεινοφροσύνη 'lies at the heart of what Christian life and community are to be', and that it is 'the cardinal virtue' of the letter.[28] While this is certainly possible, one has to take into account the fact that the virtues ταπεινοφροσύνη, ὑποταγή, and ὑπακοή are all closely tied to the local situation addressed in the letter, and therefore not necessarily applicable as 'cardinal' virtues in all Christ-believing communities. To take but a few examples of the local contingency of the virtues: at the beginning of the letter the senders praise the recipients for their conduct before the strife: '...and you walked according to the ordinances of God, submitting yourselves (ὑποτασσόμενοι) to your leaders and rendering all due honour to those who were older among you'.[29] Further, 'all of you used to be humble in mind (ἐταπεινοφρονεῖτε), not arrogant in the least, being submissive (ὑποτασσόμενοι) rather than forcing submission (ὑποτάσσοντες)'.[30] But to those responsible for the (current) faction, the senders write: 'Be subject to the presbyters (ὑποτάγητε τοῖς πρεσβυτέροις) ... Learn to be submissive (μάθετε ὑποτάσσεσθαι)'.[31] And at the closing of the letter the addressees are urged to 'assume a position of obedience (τῆς

---

[24] i.e. in 64.1. To be sure, σωφροσύνη has its cognates prior to 62.2, but only in 1.2 (σώφρων) and 1.3 (σωφρονεῖν), neither instance of which includes specific treatment of the concept itself.

[25] 1 Clem. 21.8; 30.8; 31.4; 44.3; 56.1; 58.2. Cf. ταπεινοφρονεῖν (2.1; 13.1, 3; 16.1, 2, 17; 17.2; 30.3; 48.6; 62.2), ταπεινόφρων (19.1; 38.2). Cf. also the cognates ταπεινοῦν (18.7; 19.1; 59.3), ταπεινός (30.2; 55.6; 59.3, 4), ταπείνωσις (16.7; 53.2; 55.6). According to Bowe, *Church*, 112, this latter word group (ταπειν-) refers to the *state* or *condition* of 'being low' or 'humble', whereas the former group (ταπεινοφρ-) is used to refer to the *attitude* of 'humility'. See also Walter Grundmann, 'ταπεινός κτλ', *TDNT* 8: 1–26.

[26] 1 Clem. 1.3; 37.5. Cf. ὑποτάσσειν (1.3; 2.1; 20.1; 34.5; 38.1; 57.1–2; 61.1), ὑποτεταγμένως (37.2).

[27] 1 Clem. 9.3; 10.2, 7; 19.1; 63.1. Cf. ὑπακούειν (7.6; 9.1; 57.4; 58.1), ὑπήκοος (10.1; 13.3; 14.1; 60.4; 63.2).

[28] Bowe, *Church*, 112–21 (115, 118).   [29] 1 Clem. 1.3.   [30] 1 Clem. 2.1.

[31] 1 Clem. 57.1–2.

ὑπακοῆς).… For you will make us joyful and happy if you become obedient (ὑπήκοοι) to what we have written through the Holy Spirit.'[32]

There is little doubt that the virtue ταπεινοφροσύνη (together with ὑποταγή and ὑπακοή) is of cardinal significance for the argument of the letter as a whole. But it need not tell us much more than that. It does not have to imply that, according to the letter's author, this is *the* cardinal virtue that in general and in all circumstances 'lies at the heart of Christian life and community'. Rather, ταπεινοφροσύνη (together with ὑποταγή and ὑπακοή) receives additional weight in 1 Clement on account of the letter's occasion and purpose.[33] The author might have (and certainly may have) presented some entirely different virtue as the cardinal virtue in a different letter to a different community in a different situation. In other words, the virtues above are drawn from a more general moral teaching of Christ-believing communities and suited to the Corinthian situation by the Roman ἐκκλησία.

This assessment is further strengthened by the letter's particular selection of primary vices: things that are presented as such in 1 Clement are vices that bring about and characterize *dis*unity. Notably prominent are faction (στάσις),[34] strife (ἔρις),[35] and schism (σχίσμα).[36] Precisely as the virtues ταπεινοφροσύνη, ὑποταγή, and ὑπακοή, these vices mostly occur where the Corinthian conflict is (expressly) under discussion. A good example is found in 54.2, where a voice is given to a certain imaginary addressee in Corinth: 'If I am the cause of faction (στάσις), strife (ἔρις), and schisms (σχίσματα), I will depart; I will go wherever you wish and do what is commanded by the congregation. Only allow the flock of Christ to be at peace with the presbyters who have been appointed.'[37] These words of an ideal, repenting addressee express the main purpose of the letter at the same time as they include all three terms for vices. Other notable vices in the letter include jealousy (ζῆλος),[38] envy (φθόνος),[39] arrogance (ἀλαζονεία),[40] and haughtiness (ὑπερηφανία),[41] all of which

---

[32] 1 Clem. 63.1–2.

[33] As, indeed, even Bowe seems to recognize: 'Clement's choice of ταπεινοφροσύνη as the cardinal virtue, therefore, is wholly conditioned by how he perceives and characterizes the cause of the crisis in Corinth' (*Church*, 118).

[34] 1 Clem. 1.1; 2.6; 3.2; 14.2; 46.9; 51.1; 54.2; 57.1; 63.1. Cf. στασιάζειν (4.12; 43.2; 46.7; 47.6; 49.5; 51.3; 55.1).

[35] 1 Clem. 3.2; 5.5; 6.4; 9.1; 14.2; 44.1; 54.2.   [36] 1 Clem. 2.6; 46.5, 9; 49.5; 54.2.

[37] 1 Clem. 54.2: [εἰπάτω·] εἰ δι' ἐμὲ στάσις καὶ ἔρις καὶ σχίσματα, ἐκχωρῶ, ἄπειμι, οὗ ἐὰν βούλησθε, καὶ ποιῶ τὰ προστασσόμενα ὑπὸ τοῦ πλήθους· μόνον τὸ ποίμνιον τοῦ Χριστοῦ εἰρηνευέτω μετὰ τῶν καθεσταμένων πρεσβυτέρων.

[38] 1 Clem. 3.2, 4; 4.7–13; 5.2–5; 6; 9.1; 14.1; 39.7; 43.2; 45.4; 63.2.

[39] 1 Clem. 3.2; 4.7, 13; 5.2.

[40] 1 Clem. 13.1; 14.1; 16.2; 21.5; 35.5. Cf. ἀλαζονεύειν (2.1; 38.2), ἀλαζών (57.2).

[41] 1 Clem. 16.2; 30.1; 35.5. Cf. ὑπερήφανος (30.2; 49.5; 57.2; 59.3). Specific vice lists occur in 30.1; 35.5.

frequently occur in Graeco-Roman moral discourses but are easily applied to the topic of disunity in 1 Clement.

All this implies that, when assessing the moral teaching of 1 Clement, one has to take into account that those virtues and vices that are presented as cardinal may receive their position as such mainly from the local situation addressed in the letter.

But there are other prominent virtues in 1 Clement in addition to the three leading ones listed above. There are also those that seem less contingent upon the specific situation in Corinth, such as love (ἀγάπη),[42] gentleness (ἐπιείκεια),[43] doing good (ἀγαθοποιΐα),[44] hospitality (φιλοξενία),[45] and brotherly love (φιλαδελφία),[46] along with a number of other exemplary qualities and dispositions commonly praised in early Christian literature.[47] Of these it is only ἀγάπη that occupies a position on par with the leading triad of virtues, albeit in a somewhat different way (as we shall see).

When it is first brought up explicitly as such, the virtue of ἀγάπη appears as a component of a more general moral teaching. Following an exhortation to the audience to 'do things that are good and virtuous before God in harmony' (τὰ καλὰ καὶ εὐάρεστα ἐνώπιον αὐτοῦ ποιῶμεν μεθ᾽ ὁμονοίας),[48] the Roman ἐκκλησία makes reference to certain precepts of how to conduct oneself towards 'our leaders' and the elderly (τοὺς πρεσβυτέρους), and of how to instruct and guide the youth and 'our wives'. It is in the latter two cases where the virtue of ἀγάπη occurs. As a general rule, wives should exhibit 'a character of purity, worthy of love (ἀξιαγάπητον)' and 'show their love (ἀγάπην) not with partiality'. And children are to 'partake of the discipline that is in Christ' (τῆς ἐν Χριστῷ παιδείας μεταλαμβανέτωσαν), of which three things are specifically mentioned: ταπεινοφροσύνη, ἀγάπη, and φόβος (τοῦ θεοῦ).[49] Both instances of moral instruction involve issues of general concern.

But ἀγάπη is most extensively treated in chapters 49–50, where the word itself (the noun) occurs no fewer than nineteen times. These two chapters

---

[42] 1 Clem. 21.7, 8; 33.1; 49–50; 51.2; 53.5; 54.1; 55.5; 56.4; 62.2. Cf. ἀγαπᾶν (3.1; 15.4; 18.6; 22.2; 29.1; 59.2, 3), ἀγαπητός (1.1; 7.1; 8.5; 12.8; 16.17; 21.1; 24.1, 2; 35.1, 5; 36.1; 43.6; 47.6; 50.1, 5; 53.1; 56.2, 16).

[43] 1 Clem. 13.1; 30.8; 56.1; 58.2; 62.2. Cf. ἐπιεικής (1.2; 29.1).

[44] 1 Clem. 2.2, 7; 33.1; 34.2.   [45] 1 Clem. 1.2; 10.7; 11.1; 12.1. Cf. φιλόξενος (12.3).

[46] 1 Clem. 47.5; 48.1.

[47] e.g. ἐγκράτεια (35.2; 38.2; 62.2; 64.1; cf. 30.3), ὑπομονή (5.5, 7; 62.2; 64.1; cf. 45.8), μακροθυμία (13.1; 62.2; 64.1; cf. 19.3; 49.5), μετάνοια (7.4–6; 8.1–2, 5; 57.1; 62.2; cf. 7.7; 8.3), πραΰτης (21.7; 30.8; 61.2). Specific lists of virtues are found in 35.2; 62.2; 64.1. Needless to say, there are also those that have more to do with religiosity than morality per se: εὐσέβεια (1.2; 11.1; 15.1; 32.4; cf. 2.3; 50.3; 61.2; 62.1), πίστις (1.2; 3.4; 5.6; 6.2; 10.7; 12.1, 8; 22.1; 26.1; 27.3; 31.2; 32.4; 35.2; 42.5; 55.6; 58.2; 60.4; 62.2; 64.1; cf. 9.4; 10.1; 12.7; 17.5; 27.1; 34.4; 35.5; 39.4; 42.3, 4; 43.1; 48.5; 60.1; 62.3; 63.3).

[48] 1 Clem. 21.1 (trans. mine).   [49] 1 Clem. 21.6–8.

constitute in effect a panegyrical commentary on ἀγάπη. Concise as it is, the commentary relates to ἀγάπη divine as well as human, general as well as particular. It tells of ἀγάπη as that very principle that 'binds us to God' (49.5), whose ἀγάπη, in turn, no one is able to explain (v. 2). The 'greatness of its beauty' is ineffable (v. 3; cf. 50.1–2). According to the author of 1 Clement, ἀγάπη is the term by which the proper relation between human ('us') and divine is described. It is through love that 'our' sins are forgiven by God (50.5; cf. 49.5),[50] and it was 'because of the love he had for us' that Jesus Christ gave his life 'for us' (49.6). Correspondingly, the ones who have 'love in Christ' should follow his commandments (v. 1). But no matter what one does, if it lacks ἀγάπη, it can never be pleasing (εὐάρεστον) to God (v. 5; cf. 50.5). Love of others and of God is thus a natural—*the* natural—response to God's own love for 'us'.

Thus far we have treated the general aspect of ἀγάπη in the passage. More particular is its apparent application to the Corinthian situation. In 49.5 ἀγάπη is associated with some accompanying virtues and contrasted with several vices: 'love bears all things and endures all things. There is nothing vulgar in love, nothing haughty (ὑπερήφανον). Love has no *schism* (σχίσμα), love creates no *faction* (οὐ στασιάζει), love does all things *in harmony* (ἐν ὁμονοίᾳ).' It is hardly a coincidence that ἀγάπη is here contrasted precisely with two of the letter's three primary vices, 'schism' and 'faction', the choice and weight of which, as we have seen, was mainly occasioned by the specific situation addressed. So also with 'harmony', for which the letter itself is in fact a plea. The message is of course that the individuals who are responsible for the strife in Corinth lack love. They do not have 'love in Christ' (cf. v. 1). Otherwise there would be no schism and faction, only harmony. Furthermore, it is strongly implied that since 'everyone chosen by God (πάντες οἱ ἐκλεκτοὶ τοῦ θεοῦ) has been perfected in love' (v. 5), the individuals concerned bear a risk of being cut off from God's grace.[51] After all, apart from love there is nothing that pleases God (49.5). The 'blessed' ones are those who keep 'God's commandments (τὰ προστάγματα τοῦ θεοῦ) in the harmony of love (ἐν ὁμονοίᾳ ἀγάπης)' (50.5), again combining ἀγάπη and ὁμόνοια. Those responsible for the faction, on the other hand, do not follow the commandments of Christ (τὰ τοῦ Χριστοῦ παραγγέλματα) because they lack the prerequisite 'love in Christ' (49.1). In a subsequent passage it is pointed out to the 'leaders

---

[50] 1 Clem. 50.5: . . . εἰς τὸ ἀφεθῆναι ἡμῖν δι' ἀγάπης τὰς ἁμαρτίας ('. . . that our sins may be forgiven us through love'). Interestingly, 49.5 includes exactly the same citation from Prov 10.12 (ἀγάπη καλύπτει πλῆθος ἁμαρτιῶν) as 1 Pet 4.8 (discussed in Chapter 7), but appears to interpret it somewhat differently, i.e. with reference to *God's* forgiveness of 'our' sins, instead of 'our' forgiveness of the sins of others (as I take the citation to mean in 1 Pet 4.8).

[51] cf. also 1 Clem. 50.3; 59.1.

of the faction and dissension' (ἀρχηγοὶ στάσεως καὶ διχοστασίας) that 'those who conduct themselves with reverential awe and love (μετὰ φόβου καὶ ἀγάπης) prefer to undergo torture themselves than to have their neighbours (τοὺς πλησίον) do so. They would rather have condemnation fall on themselves than on the unity that has been nobly and justly delivered over to us (τῆς παραδεδομένης ἡμῖν καλῶς καὶ δικαίως ὁμοφωνίας).'[52] And when the senders burst out in acclamation, "Ω μεγάλης ἀγάπης,[53] they proceed by posing the following (rhetorical) questions: 'Who, therefore, among you is noble (γενναῖος)? Or compassionate (εὔσπλαγχνος)? Or filled with love (πεπληροφορημένος ἀγάπης)?'[54] Their own answer has in part already been cited above: 'Let that one say: "If I am the cause of faction, strife, and schisms, I will depart…" The one who does this will have made himself eminent in Christ and will be welcomed everywhere.'[55]

In this way ἀγάπη is adapted to the local issue confronted in 1 Clement. But what is particularly noteworthy is the fact that, unlike the triad of virtues named above, ἀγάπη receives specific discussion as a concept, especially with respect to the relationship between human and divine. That is the difference I mentioned above between the author's treatment of ἀγάπη and the three virtues of ταπεινοφροσύνη, ὑποταγή, and ὑπακοή. The first is treated as a virtue of a more general kind, as a concept of more breadth.

The letter provides hardly any concrete, practical examples of ἀγάπη as a virtue. Sometimes the act of 'loving' comes close to being equated simply with doing good, as in 33.1 where the senders write: 'What then shall we do, brothers? Shall we grow idle and not do what is good (ἀργήσωμεν ἀπὸ τῆς ἀγαθοποιΐας)? Shall we abandon our (acts of) love (ἐγκαταλίπωμεν τὴν ἀγάπην)?' To these questions they themselves provide the answer: no, 'instead, we should hasten with fervour and zeal to complete every good work (πᾶν ἔργον ἀγαθὸν ἐπιτελεῖν)'. Here the phrases to 'do what is good', to 'love', and to 'complete every good work' really say the same thing. Similarly, in 54.1 the state of being 'filled with love' (πεπληροφορημένος ἀγάπης) equals the character of being 'noble' (γενναῖος) and 'compassionate' (εὔσπλαγχνος). But, on the whole, the letter does not attempt to define the concept of 'love' in specific, practical terms. It is the practical *effects* of love that are the focus of attention. This is because ἀγάπη in 1 Clement expresses a disposition of mind, a subjective motivation of the Christ-believer that, according to the author, is a prerequisite for proper conduct. As it is expressed in the letter itself, those who have love in Christ 'should do what Christ commanded', and 'apart from

---

[52] 1 Clem. 51.1–2.   [53] 1 Clem. 53.5 ('O great love!').
[54] 1 Clem. 54.1.   [55] 1 Clem. 54.2–3.

love nothing is pleasing to God'.[56] All deeds must be done on the basis of ἀγάπη.

Immediately preceding the panegyric on ἀγάπη in chapters 49–50 the senders of 1 Clement urge each and every addressee to 'seek the common good of all and not his own benefit' (ζητεῖν τὸ κοινωφελὲς πᾶσιν, καὶ μὴ τὸ ἑαυτοῦ).[57] Judging from 1 Clement, this attitude is evidently important to the Roman ἐκκλησία, the spokesmen of which find reason to praise the Corinthian readers for formerly struggling 'on behalf of the whole brotherhood' (ὑπὲρ πάσης τῆς ἀδελφότητος).[58] The character of the 'brotherhood' as a unified whole, and the need for various roles with mutual obligations within that whole, is illustrated by likening it, first, to an army, and then to the human body (chs. 37–8). With the Roman army serving as a model, the author argues that in order for the whole to function properly not all can be leaders and commanders-in-chief. There are those who are leaders—of different degrees, to be sure—and there are those who are subject to the leaders—also of different degrees—but each does his own duty in accordance with his respective position within the whole.[59] And there is a reciprocal relationship between these positions, according to 1 Clement: 'The great (οἱ μεγάλοι) cannot exist without the small (οἱ μικροί), nor the small without the great; there is a certain mixture (σύγκρασις) among all, and herein lies the advantage.'[60] To elaborate on this latter point, the metaphor of the human body is brought in as a further explanation:

Take our own body (σῶμα). The head is nothing without the feet, just as the feet are nothing without the head. And our body's most insignificant parts (τὰ δὲ ἐλάχιστα μέλη τοῦ σώματος ἡμῶν) are necessary and useful for the whole (ἀναγκαῖα καὶ εὔχρηστά εἰσιν ὅλῳ τῷ σώματι). But all parts work together in subjection to a single order (πάντα συνπνεῖ καὶ ὑποταγῇ μιᾷ χρῆται), to keep the whole body healthy [or: safe] (εἰς τὸ σώζεσθαι ὅλον τὸ σῶμα).[61]

Taken together with the preceding analogy to the army, the 'body' symbolizes, of course, the ἐκκλησία as a whole (or all the ἐκκλησίαι), whereas the 'head' represents its leaders ('the great'), and the 'feet' and the 'most insignificant parts' of the body stand for members of lower ranks ('the small'). This seems clear from the comparison with different roles and ranks within the Roman army. It is also clear that the analogy serves at least in part as an argument in favour of re-establishing the leadership and authority of the former (elder) presbyters in Corinth. However, while it is unmistakably occasioned by the

---

[56] 1 Clem. 49.1, 5.   [57] 1 Clem. 48.6 (trans. Lake).
[58] 1 Clem. 2.4; cf. 47.5; 48.1, with reference to their once famous φιλαδελφία. Cf. also 1 Pet 2.17; 5.9, where we have the word ἀδελφότης as *hapax legomena* in the whole NT.
[59] 1 Clem. 37.3.   [60] 1 Clem. 37.4 (trans. Lake).   [61] 1 Clem. 37.5.

local situation addressed in the letter, the argument nevertheless draws on general principles and describes the ideal structure of Christ-believing communities. Whereas the ideal structure accentuates not only the reciprocal dependence of different positions and roles within the communities but also the proper and necessary order of authority within them, we can see in a subsequent use of the metaphor of the body that the question of authority in this ideal structure is strongly qualified by emphasis on the aspect of mutuality: 'Why do we mangle and mutilate the members of Christ (μέλη τοῦ Χριστοῦ) and create factions in our own body (τὸ σῶμα τὸ ἴδιον)? Why do we come to such a pitch of madness as to forget that we are members of one another (μέλη ἀλλήλων)?'[62] Factions within the 'body' are still under discussion, to be sure, but the issue is not who in particular is the 'head' or who are the 'feet'. Rather, the primary argument here against factions is that Christ-believers are all 'members of Christ' and 'members of one another'. The principles of authority and mutuality go hand in hand.

This brings us to an important aspect of the moral teaching in 1 Clement, which is nicely encapsulated in the following sentence (38.1): 'Let each person be subject to his neighbour, in accordance with the gracious gift he has received' (ὑποτασσέσθω ἕκαστος τῷ πλησίον αὐτοῦ, καθὼς ἐτέθη ἐν τῷ χαρίσματι αὐτοῦ). A further explanation follows:

Let the one who is strong take care of the weak (ὁ ἰσχυρὸς τημελείτω τὸν ἀσθενῆ); and let the weak show due respect (ἐντρεπέσθω) to the strong. Let the wealthy provide what is needed to the poor (ὁ πλούσιος ἐπιχορηγείτω τῷ πτωχῷ), and let the poor offer thanks to God, since he has given him someone to supply his need. Let the one who is wise (ὁ σοφός) show forth wisdom not through words but through good deeds (ἔργοις ἀγαθοῖς).[63]

Three things require special notice here. First, it would be a mistake to infer that the passage encourages radical social change. It does not. It advocates no such thing as social or economic equality. The wealthy are neither urged to cast aside their possessions and become poor, nor to distribute their wealth evenly between fellow Christ-believers. 'Clement's' aim is not to eliminate all social inequality or to suggest some sort of egalitarianism.

Second, according to this passage, the ideal socioeconomic structure of Christ-believing communities is shaped by mutual obligations in which members contribute according to their capacity. The service called for is not unilateral (from rich to poor). The poor person is still obliged (at least) to give thanks to God for having 'given him someone [i.e. the wealthy] to supply his need', and the weak is still required to return the care of the strong with

---

[62] 1 Clem. 46.7.   [63] 1 Clem. 38.2.

'due respect'. This means, in other words, that each person (ἕκαστος) should be 'subject to his neighbour, in accordance with the gracious gift he has received', as the exhortation in 38.1 expressed. This is a quite conventional Roman perspective that mirrors the social system of patron–client relationships, one condition and demand of which was an acceptance of traditional social distinctions. The author of 1 Clement appears to accept such distinctions and to advocate a social system within the Christ-movement based on characteristic Roman patronage.[64]

Third, the series of exhortations in 38.2 is a good example of how important the social dimension is to the moral teaching of the letter. While the obligations are certainly mutual, the main attention is paid to the needs of the weak and the poor. The wealth of the wealthy, the strength of the strong, the wisdom of the wise: all are gracious gifts from God[65] and are to be used for the benefit of the needy within the group in order to 'keep the whole body healthy' (37.5). In a lengthy prayer to God at the closing of the letter (59.3–61.3), the same concern is shown for the needs of those who suffer from poverty and distress:

Save those of us who are in affliction, show mercy to those who are humble [or: lowly] (τοὺς ταπεινούς), raise those who have fallen, show yourself to those who are in need (τοῖς δεομένοις), heal those who are sick (τοὺς ἀσθενεῖς), set straight those among your people who are going astray. Feed the hungry, ransom our prisoners, raise up the weak (τοὺς ἀσθενοῦντας), encourage the despondent.[66]

These are not just abstract members of the communal 'body' or ill-defined masses of the poor, but real groups of people who are carefully identified according to the misfortune in question: the afflicted, the humble (or lowly), the fallen, the needy, the sick, the hungry, 'our' prisoners, the weak, the despondent.[67] The opposite groups are of course the so-called 'strong', 'the wealthy', and 'the wise',[68] that is, those who are better-off in most respects and are expected to utilize their resources not only for their own benefit but also for 'the common good of all'.[69] Naturally, the ethic of mutual giving and receiving does not work well unless there really *are* some Christ-believers who

---

[64] cf. Jeffers, *Conflict*, 131–4. Jeffers rightly stresses that 'Clement's idea arose not in a vacuum but from the Roman patron–client relationship' (p. 132). He also observes that '1 Clement reflects Roman ideology when it implies that those with power and wealth in the churches have far more to offer the congregation than do their powerless and poor brothers' (p. 134). Cf. also Bakke, 'Concord', 302–15. For further references on the subject of patronage in Graeco-Roman society, see Chapter 5 above.

[65] cf. 1 Clem. 59.3.　　[66] 1 Clem. 59.4.

[67] cf. also 1 Clem. 8.4 (citing Isa 1.16); 15.6 (citing Ps 11.6 [MT 12.5]).

[68] 1 Clem. 38.2 (cited above); cf. 13.1 (citing Jer 9.22 [MT 9.23]).　　[69] 1 Clem. 48.6.

are well-off and some who are 'strong' and 'wise' enough to care for the weak within the group, 'not through words but through good deeds'.[70]

As a further token of the social dimension, it is noteworthy how significant the virtue of hospitality ($\phi\iota\lambda o\xi\epsilon\nu\iota a$) seems to be for the author of 1 Clement. At the very beginning of the letter, in its *captatio benevolentiae*,[71] the senders praise the recipients for their 'character [once] so magnificent in its hospitality' ($\tau\grave{o}$ $\mu\epsilon\gamma a\lambda o\pi\rho\epsilon\pi\grave{\epsilon}s$ $\tau\hat{\eta}s$ $\phi\iota\lambda o\xi\epsilon\nu\iota as$ $\dot{\upsilon}\mu\hat{\omega}\nu$ $\mathring{\eta}\theta os$).[72] Hospitality occurs here in the midst of such weighty virtues and qualities as faith ($\pi\iota\sigma\tau\iota s$), piety ($\epsilon\dot{\upsilon}\sigma\epsilon\beta\epsilon\iota a$), and knowledge ($\gamma\nu\hat{\omega}\sigma\iota s$).[73] No less telling is the fact that when 1 Clement relates the stories of Abraham, Lot, and Rahab in chapters 10–12, their blessing and redemption is said to have resulted from their faith/piety *and hospitality*: 'Because of his faith and hospitality ($\delta\iota\grave{a}$ $\pi\iota\sigma\tau\iota\nu$ $\kappa a\iota$ $\phi\iota\lambda o\xi\epsilon\nu\iota a\nu$), a son was given to [Abraham] in his old age.'[74] 'Because of his hospitality and piety ($\delta\iota\grave{a}$ $\phi\iota\lambda o\xi\epsilon\nu\iota a\nu$ $\kappa a\iota$ $\epsilon\dot{\upsilon}\sigma\epsilon\beta\epsilon\iota a\nu$), Lot was saved out of Sodom.'[75] 'Because of her faith and hospitality ($\delta\iota\grave{a}$ $\pi\iota\sigma\tau\iota\nu$ $\kappa a\iota$ $\phi\iota\lambda o\xi\epsilon\nu\iota a\nu$) Rahab the prostitute was saved from danger.'[76] The virtue gets notable mention even if there are, in the cases of Abraham and Lot, actually no examples given (in 1 Clement) of their hospitality.[77]

Why so much attention to this particular virtue? Two possibilities come immediately to mind. On the one hand, the concern for hospitality may be motivated by the scene in Corinth, perhaps intended to expedite a proper reception of the Roman envoys.[78] However, in that case one might have expected at least some mention of hospitality in the context of the epistolary framework (e.g. among the virtues listed in ch. 64, or indeed anywhere in chs. 63–5), that is, in the very context in which the letter's external circumstances, including issues of envoys and letter carriers, were being discussed. On the other hand, the attention paid to this particular virtue may (also) say something about the Roman $\dot{\epsilon}\kappa\kappa\lambda\eta\sigma\iota a$ itself and its social setting. It may simply be

---

[70] 1 Clem. 38.2. Cf. 30.3.

[71] That is, the opening part in which an effort is made to capture the audience's goodwill.

[72] 1 Clem. 1.2 (trans. Lake).

[73] The concept is even found in the antithesis $\dot{a}\phi\iota\lambda o\xi\epsilon\nu\iota a$ (with a prefixed a: 'inhospitality'; the form is most unusual in ancient Greek literature), in a catalogue that includes such major vices as injustice ($\dot{a}\delta\iota\kappa\iota a$), lawlessness ($\dot{a}\nu o\mu\iota a$), greed ($\pi\lambda\epsilon o\nu\epsilon\xi\iota a$), strife ($\mathring{\epsilon}\rho\iota s$), malice ($\kappa a\kappa o\mathring{\eta}\theta\epsilon\iota a$), hatred of God ($\theta\epsilon o\sigma\tau\upsilon\gamma\iota a$), haughtiness ($\dot{\upsilon}\pi\epsilon\rho\eta\phi a\nu\iota a$), and arrogance ($\dot{a}\lambda a\zeta o\nu\epsilon\iota a$) (1 Clem. 35.5).

[74] 1 Clem. 10.7; cf. Gen 18.   [75] 1 Clem. 11.1; cf. Gen 19.

[76] 1 Clem. 12.1; cf. Josh 2.

[77] Apparently, the author of 1 Clement either knows or simply assumes that the Corinthian readers are well versed in these stories of the book of Genesis. The story of Rahab, on the other hand, is carefully summed up as if it is not taken for granted that the readers are equally familiar with her as an example of hospitality.

[78] See 1 Clem. 63.3; 65.1.

another token of how interwoven 1 Clement is with Roman society and patterns of thought. Hospitality had long been an important aspect of the concept of friendship among the Roman elite. It was considered a privilege of patrons and, as a virtue of civilization, became legalized in several different categories in the *ius hospitii*.[79] As a participant in the Roman system of patronage, the author of 1 Clement may well have been influenced by ideas and examples of hospitality among upper-class Romans.[80] At any rate, hospitality's place in 1 Clement is just one manifestation of many of the significance of the social dimension to the letter's moral teaching.

FROM PAUL TO 'CLEMENT': CONTINUITY AND APPLICATION OF MORAL TEACHING

The apostle Paul is held in great esteem in 1 Clement. So much in fact that when in chapter 5 the apostles Peter and Paul are introduced as examples of endurance in the face of hardships and persecution, it is Paul who receives the focus of attention. To be sure, both of them are described as the 'greatest and most upright pillars' and the 'good apostles' (vv. 2–3), and Peter is certainly praised for his persistence in suffering (v. 4). But, according to 1 Clement, it was Paul—not Peter—who 'pointed the way to the prize for endurance', and it was Paul—and not Peter—who, having 'taught righteousness to the whole world', became 'the greatest example of endurance' (vv. 5–7).

It is clear that the author(s) of 1 Clement knew at least some of Paul's letters. This is certainly true of Paul's First Letter to the Corinthians, which the senders cite explicitly: 'Take up the epistle of that blessed apostle, Paul. What did he write to you at first, at the beginning of his proclamation of the gospel?',[81] i.e. at the beginning of 1 Corinthians. What the apostle had written 'at first' in that letter is then recounted in more detail.[82] Also, the panegyric on ἀγάπη in 1 Clement 49–50 (cf. esp. 49.5) may well be based on Paul's discourse on ἀγάπη in 1 Corinthians 13 (cf. esp. vv. 4–7).[83]

Given that the Roman senders of 1 Clement had such detailed knowledge of a letter that Paul had sent to the Christ-movement in Corinth—they may even

---

[79] Oden, *Welcomed*, 18.   [80] Jeffers, *Conflict*, 127–30.

[81] 1 Clem. 47.1–2: ἀναλάβετε τὴν ἐπιστολὴν τοῦ μακαρίου Παύλου τοῦ ἀποστόλου. τί πρῶτον ὑμῖν ἐν ἀρχῇ τοῦ εὐαγγελίου ἔγραψεν;

[82] 1 Clem. 47.3–4; cf. 1 Cor 1.10–17.

[83] So also Barbara E. Bowe, 'The Rhetoric of Love in Corinth: From Paul to Clement of Rome', in *Common Life in the Early Church: Essays Honoring Graydon F. Snyder* (ed. J. V. Hills et al.; Harrisburg, PA: Trinity, 1998), 255–6; Hagner, *Use*, 200.

have had their own copy of that letter—it can almost be taken for granted that the same was true of his letter to the Romans.[84] This assumption is not merely based on logical inference, for it is strongly supported by a number of features in 1 Clement, two examples of which should suffice for the present purpose.[85] First, Romans 1 is almost certainly cited in 1 Clement 35.5–6. In 35.5 there is clearly an allusion to the catalogue of vices in Romans 1.29–30, several vices of which occur nowhere else in Paul's letters.[86] This is immediately followed in 1 Clement 35.6 by the claim that 'those who do these things are hateful to God', and then, 'not only those who do them, but also those who approve of them' (οὐ μόνον δὲ οἱ πράσσοντες αὐτά, ἀλλὰ καὶ οἱ συνευδοκοῦντες αὐτοῖς), which is practically identical to the latter part of Paul's statement in Romans 1.32: 'they not only do these things, but also approve of those who do them' (οὐ μόνον αὐτὰ ποιοῦσιν, ἀλλὰ καὶ συνευδοκοῦσιν τοῖς πράσσουσιν).

Second, the dialogical style used now and then in 1 Clement, typically through questions such as τί δὲ εἴπωμεν; ('What shall we say?' 18.1) or τί οὖν ποιήσωμεν; ('What then shall we do?' 33.1) and the like,[87] is in all probability influenced by Paul's analogous style in Romans.[88] To take but one example, the interrogative phrase τί γάρ; ('What then?') in 1 Clement 39.4 is quite uncommon in contemporary Greek literature as an independent question.[89] It does not occur in the writings of the New Testament, except on two

---

[84] cf. Hagner, *Use*, 214: 'the original manuscript itself [i.e. of Romans] was probably available to Clement.' As for other Pauline letters, Hagner concludes that the author of 1 Clement probably knew of and used Galatians, Ephesians, Philippians, 1 Timothy, and Titus, and possibly also 2 Corinthians, Colossians, and 2 Timothy (*Use*, 220–37).

[85] For further evidence, see Hagner, *Use*, 216–20.

[86] All but (the last) two vices listed in 1 Clem. 35.5 are present in Rom 1.29–30. These are: ἀδικία, πονηρία, πλεονεξία, ἔρις, κακοήθεια, δόλος, ψιθυριστής/-ισμός, κατάλαλος/-ία, θεοστυγής/-ία, ὑπερήφανος/-ία, ἀλαζών/-ονεία. Whereas several additional vices are listed in Rom 1.29–30, the word order of the two catalogues is nearly identical, and four of these words (κακοήθεια, θεοστυγής, ὑπερήφανος, ἀλαζών) are not mentioned elsewhere in Paul's letters. The two additional vices in 1 Clem. 35.5, κενοδοξία and ἀφιλοξενία, may reflect the senders' view and critique of the situation in Corinth.

[87] cf., e.g., 1 Clem. 35.3 (τίνα οὖν ἄρα...), 5 (πῶς δὲ...); 36.6 (τίνες οὖν...); 39.4 (τί γάρ); 45.6 (τί γὰρ εἴπωμεν). Note, for instance, that the question posed in 33.1 (τί οὖν ποιήσωμεν, ἀδελφοί) is answered by another question which, *à la* Romans, draws a false inference from what precedes, and is then strongly rejected with the negation μηθαμῶς (equivalent to the typical Pauline phrase μὴ γένοιτο).

[88] See esp. Rom 3.1–9, 27–31; 4.1; 6.1–2, 15; 7.7, 13; 8.31; 9.14, 19–20, 30–2; 10.18–19; 11.1, 7, 11.

[89] A *Thesaurus linguae graecae* search (TLG-E) of τί γάρ; as an independent question reveals that in the classical period the phrase was occasionally used by the great tragedians (Aeschylus, Sophocles, Euripides), by Plato, and by Xenophon, and later also by the comedian Menander. However, from the early third century BCE to the late first century CE (i.e. in Hellenistic times before the date of 1 Clement, approximately) it rarely occurs. Needless to say, a search like this has its limits and faults, but it still gives us some idea of the use of this particular phrase in (most of) the Greek literary texts we have access to from antiquity.

occasions in Paul's letters. These are Romans 3.3 and Philippians 1.18, the latter text of which, on the other hand, is not at all characterized by dialogical features. While 1 Corinthians is certainly not devoid of the dialogical style,[90] it is Paul's Letter to the Romans that is particularly characterized by this style; it differs formally from his other letters precisely in that respect.

In short, the evidence of 1 Clement's literary dependence on Romans is so compelling that it seems safe to insist that the burden of proof lies with those who would want to argue otherwise.

There are a number of close affinities between the moral teaching of 1 Clement and that of Romans. The reason, I suggest, is that 1 Clement not only alludes to Paul's letter but uses and interprets it as well. In 1 Clement we see therefore a *direct application* of Paul's moral teaching in Romans. That means also that when 1 Clement was written, Paul's teaching already enjoyed an important place in the Roman ἐκκλησία and had already contributed to the formation of the moral identity of the movement. One such contribution is Paul's proclamation to the Romans of ἀγάπη as the primary virtue. Clearly drawn also from 1 Corinthians, discussions of ἀγάπη in 1 Clement betray that, for the Roman ἐκκλησία, this virtue was already at the core of its moral teaching. Its position as a principal virtue is presupposed in the letter. The panegyric in chapters 49–50, for instance, evidently takes it for granted that ἀγάπη is worthy of such praise and that it is a prerequisite for proper morality. The latter is not argued for, only assumed and argued *from*. To be sure, there is no exact parallel in 1 Clement to Paul's downright command in Romans 13.8 to 'owe no one anything, except to love one another'. Nor is a connection made between the act of loving and fulfilling the (Jewish) Law, as in Romans 13.9 ('Love is the fulfilment of the Law'). But that comes as no surprise since the Law as such is not an issue in 1 Clement—it is nowhere even mentioned in the letter. Moreover, statements like 'apart from love *nothing* is pleasing to God' (49.5), where ἀγάπη is clearly understood as a presupposition for proper conduct, come very close to Paul's teaching in Romans 13.8–10, and may well have been inspired by that teaching in addition to 1 Corinthians 13.

Immediately following the panegyric on love in 1 Clement 49–50 we see an expression of the kind of love spoken of by Paul in Romans: as a part of the larger argument for unity in the Corinthian ἐκκλησία, the author of 1 Clement states that 'those who live in fear and love are willing to undergo torture themselves rather than to have their neighbours do so' (οἱ γὰρ μετὰ φόβου καὶ ἀγάπης πολιτευόμενοι ἑαυτοὺς θέλουσιν μᾶλλον αἰκίαις περιπίπτειν ἢ τοὺς πλησίον).[91] If led by proper φόβος and ἀγάπη, the Corinthians choose

---

[90] See esp. 1 Cor 4.7; 6.15; 7.16; 10.19; 14.15–17, 26; 15.35–6.
[91] 1 Clem. 51.2 (my trans.).

the second place for themselves behind their neighbours. They show themselves willing to place their fellow Christ-believers first. We find corresponding ideas of self-sacrifice in Romans 14–15, where Paul details some basic ways in which to put one's 'love of neighbour' in practice, and thus to imitate Christ Jesus himself. As we saw in Chapter 6 on Romans, Paul's purpose was in part to argue for the unity of the Christ-believing community, and, as a part of that argument, he urged the 'strong' to put the needs of the 'weak' in first place.[92]

It is clear that, on the surface at least, the virtue of ἀγάπη does not have quite the same prominence in 1 Clement as in Romans (not to mention 1 Peter). However, there is little doubt that ἀγάπη is essential to this author as well, and that in his eyes, too, this particular virtue is basic to proper conduct. But instead of arguing for its prominent place in the moral teaching of the Christ-movement, since it already enjoys such a position, the author focuses more directly on the *effects* of ἀγάπη, especially its social dimension of unity and mutual obligation. And here we can see some inspiration from and application of Paul's teaching in Romans (and probably 1 Corinthians as well). Like the apostle, the author of 1 Clement uses the metaphor of the 'body' to explain to his recipients that they all have different positions and functions within the community as a whole. According to 1 Clement, the differences themselves are entirely natural with respect to the structure of the whole, but it is necessary to recognize and always have in mind the mutual dependence of all positions, of all the members of the 'body', if the Christ-believing community is to function properly—πάντα συνπνεῖ.[93]

In order for the community to function as a unified whole, each and every member needs to be willing to be subject to his neighbour, states the author. He adds, however, that this must be done 'in accordance with the gracious gift (χάρισμα) he has received', that is, according to each person's position and ability. Those within the community who are 'strong' and/or wealthy must be willing to take care of and provide for the 'weak' and poor.[94] We see here an echo of Paul's argument in Romans 12–15. Precisely as Paul in Romans 12.4–8, 'Clement' moves from the body metaphor to the members' various χαρίσματα and mutual dependence. The author also applies the 'strong/weak' terminology used by Paul in Romans 14–15,[95] although there are, of

---

[92] Rom 15.1–3.   [93] 'All parts [of the body] work together', 1 Clem. 37.5.

[94] 1 Clem. 38.1–2.

[95] As observed earlier in this study (in Chapter 6), unlike many commentators today, the first-century Roman senders of 1 Clement did not take Romans 14–15 to be a discourse on 'Jewish Christian' and 'Gentile Christian' relations. There is actually no trace at all of such a reading in this earliest extant interpretation of Romans, written, it seems, only thirty-five to forty years after the reception of Paul's letter.

course, some semantic differences between the uses of the terms in Romans and 1 Clement. Whereas Paul has primarily 'the weak in faith' in mind,[96] the author of 1 Clement virtually equates 'weak' with 'poor'.[97] Specific types of behaviour are not in view in 1 Clement (as in Romans), but specific social or socio-economic groups. Hence, if the author of 1 Clement makes use of Paul's terminology in Romans of the 'strong' and the 'weak', which is likely, he prefers to focus on its economic rather than its religious aspects. Common to both letters, on the other hand, is the very attention brought to those who are worse-off in the Christ-believing community. This prominence given to the less fortunate is well reflected in 1 Clement 59.4, where the author issues a prayer to God specifically on behalf of the variously distressed groups of Christ-believers. In its requirement that the 'weak' and poor are to *repay* the 'strong' and rich in forms of 'due respect' and 'thanksgiving', however, 1 Clement follows no example from Paul's moral teaching in Romans.

It seems likely that the attitude expressed in 1 Clement towards civic authorities is partly based on Paul's discourse in Romans 13. While the author of the former is certainly influenced and motivated by other sources of inspiration from his own historical context, we see in these two texts a striking line of continuity within Roman Christianity. Significantly, the topic of the Roman authorities is the most conspicuous point of correspondence between 1 Clement and the roughly contemporary 1 Peter, and on that point they betray remarkable agreement.[98]

In sum, on the choice of terms relating to issues of unity and harmony, on the cardinal position of the virtue ἀγάπη, on the attention to and underlining of mutual social obligations, and on the proper attitude towards the civic authorities, 1 Clement is a close follow-up to Paul's Letter to the Romans. On the whole, then, the moral teaching in the Roman text of 1 Clement consti-tutes in many respects a direct continuation of the moral teaching that the apostle Paul sent to fellow Christ-believers in Rome around the middle of the first century CE.

---

[96] cf. Rom 14.1: τὸν δὲ ἀσθενοῦντα τῇ πίστει προσλαμβάνεσθε.

[97] So also Jeffers, *Conflict*, 132.

[98] But note that the view expressed in 1 Peter of civic authorities follows more closely the 'passive' attitude of Paul.

Part III

Roman Christianity and Roman Stoicism: A Comparison

9

Moral Teachings Compared

Having identified and discussed the basic features of the moral teachings of Roman Stoicism and Roman Christianity, we are now in a position to compare the two. Due to the nature of the sources themselves, that is, their varying volumes and forms,[1] the comparison is most conveniently treated thematically. Since Paul's moral teaching in Romans served in many ways as a model for the authors of 1 Peter and 1 Clement, Paul's text will have a prominent place in this investigation.

I have chosen five main themes that are most to the point for the present study and most relevant to the content of the sources themselves. The themes are discussed under the following headings: (1) 'A Particular Way of Life as Proper Worship', (2) 'Clothing Oneself with Christ and Seeking to be a Socrates', (3) 'Mutual Love and Care', (4) 'Non-Retaliation and "Love of Enemies"', and (5) 'The Social Dimension'. The question of the 'ethical scope' of the moral teachings will be treated separately in Chapter 10.

A PARTICULAR WAY OF LIFE AS PROPER WORSHIP

We have seen in Part II above that morality was integral to Christian identity. All three writings discussed there, written by and to Christ-believers, empha-size that a certain moral attitude and behaviour are an essential component of belonging to the followers of and believers in Jesus Christ. All three writings testify as well to the belief that a certain moral attitude and behaviour is *the* proper response to the acts of God through Jesus.[2] The Christ-believers' love of one another is—or should be—the natural response to God's own love for them.[3] In fact, according to these writings, correct moral action is in itself a way to worship God.

---

[1] As explained in the general introduction to this study.
[2] e.g. Rom 12.1–2; 15.7; 1 Pet 1.13–16, 22; 2.1; 1 Clem. 49.1–2; 62.2.
[3] cf. also Rom 5.1–11; 8.38–9.

Few texts express this aspect of the religion so well as Romans 12.1–2. Paul here defines the audience's 'reasonable worship' (λογικὴ λατρεία) in terms of an 'offering' of their bodies as a 'living sacrifice' (θυσία ζῶσα) to God (v. 1). That is, according to Paul, the proper way for the readers to reverence God and execute their faith is to abandon their previous manners (cf. 1.18–32) and totally devote themselves to a new way of life.[4] Such an 'offering' is a '*living sacrifice*', and if properly performed it is 'holy and acceptable to God'. Paul alludes again to this 'offering' of the audience in 15.15–16 (then with the word προσφορά), when he speaks of his own role as a 'minister of Christ Jesus to the gentiles in the priestly service of the good news of God, so that the offering of the gentiles may be acceptable, sanctified by the holy spirit'.[5] According to this thought, Paul is the 'priest' who, through his verbal 'reminder' (ὡς ἐπαναμιμνῄσκων ὑμᾶς, v. 15), effects and brings forth this προσφορά of the Roman gentile audience. Their worship of God consists to a large extent in fulfilling the moral demands of which Paul's teaching is a reminder.

Similarly, the author of 1 Peter speaks of his audience as a 'spiritual house' made of 'living stones' (λίθοι ζῶντες), and as a 'holy priesthood' offering 'spiritual sacrifices (πνευματικὰς θυσίας) acceptable to God' (2.5). Here, too, the addressees' 'sacrifices' are largely seen as 'living offerings' presented through proper morality. And in 1 Clement 'the things which befit our worship (τῇ θρησκείᾳ ἡμῶν)' are, in more general terms, clearly those things that at the same time are 'most helpful for a virtuous life (εἰς ἐνάρετον βίον)', and with which the addressees are 'bound to please (εὐαρεστεῖν) almighty God' (62.1–2), namely, proper moral deeds. As a matter of fact, all three writings stress that, rather than observing particular ritual ceremonies, the most important kind of worship is to follow God's directions for a particular way of life.[6]

We see this point of view in the Stoic sources as well. While Stoic ideas of the deity certainly differ from Christian ones in many respects—indeed the variations can be considerable within Stoicism alone—the implications of the vertical dimension (god–human, human–god) for the horizontal dimension

---

[4] cf. also Rom 6.4: οὕτως καὶ ἡμεῖς ἐν καινότητι ζωῆς περιπατήσωμεν ('so we too might walk in newness of life'); 6.6: ὁ παλαιὸς ἡμῶν ἄνθρωπος συνεσταυρώθη ('our old self was crucified with him', i.e. with Christ) (trans. NRSV).

[5] Rom 15.16: [εἰς τὸ εἶναί με] λειτουργὸν Χριστοῦ Ἰησοῦ εἰς τὰ ἔθνη, ἱερουργοῦντα τὸ εὐαγγέλιον τοῦ θεοῦ, ἵνα γένηται ἡ προσφορὰ τῶν ἐθνῶν εὐπρόσδεκτος, ἡγιασμένη ἐν πνεύματι ἁγίῳ.

[6] Note, however, the strong emphasis in 1 Clement 40–1 on the cultic service, especially in the temple of Jerusalem—which in itself is very interesting considering the (probable) date of 1 Clement, i.e. some twenty-five years after the destruction of the temple, and that this is a Christian writing (cf., e.g., the different attitude to the temple service in the roughly contemporary Hebrews).

(human–human) are nevertheless quite similar. In both cases, ethics and morality have a *theological* foundation, and the end result for human relations is strikingly similar, as are the ideas of proper worship of the deity. Needless to say, the Roman Stoics took for granted the traditional Roman ways of venerating the gods, including customary sacrificial rites,[7] but their conception of what counted as *real* service to the deity, that is, what *really* mattered to God, was quite another: 'The honour that is paid to the gods lies, not in the victims for sacrifice, though they be fat and glitter with gold, but in the upright and holy desire (*recta ac pia voluntate*) of the worshippers', Seneca states. 'Good men, therefore, are pleasing to the gods with an offering of meal and gruel; the bad, on the other hand, do not escape impiety although they dye the altars with streams of blood.'[8] It is precisely as with a gift: it is not the gift itself that truly matters, but the will and intention of the giver.[9] Moreover, according to Seneca, 'precepts are commonly given as to how the gods should be worshipped.... But God is worshipped by those who truly know Him.' For 'although a man hear what limit he should observe in sacrifice, and how far he should recoil from burdensome superstitions, he will never make sufficient progress until he has conceived a right idea of God'.[10] Hence, when Seneca proceeds by posing the question, 'Would you win over the gods?' the answer is: 'Then be a good man! Whoever imitates them, is worshipping them sufficiently (*satis*).'[11] In Seneca's opinion, then, proper worship 'does not consist in slaughtering fattened bulls, or in hanging up offerings of gold or silver, or in pouring coins into a temple treasury; rather does it consist in a will that is reverent and upright (*pia et recta voluntate*)'.[12]

Corresponding ideas of particular ways of life as a proper and sufficient worship of the deity were actually quite common among Graeco-Roman moralists of the day.[13] According to our sources, neither Musonius nor Epictetus was as critical of traditional cultic worship as was their fellow Stoic Seneca.[14] But it is nonetheless clear that for them, too, the most important way to serve God is to pursue the morally good. Above anything

---

[7] A useful overview of sacrificial cults in the Graeco-Roman world is found in Klauck, *Religious Context*, 12–42.

[8] *Ben.* 1.6.3. Cf. 4.25.1.   [9] cf. *Ben.* 1.6.1.

[10] *Ep.* 95.47: *Quomodo sint di colendi, solet praecipi.... [Sed] deum colit qui novit.... Audiat licet, quem modum servare in sacrificiis debeat, quam procul resilire a molestis superstitionibus, numquam satis profectum erit, nisi qualem debet deum mente conceperit.*

[11] *Ep.* 95.50: *Vis deos propitiare? Bonus esto. Satis illos coluit, quisquis imitatus est.*

[12] *Ep.* 115.5.

[13] See Johannes Behm, 'θύω κτλ', *TDNT* 3: 186–9; Franz-Josef Ortkemper, *Leben aus dem Glauben: Christliche Grundhaltungen nach Römer 12–13* (NTAbh 14; Münster: Aschendorff, 1980), 30–1.

[14] cf. Musonius 20.126.26–30; Epictetus, *Diss.* 1.19.24–5; 3.21.12–16. In 2.18.19–21, however, Epictetus seems to downplay the real value of cultic worship (cf. also 1.4.31–2; 1.22.15–16).

else, they claim, the proper service is to obey 'God's law' which 'bids man be good'.[15] It is to endeavour continually to imitate God as the ultimate moral being,[16] and thus be καλὸς καὶ ἀγαθός (i.e. a 'good and excellent person').[17] Whereas Epictetus does not share Seneca's highly critical stance towards traditional worship, he seems to agree that it is (sometimes) sufficient to be a morally good person. Quoting Plato's *Laws* where Plato urges his readers (among other things) to go and offer an expiatory sacrifice to the gods when an evil intention grabs hold of them,[18] Epictetus comments that 'it is enough (ἀρκεῖ) if you only withdraw "to the society of the good and excellent men," and set yourself to comparing your conduct with theirs, whether you take as your model one of the living, or one of the dead [like Socrates]'.[19] Cultic sacrifice is really unnecessary if one does what matters the most—base one's way of life on the example set by the morally good.

It is often held that there is a major difference between Graeco-Roman and Christian ethics in terms of their theological basis and motivation,[20] that is, that there is a distinctive *religious* motivation behind the latter that is more or less lacking in the ethics of the philosophical schools. This claim does not do full justice to our knowledge of Stoicism. As we have seen, especially in the discussion of Seneca and Epictetus, Stoic ethics has a strong theological foundation as it is largely based, not only on theories about God and God's presence in the world, but also on the theory of the divine origin of human-kind itself. In principle, the theory implies that no one is really superior to another, because all have equal share in the divine λόγος, and all have God as their 'father' who cares for them, helps and guides them, whoever they may be. Nature (= God) 'loves us most tenderly (*amantissima*)', Seneca declares.[21] In fact, 'we are loved (*amamur*) to the point of being spoiled'.[22] The proper response to such love and care is—or should be—to act in the same manner towards one's fellow human beings, i.e. towards other sharers of the divine. The difference between Christianity and Stoicism in this respect may there-fore be more apparent than real. In Stoicism, loving one's neighbour is nothing but a direct consequence of the doctrine of the common, divine

---

[15] Musonius 16.104.35–6: ἀγαθὸν εἶναι κελεύει τὸν ἄνθρωπον ὁ νόμος ὁ τοῦ Διός.

[16] Musonius 8.64.14; 17.108.8–18; Epictetus, *Diss.* 2.14.12–13; 2.19.26–7; 4.7.20.

[17] Epictetus, *Diss.* 3.24.95, 110.   [18] Plato, *Leg.* 9.854B.

[19] *Diss.* 2.18.19–21. Cf. also Marcus Aurelius, *Med.* 2.5.

[20] See, e.g., Schrage, *Einzelgebote*, 200–9; Horrell, *Solidarity*, 13–14, 24.

[21] *Ep.* 78.7. Cf. *Prov.* 2.7; 4.7; *Ben.* 2.29.6. On God as Nature, see *Ben.* 4.7.1.

[22] *Ben.* 4.5.1: ' "God gives no benefits," you say. Whence, then, comes all that you possess, all that you give, all that you withhold, all that you hoard, all that you steal? Whence come the countless things that delight your eyes, your ears, your mind? Whence the profusion that supplies even our luxury? For it is not merely our necessities that are provided—we are loved to the point of being spoiled!'

origin of humankind, and the natural response to God's love of human beings. Indeed, it is impossible to separate God from the virtuous life: 'No man can be good without the help of God.'[23] Modern scholarship is too much affected by an *a priori* distinction between philosophy and theology/religion that was totally alien to the ancients. Seneca explains the 'function' of philosophy as follows:

Her sole function (*opus*) is to discover the truth about things divine and things human. From her side religion (*religio*) never departs, nor duty (*pietas*), nor justice (*iustitia*), nor any of the whole company of virtues which cling together in close-united fellowship. Philosophy has taught us to worship that which is divine, to love that which is human (*haec docuit colere divina, humana diligere*); she has told us that with the gods lies dominion, and among men, fellowship.[24]

Again, of course there are features of Stoic theology that differ fundamentally from Christian theology, but the ethical occasion or motivation is nevertheless comparable. Proper morality is seen, in the former case, as a consequence of God's creation of humankind and the nature of that creation, and, in the latter, as a response to God's (recent) actions in the world on behalf of humankind. For both, the ethical outcome is practically the same, that of wholly devoting oneself to a particular way of life. Later in this chapter we shall look more closely at the very form and content of that (or those) particular way(s) of life.

Hence, when Paul, 'Peter', and 'Clement' imply that a particular way of life can count as a proper (and sufficient) worship, their words seem to echo parallel statements made by contemporary Graeco-Roman moralists, and their gentile addressees may well have made associations with such common-place statements. There is little doubt, for instance, that just a faint awareness of such statements on the part of Paul's Roman addressees would have helped them to realize that the apostle's talk about their 'bodily offering' did not involve any bloody or deadly sacrifice in the literal sense, but involved instead their 'death' to the former way of life and embodiment of the new way of life accounted for (basically) in Romans 12–15. Awareness of such statements would have better equipped them to understand Paul's message that precisely by following the moral principles presented by him they were indeed offering themselves as a 'living sacrifice'.

Could Paul's audience have read the text in this light? Is it possible, or perhaps even likely, that the audience would have made associations with current philosophical discourses as they read and listened to Paul's words?

---

[23] Seneca, *Ep.* 41.2: *Bonus vero vir sine deo nemo est.* Cf. *Ep.* 73.16: *Nulla sine deo mens bona est* ('No mind that has not God, is good').

[24] *Ep.* 90.3.

Would they have related them specifically to Stoicism? Much suggests that they may well have done so. To begin with, we must have in mind that the persons whom Paul addressed directly in his letter were of non-Jewish origin, and Paul frequently stresses that he is speaking to them as such, that is to say, specifically with respect to their non-Jewish, Graeco-Roman background.[25] As we saw in Chapter 5 above, it is not unlikely that at least a few of Paul's gentile addressees had received some education—apart from proper schooling in the Jewish (and 'Christian') tradition. It seems reasonable to infer that these more learned and better-off individuals had considerable influence on the uneducated majority when it came to things like making sense of Paul's moral teaching in Romans.

Moreover, as early as in 12.1–2 we see clear allusions, not merely to philosophical discourse in general, but to standard *Stoic* terminology. And this, we recall, is no side piece in Paul's text: there is a broad consensus among scholars that Romans 12.1–2 sets the stage for the entire moral teaching in Romans 12–15.[26] Many also agree[27] that when Paul in 12.1 uses the adjective λογικός ('rational' or 'reasonable') to define the addressees' appropriate way to serve God, their λογικὴ λατρεία, he is alluding to a well-known philosophical concept. While the concept was certainly not foreign to the other philosophical schools, it was particularly favoured among the Stoics in their efforts to explain the relationship between human beings as λογικοί and God as λόγος (*ratio*).[28] A well-known example is Epictetus' exhortation to his students to worship God with hymns and songs (quoted more fully in Chapter 4 above): 'If I were a nightingale, I should be singing as a nightingale; if a swan, as a swan. But as it is, I am a rational being (λογικός εἰμι), therefore I must be

[25] e.g. Rom 1.5–6; 6.15–23; 11.13; 15.15–16. Stowers puts it well: '[Paul] was an apostle to the Gentile peoples, and the goal of his work was communal. His concern was not the human condition and human nature but the state of the non-Jewish cultures who had, in his view, rejected the one true God' ('Paul', 284).

[26] e.g. Anton Grabner-Haider, *Paraklese und Eschatologie bei Paulus: Mensch und Welt im Anspruch der Zukunft Gottes* (NTAbh NF 4; Münster: Aschendorff, 1968), 116–17; Käsemann, *Römer*, 311; C. E. B. Cranfield, *A Critical and Exegetical Commentary on the Epistle to the Romans* (2 vols.; ICC; Edinburgh: T&T Clark, 1975–79), 2: 595; Ortkemper, *Leben*, 19; Dunn, *Romans*, 2: 707; Hans Dieter Betz, 'Das Problem der Grundlagen der paulinischen Ethik (Röm 12,1–2)', *ZTK* 85 (1988): 208–9; Michael Thompson, *Clothed with Christ: The Example and Teaching of Jesus in Romans 12.1–15.13* (JSNTSup 59; Sheffield: JSOT Press, 1991), 78; Wilson, *Love*, 129–36; Jewett, *Romans*, 724–5.

[27] e.g. Lietzmann, *Einführung*, 108–9; Käsemann, *Römer*, 316; Ortkemper, *Leben*, 27; Dunn, *Romans*, 2: 711–12; Wilson, *Love*, 137; Engberg-Pedersen, *Paul*, 263–4; Witherington and Hyatt, *Romans*, 285; Jewett, *Romans*, 730–1, with further references.

[28] See, e.g., Diogenes Laertius 7.87–8, 134, 147; Stobaeus, *Ecl.* 2.7.6 [= Arius Didymus 6; edn. Pomeroy]; Epictetus, *Diss.* 1.3.1–3; 2.8.2–3, 11–14; 3.1.25; Marcus Aurelius, *Med.* 4.4; 5.27. For Latin equivalents, cf. also, e.g., Cicero, *Nat. d.* 1.39; 2.133; Manilius, *Astronomica* 2.82–3, 105–27; Seneca, *Ep.* 66.12; 76.9–10; 92.1–2, 27; 124.23; *Nat.* 1, Pref. 14.

singing hymns of praise to God.'[29] As he clarifies elsewhere, the human being is 'a mortal animal gifted with the ability to use impressions rationally ($\lambda o\gamma\iota\kappa\hat{\omega}s$)',[30] a 'reasoning animal' (*rationale animal*), as Seneca puts it.[31] Reason, then, according to Seneca, is 'nothing else than a portion of the divine spirit set in a human body'.[32] God, in turn, says Epictetus, is 'intelligence, knowledge, right reason' ($vo\hat{v}s$, $\dot{\epsilon}\pi\iota\sigma\tau\dot{\eta}\mu\eta$, $\lambda\acute{o}\gamma os$ $\dot{o}\rho\theta\acute{o}s$), and the true nature of the good ($\tau\grave{o}$ $\dot{a}\gamma a\theta\acute{o}v$) is found where God is found.

> Here, therefore, and only here, shall you seek the true nature of the good. Surely you do not seek it at all in a plant, do you? No. Nor in an irrational creature ($\dot{\epsilon}v$ $\dot{a}\lambda\acute{o}\gamma\omega$)? No. If, then, you seek it in that which is rational ($\dot{\epsilon}v$ $\lambda o\gamma\iota\kappa\hat{\omega}$), why do you keep on seeking it somewhere else than in that which differentiates the rational from the irrational?[33]

The apostle Paul, it seems, finds it important as well to underline the rational or reasonable aspect of the worship of God to the Roman audience.[34] As one scholar comments on Romans 12.1–2,

> [w]e can safely assume that the concept of 'reasonable religion' was familiar to the Romans even in their pre-Christian situation. The concept points to attempts made by many religious cults in the Greco-Roman period to rid themselves of the stigma of superstitious primitivism and to present themselves as enlightened. Such claims were often justified by serious reforms showing compliance with standards established by the philosophers. Thus, the concept of 'reasonable religion' expresses an ideal of the Hellenistic and Roman era, which is here endorsed by Paul.[35]

If with any particular philosophical school, the Roman addressees would most likely have associated Paul's terminology here with Stoicism.[36]

Verse 2 in Paul's programmatic statement in Romans 12.1–2 continues to make allusions to popular philosophical language, Stoic in particular. Paul here proceeds by explaining that the proper way of life cannot be upheld without the *proper way of thinking*. In order to discern how God wants them to live, i.e. to determine what exactly is 'the good, acceptable, and perfect' ($\tau\grave{o}$ $\dot{a}\gamma a\theta\grave{o}v$ $\kappa a\grave{\iota}$ $\epsilon\dot{v}\acute{a}\rho\epsilon\sigma\tau ov$ $\kappa a\grave{\iota}$ $\tau\acute{\epsilon}\lambda\epsilon\iota ov$), the addressees must 'not be conformed to this world' ($\mu\dot{\eta}$ $\sigma v\sigma\chi\eta\mu a\tau\acute{\iota}\zeta\epsilon\sigma\theta\epsilon$ $\tau\hat{\omega}$ $a\grave{\iota}\hat{\omega}v\iota$ $\tau o\acute{v}\tau\omega$), but let themselves be

---

[29] *Diss.* 1.16.20–1.   [30] *Diss.* 3.1.25.   [31] *Ep.* 124.23.

[32] *Ep.* 66.12: *Ratio autem nihil aliud est quam in corpus humanum pars divini spiritus mersa.*

[33] *Diss.* 2.8.2–3.

[34] Note that the adjective $\lambda o\gamma\iota\kappa\acute{o}s$ occurs nowhere else in Paul's letters. Interestingly for the present discussion, the only other NT occurrence of $\lambda o\gamma\iota\kappa\acute{o}s$ is 1 Pet 2.2. For $\lambda a\tau\rho\epsilon\acute{\iota}a$ and cognates, cf. Rom 1.9; 9.4; Phil 3.3.

[35] Hans Dieter Betz, 'Christianity as Religion: Paul's Attempt at Definition in Romans', *JR* 71 (1991): 337.

[36] So also, e.g., Jewett, *Romans*, 730.

transformed or 'metamorphosed' (μεταμορφοῦσθε) by 'the renewing of the mind' (τῇ ἀνακαινώσει τοῦ νοός). In other words, they must completely reverse their way of thinking. Reverse it from what? From the utterly sinful and immoral existence described in 1.18–32; from the 'corrupt mind' (ἀδόκιμος νοῦς) to which they once were handed over and which made them do what is improper (τὰ μὴ καθήκοντα).[37] For, as Seneca puts it, 'it will be of no avail to give precepts unless you first remove the conditions that are likely to stand in the way of precepts'.[38] As the 'corrupt mind' is a fundamental hindrance to the proper way of life, a total intellectual 'metamorphosis' is a prerequisite for the 'reasonable worship'. Underlying these exhortations in Romans is the conception, shared by Graeco-Roman moralists, that moral behaviour is based on right learning and perception. The author of 1 Peter expresses this notion, too, when he insists that right conduct is rooted in 'the truth' (1.22), i.e. in true learning, and that the latter necessarily leads to the former.[39]

The Roman Christ-believers may have associated arguments and notions like these with current philosophical discussions about the relationship between *theory* and *praxis*. Stoics and Cynics were especially concerned with questions in that area, and both schools were widely noted for that concern. Famous was also their constant reminder to their fellow human beings (and themselves) of the need to harmonize words and deeds, as well as their sharp critique of those who (hypothetically) could not care less about such things. Compared to the Cynics, the voices of the Stoics were evidently more powerful in the city of Rome, but many of them, including Musonius and Epictetus, were much influenced by Cynicism. While the Roman Stoics sometimes downplayed the importance of theory—as a part of the argument that theory without practical application is virtually worthless—there is no question that they considered right perception essential to moral behaviour. The two were always intimately

---

[37] Rom 1.28: καὶ καθὼς οὐκ ἐδοκίμασαν τὸν θεὸν ἔχειν ἐν ἐπιγνώσει, παρέδωκεν αὐτοὺς ὁ θεὸς εἰς ἀδόκιμον νοῦν, ποιεῖν τὰ μὴ καθήκοντα ('And since they did not see fit to acknowledge God, God gave them up to a debased [or: corrupt] mind and to things that should not be done', NRSV). Note that, in Stoic ethics, τέλειον καθῆκον is a complete and appropriate moral act, in contrast to an act παρὰ τὸ καθῆκον which is ἁμάρτημα. See further the discussion in J. M. Rist, *Stoic Philosophy* (Cambridge: Cambridge University Press, 1969), 97–8.

[38] *Ep.* 95.38: *Nihil ergo proderit dare praecepta, nisi prius amoveris obstatura praeceptis.* Cf. also *Ep.* 28.9 where Seneca refers with approval to a saying of Epicurus: 'The knowledge of sin is the beginning of salvation.' 'This saying', says Seneca, 'seems to me to be a noble one. For he who does not know that he has sinned does not desire correction; you must discover yourself in the wrong before you can reform yourself.' Does this come close to what Paul is trying to express in Rom 3.20? Cf. also Seneca, *Ep.* 90.46: 'It makes a great deal of difference whether one wills not to sin or has not the knowledge to sin.'

[39] Although the matter of what 'the truth' really is needs continual reminder, according to the author of 1 Peter.

linked in their reasoning. As Musonius says, it is impossible to do anything properly if the practical execution is not in harmony with theory.[40] However, the Roman Stoics all accentuate that theory alone is not enough. 'You must learn first, and then strengthen your learning by action', Seneca insists.[41] What is needed, according to the Stoic, is a total *transformation* or *metamorphosis* of the mind. For 'one who has learned and understood what he should do and avoid, is not a wise man until his mind (*animus*) is metamorphosed (*transfiguratus est*) into the shape of that which he has learned'.[42] Similarly, Epictetus instructs his students (with his typical touch of irony) that

those who have learned the principles (τὰ θεωρήματα) and nothing else are eager to throw them up immediately, just as persons with a weak stomach throw up their food. *First digest your principles* (πρῶτον αὐτὰ πέψον), and then you will surely not throw them up this way. Otherwise they are mere vomit, foul stuff and unfit to eat. *But after you have digested these principles, show us some change in your governing principle that is due to them* (ἀλλ' ἀπ' αὐτῶν ἀναδοθέντων δεῖξόν τινα ἡμῖν μεταβολὴν τοῦ ἡγεμονικοῦ τοῦ σεαυτοῦ).[43]

Paul's words in Romans 12.2 would have sounded familiar to those who were acquainted with the Stoic notion of the transformation of the mind. As one scholar points out, 'Paul's use of μεταμορφοῦσθαι ("be transformed") is, like "rational worship," an effort to claim a Greco-Roman religious ideal for the new ethic.'[44] It seems safe to assume that (a part of) Paul's audience would have recognized that claim as such. In fact, the close relation between Paul's terminology and the philosophical tradition is further enforced, among other things, by the immediately following allusions to two of the four cardinal virtues of Greek philosophy (v. 3: φρόνησις and σωφροσύνη).[45] However, while

[40] Musonius 5.52.1–2. Cf., e.g., Seneca, *Ep.* 20.2; 95.34–5; Epictetus, *Diss.* 1.26.3; 2.11.24–5.

[41] *Ep.* 94.47: *et discas oportet et quod didicisti agendo confirmes.*

[42] *Ep.* 94.48: *qui didicit et facienda ac vitanda percepit, nondum sapiens est, nisi in ea, quae didicit, animus eius transfiguratus est.* Cf. also 6.1 where Seneca says, 'I feel, my dear Lucilius, that I am being not only reformed, but transformed' (*Intellego, Lucili, non emendari me tantum sed transfigurari*), proceeding then to speak of the primary effect of this 'transformation' that concerns his very relation to his friend: 'I should then begin to place a surer trust in our friendship (*amicitiae nostrae*)—the true friendship, which hope and fear and self-interest cannot sever... In such cases men know that they have all things in common (*omnia habere communia*), especially their troubles (*adversa*)' (2–3).

[43] *Diss.* 3.21.1–3. Epictetus uses here the standard Stoic term for the human mind, i.e. τὸ ἡγεμονικόν (lit. 'governing faculty'), the centre of the person and the seat of rationality. For general discussion of the meaning of ἡγεμονικόν in Stoic philosophy, see Julia Annas, *Hellenistic Philosophy of Mind* (Hellenistic Culture and Society 8; Berkeley, CA: University of California Press, 1992), 61–70.

[44] Jewett, *Romans*, 732.

[45] Rom 12.3: μὴ ὑπερφρονεῖν παρ' ὃ δεῖ φρονεῖν ἀλλὰ φρονεῖν εἰς τὸ σωφρονεῖν. Cf. 12.16 (τὸ αὐτὸ εἰς ἀλλήλους φρονοῦντες, μὴ τὰ ὑψηλὰ φρονοῦντες); 14.6 (ὁ φρονῶν τὴν ἡμέραν κυρίῳ φρονεῖ); 15.5 (τὸ αὐτὸ φρονεῖν ἐν ἀλλήλοις). See further Runar M. Thorsteinsson, 'Stoicism as

Paul makes it absolutely clear that the 'transformation' spoken of involves an *intellectual* renewal—a death and revival of the νοῦς—it is *not merely* intellectual; it does not stop at that. It has a broader purpose, namely, εἰς τὸ δοκιμάζειν ὑμᾶς τί τὸ θέλημα τοῦ θεοῦ, τὸ ἀγαθὸν καὶ εὐάρεστον καὶ τέλειον. That is, precisely as for the Stoics, the 'renewing of the mind' has a total *moral* transformation as the ultimate goal, pertaining to the mind as well as to the body. Paul's addressees are to demonstrate their true transformation, and thus that they really are able to discern what the will of God is, by faithfully carrying out the moral instructions presented by the apostle.

Having said this, the question needs to be asked: why does Paul present such extensive instructions to the Roman addressees if they have already adopted faith in Jesus Christ and thus (should) know already what is required of them morally? Why does the apostle first say that *they themselves* are to discern what is the will of God, that is, τὸ ἀγαθὸν καὶ εὐάρεστον καὶ τέλειον, and then go on to teach them precisely that, namely, what is τὸ ἀγαθὸν καὶ εὐάρεστον καὶ τέλειον? To put it differently, why does Paul continue with the lengthy moral teaching of 12.3–15.13 instead of simply continuing directly with words like: 'But I myself am confident about you, my brothers, that you yourselves are full of goodness (ἀγαθωσύνη), filled with all knowledge (γνῶσις), and able to admonish (νουθετεῖν) one another' (15.14)?

The answer is twofold. First, as we have seen, in Romans 12.1–2 Paul clearly alludes to his earlier description of the sinful and morally corrupt gentile world (1.18–32) and urges his addressees to totally reverse such dispositions and behaviour. In Paul's view, the addressees may indeed be (well-nigh) 'full of goodness, filled with all knowledge, and able to admonish one another', but due to their gentile background the moral instructions are nevertheless required. For they are still 'weak in the flesh'[46] and their path to τὸ ἀγαθὸν καὶ εὐάρεστον καὶ τέλειον is long and uphill, according to the apostle. It is as the Stoic Seneca explains:

The approach to these qualities is slow, and in the meantime, in practical matters, the path should be pointed out for the benefit of one who is still short of perfection, but is

a Key to Pauline Ethics in Romans', in *Stoicism in Early Christianity* (ed. T. Rasimus, I. Dunderberg, and T. Engberg-Pedersen; Peabody, MA: Hendrickson, forthcoming); idem, 'Paul and Roman Stoicism', 149–50. See also the useful discussion in Luke Timothy Johnson, 'Transformation of the Mind and Moral Discernment in Paul', in *Early Christianity and Classical Culture: Comparative Studies in Honor of Abraham J. Malherbe* (ed. J. T. Fitzgerald, T. H. Olbricht, and L. M. White; NovTSup 110; Leiden: Brill, 2003), 215–36. Note that the verb σωφρονεῖν occurs also in 1 Pet 4.7, and that the author of 1 Clement is clearly acquainted with the concept, including not only the verb σωφρονεῖν (1.3) and the adjective σώφρων (1.2; 63.3) but the noun σωφροσύνη as well (62.2; 64.1).

[46] cf. Rom 6.19: ἀνθρώπινον λέγω διὰ τὴν ἀσθένειαν τῆς σαρκὸς ὑμῶν (lit. 'I speak in human terms because of the weakness of your flesh').

making progress. Wisdom (*sapientia*) by her own agency may perhaps show herself this path without the help of admonition (*sine admonitione*); for she has brought the soul to a stage where it can be impelled only in the right direction. Weaker characters (*inbecilliores*), however, need someone to precede them, to say: 'Avoid this,' or 'Do that.'[47]

Envisaging a scene that corresponds closely to Paul's account of gentile immorality in Romans 1.18–32, Seneca explains further that,

amid this upset condition of morals (*in hac morum perversitate*), something stronger than usual is needed,—something which will shake off these chronic ills (*mala inveterata*); in order to root out a deep-seated belief in wrong ideas, conduct must be regulated by doctrines (*decretis agendum est, ut revellatur penitus falsorum recepta persuasio*). It is only when we add precepts, consolation, and encouragement (*praecepta, consolationes, adhortationes*) to these, that they can prevail; by themselves they are ineffective. If we would hold men firmly bound and tear them away from the ills which clutch them fast, they must learn what is evil and what is good (*quid malum, quid bonum sit*).[48]

That is precisely what Paul intends in Romans 12–15, namely, to teach the Roman gentile audience what is evil and what is good, and, at the same time, to aid and encourage them to root out their former (false) beliefs of what is evil and what is good. Their proper worship of God is dependent upon their renewal of the conception of what really is 'good, acceptable, and perfect' in the eyes of God. As it is, 'you know neither what God [really] is, nor what man [really] is, nor what good, nor what evil', as Epictetus explains to a student of his.[49] That is one reason why Paul includes his extensive moral teaching in the letter to the Romans.

The second reason why Paul presents this teaching to the Roman addressees, despite the fact that they have already adopted faith in Jesus Christ, is that he wants them not only to know and follow the proper moral requirements but also to fully understand the meaning of these requirements—or at least more fully understand them. Instead of just doing the proper things mechanically, so to speak, the addressees must deliberate why these things are proper in the first place. For that purpose Paul seeks to plant in the addressees the seeds of the necessary understanding and disposition to make the right judgement (cf. δοκιμάζειν) as to what they should do and why.

The attentive listener in Paul's audience would have noticed the close correspondence here with current philosophical discussions about the virtues and the ancient question—even from a first-century CE point of view—of what makes a person virtuous. For, according to a widely accepted view in

---

[47] *Ep.* 94.50.   [48] *Ep.* 95.34–5.
[49] *Diss.* 2.14.19: οὔτε τί θεός ἐστιν οἶδας οὔτε τί ἄνθρωπος οὔτε τί ἀγαθὸν οὔτε τί κακόν.

Greek philosophy, '[t]he virtuous person is not just the person who does in fact do the morally right thing, or even does it stably and reliably. She is the person who *understands* the principles on which she acts, and thus can explain and defend her actions.'[50] The virtuous person holds securely the disposition to do the right thing for the right reason. While following certain rules or instructions is usually more or less inevitable, the person who does only that without understanding those rules or instructions will not get very far in moral progress, or, in Paul's words, in the progress of discerning what is God's will in matters of morality. And to gain such an understanding, which affects one's life as a whole, requires not only intellectual renewing but intellectual development as well.

It is therefore quite to the point for Paul's purpose to proceed in 12.3 by alluding to the virtue of φρόνησις (through the verb φρονεῖν), which in Greek philosophy was generally considered most important of the four cardinal virtues.[51] This virtue was thought to underlie all the virtues because it constituted the very disposition to make right moral judgements. In ancient Greek ethical theory the virtue of φρόνησις, 'practical wisdom' or '(practical) intelligence', is 'the state the agent is in who has learned to reason well about moral matters—not in a particular sphere, but generally'.[52] For the Stoics it denoted nothing less than the skill or expertise in living.

Is it mere coincidence that Paul launches his moral lesson precisely by alluding to the virtue of φρόνησις? I think not. When he urges his audience to φρονεῖν εἰς τὸ σωφρονεῖν (12.3)[53] it is indeed the first example presented of the moral transformation called for in 12.1–2. And this first example appears to be largely programmatic for the entire community-forming ethic in Romans 12–15.[54] I find it hard to believe that the choice of terminology in such a weighty part of the text was just a matter of coincidence. In light of the widespread notion of φρόνησις as the disposition to *make right moral judgements*, it is much more likely that Paul's allusion to the virtue at the very beginning of his moral teaching was quite deliberate. Paul wanted to encourage practical wisdom and intelligence in the Christ-believing community so

---

[50] Annas, *Morality*, 67 (emphasis original).

[51] cf. Annas, *Morality*, 73: 'All ancient ethical theories agree that fully to have the virtues, or even one particular virtue, the agent has to have *phronēsis*.' See, e.g., Aristotle, *Eth. nic.* 1144b2–3: 'True virtue cannot exist without prudence (φρόνησις). Hence some people maintain that all the virtues are forms of prudence.' The (early) Stoics maintained precisely this; cf. Plutarch, *Stoic. rep.* 1034C–E.

[52] Annas, *Morality*, 73.

[53] On the virtue of σωφροσύνη, see the detailed discussion in Helen North, *Sophrosyne: Self-Knowledge and Self-Restraint in Greek Literature* (Ithaca, NY: Cornell University Press, 1966), esp. 213–31, 258–68.

[54] cf. also Johnson, 'Transformation', 221.

that the Christ-believers would be better prepared and better able to discern τὸ ἀγαθὸν καὶ εὐάρεστον καὶ τέλειον, and thus to fully embody the proper way of life as their reasonable, rational worship of God.[55] At the same time, the apostle wanted his addressees to be better able to guide and admonish one another morally, as he hints at in 15.14 (see above). It comes close to what Seneca says when he discusses the fellowship of the 'wise men': 'Good men are mutually helpful; for each gives practice to the other's virtues and thus maintains wisdom at its proper level. Each needs someone with whom he may make comparisons and investigations,'[56] even if one is making good moral progress.[57] In Stoic terms, then, one could say that Paul wished to establish in Rome (and elsewhere) a community of mutually helpful 'wise (wo)men', who recognize not only *what* to do or *how* to do it but also *why*.

In sum, for both Paul and the Stoics a particular way of life constitutes the proper worship of the deity. However, for Paul, like the Stoics, there will be no true worship without moral transformation. And there will be no true moral transformation without proper moral teaching and proper understanding of that teaching.

CLOTHING ONESELF WITH CHRIST AND SEEKING TO BE A SOCRATES

Of course, for Christ-believers all worship and all morality is intimately linked with the person and life of Christ Jesus himself. It is 'the good conduct *in Christ*' (ἡ ἀγαθὴ ἐν Χριστῷ ἀναστροφή) that is the ultimate moral purpose, as the author of 1 Peter so unequivocally explains.[58] It is 'living according to what is appropriate *in Christ*' (πολιτεύεσθαι κατὰ τὸ καθῆκον τῷ Χριστῷ), 1 Clement says.[59] And that is precisely what should be passed on to coming

---

[55] cf. also the comments of Troels Engberg-Pedersen on Rom 12.3: 'Here Paul is in effect saying, as Aristotle might have said, that his addressees must have the one basic moral (and intellectual) virtue of φρόνησις, phronēsis (moral insight), that will include the moral virtue proper of σωφροσύνη, sōphrosynē (moderation). The content of this idea is spelled out in the rest of the chapter' ('Paul, Virtues, and Vices', in *Paul in the Greco-Roman World: A Handbook* [ed. J. P. Sampley; Harrisburg, PA: Trinity Press, 2003], 627).

[56] *Ep.* 109.1: *Prosunt inter se boni; exercent enim virtutes et sapientiam in suo statu continent. Desiderat uterque aliquem, cum quo conferat, cum quo quaerat.* Cf. 7.8 ('Associate with those who will make a better man of you. Welcome those whom you yourself can improve. The process is mutual; for men learn while they teach').

[57] cf. *Ep.* 109.6: 'even one who is running well is helped by one who cheers him on'.

[58] 1 Pet 3.16.

[59] 1 Clem. 3.4. Note that the author applies here the well-known Stoic term τὸ καθῆκον.

generations, according to this author: 'Let our children partake of the discipline that is *in Christ* (τῆς ἐν Χριστῷ παιδείας).'[60]

While the apostle Paul makes only a few explicit mentions of Christ in Romans 12.1–15.14,[61] his disposition and way of life nevertheless appears as a model on which to base one's being. This is certainly not expressed openly in chapter 12, nor in the bulk of chapter 13, but it must be remembered that these chapters do not emerge from nowhere but are based on the previous discourse as a whole, i.e. Romans 1–11.[62] Also, and more to the point for the present discussion, immediately preceding chapters 14–15, in which Paul discusses relations within the Christ-believing community, he urges his readers to 'put on' or 'clothe' themselves with Jesus Christ: ἐνδύσασθε τὸν κύριον Ἰησοῦν Χριστόν (13.14). As the immediate context shows, this expression refers primarily to Christ's moral characteristics,[63] and means that in their dealings with one another the addressees are to let their actions be characterized by the example set by Christ. In particular (in Paul's text), this applies to the ethic of adaptability, that is, the necessity to adapt to the needs of others, especially those fellow believers who, in one way or another, are 'weak in faith'. Like Christ who 'did not please himself' (οὐχ ἑαυτῷ ἤρεσεν, 15.3) but impartially 'welcomed' them all (προσελάβετο ὑμᾶς, 15.7),[64] the Roman Christ-believers are to 'welcome one another' (προσλαμβάνεσθε ἀλλήλους, 15.7), and each and every member of the community must 'please' his or her fellow believer ('neighbour') for the good purpose of building up the community (15.2). The example is set by the ideal human being, Jesus Christ, whose love of others the Roman addressees are to make their own.

The Stoics, of course, did not link their morality with the person of Jesus. But they did link it with a figure of a corresponding character, namely, the ideal sage or 'wise man' (ὁ σοφός, *sapiens*),[65] whose role as an example was

---

[60] 1 Clem. 21.8. Cf. 1.2: τήν τε σώφρονα καὶ ἐπιεικῆ ἐν Χριστῷ εὐσέβειαν ('the temperate and gentle piety in Christ').

[61] Rom 12.5; 13.14; 14.9, 15, 18; 15.3, 5–8.

[62] cf. also Horrell's discussion of Christ as moral paradigm in Paul's letters, in which he remarks that the 'explicit calls to imitation of Christ, few as they are, are only the tip of a much larger iceberg' (*Solidarity*, 241). Similar remarks are also made by Thompson, *Clothed with Christ*, 238: 'The explicit example of Christ in 15.3, 7 is only the tip of a thematic iceberg for Paul. The garment metaphor in 13.14 points to Christ's moral characteristics, which by *inclusio* are implied as the goal of the transformation in 12.2.'

[63] See Thompson, *Clothed with Christ*, 149–58.

[64] cf. Glad, *Paul*, 224: 'Προσλαμβάνω is also used in 14:3 and 15:7b to encourage acceptance and mutual aid in light of divine acceptance. As God and Christ had accepted all types of gentile persons into friendship, so should the weak and strong accept each other into their circle of friends instead of rejecting each other', referring to uses of προσλαμβάνειν in familial and friendship imagery.

[65] The ideal sage is referred to with several different designations in the sources. Epictetus sometimes refers to him as ὁ φρόνιμος (cf. the cardinal virtue φρόνησις) or ὁ Κυνικός (i.e. 'the

essential to the progress leading to moral transformation. Seneca explains why this was so essential: 'We must indeed have someone according to whom we may regulate our characters; you can never straighten that which is crooked unless you use a ruler.'[66] Few Stoics, if any, claimed to have reached the state of being such an exemplary person, and the number of individuals to whom the designation 'sage' or 'wise man' was attributed was very small indeed. But there was one figure whose position as the 'wise man' par excellence was by and large consistent throughout the history of Stoicism, the philosopher Socrates.[67] Individuals like him were not only considered to be ideal philosophers but also ideal moral beings, for, as Musonius briefly puts it, 'being good is the same as being a philosopher', since philosophy is in itself nothing but 'training in nobility of character'.[68] Thus, if you are a (true) philosopher, then you are a truly good person, and vice versa. For the Stoics, then, as indeed for many others in antiquity, including the Christians,[69] Socrates was a person whose way of life (and death) presented a pattern for others to imitate.[70] He was a person to 'put on', in Paul's terminology, a person to 'clothe' oneself with. He was one of those few individuals who were 'born to be a pattern'.[71]

It is important to note that the Roman Stoics always stressed that even if one can never fully reach the sage's level of being, one should constantly have that level as the target, regardless of whether one gets off course every now and then. For *it is the very will and intention that counts.*[72] This thought is well expressed in the following statement, attributed to Epictetus: 'Even if you are

---

Cynic', idealized as the perfect 'wise man'), while Musonius often speaks of him simply as ὁ φιλόσοφος ('the philosopher').

[66] *Ep.* 11.10: *Opus est, inquam, aliquo, ad quem mores nostri se ipsi exigant; nisi ad regulam prava non corriges.*

[67] See A. A. Long, 'Socrates in Hellenistic Philosophy', *CQ* 38 (1988): esp. 150–44, 160–71. On p. 151 Long refers to the observation made by Philodemus that the Stoics actually wanted to be called 'Socratics' (Σωκρατικοὶ καλεῖσθαι θέλουσιν).

[68] Musonius 16.104.36–7 (τὸ δέ γε εἶναι ἀγαθὸν τῷ φιλόσοφον εἶναι ταὐτόν ἐστιν); 4.48.25–6 (φιλοσοφία καλοκἀγαθίας ἐστὶν ἐπιτήδευσις καὶ οὐδὲν ἕτερον). Cf. also 8.64.37–66.1; 10.78.2–3; 14.96.6–7.

[69] See Ernst Benz, 'Christus und Sokrates in der alten Kirche', *ZNW* 43 (1950–1): 195–224; Klaus Döring, *Exemplum Socratis: Studien zur Sokratesnachwirkung in der kynisch-stoischen Popularphilosophie der frühen Kaiserzeit und im frühen Christentum* (Hermes 42; Wiesbaden: Franz Steiner Verlag, 1979).

[70] Note that, whereas Seneca certainly considered Socrates a true sage (e.g. *Ben.* 5.6), the prime example of the *sapiens* in his eyes was the Roman statesman Cato the Younger (Marcus Porcius Cato Uticensis, 95–46 BCE); cf. *Ep.* 11.10; *Const.* 2.2–3; 7.1; 14.3. For further discussion, see Griffin, *Seneca*, 182–94. In *Parad.* Pref. 1, Cicero calls Cato a *perfectus Stoicus*.

[71] Seneca, *Prov.* 6.3: *nati sunt in exemplar.*

[72] Correspondingly, 'conduct will not be right unless the will to act is right; for this is the source of conduct. Nor, again, can the will be right without a right attitude of mind; for this is the source of the will' (Seneca, *Ep.* 95.57).

not yet a Socrates, still you ought to live as one who wishes to be a Socrates' (σὺ δὲ εἰ καὶ μήπω εἶ Σωκράτης, ὡς Σωκράτης γε εἶναι βουλόμενος ὀφείλεις βιοῦν).[73] The most important thing is to *consistently want and attempt* to live like Socrates, like a 'wise man'.[74] As Seneca says in a different context, 'Some people need to be taught, and we should judge it sufficient if they try, if they dare, if they are willing.'[75]

It is seldom considered in scholarship on early Christianity, but the correspondence between the role of Jesus as a moral example and the Stoic sage is strikingly close. By this I am not claiming that there ever was a figure in Stoicism who had so decisive meaning for the Stoics as Jesus Christ for the Christians. But I do claim that, in the ancient texts, Jesus and the Stoic sage had analogous functions as moral paradigms. Many Christ-believers in Rome would probably have recognized the parallel between 'putting on' Jesus Christ and 'living as one who wishes to be a Socrates' as they went through Paul's message. Some may even have recognized that, in both cases, the definite prerequisite was the kind of 'transformation' spoken of in Romans 12.2.[76] Clearly, Paul does not insist that the addressees become, as it were, perfect human beings, like Jesus, in order to have a chance before God. They are not to become 'Christs' themselves for that purpose. Rather, by 'putting on' Jesus Christ they are to become *like* him, constantly imitating his way of life and moral characteristics. As with the Stoics, here, too, it is the will and intention that counts.

Earlier we saw that the main emphasis in Romans 14–15 is on the obligation of the 'strong' towards the 'weak', and that this partly explains why Paul addresses (mainly)[77] the former directly. But there is this explanation as well: ultimately, Paul wants the audience *as a whole* to identify with the ideal 'strong' type, like himself (15.1) and Jesus (v. 3). By implication, although his message is that there will always be those within the community who are 'weak in faith', and that their needs must be met at any cost, he appears to envision that the 'weak' may in fact eventually become 'strong(er)', namely, by way of an imitation of the 'strong'. His wish is that even the 'weak' may eventually realize, as he himself does, that 'nothing is unclean in itself' (14.14) and that 'the kingdom of God is not food and drink' and so on, but something of much

---

[73] *Ench.* 51.3.

[74] cf. *Diss.* 3.13.22: ὡς σοφοὶ διάγειν ἐθέλομεν καὶ ὠφελεῖν ἀνθρώπους ('we wish to live like wise men from the very start, and to help mankind').

[75] *Ben.* 2.17.4: *quosdam doceamus et satis iudicemus, si conantur, si audent, si volunt* (the LCL trans. slightly modified).

[76] On the close link between Rom 12.1–2 and 13.11–14, see Thompson, *Clothed with Christ*, 151–3.

[77] Note that in 15.7 Paul clearly speaks to his audience as a whole: προσλαμβάνεσθε ἀλλήλους ('welcome one another').

greater consequence (v. 17). In other words, the underlying message in this respect is this (Stoic-inspired?) thought: 'Even if you are not yet strong, still you ought to live as one who wishes to be strong.' The primary pattern to follow is that of the ideal 'strong' person, Jesus Christ (and Paul himself, of course, whose paradigm, in turn, is Christ).[78] And so it is with the Stoics. No more than it is Paul's, their point is *not* that those who fail to become impeccable 'wise men' are doomed and worthless, but rather that each and every individual must continually direct his or her course towards that goal.

Needless to say, according to the Christian sources, there is a strong religious or theological dimension to Jesus' role in the world, as the very 'son of God'. But the distance from the Stoic sage in this respect is actually not as great as many would assume. A close examination of the Stoic accounts of the ideal sage reveals a decidedly theological dimension to his role as well. For instance, in a way similar to Jesus', the sage has been 'sent into the world' by God on a divine mission: 'He has been sent by Zeus to men, partly as a messenger (ἄγγελος), in order to show them that in questions of good and evil they have gone astray, and are seeking the true nature of the good and the evil where it is not.'[79] And he has been sent to human beings by God as an example, παράδειγμα, of the proper way of life: ἰδοὺ ἐγὼ ὑμῖν παράδειγμα ὑπὸ τοῦ θεοῦ ἀπέσταλμαι.[80] The relationship between the sage and the deity is indeed so close in Stoicism that Seneca describes him as a 'next-door neighbour to the gods'[81] and one who has been 'brought into nearness with God'.[82] In fact, 'why should he not call himself a son of God?' Epictetus asks (rhetorically).[83] Moreover,

when we [i.e. Stoics] have assigned to our wise man that field of public life which is worthy of him,—in other words, the universe,—he is then not apart from public life, even if he withdraws; nay, perhaps he has abandoned only one little corner thereof and has passed over into greater and wider regions; and when he has been set in the heavens, he understands how lowly was the place in which he sat when he mounted the curule chair of the judgment-seat. Lay this to heart,—that the wise man is never more active in affairs than when things divine as well as things human have come within his ken.[84]

---

[78] cf. 1 Cor 11.1: μιμηταί μου γίνεσθε καθὼς κἀγὼ Χριστοῦ ('Be imitators of me, as I am of Christ').

[79] Epictetus, *Diss.* 3.22.23: ἄγγελος ἀπὸ τοῦ Διὸς ἀπέσταλται καὶ πρὸς τοὺς ἀνθρώπους περὶ ἀγαθῶν καὶ κακῶν ὑποδείξων αὐτοῖς, ὅτι πεπλάνηνται καὶ ἀλλαχοῦ ζητοῦσι τὴν οὐσίαν τοῦ ἀγαθοῦ καὶ τοῦ κακοῦ, ὅπου οὐκ ἔστιν.

[80] Epictetus, *Diss.* 4.8.31 ('Behold, God has sent me to you as an example'), referring to the words of the ideal sage. Cf. 3.22.46, 56, 69, 82.

[81] *Const.* 8.2: *sapiens autem vicinus proximusque dis consistit*. The sage is 'like a god in all save his mortality' (*excepta mortalitate similis deo*).

[82] *Helv.* 5.2. Cf. Epictetus, *Diss.* 3.22.95.

[83] *Diss.* 1.9.6: διὰ τί μὴ υἱὸν τοῦ θεοῦ [εἴπῃ αὐτόν].   [84] Seneca, *Ep.* 68.2.

The sage's task is not only to teach human beings to recognize God but to show them how to follow God as well.[85] But towards those who make mistakes and 'sin' (*peccare*, cf. ἁμαρτάνειν), he is 'kindly and just' (*placidus et aequus*), because 'he is not the foe, but the reformer of sinners (*corrector peccantium*)'.[86]

The question of being willing and able to adapt oneself to the needs of others was commonly discussed in the Graeco-Roman world.[87] So also by the Stoics, who attributed the idea of adaptability to their ideal sage. We have already seen glimpses of how other-regarding the Stoic sage is in Seneca's description of him (despite common opinion to the contrary),[88] but for the present discussion it is helpful to take a further look at that description. Responding to earlier comments on the subject made by Epicurus, Seneca states:

The wise man, I say, self-sufficient though he be, nevertheless desires friends if only for the purpose of practising friendship (*exerceat amicitiam*), in order that his noble qualities may not lie dormant. Not, however, for the purpose mentioned by Epicurus in the letter quoted above: 'That there may be someone to sit by him when he is ill, to help him when he is in prison or in want;' but *that he may have someone by whose sick-bed he himself may sit, someone a prisoner in hostile hands whom he himself may set free* (*ut habeat aliquem, cui ipse aegro adsideat, quem ipse circumventum hostili custodia liberet*). He who regards himself only, and enters upon friendships for this reason, reckons wrongly.... For what purpose, then, do I make a man my friend? *In order to have someone for whom I may die, whom I may follow into exile, against whose death I may stake my own life, and pay the pledge, too* (*ut habeam pro quo mori possim, ut habeam quem in exilium sequar, cuius me morti opponam et inpendam*).[89]

According to Seneca, Epicurus was of the opinion that the sage was in need of friends but only for the purpose of having someone at *his* side in times of trouble or distress. Seneca's response is that, while Epicurus was right in holding that the sage does need friendship,[90] he was mistaken about the purpose for which the sage makes friends. The purpose, in Seneca's view, does not revolve around the sage himself, but quite the opposite: 'practising

---

[85] Seneca, *Ep.* 90.34.   [86] Seneca, *Ira* 2.10.7.

[87] See the survey in Clarence E. Glad, 'Paul and Adaptability', in *Paul in the Greco-Roman World: A Handbook* (ed. J. P. Sampley; Harrisburg, PA: Trinity Press, 2003), esp. 17–25, with further references.

[88] See Chapter 2 above.   [89] *Ep.* 9.8, 10.

[90] Although Seneca's opinion is still that the sage is 'self-sufficient'; cf. *Ep.* 9.3: 'There is this difference between ourselves [i.e. the Stoics] and the other school [i.e. the Cynics]: our ideal wise man feels his troubles, but overcomes them; their wise man does not even feel them. But we and they alike hold this idea,—that the wise man is self-sufficient. Nevertheless, he desires friends, neighbours, and associates, no matter how much he is sufficient unto himself.' Cf. also 9.13. The corresponding Greek term for 'self-sufficiency' is αὐτάρκεια.

friendship' is fundamentally other-regarding. It focuses on the need and want of the other. The Stoic sage makes friends for the primary purpose of being at *their* side in times of trouble and distress. To put it differently (cf. Rom 15.1–3), instead of pleasing himself or thinking only of himself, the sage is ready to bear the burdens of his friends whenever they are weak or afflicted, prepared even to give his life for them.

What are the implications of all this for the present discussion? To begin with, we should be absolutely clear about one thing: the comparison above does not imply that Jesus Christ and the Stoic sage had or were seen to have identical roles in every respect. I am not suggesting that Jesus was a Stoic sage, nor am I suggesting that the Stoic sage was perceived as a messianic redeemer in a religious sense like Jesus (i.e. as Jesus was perceived by his followers). That is not the issue here. The main point is that, in the sources compared, the two figures clearly had corresponding roles as moral examples. And an important inference drawn from that point is that (some of) the Christ-believers in Rome may well have recognized this parallel. That recognition, in turn, would have given them aid to properly interpret Paul's message in Romans 12–15 and Jesus' role in that message, his regard for others and self-sacrifice included. The portrait of Jesus as moral paradigm would not have sounded foreign to an audience already acquainted with corresponding figures from the philosophical circles, like the Stoic sage, Socrates in particular.

According to Paul, the ultimate goal of moral transformation is to become like Jesus. That goal, in turn, stands in sharp contrast to 'the ways of this world'. Seneca discusses this in relation to the Stoic sage: 'Our life should observe a happy medium between the ways of a sage and the ways of the world at large; all men should admire it, but they should understand it also.' Immediately anticipating the challenge concerning his reference to the happy medium, 'Well then, shall we act like other men? Shall there be no distinction between ourselves and the world?' Seneca replies: 'Yes, a very great one; let men find that we are unlike the common herd, if they look closely.'[91] For, as he says elsewhere, the ideal moral being, the Stoic sage, 'does not walk with the crowd (*populus*), but as the planets make their way against the whirl of heaven, so he proceeds contrary to the opinion of the world (*adversus opinionem omnium*)'.[92] If confronted with the question, 'Well then, shall we,

---

[91] *Ep.* 5.5–6: *temperetur vita inter bonos mores et publicos; suspiciant omnes vitam nostram, sed agnoscant. 'Quid ergo? Eadem faciemus, quae ceteri? Nihil inter nos et illos intererit?' Plurimum. Dissimiles esse nos vulgo sciat, qui inspexerit propius.* Seneca continues: 'If they visit us at home, they should admire us, rather than our household appointments. He is a great man who uses earthenware dishes as if they were silver; but he is equally great who uses silver as if it were earthenware.'

[92] *Const.* 14.4.

Christ-believers, act like other people, in accordance with the ways of the world?' Paul would no doubt have responded: μὴ γένοιτο· μὴ συσχηματίζεσθε τῷ αἰῶνι τούτῳ. And this is precisely what he states in Romans. The apostle underlines at the very outset of his moral teaching that the addressees must 'not be conformed to this world' (12.2). Instead, they are to act in accordance with their current position as members of the body 'in Christ' (v. 5), and thus to 'put on' not only the 'armour of light' but also Jesus Christ himself (13.12, 14). Those of Paul's addressees who were able to recognize the parallel between the Stoic thought of seeking to be a Socrates and Paul's language of 'Christ-clothing' would have had little problem with grasping the implications of that language. Instead of making a wonder about the precise meaning of Paul's phrasing, such listeners could proceed with attentiveness to learn more about the very essence of this particular 'clothing'.

In this way, Jesus' role as a moral example serves an important function in the moral instruction of Paul as he attempts to persuade his readers to take up and fully submit to a particular way of life as their 'living sacrifice' offered to God—their 'reasonable worship'. While the two are not identical in every detail, the ideal Stoic sage serves an analogous function as a model of excellence to be followed persistently on the way to the divinely ordered moral transformation. The Stoics did indeed also exhort their readers, students, and other addressees to serve the deity primarily by presenting their bodies as 'living sacrifices', that is, by leading a particular way of life, and, instead of conforming to the ways of the world at large, undergoing a total transformation in order to discern what truly is good, acceptable, and perfect in the eyes of God.

MUTUAL LOVE AND CARE

It is the concept of 'love' (ἀγάπη)[93] that in Roman Christianity is presented as something 'good, acceptable, and perfect'. First Peter clearly sees love as the primary virtue, and 1 Clement seems to do so as well, although the latter author's presentation of its primary position is more indirect due to the situational focus of the letter. As we have seen, the author of 1 Clement was very much influenced by the apostle Paul's words on love, particularly in

---

[93] Horrell complains that 'love is a vague and overused term' (referring to Richard Hays) and suggests that one speaks instead of 'other-regard' (*Solidarity*, 242). I agree that 'love' may be vague and overused, but I am not convinced about the benefits of using the phrase 'other-regard' instead, especially when comparing uses of the concept in different sources.

1 Corinthians but no doubt in Romans as well. Rather than being the subject of reasoned argument, the position of love as a primary virtue is assumed to be common knowledge, ready to be adapted to the specific issues at hand. The main attention is paid to the practical effects of love, especially in relation to the question of unity and harmony within the community. Love is perceived primarily as a disposition of mind that is prerequisite to proper conduct. Like Paul, the author of 1 Clement uses strong language to demonstrate and confirm the consequence of having this virtue: 'Apart from love *nothing* is pleasing to God' (δίχα ἀγάπης οὐδὲν εὐάρεστόν ἐστιν τῷ θεῷ).[94]

The absolute necessity of love is expressed even more strongly by the author of 1 Peter, in whose text ἀγάπη and φιλαδελφία are the key moral terms. It is the firm conception of this author that in their dealings with one another nothing is so important for the Christ-believers as love: '*Above all*, maintain fervent love for one another' (πρὸ πάντων τὴν εἰς ἑαυτοὺς ἀγάπην ἐκτενῆ ἔχοντες).[95] To express one's love for the neighbour can, according to 1 Peter, mean several things, like forgiving, helping, and showing respect and hospitality, but, precisely as in Romans and 1 Clement, the concept defies any strict definition in practical terms because the thing that it describes is essentially a subjective motivation. 'Love' denotes *the proper disposition on which all conduct is based* within Christ-believing communities. For this very reason, in Romans, Paul goes so far as to claim that the entire Jewish Law—every moral demand in the Law—is 'summed up' (ἀνακεφαλαιοῦται) in this single commandment: 'Love your neighbour as yourself' (ἀγαπήσεις τὸν πλησίον σου ὡς σεαυτόν).[96] For the Christ-believers, love represents the 'cardinal virtue'—their 'metanorm', if you will.[97]

It is not unlikely that the author of 1 Peter was, like his close contemporary 'Clement', directly influenced by Paul's emphasis on the virtue of love. To be sure, in light of the great and widespread attention to the concept of love (ἀγάπη) in early Christian writings,[98] it is not unlikely either that the Roman Christ-believers had (also) become familiar with the weight of this concept in the moral teaching of the movement through other channels. But the fact

---

[94] 1 Clem. 49.5. Cf. Rom 13.8; 1 Cor 13.1–3.   [95] 1 Pet 4.8.

[96] Rom 13.9 (from Lev 19.18).

[97] cf. Horrell, *Solidarity*, 99, 204, 274, who defines 'metanorm' as 'one which determines the moral framework within which other norms, values and customs can be articulated and practised' (following S. Benhabib). Horrell himself sees two kinds of 'metanorms' in the ethics of Paul: corporate solidarity and other-regard.

[98] cf., e.g., Matt 5.43–6; 22.39; Mark 12.31; Luke 6.27–35; 10.27; John 13.34–5; 15.12–17; Rom 13.8–10; 1 Cor 13; Gal 5.13–14; Eph 4.2; 1 Thess 3.12; 4.9–10; 2 Thess 1.3; Phlm 5; Jas 2.8; 1 Pet 1.22; 2.17; 4.8; 1 John 2.10; 3.10–18, 23; 4.7–21; 2 John 5–6; 1 Clem. 49–50; 2 Clem. 13.4; Ign. *Trall.* 8; *Diogn.* 5.11; 6.6; 10.4. Seven of these references (five authors) quote the love command in Lev 19.18 (Matt 5.43; 22.39; Mark 12.31; Luke 10.27; Rom 13.9; Gal 5.14; Jas 2.8).

remains that the earliest extant 'Christian' moral teaching in Rome is Paul's Letter to the Romans, and in that teaching love is patently presented as the primary virtue. First Peter shows many signs of literary dependence on Paul's letter, and it appears that the author of 1 Clement not only knew but directly applied much of Paul's moral teaching in Romans. Both 1 Peter and 1 Clement thus suggest that long before the close of the first century CE, the moral teaching of Paul enjoyed a significant position in Roman Christianity and had contributed much to the identity formation of the movement in terms of morality. Hence the teaching of Paul is properly treated as an ethical touchstone and point of departure for Roman Christianity.

The importance of 'love' in Paul's letter hardly needs further illustration. Neither does its place in 1 Peter and 1 Clement. For this has long been a celebrated topic through (Western, Christian) history and richly accounted for in various studies of early Christianity. Much less known, on the other hand, is Stoic thought on love, despite its observable presence in the last two millennia or so. An example of that thought in the very city of Rome around the middle of the first century CE is Seneca's teaching that one must live for one's neighbour if one would live for oneself,[99] because 'mutual love' (*amor mutuus*) is something that Nature itself (= God) has generated in human beings, creating them as it did from the same source and to the same end.[100] Mutual love, then, is a moral demand that is divinely ordained as an integral part of human existence, according to the Stoic.[101] Correspondingly, the aim of Seneca's moral teaching was to lead people to an 'all-embracing love (*amor*) of the human race even as of oneself'.[102] The thought is, in other words, simply inherent in the Stoic doctrine of the divine origin of every human being and of universal humanity. The same doctrine is behind Epictetus' radical demand that people, imitating the ideal sage, 'love' ($\phi\iota\lambda\epsilon\hat{\iota}\nu$) even those who torture them.[103]

While Epictetus uses the verb $\phi\iota\lambda\epsilon\hat{\iota}\nu$ in this context (cf. the noun $\phi\iota\lambda\acute{\iota}a$),[104] as a rule, Seneca uses the word *amor* (cf. the verb *amare*),[105] which corresponds to the Greek terms $\phi\iota\lambda\acute{\iota}a$, $\dot{a}\gamma\acute{a}\pi\eta$, and/or $\ddot{\epsilon}\rho\omega_S$ (depending on the context). As we have seen, it is the second one, $\dot{a}\gamma\acute{a}\pi\eta$, that is normally used in the Christian sources to express the concept of 'love', but it should not be

---

[99] *Ep.* 48.2: *alteri vivas oportet, si vis tibi vivere.*   [100] *Ep.* 95.52.

[101] cf. *Ep.* 102.18.   [102] *Clem.* 1.11.2. Cf. also 2.5.3.

[103] *Diss.* 3.22.54. We shall return to this text below when we turn our attention to the topic of 'love of enemies'.

[104] cf. also *Diss.* 2.22 ($\Pi\epsilon\rho\grave{\iota}$ $\phi\iota\lambda\acute{\iota}a_S$); 3.24.86; 4.2.3, 7, 10; 4.5.35.

[105] See, e.g., *Ep.* 9.6, 18; 18.15; 20.7; 35.1; 47.18; 66.24; 74.21; 78.7; 81.12; 88.30; 91.13; 95.63; 99.21; 104.11; *Clem.* 1.19.6; 2.5.3; *Ira* 1.3.6; 2.28.6; 2.31.3, 7; 2.36.6; 3.5.6; 3.28.1, 4; 3.34.3; *Prov.* 2.7; 4.7; *Marc.* 10.3; 12.2; *Brev. vit.* 19.2; *Polyb.* 16.3; *Helv.* 19.5; *Tranq.* 1.3; *Ben.* 1.2.5; 2.18.3; 3.1.5; 4.14.4; 4.17.2; 4.19.1; 4.21.2; 5.5.2; *Nat.* 1.17.6.

missed that the first term, φιλία, occurs in the composite word φιλαδελφία, 'brotherly love', which is also prominent in the moral teaching of the Christian writings.[106] There may be some difference between the Latin word *amor* and the Greek words ἀγάπη and φιλία, for the obvious reason that they belong to two different languages, but the distance between the Latin and the Greek terms should not be overstated. Studies show that the Latin *amor* (and *amare*) is more or less equivalent to the Greek φιλία (and φιλεῖν).[107] But this should hardly come as a surprise, since the terms constitute expressions of something shared by human beings, whether Latin-speaking or Greek, i.e. the proper disposition in human relations. Moreover, long before the turn of the Common Era, Roman philosophical discussions of human relations were deeply indebted to Greek discourse. And so was the use of terminology.

As for the relationship between the Greek words φιλία and ἀγάπη, it has often been held—but sometimes simply assumed—that the concept of ἀγάπη is uniquely 'Christian' and that there is a significant distinction between ἀγάπη and φιλία (and cognates),[108] that is, between 'Christian' love and 'pagan' love. However, while it is true that the noun ἀγάπη is rather rare in ancient ('pagan') Greek literature,[109] where φιλία is typically used,[110] the verb ἀγαπᾶν is actually quite common, at times even more common than the verb φιλεῖν.[111] Moreover, an increasing number of scholars are now recognizing that the two concepts, ἀγάπη/ἀγαπᾶν and φιλία/φιλεῖν, are virtually

---

[106] Rom 12.10; 1 Thess 4.9; Heb 13.1; 1 Pet 1.22; 3.8; 2 Pet 1.7 (× 2); 1 Clem. 47.5; 48.1. Cf. also, e.g., φιλόστοργος (Rom 12.10), φιλοξενία (Rom 12.13; Heb 13.2; 1 Clem. 1.2; 10.7; 11.1; 12.1; Herm. *Mand.* 38.10), φιλόξενος (1 Tim 3.2; Tit 1.8; 1 Pet 4.9; 1 Clem. 12.3; Herm. *Mand.* 38.10; *Sim.* 104.2), φιλανθρωπία (Acts 28.2; Tit 3.4), φιλανθρώπως (Acts 27.3), φιλοφρόνως (Acts 28.7), φιλόθεος (2 Tim 3.4), φιλάγαθος (Tit 1.8), φίλανδρος (Tit 2.4), φιλότεκνος (Tit 2.4; Herm. *Vis.* 3.1).

[107] cf. David Konstan, *Friendship in the Classical World* (Key Themes in Ancient History; Cambridge: Cambridge University Press, 1997), 122. The word φιλία is, of course, the standard Greek term for 'friendship', but the relationship between 'love' and 'friendship' is very close in the ancient sources. John T. Fitzgerald explains: 'In both Greek and Latin, the words for love and friendship are cognates, and love is often seen as the fount of friendship. Cicero, for instance, says that "it is love [*amor*], from which the word 'friendship' [*amicitia*] is derived, that leads to the establishing of goodwill" (*Amic.* 8.26)' ('Paul and Friendship', in *Paul in the Greco-Roman World: A Handbook* [ed. J. P. Sampley; Harrisburg, PA: Trinity Press, 2003], 338). Cf. also Cicero, *Amic.* 27.100; *Nat. d.* 1.44.122.

[108] See esp. the influential work of Ceslas Spicq, *Agapè dans le nouveau testament* (3 vols.; Paris: Gabalda, 1958–9). Cf. also his *Theological Lexicon of the New Testament* (ed. and trans. J. D. Ernest; 3 vols.; Peabody, MA: Hendrickson, 1994), 1: 8–22.

[109] See Oda Wischmeyer, 'Vorkommen und Bedeutung von Agape in der außerchristlichen Antike', *ZNW* 69 (1978): esp. 213–30.

[110] Or ἔρως, which refers mostly to love as desire and sexual passion (LSJ s.v.). The word does not occur in the NT, but cf. Ign. *Rom.* 7.2.

[111] See Robert Joly, *Le vocabulaire chrétien de l'amour, est-il original?* (Brussels: Universitaires de Bruxelles, 1968), esp. 10–29. Cf. Ethelbert Stauffer, 'ἀγαπάω κτλ', in *TDNT* 1: 35–8.

synonymous.[112] A good example of this is found already in Aristotle: 'To be loved (φιλεῖσθαι) is to be cherished (ἀγαπᾶσθαι) for one's own sake.'[113] Here Aristotle defines the state of φιλεῖσθαι by means of the verb ἀγαπᾶν. Another fine example can be seen in a speech delivered at the turn of the second century CE by the Cynic orator and former student of Musonius Rufus, Dio of Prusa (Chrysostom): 'It is somehow natural for the courageous to love (φιλεῖν) the courageous, while cowards eye them with misgiving and hate them as enemies, but welcome the base and like them (ἀγαπῶσιν).'[114] Again, the two verbs, φιλεῖν and ἀγαπᾶν, are used as virtual equivalents. The apostle Paul himself, who, as we have seen, speaks of ἀγάπη as the primary virtue of the Christ-believing communities, illustratively uses the verb φιλεῖν instead of ἀγαπᾶν at the close of his First Letter to the Corinthians (16.22): εἴ τις οὐ φιλεῖ τὸν κύριον, ἤτω ἀνάθεμα ('If anyone does not love the lord, let him be accursed!'). He does not say, 'If anyone does not ἀγαπᾷ the lord...', as one might have expected, but '*If anyone does not φιλεῖ the lord...*' Whereas this last example does not prove that Paul might as well have used φιλία/φιλεῖν instead of ἀγάπη/ἀγαπᾶν as the key concept in his moral teaching, it does indicate the closeness of the two terms in the Graeco-Roman world of thought, including Paul's.

The fact that Christian authors typically *did* prefer ἀγάπη rather than φιλία as the proper term for 'love' may indicate a wish on their part to distinguish themselves from the surrounding world by the use of characteristic terminology. That is to say, it may indicate that they wanted to use the term ἀγάπη as a certain 'stamp' for genuine Christian morality. But it need not imply that

---

[112] Joly, *Vocabulaire*, 34–47; D. A. Carson, *Exegetical Fallacies* (Grand Rapids, MI: Baker, 1984), 26, 30, 51–4; Margaret M. Mitchell, *Paul and the Rhetoric of Reconciliation: An Exegetical Investigation of the Language and Composition of 1 Corinthians* (Hermeneutische Untersuchungen zur Theologie 28; Tübingen: Mohr [Siebeck], 1991), 165 with nn.; Bakke, 'Concord', 193 with nn.; Lee, *Paul*, 178–9. See also the discussion in L&N, where the editors comment: 'Though some persons have tried to assign certain significant differences of meaning between [ἀγάπη/ἀγαπᾶν and φιλία/φιλεῖν], it does not seem possible to insist upon a contrast of meaning in any and all contexts' (p. 294). Cf. also LSJ s.v. ἀγαπάω I. On the *later* Christian distinction between ἀγάπη/ἀγαπᾶν and φιλία/φιλεῖν, see Konstan, *Friendship*, 156–73.

[113] *Rhet.* 1.11.17 (1371a): τὸ δὲ φιλεῖσθαι ἀγαπᾶσθαί ἐστιν αὐτὸν δι' αὐτόν. In *Rhet.* 2.4.1 (1380b) Aristotle defines 'love' (φιλία) as follows: ἔστω δὴ τὸ φιλεῖν τὸ βούλεσθαί τινι ἃ οἴεται ἀγαθά, ἐκείνου ἕνεκα ἀλλὰ μὴ αὑτοῦ, καὶ τὸ κατὰ δύναμιν πρακτικὸν εἶναι τούτων ('Let loving, then, be defined as wishing for anyone the things which we believe to be good, for his sake but not for our own, and procuring them for him as far as lies in our power'). Cf. Xenophon, *Mem.* 2.7.12: ὡς κηδεμόνα ἐφίλουν, ὡς ὠφελίμους ἡγάπα ('They loved him as a guardian and he liked them because they were useful').

[114] *4 Regn.* 4.15: καὶ γάρ πως πεφύκασιν οἱ μὲν θαρραλέοι τοὺς θαρραλέους φιλεῖν, οἱ δὲ δειλοὶ τούτους μὲν ὑφορῶνται καὶ μισοῦσιν ὡς ἐχθρούς, τοὺς δὲ ἀγεννεῖς προσίενται καὶ ἀγαπῶσιν. Cf. also *1 Regn.* 1.19; *3 Regn.* 3.103, 110–11. Lee offers English translations of these latter examples in *Paul*, 178 n. 52.

there actually *was* a difference of any real substance. To put it differently, the Christian preference for ἀγάπη may reflect a *claim* of difference, although the actual difference was close to none. But as history shows, the claim alone can sometimes, quite literally, *make* a difference in the conception of people.[115]

Hence, when discussing terms like ἀγάπη/ἀγαπᾶν, φιλία/φιλεῖν, and *amor/amare* in the Christian and Stoic sources, we are dealing with concepts that are largely equivalent. Needless to say, as always, each occasion is determined by the specific context in which the term in question occurs.

The Christian sources pay considerable attention to that aspect of 'love' that involves mutual help and care. Unity is also a motif intimately linked with that aspect. As we have already seen, the Stoic sources often direct their attention to these same motifs, and the outcome is fundamentally similar. The close connection between love, on the one hand, and mutual help and care, on the other, is openly expressed, too, in the Stoic writings. Thus, on one occasion Seneca pairs that which is loving together with that which advances mutual help, in contrast to that which is hostile and brings only mutual destruction: 'What is more loving (*amantius*) to others than man? What more hostile than anger? Man is born for mutual help (*adiutorium mutuum*); anger for mutual destruction.'[116] Mutual love and help go together, according to this description. And Seneca continues by adding the thought of unity: 'The one desires union (*congregari vult*), the other disunion; the one to help (*prodesse*), the other to harm',[117] and so on. In agreement with the thought and language of 1 Clement, the Stoic philosopher emphasizes that human life is based on kindness (*beneficium*) and concord (*concordia*), and in agreement with the argument of 1 Peter, the prerequisite for mutual alliance and help, according to Seneca, is mutual love (*amor mutuus*).[118] Quoting the Stoic Hecato (early first century BCE),[119] his advice is: 'If you would be loved, love' (*si vis amari, ama*).[120] Here we are reminded of Paul's words on mutual love in Romans 13.8–10, where the apostle stated that the moral code of the Jewish Law as a whole is fulfilled in this one commandment, from Leviticus 19.18: 'Love your neighbour as yourself'. The apostle then went on to explain what the commandment of love meant in actual practice (chs. 14–15): it meant mutual help and care, and adaptation to the needs of the others, especially the (more) 'weak' ones. Similarly, Seneca's reference to the corresponding Stoic rule, 'If you would be loved, love', is made in an epistolary discourse on the topic of friendship, and it is in this very discourse that he underlines so distinctly the

---

[115] cf. my discussion in Thorsteinsson, 'Role of Morality', esp. 145–57.
[116] *Ira* 1.5.2.   [117] *Ira* 1.5.2. Cf. 3.5.6.   [118] *Ira* 1.5.3.
[119] Hecato of Rhodes was a student of Panaetius and associate of Posidonius.
[120] *Ep.* 9.6.

active side of love and care, i.e. that the Stoic sage—and thus everyone else—desires friends so that he can love and care for *them* whenever *they* are in need. Here, too, the stress is laid on the needs of the 'weak' and the less fortunate: the sage desires friends 'that he may have someone by whose sick-bed he himself may sit, someone a prisoner in hostile hands whom he himself may set free'.[121] We saw this text quoted more fully in the previous section.

For Epictetus, in their application of love, human beings have clear patterns to follow in such virtuous individuals as Socrates and Diogenes the Cynic, whose love of others was rooted not only in their character as human beings but also in their specific relationship with God. Responding to an interlocutor's question of how one should become 'affectionate' (φιλόστοργος),[122] Epictetus reminds him of his duty to love (φιλεῖν) all fellow human beings, precisely as Diogenes had done, a sage who was so gentle and benevolent (ἥμερος καὶ φιλάνθρωπος) that he willingly took upon himself great physical pain and suffering for the sake of the common welfare of humanity (ὑπὲρ τοῦ κοινοῦ τῶν ἀνθρώπων). 'But what was the manner of his loving (φιλεῖν)?' the Stoic teacher then asks, providing the answer himself: 'As became a servant of Zeus, caring for men indeed, but at the same time subject unto God' (ὡς τοῦ Διὸς διάκονον ἔδει, ἅμα μὲν κηδόμενος, ἅμα δ' ὡς τῷ θεῷ ὑποτεταγμένος).[123] According to Epictetus, this is also the reason why for Diogenes the whole world, and not some particular place in the world, was his fatherland (πατρίς), implying that the sage saw the whole humankind as his family.[124]

As we have seen time and again, the Stoics agree that human beings are both social beings and good by nature, and thus that it lies in their very nature to care for and help their neighbours. This is an essential aspect of the Stoic theory of *oikeiōsis*, a theory that is fundamentally other-regarding and community-oriented.[125] The theory is grounded in the principle of universal humanity, which teaches that, as all have equal share in the divine and all-pervading λόγος (*ratio*), every human being is sacred simply on account of his or her being. Morality is so firmly rooted in the order of Nature itself that it cannot be understood apart from it. As Epictetus explains, the Stoic opinion is that each and every person is by nature a social and affectionate being, and that human beings are created to do good, to cooperate, and to pray for the well-being of each other.[126] It follows that a work that is beneficent, of

---

[121] *Ep.* 9.8. Seneca continues: 'He who regards himself only, and enters upon friendships for this reason, reckons wrongly.'

[122] Note that Paul uses this concept in Rom 12.10 (τῇ φιλαδελφίᾳ εἰς ἀλλήλους φιλόστοργοι).

[123] *Diss.* 3.24.58–65. A useful discussion of the love of the Stoic sage is found in William O. Stephens, 'Epictetus on How the Stoic Sage Loves', *OSAP* 14 (1996).

[124] *Diss.* 3.24.66. Cf. also 3.22.81–2.

[125] See the discussion on Seneca in Chapter 2 above.   [126] *Diss.* 3.13.5; 4.1.122.

common utility, and noble is the work which 'befits a human being' (ἀνθρωπικόν).[127] A human being looks to the interests of the other and seeks to benefit her neighbour. The Stoics are optimistic about human capacity to live virtuously, agreeing that this pertains to humanity as a whole, without exception. Everyone has an inborn inclination towards 'goodness and nobleness' (καλοκἀγαθίαν), and there are 'seeds of virtue' (σπέρμα ἀρετῆς) in each and everyone,[128] Musonius declares. According to the Stoics, then, every human being has a natural disposition to virtue, and there are bonds between people that have come into existence long before the formation of any concrete communities.[129] Influenced as he was by the ethics of the Stoics, Cicero called this bond the 'universal brotherhood of mankind' (*communem humani generis societatem*).[130] The aim of Stoic ethics was to preserve this universal brotherhood, this natural bond of mutual love. Seneca puts the Stoic position in plain terms: 'Nature begot me loving (*amantem*) all people.'[131]

It would almost certainly be wrong to go so far as to say that the Stoics had made the virtue of love into a 'cardinal virtue', even though some of them did not hesitate to subdivide and add rather freely to the virtues.[132] For them, in theory at least, the cardinal virtues remained the four traditional ones, namely, φρόνησις/*prudentia*, σωφροσύνη/*temperantia*, δικαιοσύνη/*iustitia*, and ἀνδρεία/*fortitudo*, of which the first one was the pre-eminent virtue. However, it would be equally wrong to hold that the virtue of love was not important to Stoic moral teaching. On the contrary, there is little doubt that the Stoics in Rome would have agreed wholeheartedly with Paul, 'Peter', and 'Clement' about love being a proper moral principle on which to base the community. And there is no good reason to presume that, if confronted with the Stoic moral teaching, the Roman Christ-believers would have needed detailed theoretical knowledge of the doctrine of *oikeiōsis* in order to recognize the similarity of thought in this respect between their own moral teaching and that of the Stoics. They may, on the other hand, have recognized

---

[127] *Diss.* 4.10.12. Cf. 1.19.13; 2.10.23.

[128] Musonius 2.38.12–14. Cf. 2.38.1–3; 17.108.8–18; Epictetus, *Diss.* 1.19.12–13; 1.23.1; 2.10.23; 2.20.6; 3.7.27; 3.13.5; 3.24.12; 4.7.8; 4.10.12; 4.11.1.

[129] cf. Lee, *Paul*, 88. On p. 76 she comments: 'The Stoics did not seek to create a moral order as much as to teach people how to recognize and preserve the order which already existed.' On Seneca in particular, Lee writes: 'Seneca does not advocate a certain type of social behavior in order to create unity, but rather he sees it as inherent, a result of being a human being' (p. 87).

[130] *Off.* 3.6.28.

[131] *Ep.* 102.18: *Natura me amantem omnium genuit* (my translation above). Cf. *Ep.* 48.2; *Clem.* 1.3.2; *Ben.* 7.1.7. Cf. also Cicero, *Fin.* 3.65.

[132] cf., e.g., Seneca, *Ep.* 92.19 (*iustitia, pietas, fides, fortitudo, prudentia*); *Ben.* 2.31.1 (*pietas, fides, iustitia*); 4.8.3 (*iustitia, probitas, prudentia, fortitudo, frugalitas*).

a certain difference between the two moral teachings with respect to the ethical scope of 'love' (see the discussion in Chapter 10 below).

As we have seen, the manner in which these two parties express their moral teachings points to shared tenets of thought. Thus both favour the metaphor of the 'body' (σῶμα, *corpus*) to describe their notions of the ideal structure of the community or of human relations in general. Seneca applied it as he laid down his formula for proper duties in human relationships, stressing that all are related by nature as members of one and the same 'body', i.e. the universe as a whole, and he applied it when he wanted to demonstrate the reciprocal responsibility of society and individual members thereof.[133] Epictetus used the metaphor to illustrate the essence of universal humanity, emphasizing each and every part's integral relation to the whole.[134] Paul chose to describe his community-oriented ethic in Romans by way of the metaphor of the body, explaining that all roles and functions within the community were interconnected and interdependent, always working for the benefit of the whole.[135] The author of 1 Clement made use of the metaphor as an argument against factions within the community, underlining the aspects of oneness and mutuality.[136] In all cases, the use of the metaphor calls for unity and mutual love and care by illustrating that each and every individual in the community or society has a certain function within the whole without which the whole cannot function properly, and that each and every part of the whole is related to the other parts and has obligations towards them, regardless of position. What image could be more appropriate than the 'body' to underline the need for diversity and, at the same time, to illustrate proper corporate unity? All parties involved would have agreed that the community as a whole is sustained 'only by the mutual protection and love of its parts (*amore partium*)'.[137]

What does it tell us that the metaphor of the body is so richly used by the Stoics and Christians alike? To begin with, it should be absolutely clear that the use of the metaphor by both parties need not imply any direct relationship between the two. After all, the metaphor was widely known in the ancient world, whether from writings or public speeches, and it was used by different groups of people in different places. According to our sources, this was particularly the case in the city of Rome, where the metaphor was popularized through the Menenius Agrippa fable, famously accounted for in Livy's *History of Rome* in the late first century BCE and shortly thereafter by Dionysius of

---

[133] *Ep.* 95.51–3; *Ira* 2.31.7. Cf. the discussion in Chapter 2 above.
[134] *Diss.* 2.5.24–6; 2.10.4. Cf. the discussion in Chapter 4 above.
[135] Rom 12.4–5 (cf. 1 Cor 12.12–31). Cf. the discussion in Chapter 6 above.
[136] 1 Clem. 37.5; 46.7. Cf. the discussion in Chapter 8 above.   [137] Seneca, *Ira* 2.31.7.

Halicarnassus, among others.[138] Hence we cannot simply assume that when Christ-believers made use of the metaphor they did so because they had some specific, close connection to those 'pagans' who also applied it, like the Stoics who did so to a notable extent. Nevertheless, the analogous applications of the metaphor by the two groups underline further the resemblance of thought and means of argument. Roman Christian readers of Paul's letter(s), like the author of 1 Clement, may well have associated his body metaphor with earlier and current uses of it in Rome, not necessarily by the Stoics, but quite likely so.[139] Moreover, precisely in light of how well the metaphor was known in Rome, its use by Christ-believers suggests not only that, in this case at least, they felt quite comfortable with applying traditional Graeco-Roman material, but also that they did not desire or see reasons to differentiate themselves from Roman society as a whole in this respect.

Of course, the Christian authors do not apply the body metaphor as an illustration of universal humanity, as the Stoics frequently do. The former are primarily concerned with the community of Christ-believers and thus speak of the unity of that particular community as one body 'in Christ'. The Stoics spoke more broadly of one body 'in Nature', so to speak, or one body 'in God', which is the very same thing.[140] While the underlying thought may coincide, the manner of expression is not the same. There is a resemblance, however, in the fact that, although the Christian 'body' definitely includes a more narrow reference in moral terms (cf. the discussion in the final chapter of this study), both the Christians and the Stoics believe that the 'body' is pervaded with a divine 'spirit' or 'breath' ($\pi\nu\epsilon\hat{\upsilon}\mu\alpha$, *spiritus*), which holds it together and makes it a unified whole. For the Stoics, their 'origin upward' is the divine $\pi\nu\epsilon\hat{\upsilon}\mu\alpha/$ *spiritus* which permeates everything, including the human mind, which is a fragment of the 'spirit'.[141]

Just as the universe as a whole has *tonos*, *pneuma*, and *logos* holding it together, so each individual thing in the universe has its own *tonos*, *pneuma*, and *logos*, regulating its

---

[138] Livy, *Ab urbe cond.* 2.32.8–12; Dionysius of Halicarnassus, *Ant. rom.* 6.86. Cf. also Plutarch, *Cor.* 6; Florus, *Epit.* 1.17. See further Wilhelm Nestle, 'Die Fabel des Menenius Agrippa', *Klio* 21 (1927): 350–60.

[139] The fact that passages like 1 Clement 20 show strong signs of Stoic influences (here in terms of cosmology) does not speak against such an association on the part of this author. For further discussion of potential Stoicism in 1 Clement 20, see W. C. van Unnik, 'Is 1 Clement 20 Purely Stoic?' *VC* 4 (1950): 181–9; Werner Jaeger, *Early Christianity and Greek Paideia* (Cambridge, MA: Belknap, 1961), 14–16; Lampe, *From Paul*, 208–17; Bakke, 'Concord', 160–2; Meiser, 'Christentum', 146–52.

[140] cf., e.g., these words of Seneca, *Ep.* 92.30: 'All this universe which encompasses us is one, and it is God; we are associates of God; we are his members' (*totum hoc, quo continemur, et unum est et deus; et socii sumus eius et membra*).

[141] cf. Reydams-Schils, *Roman Stoics*, 36.

physical and metaphysical metabolism, so to speak, keeping it within its own skin, and accounting for its vital functions. All things are thus related to the cosmic *pneuma* and to each other, since *tonos* and *pneuma* are the same whether operating on a cosmic level or on the level of the individual being.[142]

While the πνεῦμα/*spiritus* may certainly have different connotations for the Christians and the Stoics,[143] for both the divine origin of the πνεῦμα/*spiritus* and its unifying role within the 'body' is in essence the same. As the author of 1 Clement says, 'All parts [of the body] work together in subjection to a single order, to keep the whole body healthy', using the wording πάντα συνπνεῖ, which literally means 'all parts *breathe* together', the verb συμ-πνεῖν being cognate with the noun πνεῦμα.[144] And as Paul says in Romans, it is through the πνεῦμα that God's love is 'poured' into the hearts of believers,[145] whose possession of the πνεῦμα (God's and Christ's πνεῦμα 'within' them),[146] in turn, leads to their mutual love and care. Thus, for Christians and Stoics alike, the metaphor of the body constitutes an attempt to provide an inclusive illustration not only of people's (proper) relationship to each other but also of their (proper) relationship to the divine.

NON-RETALIATION AND 'LOVE OF ENEMIES'

There are few topics that so clearly betray the common traits in the Christian and Stoic texts under discussion as the demand of non-retaliation. To be sure,

---

[142] Colish, *Stoic Tradition*, 27. *Tonos* (τόνος) is a designation sometimes used by the Stoics of the deity. It denotes 'the vital tension holding each thing together within itself and making the whole universe cohere' (ibid., 24). Cf. also David E. Hahm, *The Origins of Stoic Cosmology* (Columbus, OH: Ohio State University Press, 1977), 240–8.

[143] Space does not allow me to discuss this complicated issue in any detail, but see the discussion in Lee, *Paul*, esp. 49–58, 86, 116–52, 158–66; Troels Engberg-Pedersen, 'A Stoic Understanding of *Pneuma* in Paul', in *Philosophy at the Roots of Christianity* (ed. T. Engberg-Pedersen and H. Tronier; Copenhagen: University of Copenhagen, 2006), 101–23; idem, 'The Material Spirit: Cosmology and Ethics in Paul', *NTS* 55 (2009): 179–97. For a general survey of πνεῦμα in Stoic cosmology, see Michael Lapidge, 'Stoic Cosmology and Roman Literature, First to Third Centuries A.D.', *ANRW* 36.3: 1383–5 and *passim*.

[144] 1 Clem. 37.5. Cf. 21.9: ἡ πνοὴ αὐτοῦ [i.e. τοῦ θεοῦ] ἐν ἡμῖν ἐστίν ('His [i.e. God's] breath is in us'). The noun πνοή ('breath') is also a cognate of the verb πνεῖν. See also Bakke, 'Concord', 183, where he discusses the Graeco-Roman political context of phrases like πάντα συνπνεῖ in relation to the body metaphor.

[145] Rom 5.5: ἡ ἀγάπη τοῦ θεοῦ ἐκκέχυται ἐν ταῖς καρδίαις ἡμῶν διὰ πνεύματος ἁγίου τοῦ δοθέντος ἡμῖν ('God's love has been poured into our hearts through the holy spirit that has been given to us').

[146] Rom 8.9–11.

the topic is not addressed as such in 1 Clement,[147] but all the other authors include at least a general reference to this demand, and some are willing to reflect further on its meaning.

As we have seen, in his moral instruction sent to Rome, Paul strongly rejects any form of retaliation on the part of Christ-believers. According to him, they should never repay evil for evil (μηδενὶ κακὸν ἀντὶ κακοῦ ἀποδιδόντες),[148] regardless of who is responsible for this evil. Likewise, the author of 1 Peter urges that under no circumstances should one render evil for evil (μὴ ἀποδιδόντες κακὸν ἀντὶ κακοῦ), using almost exactly the same expression as Paul in Romans, adding also that neither should one repay 'abuse for abuse' (λοιδορίαν ἀντὶ λοιδορίας).[149] In addition to some other potential Christian writings or oral traditions, it is not unlikely that the author of 1 Peter was here directly influenced by Paul's words in Romans. But it is also quite possible that both of these authors were shaped by a wider circle of moral discourse, and that they may even have been conscious that they were agreeing to and proclaiming a moral demand that was widely expressed in the ancient world.[150] At any rate, those of Paul's readers in Rome—possibly including the authors of 1 Peter and 1 Clement—who may have been in some contact with the more philosophically inspired environment of the city would not have found his demand of non-retaliation to be anything unusual, let alone unique. On the contrary, they would probably have understood him to be simply agreeing with the wider Graeco-Roman moral tradition that rejected all forms of retaliation, the background of which can be traced to Plato's account of Socrates in *Crito*: 'Then we ought neither to requite wrong with wrong nor to do evil to anyone, no matter what he may have done to us.'[151]

We have already seen that, in the milieu to which Paul sent his letter, and in the milieu in which the authors of 1 Peter and 1 Clement lived, it was the Stoic school that provided the most prominent and influential ethical system, and it is evident that the Roman Stoics firmly advocated Socrates' ethic of non-retaliation. Thus, at the same time that Paul's letter arrived in Rome, Seneca

---

[147] Although it may perhaps be argued that the topic of non-retaliation is *indirectly* included in the senders' objections to 'faction', 'strife', and 'schism' within the Corinthian community.

[148] Rom 12.17. Cf. v. 19: μὴ ἑαυτοὺς ἐκδικοῦντες. Cf. also 1 Thess 5.15. For a list of non-retaliatory responses to offences in the letters of Paul, see Gordon M. Zerbe, *Non-Retaliation in Early Jewish and New Testament Texts: Ethical Themes in Social Contexts* (JSPSup 13; Sheffield: JSOT Press, 1993), 215–16.

[149] 1 Pet 3.9. On λοιδορία, cf. 2.23; 1 Cor 4.12.

[150] See the references, Jewish as well as non-Jewish, collected in Wilson, *Love*, 187–9 with nn.; Zerbe, *Non-Retaliation*; Söding, *Liebesgebot*, 80–2.

[151] Plato, *Crito* 49C: οὔτε ἄρα ἀνταδικεῖν δεῖ οὔτε κακῶς ποιεῖν οὐδένα ἀνθρώπων, οὐδ' ἂν ὁτιοῦν πάσχῃ ὑπ' αὐτῶν. See further Marius Reiser, 'Love of Enemies in the Context of Antiquity', *NTS* 47 (2001): 417–18.

was proclaiming forcefully that it can never be right to render evil for evil.[152] 'If someone strikes you, step back', he advised.[153] In fact, long before Seneca, Cicero had presented precisely this view to the Romans as the orthodox Stoic view.[154] Correspondingly, around the time of the authorship of 1 Peter and 1 Clement, Musonius was teaching his Roman students to renounce the old and widely fostered 'eye for an eye' attitude, which he described as characteristic not of human beings but of wild beasts.[155] Shortly thereafter, Musonius' teaching was promoted by Epictetus as well.[156] Hence, whether they knew it or not, when Paul and 'Peter' urged their audience to adopt and/or be faithful to an ethic of non-retaliation, they were expressing agreement with a widespread moral tradition that in the city of Rome was particularly associated with the Stoic school.

But *how* should one meet evil, according to these sources, and how should one treat evildoers? While Socrates (in Plato's account) does not take the step to address this question, on this point, too, our Stoic and Christian authors are in fundamental agreement: evil must be met and overcome *with good*. Seneca is very clear on this in his treatise 'On Anger' (*De Ira*): responding to an (imaginary) interlocutor who claims that 'it is sweet (*dulce*) to return a smart', Seneca says:

Not at all (*minime*); for it is not honourable, as in acts of kindness to requite benefits with benefits, so to requite injuries with injuries. In the one case it is shameful to be outdone, in the other not to be outdone. 'Revenge' (*ultio*) is an inhuman word and yet one accepted as legitimate, and 'retaliation' (*talio*) is not much different except in rank; the man who returns a smart commits merely the more pardonable sin.[157]

Seneca then goes on to recount an incident when Marcus Cato (Seneca's paradigmatic sage) chose to follow this very principle, namely, not to match fault with fault. Seneca's message is that each and every human being should follow in the footsteps of the sage[158] and treat the 'sins' and misdeeds of other people with its opposite—with good. After all,

we are all inconsiderate and unthinking, we are all untrustworthy, discontented, ambitious—why should I hide the universal sore by softer words?—we are all wicked. And so each man will find in his own breast the fault which he censures in another.... And so let us be more kindly toward one another; we being wicked live among the wicked. Only one thing can bring us peace—the compact of mutual indulgence (*mutuae facilitatis conventio*).[159]

---

[152] *Ira* 1.16.1; 2.32.1; 3.27.1.   [153] *Ira* 2.34.5 (*Percussit te, recede*).
[154] *Fin.* 3.71: *alienumque esse a sapiente non modo iniuriam cui facere verum etiam nocere* ('it is foreign to the nature of the Wise Man not only to wrong but even to hurt anyone').
[155] Musonius 10.78.26–8.
[156] *Diss.* 4.1.122, 167; *Ench.* 43. Cf. also Marcus Aurelius, *Med.* 6.6; 7.52; 11.13.
[157] *Ira* 2.32.1.   [158] See *Ira* 2.10.6–7.   [159] *Ira* 3.26.4. Cf. also 2.28.

People who do bad things and harm their fellow human beings do so primarily out of ignorance and false opinion. They know not what they are doing.[160] And that is precisely why there can be no real justification for retaliation, according to the Stoic.[161] In short, 'unkindness must be treated with kindness' (*mansuete immansueta tractanda sunt*).[162]

Paul's discussion of the topic does not belong to a philosophical treatise or schoolroom lesson in ethics, and is naturally therefore more concise and less systematic than the Stoic discussions above. But it can nonetheless be seen that one of Paul's main points in Romans 12–13 is also to 'overcome evil with good' (νίκα ἐν τῷ ἀγαθῷ τὸ κακόν).[163] He, too, shares the view not only that it is possible to lead the evildoer towards a better course, but that one is obliged to do so as well. He believes that by doing good to the evildoer one can cause him to repent and change his ways.[164] To put it differently, the apostle agrees in essence with the judgement of the Stoic philosopher Musonius that by meeting evil with good one can be 'a source of good hope' to the person who treats one badly,[165] and thus possibly bring about the latter's conversion to a better behaviour and proper way of life. Seneca puts this conviction of the Stoics well when he insists that 'persistent goodness wins over bad men (*vincit malos pertinax bonitas*), and no one of them is so hardhearted and hostile to kindly treatment as not to love (*amet*) a good man even while they wrong him'.[166] Seneca's choice of the verb *vincere* (to 'win' or 'overcome') in this context corresponds to Paul's use of the verb νικᾶν (to 'overcome' or 'win'). Needless to say, the thought itself has roots in Jewish traditions as well, but it is telling in Paul's case that the closest parallel to his use here of the verb νικᾶν appears to be in 4 Maccabees,[167] a (roughly) contemporary Jewish writing that is marked precisely by the close combination, at times even full synthesis, of Jewish traditions and Greek philosophy (esp. Stoicism and Platonism).

While the treatment of the subject in 1 Peter is certainly brief, expressed mostly in clear-cut imperatives, the author underlines the importance of forgiveness in this respect, an act that he seems to present as one aspect of the virtue of love.[168] The close contemporaries of this author, Musonius and

---

[160] cf. the parallel thought in Rom 7.14–25.

[161] Seneca, *Ep.* 20.4–6; 28.9; 50.4–9; 61.3–4; cf. Epictetus, *Diss.* 1.18.3–4; 2.22.1–3; 2.26; 4.1.3; *Ench.* 42. The Stoics follow here in the footsteps of their ideal philosopher, Socrates.

[162] *Ira* 3.27.3.   [163] Rom 12.21.

[164] Rom 12.20. On this reading of the verse, see the discussion in Chapter 6 above. Cf. also 1 Pet 2.12, 15.

[165] Musonius 10.78.32–3 (αἴτιον εἶναι αὐτοῖς ἐλπίδος χρηστῆς).

[166] *Ben.* 7.31.1. Cf. also *Ira* 1.14.3.

[167] See Zerbe, *Non-Retaliation*, 236 n. 102, 249 n. 146. The verb is used in this context in 4 Macc. 1.11; 9.30; 16.14. Cf. also 6.10; 7.11; 9.6; 11.20.

[168] 1 Pet 4.8. On this reading of the verse, see the discussion in Chapter 7 above.

Epictetus, also find the act of forgiving essential to the principle of treating bad with good. According to the former, it is the Stoic sage who shows the way by deeming worthy of forgiveness (συγγνώμης ἀξιοῦν) anyone who does him wrong, regardless of who that person is.[169] It is probably safe to presume that forgiveness is also one of the things which Paul had in mind when he in Romans 14–15 pleaded for unity among the Christ-believers in Rome and urged them to cease passing judgements on one another.[170] For Paul, it was Jesus Christ who set the example to be followed in this regard,[171] precisely as the Stoic sage did for Musonius.[172]

Paul, however, has some afterthoughts regarding the degree and nature of this forgiveness. Having expressed his wish in Romans 12.17 that the Roman audience should never render evil for evil, and having repeated that wish in v. 19 with the words 'do not avenge yourselves' (μὴ ἑαυτοὺς ἐκδικοῦντες), he nevertheless allows for and expresses the belief that the evildoer *will* eventually receive due punishment, that is, through the 'wrath of God' for which the audience is to leave room (δότε τόπον τῇ ὀργῇ). Paul cites the words of none other than God as witness: ' "Vengeance is mine (ἐμοὶ ἐκδίκησις)! I will repay (ἐγὼ ἀνταποδώσω)!" says the Lord.'[173] The apostle thus assures his addressees that even though they themselves should never apply the 'eye for an eye' principle, in the end *God* will do so in their stead.[174] It is not unlikely that Paul here alludes to God's final judgement at the end of times, i.e. that Romans 12.19 is grounded in traditional Jewish eschatological discourse,[175] but it is even more likely that he (also) has in mind divine punishment that will take place in the very near future. Indeed, such punishment is what he refers to in

---

[169] Musonius 10.78.34–80.1. Cf. Epictetus, *Diss.* 2.22.36. Cf. also Seneca, *Ira* 2.10.2.

[170] Rom 14.3–4, 10, 13; 15.2. On the topic of forgiveness, cf. also 2 Cor 2.5–11.

[171] cf. Rom 13.14; 14.15; 15.1–7.

[172] Discussing Rom 12.14, 17–21, Esler asserts in his recent book on Romans: 'Whereas the Stoics advised the wise man not to pardon those who injured him, Paul urges a different approach' (*Conflict*, 327). This is a strange claim. Besides the fact that the Stoics would never 'advise' the wise man about anything (the basic idea is, of course, precisely the opposite!), the examples in my discussion above should suffice to show how badly mistaken Esler is in this respect.

[173] Rom 12.19, citing Deut 32.35, apparently from a version of the LXX that is not available to us (it differs also slightly from the MT); see further Dunn, *Romans*, 2: 749–50.

[174] This is a thought that some New Testament scholars seem to have more problems with than Paul himself, which, in turn, has resulted in some curious cases of theodicy. For instance, in his recent commentary on Romans, Jewett refers to an article by Robert Hamerton-Kelly who comments thus on Rom 12.19: 'The wrath [of God] works by self-inflicted harm. God gives sinners up to the consequences of their self-destructive actions.... Thus there is no actual violence in God, and the quotation, "vengeance is mine, I shall repay" must, therefore, be taken loosely.' Jewett himself ends up with the solution that the divine wrath spoken of in Rom 12.19 'belongs in that arena of unsearchable mystery celebrated at the end of Rom 11' (*Romans*, 777).

[175] cf. Rom 2.5–6; 5.9. Cf. also 1 Thess 1.10; 2.16.

the immediately following discussion of the Roman authorities, when he explains that the authorities serve as God's instrument, not only to reward those who do good but also, and not least, to punish those who do evil.[176] That is (partly) how God chooses to punish evildoers *before* the arrival of the day of judgement, i.e. through the Roman authorities. It is probably no mere coincidence that we can see a similar line of thought in the moral teaching and theology of 1 Peter. According to this author, God will eventually judge all people, whether they are responsible for good things or bad.[177] The end is near,[178] but until that day God makes use of the civic authorities to punish all evildoers, including those who are Christian.[179] To be sure, we do not see in this writing the same promise to the audience, so to speak, of divine revenge as in Romans. Unlike Paul, the author of 1 Peter does not explicitly assure or remind his addressees that the evildoers whom they must forgive and treat well will eventually receive their punishment anyway. But the notion is still there, albeit implicitly.

Despite the basic similarities between Roman Christianity and Roman Stoicism with respect to the topic of non-retaliation, an important difference emerges here between the two: it is quite difficult to find corresponding justification for revenge in the writings of the Roman Stoics, whether the revenge is thought to take place in the present or in the future.[180] This is without doubt partly due to theological differences between the two systems of thought, especially different ideas of the manner and extent to which the deity intervenes in human affairs and history. In the Judeo-Christian tradition God does so frequently, by direct as well as by indirect means. This is clearly seen in the narrative writings of the Hebrew Bible (the 'Old Testament' in the Christian tradition), which are basically stories about God's intervention in the history of humankind and of Israel. Generally speaking, in Stoic thought such intervention is much more indirect, which is also probably why Stoicism gives little room for belief in divine vengeance.[181]

---

[176] Rom 13.4: θεοῦ γὰρ διάκονός ἐστιν ἔκδικος εἰς ὀργὴν τῷ τὸ κακὸν πράσσοντι ('for it [i.e. the authority] is a servant of God to execute wrath on the evildoer').

[177] 1 Pet 3.12 (quoting Ps 33.16–17 [мт 34.15–16]); 4.5.

[178] 1 Pet 4.7: πάντων δὲ τὸ τέλος ἤγγικεν.   [179] 1 Pet 2.13–17.

[180] In addition to examples from Jewish and Christian writings, Zerbe claims that 'the grounding notion of deferring vengeance to God is associated with exhortations to non-retaliation in... popular Greek philosophy', but mentions only Epictetus, *Diss.* 3.22.54 in that respect, which, on the other hand, includes no clear example of such association (*Non-Retaliation*, 236). According to Meeks, Plutarch accused the Stoic Chrysippus of inconsistency because he attacked the idea of divine punishment of evil in Plato's *Republic* while stating the idea himself elsewhere (see further Meeks, *Origins*, 85).

[181] cf. Schnackenburg, *Moral Teaching*, 301: '[N]o one can say that punishment by the gods in the world to come was a dominant concept in Hellenism; the Epicureans and Stoics were at one in rejecting the concept of the wrath of the gods.'

Having said this, a reminder is in order not to lapse into stock assumptions and generalizations about the Stoics. As we have seen in the discussion above, the Stoic deity is not as 'passive' as many would think or claim. The intimate ways in which Epictetus speaks about the divine surely suggest otherwise (see Chapters 1 and 4 above).[182] Moreover, at the very close of his discussion of proper benefits (*De Beneficiis*), Seneca urges his readers to imitate the gods, 'those glorious authors of all things', in giving benefits to all, including even those who do not know the gods at all, as well as those who are ungrateful for what they receive. Then he says:

Some reproach them [i.e. the gods] with indifference to us (*neclegentiam nostri*), others with injustice (*iniquitatem*); some place them outside of their world (*extra mundum suum*), and abandon them to sloth and languor, leaving them without light, without any task.... Yet, none the less, like the best of parents, who only smile at the spiteful words of their children, the gods do not cease to heap their benefits upon those who are doubtful about the source of benefits, but distribute their blessings among the nations and peoples (*per gentes populosque*) with unbroken uniformity. Possessing only the power of doing good, they sprinkle the lands with timely rains, they stir the seas with their blasts, they mark off the seasons by the course of the stars, they modify the extremes of summer and winter by interposing periods of milder temperature, and, ever gentle and kindly, bear with the errors of our feeble spirits.[183]

It is evident that such a description of the deity does not accord with common opinion about Stoic theology. More to the point for the topic of non-retaliation, we see in this and the subsequent passage a clear exhortation to imitate the gods in giving benefits 'even to those at whose hands we have suffered loss', i.e. those who do evil, but there is no implication whatsoever that such evildoers will eventually receive due punishment through divine vengeance.[184] In general, such conceptions seem to have been alien to Stoic theology and ethics. Seneca for one would probably have disliked Paul's implied 'promise' of God's eventual revenge against the evildoer, judging from what he himself wrote in *De Beneficiis*: 'You treat a man very badly in wishing him to be injured by the gods.'[185]

---

[182] cf. also Seneca, *Ep.* 41.2, 4–5; 95.48–50; *Prov.* 1.5–6; 3.1; 4.7–8, 11–12; *Ben.* 2.29.6; 4.5.1– 6.6; 4.8.1–2; 4.25.1–2; 6.27.5; Musonius 8.64.14–15; 17.108.8–18; 53.144. On Marcus Aurelius, see Chapter 1 above.

[183] *Ben.* 7.31.2–4. Cf., e.g., Epictetus, *Diss.* 4.1.103–4.

[184] On divine punishment (in the present), see, however, Seneca, *Ep.* 95.50; 110.2. Seneca rejects the notion that human beings will be judged after death. According to him, such notions are 'the fancies of the poets, who have harrowed us with groundless terrors' (*Marc.* 19.4). In *Diss.* 3.24.41–3 Epictetus speaks indirectly of divine punishment (in the present) when he describes how those who violate 'the divine and mighty and inescapable law' (ὁ νόμος θεῖος καὶ ἰσχυρὸς καὶ ἀναπόδραστος) and disobey 'the divine governance' (τῇ θείᾳ διοικήσει) are punished.

[185] *Ben.* 6.27.5: *Pessime cum eo agis, cui vis a dis noceri.*

The Stoic demand is clear: one should love *all* human beings without exception, and never render evil for evil. Founding their ethics on the principle of universal humanity, the Roman Stoics all stress that one is even obliged to treat one's *enemies* well and to help them in any possible way. Musonius firmly rejects the opposite view: 'To share the common notion that we shall be despised by others if in every way we do not strive to harm the first enemies (ἐχθρούς) we meet is the mark of mean-minded and ignorant men.' His own teaching is instead that, whereas 'we [commonly] say that the despicable man is recognized among other things by his inability to harm his enemies,... actually he is much more easily recognized by his inability to help them (ὠφελεῖν)'.[186] It is, in other words, a mark of the genuinely good and noble person ever to be ready to help one's enemies. Seneca, too, proclaims this to be the only proper disposition. In his (relatively) short writing 'On Leisure' (*De Otio*), he states, 'We shall never cease to work for the common good (*communi bono*), to help each and all (*adiuvare singulos*), to give aid even to our enemies (*inimicis*) when our hand is feeble with age.'[187] But most radical in this respect among the Stoics is Epictetus, who goes so far as to demand not merely that people should help their enemies but that they must *love* them as well. As the Stoic teacher puts it himself, the sage (i.e. the ideal philosopher and human being) 'must needs be flogged like an ass, and while he is being flogged he must *love* (φιλεῖν) the men who flog him, as though he were the father or brother of them all (ὡς πατέρα πάντων, ὡς ἀδελφόν).'[188] To be sure, Epictetus does not use the word 'enemies' here, but it seems reasonable to take 'the men who flog' the sage 'like an ass', i.e. those who torture him in a most vicious and heartless manner, as roughly equivalent to those who are normally considered enemies.

The apostle Paul expresses almost as radical a viewpoint in his letter to the Romans when he urges his addressees to 'bless those who persecute you' (εὐλογεῖτε τοὺς διώκοντας ὑμᾶς),[189] and exhorts them to give aid to their enemies whenever the latter are in need.[190] It has often been claimed that Paul is here calling for an ethic of 'love of enemies'.[191] It has also often been

---

[186] Musonius 41.136: φαμὲν γὰρ τὸν εὐκαταφρόνητον νοεῖσθαι μὲν καὶ κατὰ τὸ ἀδύνατον εἶναι βλάψαι [τοὺς ἐχθρούς]· ἀλλὰ πολὺ μᾶλλον νοεῖται κατὰ τὸ ἀδύνατον εἶναι ὠφελεῖν. Cf. Epictetus, frg. 7.

[187] *Otio* 1.4. Cf. also 8.2; *Vit. beat.* 20.5; *Ben.* 7.31.1, 5; *Ira* 2.28.4; *Ep.* 120.10.

[188] *Diss.* 3.22.54. As is often the case in Epictetus' lectures, the sage is here represented by the ideal 'Cynic'. Cf. also 3.24.64–5.

[189] Rom 12.14a, immediately followed by εὐλογεῖτε καὶ μὴ καταρᾶσθε ('bless and do not curse [them]').

[190] Rom 12.20: ἐὰν πεινᾷ ὁ ἐχθρός σου, ψώμιζε αὐτόν· ἐὰν διψᾷ, πότιζε αὐτόν ('if your enemy is hungry, feed him; if he is thirsty, give him something to drink'; cf. Prov 25.21).

[191] e.g. Piper, 'Love Your Enemies', 102–19 (Piper even sees 'a specific command of enemy love' in 1 Pet 3.9; p. 122); Schrage, *Einzelgebote*, 252, 263; Sevenster, *Paul and Seneca*, 183–5;

claimed—but no less often simply assumed—that such an ethic was some-thing unheard of in the 'pagan' moral tradition. Neither claim is true. While the idea that 'love of enemies' was unique to Christian ethics is as old as Christianity itself,[192] it is altogether false, as these examples from the Stoic texts suggest. A careful investigation of the ancient sources, Christian as well as non-Christian, shows instead that 'the pertinent conception was deeply entrenched in the popular morality of the ancient world'.[193] Needless to say, the 'eye for an eye' principle was still widely held and applied in Graeco-Roman societies, which also explains why certain people found it necessary to argue so firmly against it in the first place, but it is a grave mistake to attribute the ethic of enemy love exclusively to the Judeo-Christian tradition. Scholars who do so either ignore the 'pagan' sources altogether[194] or apply very different and unbalanced criteria to the ancient texts, depending, it seems, on the origin and/or religious bearings of the texts, that is, whether they are (Judeo-)Christian or not.[195] A recent, more balanced, study of the principle of 'love of enemies' in pre-Christian antiquity suggests that 'the third level [i.e. "Never take revenge, love your enemy—with all the consequences"] is reached only by Socrates, a few Roman Stoics, Lev 19.18 and Jesus.... Even Chris-tianity, seen as a whole, rarely transcended the second level ["Try not to pay back evil with evil"] and often enough fell back to the first level ["Love your friend, hate your enemy"].'[196]

As for Paul's statements in Romans—and this applies to 1 Peter, too (cf. 3.9)—it is clear that the apostle wants his addressees to be well disposed towards all people, including persecutors and enemies, but it is important to pay notice to the fact that he does not speak of 'love' in this regard. He calls for a 'blessing' of persecutors and a help offered to enemies (at least until they receive due punishment from God), but there is no such thing as a demand

---

Lietzmann, *Einführung*, 111. More recently, e.g., Wilson, *Love*, 172–7, 198–9; Söding, *Liebesgebot*, 241–50.

[192] cf. Tertullian, *Scap.* 1.3: *Amicos enim diligere omnium est, inimicos autem solorum chris-tianorum* ('All men love their friends; Christians alone love their enemies').

[193] Whittaker, 'Christianity and Morality', 211. Whittaker's important article should be included in any serious investigation of this topic.

[194] This is the case, for instance, in Stark, *Rise* (see, e.g., pp. 209–15). For a critique of this work, see Thorsteinsson, 'Role of Morality'.

[195] As, e.g., in Piper, '*Love Your Enemies*' (cf. esp. pp. 20–7 with my discussion of the Stoics above).

[196] Reiser, 'Love of Enemies', 426. Cf. Ramsay MacMullen, 'What Difference did Christianity Make?' in *Changes in the Roman Empire: Essays in the Ordinary* (Princeton, NJ: Princeton University Press, 1990), 154: 'If we look to deeds...and try to see patterns of action in the population at large that clearly reflect Christian preaching, we are hard put to find anything very significant. Of that most aspiring virtue, charity to the point of loving one's enemies—hardly a sign.'

for enemy *love* in these verses.[197] It is possible, as some scholars argue, that Paul here draws on an earlier Jesus tradition of enemy love (as later related in the Gospels of Matthew and Luke),[198] knowledge of which he could then assume on the part of his audience. But this seems unlikely.[199] The fact remains that he does not refer explicitly to such a tradition, and he never speaks of 'love of enemies' in this text (as do Matthew and Luke). Nor do we know of any first-century Roman Christian source that includes such a tradition.[200] What we *do* know, on the other hand, is that there circulated a corresponding moral teaching in Rome in the first century, namely, the Stoic one, and if there were people in Paul's audience who knew about *that* teaching they may well have made associations between his message in Romans and the Stoic teaching. Indeed, it is quite possible that for the audience in Rome the line of thought in this respect between Paul and the Stoics was more lucid and direct than between Paul and Jesus.

THE SOCIAL DIMENSION

In the discussion above I have touched briefly on a number of examples of the social dimension of the moral teachings of Roman Stoicism and Roman Christianity. But there is more to be said, although it should be clear at the outset that I do not pretend to be able to address all or even most topics that are relevant to the subject.[201] My aim in this section is rather to provide a general comparison, and to discuss a selection of specific topics that, in my judgement, are important both for the sources concerned as well as for the purposes of the present study.

New Testament scholars and other scholars of early Christianity often charge the Stoics with having been haughty figures with little or no real interest in social issues. Stoic philosophers, it is claimed, rarely discuss topics that have to do with social aspects of life, and when they do they don't really mean what they say—unlike the Christian authors who truly mean

---

[197] cf. Thorsteinsson, 'Paul and Roman Stoicism', 144–6, 156–8. See also Engberg-Pedersen, 'Relationship', 58; idem, *Paul*, 265–9, 276–7, 287–9; Zerbe, *Non-Retaliation*, 216.

[198] Matt 5.44; Luke 6.27–8. Cf. *Did.* 1.3.

[199] See the discussion in Wilson, *Love*, 165–71.

[200] Note that the Gospel of Mark, which many scholars associate with the city of Rome, includes no words of Jesus on enemy love. Note also that, if the authors of 1 Peter and 1 Clement knew of such a tradition, they make no mention of it.

[201] Space does not allow me, for instance, to discuss here in any detail the important topic of the status of women in antiquity, a topic that I nonetheless touched on in my survey of the moral teachings of Musonius Rufus and 1 Peter (see Chapters 3 and 7 above).

what they say.[202] This view of the Stoics has become so widespread a cliché that one can quite easily follow its route as it travels from one exegetical study to another, being more or less copied without much consideration of the sources themselves and without much protest from the rest of the scholarly community. But it is false, and it needs to be corrected. The Stoicism of the first and second centuries CE, that is, Stoicism as it was understood and experienced when the earliest Christian writings were penned, was very much concerned with social matters, and there is no good reason to believe that the Stoics were less serious or less sincere in their discussions of those matters than were Christian authors.

This is not to say that the social settings of Roman Christianity and Roman Stoicism were identical. Clearly they were not, although we should be careful not to overstate the case: the Stoic Epictetus did not belong to the Roman elite; he was a former slave. Moreover, some of the Christ-believers were probably relatively well-off economically and socially (see Chapter 5 above). Nonetheless, there can be little doubt that, generally speaking, the social difference was considerable between the two groups concerned. Thus, when equestrian Stoics like Seneca and Musonius describe material poverty, as they sometimes do, in positive and somewhat idealized terms, they are clearly not speaking out of personal experience. They knew not what true, more or less permanent, non-voluntary poverty was. Otherwise, their descriptions would doubtless have been quite different. However, it is important to keep in mind that the fact that most of the Stoic authors were better-off socially and economically does not, as it were, automatically make them less concerned with social issues or less sincere in their treatment of such issues. This is something that cannot be taken for granted, although it frequently is. Moreover, one must also take into consideration the way in which these particular individuals may have affected their social surroundings by their teachings and/or deeds. Musonius, for instance, did not think it sufficient only to preach the Stoic teaching of proper disposition towards material wealth, but went further by harshly criticizing those Romans who, in his opinion, spent too much money on buying expensive things such as luxurious houses, furniture, clothing, and so on, the cost of which, according to him, would have served better to aid less fortunate citizens.[203] This criticism accords well with Musonius' emphasis on the cardinal virtue of justice ($\delta\iota\kappa\alpha\iota\sigma\sigma\upsilon\nu\eta$), which he interpreted in decidedly social terms.[204] Whereas scholars today often tend to tone down the implications of Musonius' social criticism, first-century

---

[202] cf. the discussion in the general introduction to this study.
[203] Musonius 19.120–2; 20.124–6 (see further Chapter 3 above).
[204] Musonius 3.40.25–33; 4.44.12–16; 4.48.9–12; 6.52.17–18; 14.92.20–55.

Roman authorities appear to have taken his critique of society quite seriously; so much so that they expelled him from the city of Rome, seeing in him not only a political threat but also a social one.[205] It is a curious thing that scholars do not take his message more seriously in this respect despite all the information we have about the nature and content of his lectures, which devote an unusual amount of attention to social matters, including questions relating to the family, such as marriage, parenthood, and the relationship between children and parents, as well as questions regarding the status of women in society. These were issues of no peripheral importance to this philosopher, who saw in the institution of family and marriage the very cornerstone of society. And, as we have seen, Musonius was remembered and revered by subsequent generations, 'pagans' and Christians alike, precisely for his moral integrity, for taking his own teaching seriously and living up to it. While his fellow Stoic Seneca has in recent times emerged as the stereotype of the 'hypocritical rich moralist', he, too, was very much concerned with social issues,[206] not least of which was the proper treatment of slaves. And the fact remains that there are few discourses, if any, from antiquity that speak so strongly in favour of a better and more humane treatment of slaves than do those of Seneca (and we shall return to this below).

There is no sustainable reason, then, to suspect that the Stoics were only vaguely interested in social matters or that their interest was only on the surface. Quite to the contrary, we see in the texts of the Roman Stoics a very strong and consistent concern for questions relating to social issues. This should come as no surprise, since the social dimension is merely a natural consequence of the Stoic doctrine of universal humanity and human share in the divine Reason. As noted earlier in this study, the social dimension is in actual fact *inescapable* because of this doctrine.[207] For the Stoic, to be rational *is* to be social.[208] Epictetus explains this aspect of human existence through a

---

[205] cf. Lutz, 'Musonius Rufus', 24: 'His very prominence in public life, his active concern with the problems of his day, and his keen sense of duty to society necessarily made him an object of Nero's persecution.' Cf. also Pohlenz, *Stoa*, 302–3.

[206] cf. Miriam T. Griffin, 'Seneca and Pliny', in *The Cambridge History of Greek and Roman Political Thought* (ed. C. Rowe and M. Schofield with S. Harrison and M. Lane; Cambridge: Cambridge University Press, 2000), 533: 'In fact, Seneca frequently subjects to ethical scrutiny areas of conduct that are more social than individual, more public than private.'

[207] cf. Colish, *Stoic Tradition*, 38. Cf. also Martha C. Nussbaum, 'The Worth of Human Dignity: Two Tensions in Stoic Cosmopolitanism', in *Philosophy and Power in the Graeco-Roman World: Essays in Honour of Miriam Griffin* (ed. G. Clark and T. Rajak; Oxford: Oxford University Press, 2002), 38, who observes that 'respect for humanity has implications for social and educational reform. Thus Musonius Rufus uses Stoic cosmopolitanism to defend the equal education of boys and girls and the higher education of married women, arguing that rational and moral nature needs educational development.'

[208] cf. Reydams-Schils, *Roman Stoics*, 74–5.

dialogue with an imaginary interlocutor who (eventually) comes to the conclusion that he is indeed a rational creature ($\lambda o\gamma\iota\kappa\acute{o}v$ $\epsilon\mathcal{i}\mu\iota$ $\zeta\tilde{\omega}ov$). Epictetus then reminds him of his duties as such: 'What, then ($o\tilde{v}v$), are the demands upon you? Rehearse your actions. '"Where did I go wrong?" in matters conducive to serenity? "What did I do" that was unfriendly ($\breve{a}\phi\iota\lambda ov$), or unsocial ($\dot{a}\kappa o\iota v\acute{\omega}v\eta\tau ov$), or unfeeling ($\breve{a}\gamma v\omega\mu ov$)? "What to be done was left undone" in regard to these matters?" '[209] Epictetus' response to the interlocutor implies that sociability is incorporated in Reason itself. It is simply an intrinsic part of being a rational creature. With reference to Epictetus' application and clarification of the Stoic theory of *oikeiōsis* in *Discourse* 1.19.11–15, one scholar explains as follows:

Working for the well-being of one's fellow is to him [i.e. Epictetus] therefore not a merely accidental or optional part of morality, but the indispensable condition for the attainment of one's own blissful happiness. Just as god cannot do otherwise than be useful and do good, so too does the impulse to that end lie in human nature, simply because it is rational: for everything rational and good is at the same time useful ([*Diss.*] II, 8, 1 $\tau\grave{o}$ $\dot{a}\gamma a\theta\grave{o}v$ $\dot{\omega}\phi\acute{e}\lambda\iota\mu ov$). Epictetus... also grounds the duty of altruism on the equality of human beings as the children of a heavenly father, and in this way comes very close to the Christian idea of the kingdom of God as a community comprising god and human beings.[210]

In the texts of the Roman Stoics we also see how important it was for them to focus on the practical aspects of their moral teaching, and to urge their students and followers not to fix their eyes solely on ethical theory but to go directly to the scene of action and apply that theory. The Roman Stoics were 'practical men of action', as one scholar puts it.[211] Recurrent references to this emphasis on practical ethics in their texts refute the claim that the Stoics were only vaguely concerned with real life when they put forth their moral lessons.[212] The evidence points in fact in the opposite direction: 'The Roman Stoics... successfully established a connection between a philosophical ideal and ordinary, everyday-life circumstances, and between a community shaped by Stoic wisdom and society as it is.'[213] The Stoics, however, like everyone else,

---

[209] *Diss.* 4.6.34–5.   [210] Bonhöffer, *Ethics*, 204.

[211] Sandbach, *Stoics*, 19: 'The early Stoics had intended their philosophy to form a guide to life, but the very nature of the evidence makes them appear as theoreticians. Many of the later [= Roman] Stoics were practical men of action and one can see the relevance of their beliefs to their doings. Even those who were primarily teachers were mainly concerned with the practical problems of life which faced them and their pupils.' Cf. also Malcolm Schofield, 'Stoic Ethics', in *The Cambridge Companion to the Stoics* (ed. B. Inwood; Cambridge: Cambridge University Press, 2003), 253–6.

[212] See, e.g., Seneca, *Ep.* 6.5; 16.3; 20.1–2; 34.4; 52.8; *Ben.* 7.1.3; Musonius 1.36.10–12; 5.52.2–4; 6.52.7–8; 14.96.6–7; Epictetus, *Diss.* 2.1.29–31; 2.11.24–5; 3.21.4–6.

[213] Reydams-Schils, *Roman Stoics*, 1.

addressed questions relating to life in society on the basis of their own social situation and their own understanding and experience. And so did the Roman Christian authors with whom we are concerned in the present study, whose socio-economic situation, we should remember, was *not* in absolute contrast to that of the Stoics, although it was different. Neither 'Peter' nor 'Clement' lived in the lowest slums of Rome.[214]

In the chapter on Paul's Letter to the Romans above, we saw that the apostle's community-oriented ethic lays great weight on 'social moderation', that is, the Christ-believers' moderate opinion of themselves as individuals and members of the 'body in Christ', and their humble attitude towards and respect for one another. This is one of the main themes of Romans 12–15.[215] A significant part of Paul's argument—indeed the point of departure in his argument for social moderation—is his allusion in 12.3 to the virtues of φρόνησις and σωφροσύνη, which he adopts and adapts to his own purposes. Paul wants the Christ-believers to φρονεῖν εἰς τὸ σωφρονεῖν ('think with proper moderation'), which is here put in contrast to ὑπερφρονεῖν παρ' ὃ δεῖ φρονεῖν ('think highly of oneself beyond what one ought to think') and thus refers primarily to interpersonal dealings. That Paul is here primarily concerned with interpersonal dealings is further confirmed by the immediately following references to social relations within the Christ-movement, especially through the 'body' metaphor and the discussion of different functions and roles within the community. Paul's allusion to σωφροσύνη appears thus to differ somewhat from contemporary understanding of the virtue, where the attention was particularly aimed at the aspect of self-control or self-restraint,[216] and to reflect instead the earlier, classical usage, in which the social or interpersonal aspect was emphasized.[217] According to the apostle, the fact that some within the community of believers have received certain gifts (χαρίσματα), like the gift of 'prophecy' for instance, does not grant them the right to be overbearing towards their fellow believers, whatever the position or (lack of) gifts of the latter. Paul's point is not that the Christ-believers should in any way decry the gifts themselves or to disclaim their own share in them, but rather that they should embrace the gifts and use them for the sake of the community as a whole—but only for that sake. In other words, Paul does not argue against the fact that there are different roles, functions, and positions within the community. Rather, he underlines that each and

---

[214] Although many of their fellow Roman Christ-believers may have done so, of course; cf. the discussion in the introductions to Chapters 7 (on 1 Peter) and 8 (on 1 Clement).

[215] cf. also 1 Pet 4.8–11.

[216] See, e.g., Musonius 3.40.17–25; 4.44.16–22; 6.52.15–17; 8.62.10–23. For Jewish and Christian parallels, see 4 Macc. 1.31; 5.23; 1 Tim 2.9, 15.

[217] Jewett, *Romans*, 739–42.

every member of the community must always consider his or her role, function, and position in relation to the other members. That is how they 'ought to think' ($\delta\epsilon\hat{\imath}$ $\phi\rho o\nu\epsilon\hat{\imath}\nu$). And that is how the ethic of love is actualized, according to Paul. As he explains in chapters 14–15, Christ-believers are obligated to show mutual thoughtfulness and respect, and to bear the burdens of those within the community who may be 'weak'. Like Jesus Christ himself, the 'strong' must view their position and role with proper moderation and give priority to the needs of the 'weak'.

It is clear that when Paul here uses the term 'weak' he is referring to individuals who are or may be 'weak' *in faith* ($\tau\hat{\eta}$ $\pi\acute{\iota}\sigma\tau\epsilon\iota$), that is, in their attitude towards and practice of their faith. He is, in other words, primarily alluding to certain dispositions within the Christ-believing community, rather than social positions. Nevertheless, there is undeniably a social dimension to Paul's message as well. It has some very important social implications: the call for adaptability on the part of the 'strong' means in effect that they must disregard their own social status, whatever that may be, with respect to the needs of the 'weaker' brothers and sisters, whatever *their* social position may be. Social difference is not rejected as such, but it is judged indifferent in this respect. As the apostle explained in chapter 12, no member of the Christ-believing community should 'think too highly' of him- or herself with respect to others. All members constitute 'one body in Christ', irrespective of their social (or socio-religious) position, and true love of neighbour makes no distinction between individual members—it is 'unhypocritical' ($\dot{\alpha}\nu\upsilon\pi\acute{o}\kappa\rho\iota\tau o\varsigma$).[218]

If Paul applies the terms 'weak' and 'strong' only indirectly in a social sense, the same cannot be said of the author of 1 Clement, who uses them as virtual equivalents to 'poor' and 'wealthy', respectively: 'Let the one who is strong take care of the weak; and let the weak show due respect to the strong. Let the wealthy provide what is needed to the poor, and let the poor offer thanks to God, since he has given him someone to supply his need.'[219] As we have seen, neither is it the purpose of this author to speak against social differences. Rather, 'Clement' presupposes the traditional Roman social system of patron–client relationships and bases the social structure of the Christ-believing community largely on that system. But, in agreement with Paul's emphasis in Romans, the main attention in 1 Clement is paid to the needs of the 'weaker' and 'poorer' members of the community, although 'Clement' is careful to add that the more inferior members are expected to repay the more superior members for their care in the form of due respect and expressed gratitude (expressed through thanksgiving to God). Paul's concern in Romans 14–15 is,

---

[218] Rom 12.3–5, 9.   [219] 1 Clem. 38.2.

as it were, more unilateral, as it addresses almost solely the duty of the 'strong' towards the 'weak' (although the basic principle, of course, is *mutual* respect, love, and care). In this regard, the influence of Roman ideology and society on the author of 1 Clement is clear. The way in which 'Clement' underlines the virtue of 'hospitality' is probably also the result of the influence of Roman ideology, particularly aristocratic notions of friendship.[220] The same was probably true of the author of 1 Peter, who devotes about the same proportion of space to the virtue of 'hospitality' as 'Clement' does. Considering the strong social mixture in the city of Rome, due partly to the vertical structure of Roman society (see Chapter 5 above), such an influence on the author of 1 Peter should come as no surprise. As we have seen, 'Peter' is very conscious of his social surroundings and shows great concern for Christians' relation to outsiders, urging his readers to behave honourably 'among the gentiles' and to willingly submit to the Roman authorities.

In his letter to the Romans, Paul uses a significant social term in chapter 12 when he advises the audience, 'Do not be haughty ($\mu\dot{\eta}$ $\tau\dot{\alpha}$ $\dot{v}\psi\eta\lambda\dot{\alpha}$ $\phi\rho o\nu o\hat{v}\nu\tau\epsilon\varsigma$), but associate with the lowly ($\dot{\alpha}\lambda\lambda\dot{\alpha}$ $\tauo\hat{\imath}\varsigma$ $\tau\alpha\pi\epsilon\iota\nuo\hat{\imath}\varsigma$ $\sigma\upsilon\nu\alpha\pi\alpha\gamma\acute{o}\mu\epsilon\nuo\iota$).'[221] Here the word $o\acute{\iota}$ $\tau\alpha\pi\epsilon\iota\nuo\acute{\iota}$ ('the lowly') appears to refer to those Christ-believers who are socially inferior, which, in turn, may suggest that Paul did presume or even know that there were perceptible social differences within the Christ-believing community in Rome.[222] Paul does not use the cognate noun $\tau\alpha\pi\epsilon\iota\nuo\phi\rhoo\sigma\acute{v}\nu\eta$ ('humility') in this context, but he does so in his Letter to the Philippians, where $\tau\alpha\pi\epsilon\iota\nuo\phi\rhoo\sigma\acute{v}\nu\eta$ emerges as a key term in Paul's discussion of proper behaviour towards fellow believers.[223] This text appears to be the primary source for the use of the term in 1 Clement,[224] in which $\tau\alpha\pi\epsilon\iota\nuo\phi\rhoo\sigma\acute{v}\nu\eta$ definitely receives a primary position among other virtues, especially in relation to the letter's immediate purpose. Similarly, 'Peter', who, like Paul, stresses the ethic of mutual aid and respect, underlines very clearly the importance of $\tau\alpha\pi\epsilon\iota\nuo\phi\rhoo\sigma\acute{v}\nu\eta$ for interpersonal dealings in Christ-believing

---

[220] Jeffers, *Conflict*, 127–30.

[221] Rom 12.16 (trans. NRSV). As noted in the NRSV translation, it is also possible to translate $\tauo\hat{\imath}\varsigma$ $\tau\alpha\pi\epsilon\iota\nuo\hat{\imath}\varsigma$ $\sigma\upsilon\nu\alpha\pi\alpha\gamma\acute{o}\mu\epsilon\nuo\iota$ as 'give yourselves to humble tasks' (reading $\tauo\hat{\imath}\varsigma$ $\tau\alpha\pi\epsilon\iota\nuo\hat{\imath}\varsigma$ as the neuter $\tau\dot{\alpha}$ $\tau\alpha\pi\epsilon\iota\nu\acute{\alpha}$). But in this context of interpersonal relations it seems better to take it, as most commentators do, as a masculine plural, thus referring to a certain group of people. For a different reading of $\tau\dot{\alpha}$ $\dot{v}\psi\eta\lambda\dot{\alpha}$ (i.e. as 'the exalted things, heights'), see Jewett, *Romans*, 770.

[222] cf. Lampe, *From Paul*, 80: 'Social differences, a social stratification, is presupposed in Roman church life, already by Paul, when he calls for the better-off to give alms to the poorer (Rom 12:13, 8)'.

[223] Phil 2.3: $\tau\hat{\eta}$ $\tau\alpha\pi\epsilon\iota\nuo\phi\rhoo\sigma\acute{v}\nu\eta$ $\dot{\alpha}\lambda\lambda\acute{\eta}\lambdao\upsilon\varsigma$ $\dot{\eta}\gammao\acute{v}\mu\epsilon\nuo\iota$ $\dot{v}\pi\epsilon\rho\acute{\epsilon}\chio\nu\tau\alpha\varsigma$ $\dot{\epsilon}\alpha\upsilon\tau\hat{\omega}\nu$ ('in humility regard others [i.e. other fellow believers] as better than yourselves'). Philippians is a letter which Paul *may* have written in Rome. Cf. also the uses of $\tau\alpha\pi\epsilon\iota\nuo\phi\rhoo\sigma\acute{v}\nu\eta$ in Col 3.12; Eph 4.2.

[224] So Bowe, *Church*, 114.

communities.[225] Noteworthy is the fact that in 5.5 ταπεινοφροσύνη emerges from the author's discussion of the proper relationship between the 'elders' (πρεσβύτεροι) and the 'younger' (νεώτεροι), which he concludes with the words, νεώτεροι, ὑποτάγητε πρεσβυτέροις ('you who are younger, submit to [the authority of] the elders'). This corresponds closely to the main interest of 1 Clement, where ταπεινοφροσύνη goes hand in hand with ὑποτάσσειν. In short, then, according to all three authors, Paul, 'Peter', and 'Clement', ταπεινοφροσύνη is a virtue that should be embraced by Christians.

On this point, scholars are eager to point out, we encounter a difference between Christian moral teaching and 'Graeco-Roman ethics' (typically clustered into a single mass). As one scholar puts it: 'This "social humility", that is, the lowering of oneself before (and for the sake of) those who are socially equal or inferior is *not*, it is widely agreed, seen as positive or morally commendable in Graeco-Roman ethics.'[226] This is true to the extent that there seems to be some difference in the use of the words themselves, ταπεινός and ταπεινοφροσύνη: Christian authors often apply them in a more positive sense than is usual in Greek texts. But we should avoid generalizations in this respect, as in so many others, because when the ancient material is carefully examined it turns out that things are not quite as black and white as many would have it: first, while the noun ταπεινοφροσύνη is rather uncommon in Greek sources, as a rule, the adjective ταπεινός has the same negative sense in the Greek translation of the Hebrew Bible (LXX) as it normally does in non-Judeo-Christian texts.[227] Second, even Paul uses the adjective in a derogatory sense,[228] which suggests that its meaning is more context-bound than usually thought. Third, there are instances in which non-Judeo-Christian Greek texts apply ταπεινός in a positive sense. In these instances the word means 'modest' or 'obedient',[229] and it occurs in contexts in which questions of obedience to authorities are under discussion, corresponding closely to the specific contexts in which the concept is used in 1 Peter and 1 Clement.

All this indicates that the use of ταπεινός (and ταπεινοφροσύνη) must not be put in 'either/or' categories, that is, either Christian and positive or 'pagan' and negative. There are more 'grey areas' here than usually assumed or acknowledged. This is not to deny the differences altogether. It is clear, for

---

[225] 1 Pet 3.8; 5.5–6.

[226] Horrell, *Solidarity*, 210–11 (italics original). Cf. also, e.g., Grundmann, 'ταπεινός', 11–12; Käsemann, *Römer*, 335; Dunn, *Romans*, 2: 747; Bowe, *Church*, 113; Gerd Theissen, *The Religion of the Earliest Churches: Creating a Symbolic World* (trans. J. Bowden; Minneapolis, MN: Fortress, 1999), 71–80.

[227] See Grundmann, 'ταπεινός', 9.   [228] 2 Cor 10.1; cf. 11.7; 12.21.

[229] See Grundmann, 'ταπεινός', 4, who cites examples from Aeschylus, Plato, Xenophon, Isocrates, and Plutarch.

instance, that the Stoic Epictetus uses both the adjective ταπεινός and the noun ταπεινοφροσύνη in a negative sense (the latter occurs only once).[230] But I see a certain danger here of unwarranted generalization about the Stoics and Stoicism as a whole (not to mention 'Graeco-Roman ethics') on the sole basis of Epictetus' use of the terms. A widespread opinion runs as follows: 'The classical and Hellenistic usage of ταπεινός, is, for the most part, entirely negative. This is *especially true* for the Stoic use of the terms where, *for example*, Epictetus is *most explicit* in his negative evaluation of this word group' (emphases mine).[231] We see here how Epictetus is used as an 'example' of *the* Stoic opinion. The problem, however, is that no other instances are quoted in the scholarly literature from the Stoic texts. It is therefore questionable whether his usage can be cited as an 'example' of the typical Stoic point of view, rather than an example of *a* view of a certain Stoic or a certain individual philosopher.

Moreover, it may be a serious mistake to make generalizations about basic conceptions from the use of particular words.[232] That is, even if Epictetus and other (non-Stoic) philosophers use the words ταπεινός and ταπεινοφροσύνη in a negative sense, that does not necessarily mean that the basic conception of 'social humility', i.e. 'the lowering of oneself before (and for the sake of) those who are socially equal or inferior', was totally lacking in (all cases of) 'Graeco-Roman ethics'.[233] It may well be correct that the use and meaning of the words ταπεινός and ταπεινοφροσύνη was somewhat different in Christian sources, and that Christians did go a step further with their emphasis on 'humility',[234] but the case must not be pressed too far.

As a matter of fact, we see Seneca arguing for, if not 'social humility', then a closely corresponding social moderation in his *De Clementia*, which was addressed to none other than Nero himself, who was then (in 55/56 CE) newly throned and untried as an emperor.[235] The main topic of Seneca's address is the virtue of *clementia* or 'mercy', which, according to him, the young emperor should make his own as the sovereign ruler of Rome. In Seneca's view, 'in a position of unlimited power [true mercy] is in the truest sense self-control (*temperantia*) and an all-embracing love of the human race

---

[230] *Diss.* 3.24.56 (ταπεινοφροσύνη); 1.3.8; 1.4.25; 1.9.10; 2.16.18; 3.2.14; 3.24.43, 58; 4.1.2, 54; 4.4.1; 4.7.11; 4.12.20 (ταπεινός).

[231] Bowe, *Church*, 113.   [232] cf. the useful discussion in Carson, *Fallacies*, 44–5.

[233] cf. Horrell's argumentation above.

[234] On this further step, Horrell observes (in relation to Paul): 'it is notable how this most distinctively Christian morality in Paul has at least the potential to legitimate and sustain patterns of suffering and oppression through an appeal to imitate Christ's self-giving through suffering' (*Solidarity*, 244).

[235] The purpose of Seneca's writing was to serve as a 'mirror' to the young emperor (*Clem.* 1.1.1). But eventually, of course, Nero crushed the mirror into a thousand pieces.

even as of oneself (*humani generis comprendens ut sui amor*).[236] An emperor should model himself on the standards of the gods, who are good and merciful to mortal human beings: 'He should wish so to be to his subjects (*civibus*), as he would wish the gods to be to himself.'[237] Discussing the proper duties of an emperor towards his subordinates, Seneca then states: 'To his subjects (*civibus*), to the obscure (*ignotis*), and to the lowly (*humilibus*) he should show the greater moderation (*moderatius agendum est*).'[238] Again, it would almost certainly be a mistake to claim that Seneca is here calling for social 'humility' on the part of the emperor, but there can be no doubt that he insists on social moderation, including towards such inferior groups as the 'obscure' and the 'lowly'. Thus, much like Paul in Romans, Seneca takes up the situation of the 'lowly' in society (whatever their degree of 'lowliness') and speaks on their behalf. Moreover, at the beginning of his address to the emperor, Seneca establishes his argument by employing the metaphor of the body, where Nero is portrayed as the 'head' (*caput*) and 'soul' (*animus*) of the state, while the state itself is his 'body' (*corpus*).[239] By means of this metaphor Seneca makes a case for an inescapable, natural responsibility on the emperor's part towards his subordinates (i.e. Roman citizens), which, in turn, means that 'even reprobate citizens (*improbandis civibus*) should have mercy as being the weak members of the body' (*membris languentibus*).[240] According to the Stoic teacher and counsellor, *every* member of the body should be subject to the emperor's mercy, even the 'reprobate'.[241]

Seneca's concern for the 'weak members of the body' is expressed elsewhere, too, in his writings. For him, the primary purpose of philosophy is to lead people towards the virtuous path of unity and mutual care, for 'the first thing which philosophy undertakes to give is fellow-feeling with all men (*sensum communem*); in other words, sympathy and sociability (*humanitatem et congregationem*).'[242] We have already seen samples of Seneca's urging for humane treatment of slaves (and shall see more below). We have also overheard his directions to his friend Lucilius (and other potential readers) to give aid to people who are lost and starving or in need of any help at all.[243] Nature,

---

[236] *Clem.* 1.11.2. Cf. 1.19.6: *Unum est inexpugnabile munimentum amor civium* ('His [i.e. the king's] one impregnable defence is the love of his countrymen'). In 2.3.1 Seneca defines *clementia* as follows: 'Mercy means restraining the mind from vengeance when it has the power to take it, or the leniency of a superior towards an inferior in fixing punishment.'

[237] *Clem.* 1.7.1.

[238] *Clem.* 1.21.4 (the LCL trans. slightly modified: LCL has 'fellow-countrymen' instead of 'subjects').

[239] *Clem.* 1.4.3; 1.5.1; cf. 2.2.1.   [240] *Clem.* 1.5.1.

[241] cf. also *Clem.* 1.13.4: 'he whose care embraces all (*cui curae sunt universa*) ... fosters each and every part of the state as a portion of himself (*nullam non rei publicae partem tamquam sui nutrit*)'.

[242] *Ep.* 5.4.   [243] *Ep.* 95.51–2. See further Chapter 2 above.

he says, established fairness and justice (*aequum iustumque*), and 'through her orders, let our hands be ready for all that needs to be helped'.[244] Seneca repeatedly underlines the weight of virtues like *clementia* and *humanitas*, the latter of which occurs in one of his letters along with two of the cardinal virtues, *temperantia* (= σωφροσύνη) and *fortitudo* (= ἀνδρεία), as well as with *fides* (= πίστις), where *humanitas* is defined as follows: it 'forbids you to be over-bearing towards your associates (*superbum esse adversus socios*), and it forbids you to be grasping'.[245] Elsewhere Seneca condemns such vices as 'haughtiness (*insolentiam*), a too high opinion of one's self (*nimiam aestima-tionem sui*) and a puffed-up superiority to others (*tumoremque elatum super ceteros*)' together with 'a blind and unthinking devotion to one's own interests'.[246]

What we see in all these references is Seneca's appeal to social moderation, very similar to that of Paul in Romans. We also see in Seneca's writings a corresponding use of the 'strong/weak' terminology as we witnessed in Romans and, especially, in 1 Clement. In a portrait of past generations in human history, as compared with the current one, he writes: 'Not yet had the stronger (*valentior*) begun to lay hands upon the weaker (*infirmiori*); not yet had the miser... begun to shut off his neighbour from even the necessities of life; each cared as much for his neighbour as for himself (*par erat alterius ac sui cura*).'[247] Whatever the historical basis for this rather typical 'Golden Age' description,[248] it demonstrates well Seneca's own notion of the ideal society. Or, rather, it shows aspects of human relations that he seeks to condemn as unacceptable. The ideal scene, we may gather, would include 'strong' people who take care of the 'weak'; powerful people who care as much for the powerless as for themselves. According to this Stoic teaching, then, the well-to-do are obliged to aid their less fortunate neighbours. The rich should take care of the poor.

Hence, despite all differences of social settings, the social aspect of Seneca's moral teaching has some fundamental similarities to that of Paul in Romans 12–15 as well as that of 1 Clement. The Stoic *eques* also gives heed to people who are worse-off in society. As he explains in his extensive treatise on proper

---

[244] *Ep.* 95.52: *ex illius imperio paratae sint iuvandis manus.*   [245] *Ep.* 88.29–30.

[246] *Vit. beat.* 10.2.

[247] *Ep.* 90.40. Cf. also Epictetus, *Diss.* 4.5.34–5: 'This control over the moral purpose is my true business, and in it neither shall a tyrant hinder me against my will, nor the multitude the single individual, nor the stronger man the weaker (ὁ ἰσχυρότερος τὸν ἀσθενέστερον); for this has been given by God to each man as something that cannot be hindered. These are the judgements which produce love (φιλίαν) in the household, concord (ὁμόνοιαν) in the State, peace among the nations, make a man thankful toward God...'

[248] This was a common motif in Greek and Latin literature; see Stowers, *Rereading*, 85, with further references.

benefits, *De Beneficiis*, which, it should be noted, is not merely about the system of benefaction as such but about the ethic of other-concern as well:[249] 'If we made contributions with the expectation of receiving a return, we should give, not to the most worthy, but to the richest men; as it is (*nunc vero*), we prefer a poor man to an importunate rich man (*diviti importuno pauperem praeferimus*).'[250] The words *nunc vero* suggest that Seneca's statement is not just put forth for the sake of the argument but reflects his genuine concern for the less fortunate (whatever his understanding of the term *pauper*, 'poor').

Contrary to common (modern) opinion of the well-to-do equestrian, Seneca underlines very clearly that the principle of mutual love does not differentiate between certain individuals or certain groups of people. On the contrary, he says, it speaks against any such differentiation, whether social, physical, or otherwise:

You would not, I fancy, love (*amare*) a good man if he were rich any more than if he were poor, nor would you love a strong and muscular person more than one who was slender and of delicate constitution.... Or, if you do this, you will, in the case of two equally good men, care more for him who is neat and well-groomed than for him who is dirty and unkempt. You would next go so far as to care more for a good man who is sound in all his limbs and without blemish, than for one who is weak or purblind; and gradually your fastidiousness would reach such a point that, of two equally just and prudent men, you would choose him who has long curling hair![251]

Indicating that this impartiality emerges from the order of Nature itself, Seneca then refers to the care of parents for their offspring:

Would any man judge his children so unfairly as to care more for a healthy son than for one who was sickly, or for a tall child of unusual stature more than for one who was short or of middling height? Wild beasts show no favouritism among their offspring; they lie down in order to suckle all alike; birds make fair distribution of their food.[252]

Of course, this does not mean that, in real life, Seneca would have made no distinction whatsoever between certain groups of people, for example Roman senators, on the one hand, and household slaves, on the other. To insist on such *de facto* total impartiality on his part—or on anyone's part for that

---

[249] cf. Troels Engberg-Pedersen, 'Gift-Giving and Friendship: Seneca and Paul in Romans 1–8 on the Logic of God's Χάρις and Its Human Response', *HTR* 101 (2008): 18–19.

[250] *Ben.* 4.3.1.

[251] *Ep.* 66.24–5: *Non, puto, magis amares virum bonum locupletem quam pauperem, nec robustum et lacertosum quam gracilem et languidi corporis.... Aut si hoc est, magis diliges ex duobus aeque bonis viris nitidum et unctum quam pulverulentem et horrentem. Deinde hoc usque pervenies, ut magis diligas integrum omnibus membris et inlaesum quam debilem aut luscum. Paulatim fastidium tuum illo usque procedet, ut ex duobus aeque iustis ac prudentibus comatum et crispulum malis.*

[252] *Ep.* 66.26.

matter—would not only be historically naïve but a highly unfortunate invitation to anachronism as well. Seneca lived in the first century, long before any serious doubts about the institution of slavery began to arise, and he did not question the slaves' social position as such.

But neither did other ancients, like the Christians, who nevertheless have often been accredited with some radical innovations of thought in this respect: 'It is often said that Christianity introduced an entirely new and better attitude towards slavery. Nothing could be more false.' As a matter of fact, 'the yoke of slavery is fastened even more firmly upon Christian slaves as the emphasis on obedience to their masters becomes even more absolute'.[253] This is indeed what we see in the text of 1 Peter, where (Christ-believing) household slaves are urged to submit to their owners 'in all fear' (ἐν παντὶ φόβῳ), even if the owners treat them badly.[254] According to this author, it is a 'gracious thing in the eyes of God' (χάρις παρὰ θεῷ) if a slave endures patiently when treated unjustly at the hands of his or her master. Thus, rather than speaking in favour of a better treatment of slaves, 'Peter' advances an argument that, in effect, can justify owners' maltreatment of slaves.

The fact is that in antiquity no one questioned the institution of slavery as such. However, there were certain individuals who tried to speak in favour of a better treatment of slaves. Among them was Seneca, in particular, but also to some extent his fellow Stoic Musonius Rufus. The latter did so, for instance, when he disputed the (male) slaveowner's right to treat his female slave according to his will: 'In this category [i.e. of wrongdoers] belongs the man who has relations with his own slave-maid, a thing which some people consider quite without blame, since every master is held (δοκεῖ) to have it in his power to use his slave as he wishes.'[255] There is little doubt that Musonius would have shocked his (male, mostly upper-class) students with this almost unheard-of moral teaching that denied the slaveowner his right and 'power' to treat his slaves in any way he liked—a *female* slave on top of that! The contemporary author of 1 Peter, on the other hand, appears to have been in agreement with the majority who 'held' that a slave-maid could be treated according to her master's will. Musonius' teaching was a strike against views of this sort.

---

[253] G. E. M. de Ste. Croix, *The Class Struggle in the Ancient Greek World from the Archaic Age to the Arab Conquests* (London: Duckworth, 1981), 419. Having discussed texts and authors including Galatians, Colossians, Ephesians, the *Epistle of Barnabas*, *Didache*, Ignatius, Ambrose, and especially Augustine of Hippo, de Ste. Croix writes: 'I have not been able to find in any early Christian writer anything like a demand for the abandonment of slavery or even for a general freeing of existing slaves' (p. 421).

[254] 1 Pet 2.18–20.

[255] Musonius 12.86.29–32: οἷος οὐχ ἥκιστά ἐστι καὶ ὁ δούλῃ ἰδίᾳ πλησιάζων, ὅπερ νομίζουσί τινες μάλιστά πως εἶναι ἀναίτιον, ἐπεὶ καὶ δεσπότης πᾶς αὐτεξούσιος εἶναι δοκεῖ ὅ τι βούλεται χρῆσθαι δούλῳ τῷ ἑαυτοῦ. Cf. the discussion in Chapter 3 above.

Returning to Seneca, time and again we have seen the unqualified impartiality in his principle of mutual love. While a principle of that sort is of course just a *principle*, there are strong indications that Seneca took this principle quite seriously—remarkably seriously with respect to the social milieu of the time. In his 47th *Letter* to Lucilius, which contains 'one of the most humane statements on slavery preserved from antiquity',[256] Seneca insists not merely that slaveholders should dine with their slaves, which was quite a peculiar thing to say,[257] but also that slaves should be included in the group of potential friends (*amici*): 'You need not, my dear Lucilius, hunt for friends only in the forum or in the Senate-house; if you are careful and attentive, you will find them at home also', i.e. among the household slaves.[258] As Seneca sees it, every slaveholder must treat his (or her) slaves as he would be treated by his superiors, and, precisely as any other human beings, slaves should be valued according to their character (*moribus*) and not according to their duties (*ministeriis*).[259] The slaveholder is certainly their superior, i.e. socially (but not necessarily otherwise),[260] but he should treat his slaves in a way that gives rise to respect rather than fear, the former of which, in turn, leads to love (*amor*): 'Respect means love, and love and fear cannot be mingled' (*qui colitur, et amatur; non potest amor cum timore misceri*).[261]

Once again we see a striking contrast in this respect between the views expressed by the Stoics, on the one hand, and the Christian author of 1 Peter, on the other, the latter of whom saw 'fear' as something that should characterize Christ-believing slaves' submission to their masters.[262] As for Seneca,

[he] does not merely condemn cruelty. He asks that slaves be regarded as individuals with different moral capacities, as potential friends whose relations with the master are based on love or respect rather than fear, generosity on one side being matched by loyalty on the other. The slave should find in the home, not only a master, but a society with responsibilities, honours, and a sense of community.[263]

---

[256] Griffin, 'Seneca', 554.

[257] Even more so was his habit of 'kissing the hands of other men's slaves' (*Ep.* 47.13).

[258] *Ep.* 47.16: *Non est, mi Lucili, quod amicum tantum in foro et in curia quaeras; si diligenter adtenderis, et domi invenies.* Note that the word *amicus* carried no inherent notions of differential social status; see Saller, *Patronage*, 11–15.

[259] *Ep.* 47.11, 15.

[260] cf. *Ep.* 47.10: 'Kindly remember that he whom you call your slave sprang from the same stock, is smiled upon by the same skies, and on equal terms with yourself breathes, lives, and dies. It is just as possible for you to see in him a free-born man as for him to see in you a slave'!

[261] *Ep.* 47.18. Cf. *Ben.* 4.19.1: *nec quisquam amat, quos timet* ('no one loves those whom he fears'); *Ep.* 123.16.

[262] 1 Pet 2.18. Cf. also 2.17 (τὴν ἀδελφότητα ἀγαπᾶτε, τὸν θεὸν φοβεῖσθε). A further, but another, kind of 'mingling' of fear and love can be seen in 1 Clem. 51.2.

[263] Griffin, *Seneca*, 256.

Again, Seneca does not intend to argue against slavery per se. Slaves are not to cease to be slaves and their masters are not to cease to be masters. Rather, his point concerns the reciprocal mind-set between master and slave, and particularly the question of how the former treats the latter. 'Only dumb animals need the thong', not human beings, he reminds the reader.[264] To treat the slave well creates respect instead of fear. A good practical rule and, in fact, 'the kernel' (*summa*) of Seneca's advice is this: 'Treat your inferiors as you would be treated by your superiors.'[265] This is part of what it means to 'live in accordance with Nature' in the Stoic sense. Seneca's point of departure here is the philosophical principle that there are no natural slaves.[266] The idea itself was not new, to be sure. But Seneca went further than most of his predecessors and contemporaries in this respect,[267] as is suggested in his letter by his anticipation of critical voices from other slaveholders: 'Some may maintain that I am now offering the liberty-cap to slaves in general and toppling down lords from their high estate, because I bid slaves respect their masters instead of fearing them. They say: "This is what he plainly means: slaves are to pay respect as if they were clients or early-morning callers!"' Seneca's immediate response is that such (potential) critics forget that 'what is enough for a god cannot be too little for a master'.[268] According to the Stoic philosopher, the virtues of *humanitas* and *clementia* should govern all relations with slaves as with other people.[269]

We see from this discussion that moral responsibility in terms of looking to the interests and well-being of the other, largely irrespective of social status, was shared by Stoic and Christian authors. The larger moral framework was fundamentally similar,[270] and, despite all differences of social setting, so was its social dimension.

It remains to examine if this fundamental similarity also applies to the ethical scope of Roman Stoicism and Roman Christianity. This is the subject of the next and final chapter of this study.

---

[264] *Ep.* 47.19.

[265] *Ep.* 47.11: *sic cum inferiore vivas, quemadmodum tecum superiorem velis vivere* (the word *superiorem* is translated as 'betters' in the LCL trans.). Cf. *Clem.* 1.7.1; *Ep.* 94.43. Cf. also the contemporary Petronius, *Sat.* 71.1, in which this point of view is alluded to.

[266] Contrast Aristotle, *Pol.* 1253b32–54a15.

[267] See C. E. Manning, 'Stoicism and Slavery in the Roman Empire', *ANRW* 36.3: 1525–9. Cf. also the helpful discussion in Griffin, *Seneca*, 256–85.

[268] *Ep.* 47.18.   [269] cf. Griffin, *Seneca*, 258–9.

[270] Comparing Pauline ethics with Graeco-Roman ethics, Horrell states: 'The degree of similarity should not be over-pressed; as is often noted, Paul does not include in his lists the four cardinal virtues of Greek morality' (*Solidarity*, 161). But neither does Epictetus (cf. Chapter 4 above)! And yet, who would seriously claim that Epictetus was unaware of the cardinal virtues or that they played no role in his moral teaching?

10

Ethical Scope Compared

We have now seen how fundamentally similar the moral teachings of Roman Stoicism and Roman Christianity were, as reflected in the texts of Seneca, Musonius, Epictetus, Romans, 1 Peter, and 1 Clement. In this final chapter we shall turn our attention specifically to the question of the ethical scope of these texts, that is, the question whether their ethics extend unconditionally to humanity as a whole or not. In other words, do the authors of these texts teach universal humanity? Or is their moral teaching somehow more restricted or conditioned in any way?

In the following, we shall first briefly recall the ethical scope in Roman Stoicism. Since this has frequently been touched on in the discussion above, there is no need to dwell on this part of the enquiry. Instead we shall promptly move on to the question of the ethical scope of our Christian texts, which has not been addressed specifically in the above, and is in need of a more detailed discussion. We shall see that there is a considerable difference between Roman Stoicism and Roman Christianity in this respect.

ETHICAL SCOPE IN ROMAN STOICISM: UNIVERSAL HUMANITY

Common assumptions are by definition and nature both widespread and hard to change. And so it is with the typical conception of the ethical scope of Graeco-Roman philosophy: 'It is very often assumed that ancient theories must be, at some level, egoistic, just because their starting point is the agent's reflections on his life, and because they demand that the agent have concern for his acquisition of virtue.'[1] As for the Stoics in particular compared to the Christians, the common opinion runs like this: 'Stoicism was a philosophy for an exclusive circle of the elect, whereas Christianity taught universal

---

[1] Annas, *Morality*, 12. Cf. Engberg-Pedersen, *Paul*, 290, on Paul and the Stoics: 'Pauline scholars regularly contrast the idea of an outward-directedness (to be found in Paul) with that of an inward-directedness (to be found in the Stoics). That is a misunderstanding.'

salvation.'[2] It remains to be seen if the latter applies to the Christian texts considered in this study, but our survey of the Stoic sources has shown that the common opinion of Stoicism is utterly false and in urgent need of correction. There can be no mistake that Stoic theory teaches that 'other-concern will extend beyond the range of personal acquaintance and commitment, and eventually result in the virtuous agent having concern, from the moral point of view, for any rational being.'[3] In fact, '[t]he Stoics are the first ethical theorists clearly to commit themselves to the thesis that morality requires impartiality to all others from the moral point of view.'[4] For them this is nothing but a natural consequence of the process of social *oikeiōsis* in which the distinction between self-interest and altruism is vanquished.

This is precisely what we have seen time and again in the sources of Roman Stoicism. The sources reveal clearly how basic the tenet of universal humanity was to the Stoic moral teaching, and how strongly the Stoics emphasized impartiality in human relations. This line of thought becomes particularly clear and prominent in Roman Stoicism. 'Nature begot me loving all people', Seneca said,[5] referring, of course, not just to himself but to *all* humans, who by nature love all fellow humans simply on account of their being human and nothing else. Since this is clearly not the actual state of the world, due to many external reasons, it is one of the main purposes of philosophy to guide people and lead them to an all-embracing love (*comprendens amor*) of the entire human race (*humani generis*).[6]

With this teaching, Seneca and his fellow Stoics sought to point out to people something that was inherent in human life itself, something that already existed as part of the creation of the world.[7] According to the Stoics, then, if properly informed and motivated, people will (re)discover their true nature as human beings and act accordingly. At the same time, they will (re)discover the natural equality between all 'sorts' of people, 'Greek and Barbarian, man and woman, noble and commoner, free man and slave.'[8] There can thus be no ethical partiality between people of different race, nationality, gender, social status, or, we may add, religion. The cardinal virtues of the Roman Stoics and their highest ethical ideals are not reserved for particular individuals or particular groups of people, but are meant to reach to and include 'each and all'—*universis singulisque.*[9]

---

[2] Hubertus R. Drobner, 'Christian Philosophy', in *The Oxford Handbook of Early Christian Studies* (ed. S. A. Harvey and D. G. Hunter; Oxford: Oxford University Press, 2008), 683.
[3] Annas, *Morality*, 13.　　[4] Annas, *Morality*, 265.
[5] *Ep.* 102.18: *natura me amantem omnium genuit* (my translation above).
[6] Seneca, *Clem.* 1.11.2.　　[7] cf. Lee, *Paul*, 74, 87–8.
[8] Christensen, 'Equality', 46.　　[9] Seneca, *Clem.* 2.5.3. Cf. Chapter 2 above.

In short, Stoic theory is decidedly universalistic in its scope and makes no ethical differentiation between particular groups of people.

ETHICAL SCOPE IN ROMANS: 'UNIVERSAL LOVE'?

In the discussion of Paul's Letter to the Romans in Chapter 6 above, we saw that 'love' (ἀγάπη) was the main principle upon which Paul based his moral teaching for the Christ-believing community in Rome. As the apostle envisioned it, the 'cardinal virtue' for Christ-believers was mutual love: μηδενὶ μηδὲν ὀφείλετε εἰ μὴ τὸ ἀλλήλους ἀγαπᾶν· ὁ γὰρ ἀγαπῶν τὸν ἕτερον νόμον πεπλήρωκεν. ... πλήρωμα οὖν νόμου ἡ ἀγάπη.[10] From other letters authored by Paul it can be seen that he thought the same should apply to other Christ-believing communities. It suffices to mention Paul's well-known panegyric of love in 1 Corinthians 13, in which he declares, among other things, that even if a person has powers of prophecy or knowledge, or is filled with faith, but does not have love, that person is *nothing* (οὐθέν). Indeed, of the three core principles of faith, hope, and love (πίστις, ἐλπίς, ἀγάπη), love is the greatest (μείζων δὲ τούτων ἡ ἀγάπη).[11]

But did Paul maintain that the virtue of ἀγάπη should extend beyond the fellowship of Christ-believers to outsiders as well? Did he urge his addressees to 'love' not only one another but also their non-believing neighbours? According to the traditional interpretation the answer is clear: Paul's love ethic is decidedly universalistic.[12] The Pauline ἀγάπη embraces all humanity, it is claimed or assumed, including even persecutors, as Romans 12.14 states. On a closer examination, however, this is actually far from evident. I have already noted how ἀγάπη is mentioned mostly in passing in Romans 12.9a, that it relates mainly to what precedes, and that its frequently alleged 'introductory' function for the subsequent discourse has little support in the text itself. This is important for the present discussion because it is mainly by reading such an 'introductory' function of ἀγάπη into Paul's text that scholars have been able to bolster their interpretation of Romans 12.9–21 as an

---

[10] Rom 13.8–10 ('Owe no one anything, except to love one another. For the one who loves the other has fulfilled the Law.... Therefore, the fulfilment of the Law is love').

[11] 1 Cor 13.13.

[12] So, e.g., Furnish, *Love Command*, 107. Furnish refers in this respect to Rom 12.18, but it needs to be pointed out that in 12.18 Paul does not exhort his addressees to 'love' all people but to *live at peace* with all people: εἰ δυνατὸν τὸ ἐξ ὑμῶν, μετὰ πάντων ἀνθρώπων εἰρηνεύοντες ('if possible for your part, live at peace with all people'). There is no mention of 'love' in this verse, nor in its immediate context.

example of Paul's 'universalistic love ethic'. One scholar claims, for instance, that 'in Romans 12, Paul explicitly extends the application of ἀγάπη to one's dealings with outsiders, people in general, even enemies and persecutors'.[13] But Paul does no such thing in Romans 12, let alone 'explicitly'. As we have seen, the weight of ἀγάπη in 12.9a is hardly such that it can be taken as a determining concept for the entire discourse in 12.9b–21. It is not until 13.8 that such a thing takes place, and then in a very explicit manner. The diverse moral exhortations in 12.9–21, on the other hand, need to be considered individually, each in its own right.

We have already seen above how unsystematic Paul is in his treatment of in-group and out-group relations in Romans 12. While vv. 3–13 are devoted solely to the former, vv. 14–21 allude to both groups.[14] In 12.9a ἀγάπη is used within the context of in-group relations, but in vv. 14–21 there is no reference at all to that particular concept. When in v. 14 Paul urges his audience to 'bless those who persecute you; bless and do not curse them' (εὐλογεῖτε τοὺς διώκοντας ὑμᾶς, εὐλογεῖτε καὶ μὴ καταρᾶσθε), it does not involve a demand to 'love' these people, as has commonly been claimed. There is no 'love of enemies' witnessed in this verse.[15] Certainly Paul exhorts his addressees to bless (or 'speak well of') potential persecutors (who are a sort of 'enemies'), but ἀγάπη is simply not the issue here. The same holds true of vv. 17–21, in which Paul teaches proper relations with people in general. It is clear that there is an explicit universal reference in v. 17b ('all people'), but it should be equally clear that Paul is not referring to 'universal love' or anything like that in this verse. Rather, he is speaking of the Christ-believers' noble appearance in the sight of all people (προνοούμενοι καλὰ ἐνώπιον πάντων ἀνθρώπων). In v. 18, then, he follows this up by expressing his concern that the addressees do their best (εἰ δυνατὸν τὸ ἐξ ὑμῶν) to 'be at peace with all people' (μετὰ πάντων ἀνθρώπων εἰρηνεύοντες),[16] that is, that they always try to avoid unnecessary conflict with the outside world.

In other words, the virtue of ἀγάπη is nowhere mentioned in vv. 14–21. The most reasonable explanation for this seems to be that, for Paul, ἀγάπη was not a concept that applied to the Christ-believers' relations to outsiders. Instead, it

---

[13] Wilson, *Love*, 131. This is a common misunderstanding the grounds of which are rarely considered, but simply taken for granted. Cf., e.g., the recent example in Hubert Meisinger's 'Christian Love and Biological Altruism' (*Zygon* 35 [2000]: esp. 748–51).

[14] The demand in v. 13b to practise hospitality (τὴν φιλοξενίαν διώκοντες) may also apply to outsiders, but I find that less likely.

[15] cf. the discussion on 'Non-Retaliation and "Love of Enemies" ' in Chapter 9 above.

[16] Note the close parallel in Epictetus, *Diss.* 4.5.24: εἰρήνην ἄγεις πρὸς πάντας ἀνθρώπους. The difference is that while Paul cautiously adds the condition 'if possible for your part' (εἰ δυνατὸν τὸ ἐξ ὑμῶν), Epictetus includes no such condition, but specifically underlines the absolute nature of the peace demand: 'no matter what they do' (ὅ τι ἂν ἐκεῖνοι ποιῶσι).

was an *in-group term*.[17] The act of 'loving' concerned in-group relations, and in-group relations only: 'Owe no one anything, except to *love one another* (τὸ ἀλλήλους ἀγαπᾶν)', he instructs his addressees in 13.8. Thus 'the other' (ὁ ἕτερος) and 'the neighbour' (ὁ πλησίον [sc. ὤν]) spoken of in 13.8–10, whom the addressees are obliged to 'love', are persons who belong to a very specific part of humankind: they are fellow believers in Christ. In this way, the verb ἀγαπᾶν denotes preference.[18]

That this was Paul's understanding of the virtue of ἀγάπη is confirmed by his other writings where he discusses human relations. Contrary to common opinion, very few of these texts tell anything about human relations in general, of how Christ-believers should behave not only towards themselves, but towards others as well. And when they do tell something about such relations, the concept of ἀγάπη is not applied. Thus, in Galatians 5.14 where Paul refers to the command to love (ἀγαπᾶν) one's neighbour as oneself (from Lev 19.18) with the same message as in Romans 13.9, namely, that the Jewish Law is fulfilled in this single commandment, he is solely concerned with in-group relations. This is strongly suggested by the context, for in the preceding verse he urges the Galatian addressees to 'serve one another through love' (διὰ τῆς ἀγάπης δουλεύετε ἀλλήλοις), and in the verse immediately following the love command in v. 14, he continues: 'If you bite and devour one another (ἀλλήλους), take care not to be consumed by one another (ὑπ' ἀλλήλων).'[19] Relations with outsiders are not discussed in this text. The 'neighbour' is a fellow Christ-believer. The same is most likely true of a passage in 1 Thessalonians that is nonetheless quite routinely cited as an example of the Pauline 'universal love'. In 3.12 Paul expresses his wish that the Thessalonian addressees may abound in love (ἀγάπη) 'for one another and for all' (εἰς ἀλλήλους καὶ εἰς πάντας). At first sight, the phrase εἰς πάντας ('for all') may seem to imply an appeal to a love of all human beings, but the clause immediately following

---

[17] cf. Thorsteinsson, 'Paul and Roman Stoicism', 144–6; Engberg-Pedersen, *Paul*, 265–9, 276–7, 287–9; idem, 'Relationship', 58. Cf. also Michael Ebersohn, *Das Nächstenliebegebot in der synoptischen Tradition* (Marburger Theologische Studien 37; Marburg: Elwert, 1993), 245 n. 502.

[18] cf. Stauffer, 'ἀγαπάω', 36–7, where he discusses the use of ἀγαπᾶν in pre-biblical Greek: 'Particularly characteristic are the instances in which ἀγαπᾶν takes on the meaning of "to prefer," "to set one good or aim above another," "to esteem one person more highly than another." Thus ἀγαπᾶν may be used of the preference of God for a particular man. The ἠγαπημένος ὑπὸ τοῦ θεοῦ has a position of preference before God. He is blessed by God with particular gifts and possessions.... Ἀγαπᾶν is a love which makes distinctions, choosing and keeping to its object.' Cf. also p. 51, on the Pauline 'love': 'Neighbourly love, once a readiness to help compatriots in the covenant people of Israel, is now service rendered to fellow-citizens in the new people of God. It implies making the welfare of the brotherhood the guiding principle of conduct. Ἀγαπητός and ἀδελφός become interchangeable terms (1. Th. 2:8; Phlm. 16).'

[19] Gal 5.15: εἰ δὲ ἀλλήλους δάκνετε καὶ κατεσθίετε, βλέπετε μὴ ὑπ' ἀλλήλων ἀναλωθῆτε. On the 'biting', cf. Musonius 10.78.27–8 (ἀντιδήξεταί τις τὸν δακόντα).

suggests that these 'all' are in fact *all fellow Christ-believers.*[20] For Paul adds the motivation 'just as we [abound in love] for you' (καθάπερ καὶ ἡμεῖς εἰς ὑμᾶς). That is, Paul's point is that precisely as he and his co-senders abound in love for the Christ-believers in Thessalonica, so should they abound in love as well, not only for one another, but also for all other fellow believers.[21] That Paul's perspective here is still an in-group perspective is also suggested by the fact that when he, shortly after this passage, applauds the addressees because of their 'brotherly love' (φιλαδελφία),[22] he explains that their praise is merited because they do not stop at loving one another (τὸ ἀγαπᾶν ἀλλήλους) but love even 'all the brothers throughout Macedonia' (πάντας τοὺς ἀδελφοὺς τοὺς ἐν ὅλῃ τῇ Μακεδονίᾳ), i.e. all fellow Christ-believers in the Macedonian province. But when he turns to speak of the addressees' relationship with non-believers, he finds it sufficient to urge the audience to 'behave honourably towards outsiders' (περιπατῆτε εὐσχημόνως πρὸς τοὺς ἔξω) and to 'be in need of no one [or: nothing]' (μηδενὸς χρείαν ἔχητε).[23] There is no reference to 'love' in this latter context. In 5.15 Paul may certainly mean people in general when he exhorts the addressees to do good 'to all' (εἰς πάντας), but, again, the virtue of ἀγάπη is not the issue here either, but, more generally, τὸ ἀγαθόν: 'See that no one renders anyone evil for evil, but always seek to do good to one another and to all' (ὁρᾶτε μή τις κακὸν ἀντὶ κακοῦ τινι ἀποδῷ, ἀλλὰ πάντοτε τὸ ἀγαθὸν διώκετε καὶ εἰς ἀλλήλους καὶ εἰς πάντας).[24] The same goes for Galatians 6.10 where he, on the other hand, expresses a certain distinction between humankind as a whole ('all') and a particular portion of that whole: 'Let us do good

---

[20] Somewhat differently Malherbe, who suggests that '[r]ather than all people generally, it is likely that Paul has in mind pagans who were present in the Christian assemblies' (*Thessalonians*, 213). Similarly also Victor Paul Furnish, 'Inside Looking Out: Some Pauline Views of the Unbelieving Public', in *Pauline Conversations in Context: Essays in Honor of Calvin J. Roetzel* (ed. J. C. Anderson, P. Sellew, and C. Setzer; JSNTSup 221; Sheffield: Sheffield Academic Press, 2002), 109.

[21] cf. 2 Cor 8.24; Phlm 5. One may also compare Eph 1.15; 4.2; Col 1.4; 3.13–14; 2 Thess 1.3.

[22] 1 Thess 4.9–10.

[23] 1 Thess 4.12. Standard translations of this verse vary somewhat, as the following examples indicate: 'so that you may behave properly toward outsiders and be dependent on no one' (NRSV); 'that ye may walk becomingly toward them that are without, and may have need of nothing' (ASV); 'so that your daily life may win the respect of outsiders and so that you will not be dependent on anybody' (NIV); 'So sollt ihr vor denen, die nicht zu euch gehören, ein rechtschaffenes Leben führen und auf niemand angewiesen sein' (EIN); 'damit ihr anständig wandelt gegen die draußen und niemanden nötig habt' (ELB); 'en sorte que vous vous conduisiez honnêtement envers ceux du dehors, et que vous n'ayez besoin de personne' (NEG). The adverb εὐσχημόνως has the basic sense 'with grace and dignity, like a gentleman' (LSJ, s.v. εὐσχήμων II).

[24] cf. Rom 12.17, 21.

to all, but especially to those who are of the household of the faith' (ἐργαζώμεθα τὸ ἀγαθὸν πρὸς πάντας, μάλιστα δὲ πρὸς τοὺς οἰκείους τῆς πίστεως).

In sum, whereas ἀγάπη can rightly be described as Paul's primary virtue, he clearly makes a distinction between insiders and outsiders in his moral teaching, and there is no positive evidence that he ever taught that the primary virtue, ἀγάπη, should extend to outsiders as well. In none of his letters does he urge his addressees to *love* (ἀγαπᾶν) anyone other than fellow Christ-believers. The common notion that the apostle advocated unconditional 'universal love' needs to be reconsidered.

Returning to Paul's Letter to the Romans, we are now in a better position to assess what he appears to be saying to his Roman addressees about proper relations to the outside world. First of all, according to Paul, Christ-believers are not to render evil for evil to anyone, including outsiders (μηδενὶ κακὸν ἀντὶ κακοῦ ἀποδιδόντες, 12.17a; μὴ καταρᾶσθε [τοὺς διώκοντας ὑμᾶς], v. 14b; μὴ ἑαυτοὺς ἐκδικοῦντες, v. 19a), but to render good for evil (εὐλογεῖτε τοὺς διώκοντας ὑμᾶς, v. 14a; ἐὰν πεινᾷ ὁ ἐχθρός σου, ψώμιζε αὐτόν· ἐὰν διψᾷ, πότιζε αὐτόν, v. 20) and by so doing defeat the evil (νίκα ἐν τῷ ἀγαθῷ τὸ κακόν, v. 21). Any vengeance, however, is God's and God's alone (v. 19). Second, but no less significantly, followers of Christ are to behave nobly and honourably in society (προνοούμενοι καλὰ ἐνώπιον πάντων ἀνθρώπων, v. 17b) and conduct themselves as peacefully as they can before people around them (εἰ δυνατὸν τὸ ἐξ ὑμῶν, μετὰ πάντων ἀνθρώπων εἰρηνεύοντες, v. 18). Such conduct is desired also in order not to arouse any unnecessary hostility on behalf of the Roman authorities (13.1–4), to which the Christ-believers should do their proper duties, including paying taxes (vv. 6–7).

Paul's discourse on appropriate behaviour towards outsiders in Romans 12–13 is the most specific and most extensive of its kind in his letters. (Convinced that Paul would never have done so himself, I do not include Jews as 'outsiders' in the present discussion.) We have already seen glimpses of Paul's comments on the subject in Galatians and 1 Thessalonians. In 1 Thessalonians 4.11–12 he urges the audience to 'endeavour to live quietly (φιλοτιμεῖσθαι ἡσυχάζειν), to mind your own affairs (πράσσειν τὰ ἴδια), and to work with your own hands (ἐργάζεσθαι ταῖς ἰδίαις χερσὶν ὑμῶν), as we commanded you, so that you may behave honourably towards outsiders and be in need of no one (ἵνα περιπατῆτε εὐσχημόνως πρὸς τοὺς ἔξω καὶ μηδενὸς χρείαν ἔχητε).' These words, which come close to the main message in Romans 12–13, seem quite characteristic of Paul's general view in this respect. So does also the brief remark in Galatians 6.10 in which he exhorts the audience to 'do good to all', where, as we saw above, the word 'all' (πάντες) appears to refer to people in general.

It is true that Romans 12–13 (together with 1 Thess 4.11–12 and Gal 6.10) may be somewhat misleading as an illustrative example of Paul's own perspective due to the remarkably positive views expressed of the outside world. For we do have texts by Paul that show much less sympathy for outsiders: 'Do not be mismatched with unbelievers (μὴ γίνεσθε ἑτεροζυγοῦντες ἀπίστοις). For what partnership is there between righteousness (δικαιοσύνη) and lawlessness (ἀνομία)? Or what fellowship is there between light and darkness? What agreement does Christ have with Beliar? Or what does a believer (πιστός) share with an unbeliever (ἄπιστος)?'[25] Nevertheless, whereas texts like this certainly leave us with a picture of Paul himself that is more complex and composite than otherwise, it is the text of Romans that is under discussion in this study because it was that particular text that the apostle sent to the Roman Christ-believers in the middle of the first century. And in that text Paul was in general quite positive in his comments on the outside world, on Roman authorities, and on Roman society at large, although he did make a distinction between Christ-believers and others in terms of moral obligations. We have seen how this distinction is expressed through his application of ἀγάπη in discussions of in-group relations only. Nowhere is this concept used to describe proper disposition towards outsiders. Texts such as 2 Corinthians 6.14–15 (cited above) make it more understandable to modern readers why there is such a differentiation between Christ-believers and others even in Romans. It explains why Paul's ethic of love was, as it were, more particular than 'universal'—at least it speaks against the latter.[26]

In brief, then, according to Paul's moral teaching in Romans it is most beneficial and wise for the followers of Jesus Christ to behave honourably in the larger society. However, this is not the whole story. This does not express what is most important for the Roman addressees, according to Paul. What really counts is not how they behave towards outsiders, but how they treat one another. In general, they should conduct themselves in a noble manner and live as peacefully as they can, always showing proper submission to civic authorities, but none of this is what matters the most. Indeed, these are all

---

[25] 2 Cor 6.14–15 (trans. NRSV).

[26] It is interesting to note that in his comparison of Paul and Seneca, Sevenster came to the conclusion that Paul's conception of fellowship seems indeed to have differed in scope from Seneca's, since Paul had 'the Church' primarily in mind, while Seneca was thinking of humanity as a whole (*Paul and Seneca*, 173). Nevertheless, Sevenster then manages to turn it all on its head by implying that while Seneca's ethics *really* was particular and restricted (because Seneca really did not mean what he said; it was rather a question of 'the superficially broader universalism of Seneca and other Stoics', p. 174), Paul's moral teaching *really* was universal (see p. 218).

adiaphora.[27] The decisive thing is rather the Christ-believing community itself and relations within that community. That is also the issue of Paul's ethical instructions in 13.8 and following, at which point he returns to the discussion of in-group relations, and at which point the concept of ἀγάπη reappears. While Romans 12.3–13.7 speaks of issues that concern both relations with fellow Christ-believers and relations with outsiders, the text in 13.8–15.14 is confined to the former. And as a further token of the in-group relevance of ἀγάπη, we encounter the virtue again precisely in the middle of the latter discourse,[28] where Paul emphasizes that if you do not adapt yourself to the needs of other members of the Christ-believing community, 'you are no longer walking in love' (οὐκέτι κατὰ ἀγάπην περιπατεῖς).

ETHICAL SCOPE IN 1 PETER: LOVING
THE 'BROTHERHOOD'

It should be clear from the discussion in Chapter 7 above that for the author of 1 Peter ἀγάπη was the primary Christian virtue. But who were the persons who were to be 'loved'? Were they exclusively fellow believers in Christ (as in Paul's letter)? Or did ἀγάπη extend to other people as well? If not, how did the author of 1 Peter conceive the proper Christian relation to and behaviour towards outsiders?

To begin with, there can be no doubt that 1 Peter 1.22 concerns fellow believers and fellow believers only. This is explicit enough in the text. The Christ-believing addressees are told to 'love one another' (ἀλλήλους ἀγαπήσατε) as their 'brotherly love' (φιλαδελφία) requires of them. Other people do not come into focus here.[29]

The same must be said about the specific demand to 'love' in 2.17, even though the issue is not as straightforward as in 1.22. The immediate context, beginning in 2.11, is quite different, since it mostly regards the Christ-movement's relation to outsiders, including civic authorities. According to the author, the proper attitude is to conform to the will of rightful authorities and behave nobly in society in general. He does not specify more precisely

---

[27] On the submission to the Roman authorities as *adiaphoron*, see esp. Troels Engberg-Pedersen, 'Paul's Stoicizing Politics in Romans 12–13: The Role of 13.1–10 in the Argument', *JSNT* 29 (2006): 163–72, where Engberg-Pedersen reads Rom 13.1–7 in the light of Seneca's *Clem.* 1.1–4.

[28] Rom 14.15.

[29] As for 2.1, nothing in the text indicates a shift of focus away from the addressees in 1.22–5.

what he considers to be 'noble conduct' or 'good works' etc. (ἡ ἀναστροφὴ
καλή, τὰ καλὰ ἔργα, ἀγαθοποιεῖν),[30] but the 'good' itself does not seem to be
the ultimate objective. Rather, the decisive thing is the way in which the
'brotherhood' of Christ-believers is seen by society at large, by those who (yet)
are unbelievers.[31] The purpose for such noble behaviour towards the outside
world is twofold: to prevent any undue criticism, and to win converts to the
Christ-believing community. In 2.17, then, the author urges his addressees to
'honour everyone' (πάντας τιμήσατε), including the emperor (τὸν βασιλέα
τιμᾶτε). I take the former to mean 'behave honourably towards everyone' or
'treat everyone with proper honour', thus rephrasing the main point of the
text immediately preceding.[32] But when the author of 1 Peter proceeds to the
Christ-movement and relations within that group it is no longer τιμή
('honour') that counts as most imperative, but ἀγάπη: τὴν ἀδελφότητα
ἀγαπᾶτε ('love the brotherhood'). Again, the readers are specifically told to
love one another and all fellow believers ('the brotherhood'). Whereas honour
and honourable behaviour are definitely called for in relation to non-believers, love is not. The latter is confined to the Christian fellowship.

The series of exhortations initiated in 3.8 gives us some difficulties with
respect to the question of ethical scope in 1 Peter. Against whom are the

---

[30] Bruce W. Winter has suggested that the text urges well-to-do Christians to (continue to)
provide benefactions for the common good, something that was honoured in public with
customary civic conventions (*Seek the Welfare of the City: Christians as Benefactors and Citizens*
[Grand Rapids, MI: Eerdmans, 1994], esp. 21–3, 33–40, 200–3). According to Winter, this
means that the author of 1 Peter does not encourage his readers to withdraw from society, as has
often been held, but precisely to *be involved* in society: 'Conversion to Christianity did not mean
that civic benefactors ceased to seek the welfare of their earthly cities.... It was an ethical
imperative which Christians were commanded to fulfil within this aspect of *politeia*, and as a
result would have made them very visible in the public place' (pp. 39–40).

[31] cf. 1 Pet 2.12: τὴν ἀναστροφὴν ὑμῶν ἐν τοῖς ἔθνεσιν ἔχοντες καλήν, ἵνα ἐν ᾧ καταλαλοῦσιν
ὑμῶν ὡς κακοποιῶν ἐκ τῶν καλῶν ἔργων ἐποπτεύοντες δοξάσωσιν τὸν θεὸν ἐν ἡμέρᾳ ἐπισκοπῆς
('Conduct yourselves honorably among the Gentiles, so that, though they malign you as
evildoers, they may see your honorable deeds and glorify God when he comes to judge';
trans. NRSV). Cf. also v. 15.

[32] Building on Stanley Porter's studies of Greek verbal aspect, Scot Snyder argues that the
aorist τιμήσατε in v. 17a (with the general object πάντας) expresses general action, while the
present tenses ἀγαπᾶτε, φοβεῖσθε, and τιμᾶτε in v. 17b–d (all with particular objects) serve to
specify that action. 'Hence, he says, "honour all: (yes, as was already directed) love the brethren
and fear God and (also) honour the king"'. This means that 'πάντας does not refer to the pagans,
but to those whom the Christians are to honour (i.e., the brethren, God, the king) in main-
taining ἀναστροφὴν καλήν' ('1 Peter 2:17: A Reconsideration', *FN* 4 [1991]: 213, 214). Snyder's
suggestion is certainly worth considering, but the problem is that it necessarily makes 'love' and
'fear' two specific sub-types of 'honour', which seems unlikely. The demand to 'honour the
emperor' may fit well with Snyder's reading (although it seems superfluous to repeat the word
'honour'), but it is quite clear that the readers are not told to 'honour' the brotherhood and God
but to *love* and *fear* them respectively. For further discussion, see Achtemeier, *1 Peter*, 187–8.

addressees not to render 'evil for evil' or 'abuse for abuse' in v. 9? Against each other or (also) against outsiders? The two groups of insiders and outsiders seem somewhat fused in this verse. We must look to the immediate context: in the preceding passage (2.18–3.7) the author had addressed particular groups of people among the letter's recipients (slaves, wives, husbands). In 3.8 he turns again to the audience as a whole with the word πάντες ('all of you')[33] and exhorts them to be such and such: ὁμόφρονες, συμπαθεῖς, φιλάδελφοι, εὔσπλαγχνοι, ταπεινόφρονες (i.e. to have unity of mind, sympathy, and brotherly love, and to be kind-hearted and humble-minded). The words ὁμόφρονες and φιλάδελφοι in particular show that what is stated in this verse must concern in-group relations.[34] However, the subsequent context suggests that the exhortation in v. 9, μὴ ἀποδιδόντες κακὸν ἀντὶ κακοῦ ἢ λοιδορίαν ἀντὶ λοιδορίας, τοὐναντίον δὲ εὐλογοῦντες,[35] has to do with out-group relations as well, perhaps even primarily. For following the scriptural citations in vv. 10–12, the author poses the rhetorical question, 'And who will do you evil if you are eager to do what is good?' (καὶ τίς ὁ κακώσων ὑμᾶς ἐὰν τοῦ ἀγαθοῦ ζηλωταὶ γένησθε;), and then goes on to speak of the readers' proper response to outside evil and abuse.[36] This suggests that out-group relations are already in view when the author tells the readers not to render 'evil for evil' in v. 9. The distinction between insiders and outsiders is fused in this verse because there is no clear-cut division between v. 8 and v. 9 (despite the asyndeton), and because it becomes discernible only in the following discourse that outsiders were (also) in view in v. 9. It is important to note that there is no question here of 'loving' those outside the Christian brotherhood. Precisely as Paul's audience, the addressees of 1 Peter are urged to 'bless' (εὐλογεῖν) those who do them harm, but they are not urged to *love* them. Both here and in the subsequent discussion of relations with outsiders the basic advice is caution and 'passivity': '*If* they act so and so, *then* you should (not) do so and so', is the main message.

If there is some uncertainty about the ethical scope in 3.9, the same cannot be said of 4.8–11. This text solely concerns morality within the fellowship of Christ-believers, and does so very explicitly: as fellow believers the addressees are to have fervent love for 'each other' (εἰς ἑαυτούς), to be hospitable to 'one another' (εἰς ἀλλήλους), and to serve 'each other' (εἰς ἑαυτούς). Everything in

---

[33] It is also possible that πάντες refers to the three groups addressed in the preceding, i.e. 'Finally, all of you, slaves, wives, and husbands,...', but such a reading seems less likely, especially with respect to the content of the ensuing exhortations.

[34] The word ταπεινόφρονες may also imply this; cf. 5.5–6 where its cognates are used of relations within the group.

[35] i.e. 'Do not repay evil for evil or abuse for abuse; on the contrary, repay with a blessing'.

[36] 1 Pet 3.13–17.

this passage speaks of in-group relations. Furthermore, once again, the concept of ἀγάπη is used in that respect. It is even stated that, as 'the end of all things' draws near, there is nothing of so much consequence as the Christ-believers' love for one another: πρὸ πάντων τὴν εἰς ἑαυτοὺς ἀγάπην ἐκτενῆ ἔχοντες ('Above all, maintain fervent love for one another'). This understanding is skilfully sealed at the closing of the letter with the words, 'greet one another with a kiss of love' (ἀσπάσασθε ἀλλήλους ἐν φιλήματι ἀγάπης).[37]

In sum, for the author of 1 Peter and for (some of) his fellow believers in Rome, the primary virtue of ἀγάπη is confined to fellow believers. The letter's recipients are urged to behave honourably in society and to do 'good' to all, but nowhere is it required of them to direct the Christian primary virtue towards those who stand outside the Christian brotherhood. This point of view agrees in all its basics with Paul's moral teaching in Romans, with which the author of 1 Peter was in all likelihood well acquainted.

ETHICAL SCOPE IN 1 CLEMENT:
THE 'BROTHERHOOD' AND ROMAN SOCIETY

Unlike both Paul's Letter to the Romans and 1 Peter, there is little advice in 1 Clement that specifically and unmistakably concerns the question of how to behave towards non-believers and in society in general. The letter focuses almost entirely on the fellowship of Christ-believers and relations within that group, whether in Corinth or elsewhere. It is therefore difficult to tell if the author of 1 Clement thought differently of in-group relations and relations with outsiders. Still, a few passages may offer some clues in this respect.

In 48.5–6 a brief description is given of an ideal Christ-believer with the closing comment that he should 'seek the common good of all (τὸ κοινωφελὲς πᾶσιν) and not his own benefit'.[38] It is possible that the word 'all' (πᾶς) alludes here to all people, including outsiders, but the immediate context speaks strongly against such reading.[39] Instead, the word 'all' most likely refers to *all fellow Christ-believers*, either those in Corinth specifically or followers of Christ at large as a collective whole. That does not necessarily mean that,

---

[37] 1 Pet 5.14. The letter ends with a peace wish: εἰρήνη ὑμῖν πᾶσιν τοῖς ἐν Χριστῷ.

[38] Trans. Lake.

[39] The chapter begins with an exhortation to put an end to the strife within the Corinthian community and to return to the practice of 'brotherly love' (φιλαδελφία) (48.1), a term that is almost certainly used here of in-group relations. What we have then is the statement that the only 'gate of righteousness' is 'the one that is in Christ' (v. 4), followed by the description of the ideal Christ-believer, whose duty it is not only to seek the common good of all but also to 'be

according to 1 Clement, the ideal believer should *not* seek the good of non-believers as well. It simply means that the latter are not under consideration in this particular passage.

The case is somewhat different in 62.2, where 'our fathers' are praised as prototypes of proper conduct, as they were 'well-pleasing in their humility (εὐηρέστησαν ταπεινοφρονοῦντες) towards God...and towards all men ([πρὸς] πάντας ἀνθρώπους)'.[40] There is little doubt that the phrase πάντες ἄν·θρω·ποι refers here to all people, i.e. humanity as a whole, implying that the letter's recipients are encouraged to be 'well-pleasing' and humble in their dealings not only with fellow believers but with other people as well. While the text does not dwell further on the issue, at least it betrays a friendly disposition towards outsiders.

This friendly attitude agrees rather well with some scattered remarks in the letter that, directly or indirectly, allude to Graeco-Roman culture and society. Amidst all in-group examples of virtuous behaviour, in 55.1 the Roman senders of 1 Clement note that they find it only fitting to bring in 'examples from the gentiles' (ὑποδείγματα ἐθνῶν) as well. These are no ordinary examples from the masses, to be sure, but kings and rulers (βασιλεῖς καὶ ἡγούμενοι) who, after having had divine directions to do so, are said to have offered their lives and homes for the sake of their fellow citizens. No negative comment is added whatsoever, not even a warning about the otherwise bad habits of the gentiles. The text portrays gentile kings and rulers as equally worthy examples to follow as the in-group examples.

Similar implications are in view when the community of Christ-believers is likened to the Roman army (37.1–4), the leaders of which are even referred to as 'our' leaders. Indeed, the army as a whole serves as a prototype of order, submission, and authority structure for the Christ-believing community:

Let us consider those who serve our generals (τοὺς στρατευομένους τοῖς ἡγουμένοις ἡμῶν), with what good order (εὐτάκτως), habitual readiness (ἐκτικῶς), and submissiveness (ὑποτεταγμένως) they perform their commands. Not all are prefects, nor tribunes, nor centurions, nor in charge of fifty men, or the like, but each carries out in his own rank the commands of the emperor and of the generals (τοῦ βασιλέως καὶ τῶν ἡγουμένων).[41]

humble' (ταπεινοφρονεῖν), a virtue closely tied to the situation in Corinth, as we saw in Chapter 8 above. Furthermore, immediately following the comment in 48.6 is the panegyric on ἀγάπη that begins with the (in-group) terminology ὁ ἔχων ἀγάπην ἐν Χριστῷ ('the one who experiences love in Christ', 49.1). This context of in-group discourse suggests that the ideal believer described in 48.6 is thought of as a person who seeks the common good of all fellow Christ-believers.

[40] Trans. Lake.

[41] 1 Clem. 37.2–3 (trans. Lake). Note that an office of πεντηκόνταρχοι (i.e. those 'in charge of fifty men') did not exist in the Roman army, which suggests that the author of 1 Clement never

This is also fully in line with the positive attitude towards civic authorities that we see elsewhere in 1 Clement. As a part of the lengthy prayer at the closing of the letter, the senders appeal to God to grant that they may be 'obedient... to those who rule and lead us here on earth' (ὑπηκόους γινομένους ... τοῖς τε ἄρχουσιν καὶ ἡγουμένοις ἡμῶν ἐπὶ τῆς γῆς).[42] There is no sign of constraint or affliction in these words. On the contrary, as the subsequent expression clearly shows, the authority of the earthly rulers is considered anything but controversial because it has been given to them by none other than God:

> You have given them, O Master, the authority to rule (σύ, δέσποτα, ἔδωκας τὴν ἐξουσίαν τῆς βασιλείας αὐτοῖς) through your magnificent and indescribable power, that we may both recognize the glory and honor you have given them (τὴν ὑπὸ σοῦ αὐτοῖς δεδομένην δόξαν καὶ τιμήν) and subject ourselves to them (ὑποτάσσεσθαι αὐτοῖς), resisting nothing that conforms to your will. Give to them, O Lord (οἷς δός, κύριε), health, peace, harmony, and stability, so that without faltering they may administer the rule that you have given to them (τὴν ὑπὸ σοῦ δεδομένην αὐτοῖς ἡγεμονίαν).... O Lord, make their plan conform with what is good and acceptable (καλὸν καὶ εὐάρεστον) before you, that when they administer with piety the authority you have given them (τὴν ὑπὸ σοῦ αὐτοῖς δεδομένην ἐξουσίαν), in peace and meekness, they may attain your mercy.[43]

It should be noted that most scholars today reject the earlier view that 1 Clement was written in a context of persecution on the part of Roman authorities (emperor Domitian), a view largely based on the senders' reference at the opening of the letter to their own 'sudden and repeated misfortunes and setbacks',[44] which does not have to refer to persecutions of any sort. It is also highly unlikely that such a context would have given birth to the unmistakably positive statements about the Roman authorities quoted above.

Thus, seen in the light of Paul's exhortations in Romans 12–13, the attitude in 1 Clement towards outsiders appears to agree roughly with that advocated by the apostle, but there is nonetheless a significant difference between the two texts. The author of 1 Clement clearly sees out-groups in a more positive

served in it. His intimate familiarity with the Jewish scriptures, and thus with descriptions of the (ideal) structure of Israel's leadership (cf. Exod 18.21, 25; Deut 1.15), probably caused this error of his concerning the organization of the Roman army; cf. Jeffers, *Conflict*, 139–40; Bakke, 'Concord', 174–5.

[42] 1 Clem. 60.4. The exhortation 'we should respect our leaders' (τοὺς προηγουμένους ἡμῶν αἰδεσθῶμεν) in 21.6, on the other hand, probably refers to in-group leaders (cf. the immediate context, e.g. the following τοὺς πρεσβυτέρους τιμήσωμεν).

[43] 1 Clem. 61.1–2.

[44] 1 Clem. 1.1: διὰ τὰς αἰφνιδίους καὶ ἐπαλλήλους γενομένας ἡμῖν συμφορὰς καὶ περιπτώσεις. On the scholarly discussion, see Ehrman, 'Introduction', 24. Cf., however, allusions to earlier persecutions (of Peter and Paul, among others) in 1 Clement 5–6.

light than does Paul, whose notion of the proper attitude towards outsiders is certainly friendly but still rather 'passive', dominated as it is by the apostle's opinion of the question as an *adiaphoron*. Paul's message is, in essence, 'In general, do what is required of you by the larger society, that is, what is necessary in order for you to survive and prosper as Christ-believers, but, otherwise, let the outer society be a matter of indifference. What really matters is the Christ-movement itself and relations between fellow believers.' There is thus an easily recognized line between the in-group and out-groups in Paul's discourse. In 1 Clement the boundaries between insiders and outsiders are much more blurred. The author of 1 Clement is evidently more associated with and committed to Roman society than the apostle (expressly, at least). For instance, when Paul applies moral examples from outside groups (gentiles), they, as a rule, constitute illustrations of improper disposition and negative behaviour. In 1 Clement, on the other hand, moral examples drawn from the gentiles (ὑποδείγματα ἐθνῶν) are presented in 55.1 as equally good patterns to follow as Jewish and Christian examples. Moreover, unlike the 'passive' attitude of Paul towards civic authorities, the author of 1 Clement not only advocates submission and good behaviour towards the authorities (as Paul does) but actively issues a prayer on their behalf (61.1–2), thus inciting the audience to be active in that manner as well.

While the comments on civic authorities remain perhaps on the fringes of *moral* teaching in 1 Clement, they add to our scanty information about the author's perception of and attitude towards outsiders. One should be aware, however, that these comments can be somewhat misleading. For judging from them it is easy to get the impression that all is well with outsiders in the eyes of 'Clement', and that the ethical scope of 1 Clement applies in equal measure to all, even gentiles (non-believers). That is not entirely the case. Some remarks evince that outsiders are still outsiders, and that gentiles are precisely that— gentiles. So, in 59.3 God is praised as the one who, among other things, 'destroys the reasonings of the gentiles (λογισμοὺς ἐθνῶν)'.[45] And when in 21.6–7 it is stated that Christ-believing women ('our wives') should 'show their love not with partiality (τὴν ἀγάπην αὐτῶν μὴ κατὰ προσκλίσεις)', it is not a question of them showing their love equally to all (i.e. loving even outsiders), but 'equally to *all those who stand in reverential awe of God in a holy way*' (πᾶσιν τοῖς φοβουμένοις τὸν θεὸν ὁσίως ἴσην),[46] that is, only to those within the 'brotherhood' (ἀδελφότης).[47] The old Hebrew view of

---

[45] Or: 'reasonings of the nations', as Ehrman translates (cf. Lake: 'imaginings of nations').

[46] Lake translates as follows: 'let them not give their affection by factious preference, but in holiness to all equally who fear God'.

[47] 1 Clem. 2.4.

non-believers as adverse and immoral others still lingers about in this late first-century CE Roman Christian writing. Similarly, at the end of the cosmological description in 1 Clement 20 we see a clear distinction made between 'us' and the rest of the world: 'The great Creator and Master of all appointed all these things [of the cosmos] to be in peace and harmony, bringing great benefits to all things, *but most especially to us*, who flee to his compassion through our Lord Jesus Christ.'[48] Despite all positive comments on outsiders, the 'brotherhood' retains its character of exclusiveness.

Two things become apparent from this discussion. On the one hand, the details in the letter are hardly frequent or solid enough to allow us to draw any general conclusion about the letter's view of outsiders and the proper attitude towards them. First Clement is a situational letter that simply is not concerned enough with the question of outsiders in general. On the other hand, those remarks that nonetheless show some such concern mostly testify to and encourage a friendly disposition towards outsiders, especially the Roman authorities, whose characterization is remarkably positive. At the same time, however, the typical and somewhat expected distinction between insiders (believers) and outsiders (non-believers) is hinted at as well.

ETHICAL SCOPE IN ROMAN CHRISTIANITY: CONCLUDING SUMMARY

In general, the texts of Romans, 1 Peter, and 1 Clement reveal a quite friendly disposition towards society at large. In their moral teachings, the authors (at least Paul and 'Peter') strongly emphasize that Christ-believers should behave honourably and peacefully in society, always endeavouring to return bad with good rather than rendering evil for evil. Common to all the letters is the almost surprisingly positive attitude towards the civic authorities, including even an insistence on total submission to them.

However, a closer examination of the texts shows that in both Romans and 1 Peter, and to a certain extent in 1 Clement as well, there is a fundamental division between those *within* and those *outside of* the Christ-believing community. The question is somewhat uncertain in 1 Clement because the issue as such is not specifically addressed in that letter. But the authors of Romans and 1 Peter both agree and underline quite clearly that the highest ethical

---

[48] 1 Clem. 20.11: ταῦτα πάντα ὁ μέγας δημιουργὸς καὶ δεσπότης τῶν ἁπάντων ἐν εἰρήνῃ καὶ ὁμονοίᾳ προσέταξεν εἶναι, εὐεργετῶν τὰ πάντα, ὑπερεκπερισσῶς δὲ ἡμᾶς τοὺς προσπεφευγότας τοῖς οἰκτιρμοῖς αὐτοῦ διὰ τοῦ κυρίου ἡμῶν Ἰησοῦ Χριστοῦ.

ideal of the Christian community, the virtue of ἀγάπη, applies to relationships within that community. There are no clear examples of the 'Christian cardinal virtue' occurring where relations to outsiders are considered. Instead, it occurs in contexts in which the relationship between Christ-believers themselves is under discussion, and only in such contexts.

In short, the conclusion must be that the moral teaching of Roman Christianity does *not* teach unconditional universal humanity. It is conditioned by adherence to a particular religion.

Conclusion

In this study I have presented, examined, and compared the moral teachings of Roman Stoicism and Roman Christianity (primarily) in the first century CE. The sources for the former included Seneca, Musonius Rufus, and Epictetus, whereas the sources consulted for Roman Christianity were Paul's Letter to the Romans, the First Letter of Peter, and the First Letter of Clement. Parts I and II presented and examined Stoic and Christian moral teachings, respectively, while Part III included the comparison between the two.

Subsequent to a general introduction to Roman Stoicism in Chapter 1, in Chapter 2 I provided an overview of the moral teaching of Seneca, who wrote extensively on ethics in the middle of the first century and left behind an impressive collection of writings of various genres. Seneca has often been referred to as a shallow hypocrite, even to the extent of being *the* typical hypocrite, but I have argued that, if one aims to follow the ancient sources, this must be a mistake. The fact that he was a very wealthy person does not automatically make him a hypocrite, and while his social situation naturally influenced his thoughts, little suggests that Seneca was less sincere than others in his morality and moral teaching. According to him, people are by nature inclined to love other people, because, as the Stoic tenet says, Nature engendered in them mutual love (*amor mutuus*). This thought runs like a red thread through the entire moral teaching of Seneca, strongly guiding his view and discussion of various topics, including social issues.

In Chapter 3 we focused on another Stoic of the Roman elite, Musonius Rufus. Musonius was a towering figure in Roman Stoicism, and widely celebrated in antiquity for his moral integrity, including among the so-called church fathers. The sources on Musonius reveal a teacher of philosophy who was particularly concerned with social affairs. While he remained true to the philosophical tradition that considered the four cardinal virtues more or less sufficient as the basis for ethics, he could also define virtue as humanity and concern for the welfare of one's fellow human beings. This definition of virtue was wholly in line with Musonius' heavy emphasis on concrete social matters, like questions concerning the family, the status of women, and the situation of the less fortunate in society.

Chapter 4 offered a survey of the moral teaching of Epictetus, who was also a teacher of philosophy, although originally a slave. Like his fellow Stoics, Epictetus points to the divine origin of human beings as basic to the principle of other-regarding morality, but he places more weight on the theological foundation of ethics than any other Stoic we know of. All three Stoics discussed in this study agree that it can never be right to render evil for evil, and that one must always forgive those who treat one badly, but Epictetus takes a step further when he insists that one must even *love* such persons. The Stoic teacher thus comes close to advocating an ethic of 'enemy love'.

In Chapter 5 we turned our attention to the Christian sources, beginning in that chapter with a general discussion of the origin, social setting, and sources of Roman Christianity. In Chapter 6, then, Paul's Letter to the Romans was under consideration, in particular the apostle's moral teaching in Romans 12–15. It became clear that, for Paul, 'love' was the primary virtue. In his moral teaching, Paul urges mutual love and respect among the members of the Christ-believing community, specifically stressing that the 'stronger' must adapt to the needs of the 'weaker' members. Paul's teaching in Romans 12–15 appears to have played a central role in the formation of Roman Christian identity in terms of morality.

Chapter 7 concentrated on the First Letter of Peter, an encyclical letter containing general exhortations to fellow Christians, which shows many signs of Pauline influence. An analysis of the letter revealed a moral teaching in which 'love' unmistakably presented itself as the primary virtue. Like Paul in Romans, the author of 1 Peter is of the opinion that Christ-believers should behave honourably in society, strive to do good to all, and submit to the civic authorities.

Chapter 8 dealt with the First Letter of Clement, the author of which directly applies Paul's moral teaching in Romans. First Clement, too, emphasizes the virtue of 'love', albeit in a more indirect manner due to the letter's focus on the local situation (in Corinth) that it addresses. The moral teaching of 1 Clement speaks primarily in favour of unity, mutual love, and social obligation within the Christ-believing communities. By emphasizing the reciprocal relationship between rich and poor, 'strong' and 'weak', 'great' and 'small', the author advocates a social model that largely mirrors the traditional Roman system of patronage. Correspondingly, the author urges total submission to the Roman authorities, even more so than Paul and 'Peter' had done.

In the longest chapter of the study, Chapter 9, a number of aspects of the moral teachings of Roman Christianity and Roman Stoicism were compared under the headings of five broader themes. These themes included questions of similarities and differences with respect to Christian and Stoic views about

(a) a particular morality or way of life as proper worship of the deity; (b) certain individuals (like Jesus and Socrates) as paradigms for the proper way of living; (c) the importance of mutual love and care; (d) non-retaliation and 'love of enemies'; and (e) the social dimension of ethics. In all cases the comparison revealed a fundamental similarity between the Christian and Stoic sources. In other words, given the present choice of primary sources as well as of subjects to be compared, *Roman Christianity and Roman Stoicism are fundamentally similar in terms of morality or ethics.* This conclusion does not mean that there are no differences whatsoever between the two. Of course there are differences, and the study has revealed some of them, too. But these are minor variations that do not affect the basic moral agreement seen in the teachings of Roman Christianity and Roman Stoicism—except for one difference, which indeed was vital enough to be treated separately in the final chapter of the study.

The final chapter, Chapter 10, discussed the ethical scope of the Christian and Stoic texts, that is, the question of whether the texts teach unqualified universal humanity or not. It was concluded that, contrary to common opinion, there can be no doubt that the Stoic texts teach such universal humanity, while the Christian texts do not. The latter reserve the application of their primary virtue for fellow believers, and thus set an important condition in terms of religious adherence. This condition, in turn, reveals a fundamental distinction between 'us' and 'them' in Christian moral teaching. Such a distinction is not found in Roman Stoic ethics, for which unconditional universal humanity is absolutely basic. Here at last, then, we encountered a difference of considerable importance between the moral teachings of Roman Christianity and Roman Stoicism.

Bibliography

Abel, Karlhans. 'Seneca: Leben und Leistung'. *ANRW* 32.2:653–775. Part 2, *Principat*, 32.2. Edited by H. Temporini and W. Haase. New York: de Gruyter, 1985.

Achtemeier, Paul J. *1 Peter*. Hermeneia. Minneapolis, MN: Fortress, 1996.

Algra, Keimpe. 'Stoic Theology'. Pages 153–78 in *The Cambridge Companion to the Stoics*. Edited by B. Inwood. Cambridge: Cambridge University Press, 2003.

Alvarez Cineira, David. *Die Religionspolitik des Kaisers Claudius und die paulinische Mission*. Herders biblische Studien 19. Freiburg: Herder, 1999.

Annas, Julia. *Hellenistic Philosophy of Mind*. Hellenistic Culture and Society 8. Berkeley, CA: University of California Press, 1992.

—— *The Morality of Happiness*. New York: Oxford University Press, 1993.

—— 'Ethics in Stoic Philosophy'. *Phronesis* 52 (2007): 58–87.

Arnold, E. Vernon. *Roman Stoicism*. Cambridge: Cambridge University Press, 1911.

Aune, David E. *The New Testament in Its Literary Environment*. LEC 8. Philadelphia, PA: Westminster, 1987.

Bakke, Odd M. *'Concord and Peace': A Rhetorical Analysis of the First Letter of Clement with an Emphasis on the Language of Unity and Sedition*. WUNT 2.143. Tübingen: Mohr (Siebeck), 2001.

Balch, David L. 'Paul, Families, and Households'. Pages 258–92 in *Paul in the Greco-Roman World: A Handbook*. Edited by J. P. Sampley. Harrisburg, PA: Trinity Press, 2003.

Balsdon, J. P. V. D. *Life and Leisure in Ancient Rome*. London: Phoenix, 1969.

Basore, John W. 'Introduction'. Pages vii–xvi in vol. 1 of *Seneca: Moral Essays*. Translated by J. W. Basore. 3 vols. LCL. Cambridge: Harvard University Press, 1928.

Behm, Johannes. 'θύω κτλ'. Pages 180–90 in vol. 3 of *TDNT*. Edited by G. Kittel and G. Friedrich. Translated by G. W. Bromiley. 10 vols. Grand Rapids, MI: Eerdmans, 1965.

Benko, Stephen. 'Pagan Criticism of Christianity During the First Two Centuries A.D.' *ANRW* 23.2:1055–1118. Part 2, *Principat*, 23.2. Edited by H. Temporini and W. Haase. New York: de Gruyter, 1980.

—— *Pagan Rome and the Early Christians*. Bloomington, IN: Indiana University Press, 1984.

Benz, Ernst. 'Christus und Sokrates in der alten Kirche'. *ZNW* 43 (1950–1): 195–224.

Betz, Hans Dieter. 'Das Problem der Grundlagen der paulinischen Ethik (Röm 12,1–2)'. *ZTK* 85 (1988): 199–218.

—— 'Christianity as Religion: Paul's Attempt at Definition in Romans'. *JR* 71 (1991): 315–44.

Bonhöffer, Adolf F. *Epiktet und das Neue Testament*. Religionsgeschichtliche Versuche und Vorarbeiten 10. Gießen: Töpelmann, 1911.

—— *The Ethics of the Stoic Epictetus*. Translated by W. O. Stephens. Revisioning Philosophy 2. New York: Peter Lang, 1996 [first published in 1894 as *Die Ethik des Stoikers Epiktet*].

Botermann, Helga. *Das Judenedikt des Kaisers Claudius: Römischer Staat und Christiani im 1. Jahrhundert*. Hermes 71. Stuttgart: Franz Steiner, 1996.

Bowe, Barbara E. *A Church in Crisis: Ecclesiology and Paraenesis in Clement of Rome*. Harvard Dissertations in Religion 23. Minneapolis, MN: Fortress, 1988.

—— 'The Rhetoric of Love in Corinth: From Paul to Clement of Rome'. Pages 244–57 in *Common Life in the Early Church: Essays Honoring Graydon F. Snyder*. Edited by J. V. Hills et al. Harrisburg, PA: Trinity, 1998.

Boys-Stones, George R. *Post-Hellenistic Philosophy: A Study of its Development from the Stoics to Origen*. Oxford: Oxford University Press, 2001.

—— '*Fallere sollers*: The Ethical Pedagogy of the Stoic Cornutus'. Pages 77–88 in vol. 1 of *Greek and Roman Philosophy 100 BC – 200 AD*. Edited by R. Sorabji and R. W. Sharples. 2 vols. Bulletin of the Institute of Classical Studies Supplement 94. London: Institute of Classical Studies, University of London, 2007.

Brändle, Rudolf, and Ekkehard W. Stegemann. 'The Formation of the First "Christian Congregations" in Rome in the Context of the Jewish Congregations'. Pages 117–27 in *Judaism and Christianity in First-Century Rome*. Edited by K. P. Donfried and P. Richardson. Grand Rapids, MI: Eerdmans, 1998.

Braund, Susanna Morton. 'Introduction'. Pages 1–39 in *Juvenal and Persius*. Edited and translated by S. M. Braund. LCL. Cambridge, MA: Harvard University Press, 2004.

Brennan, Tad. 'The Old Stoic Theory of Emotions'. Pages 21–70 in *The Emotions in Hellenistic Philosophy*. Edited by J. Sihvola and T. Engberg-Pedersen. The New Synthese Historical Library 46. Dordrecht: Kluwer, 1998.

—— *The Stoic Life: Emotions, Duties, and Fate*. Oxford: Clarendon Press, 2005.

Brown, Raymond E. *An Introduction to the New Testament*. Anchor Bible Reference Library. New York: Doubleday, 1997.

—— and John P. Meier. *Antioch and Rome: New Testament Cradles of Catholic Christianity*. New York: Paulist Press, 1983.

Bruce, F. F. 'The Romans Debate—Continued'. Pages 175–94 in *The Romans Debate*. Rev. and exp. edn. Edited by K. P. Donfried. Peabody, MA: Hendrickson, 1991.

Brunt, P. A. 'From Epictetus to Arrian'. *Athenaeum* 55 (1977): 19–48.

Burkert, Walter. *Greek Religion: Archaic and Classical*. Translated by J. Raffan. Oxford: Blackwell, 1985.

Cappelletti, Silvia. *The Jewish Community of Rome: From the Second Century B.C. to the Third Century C.E.* JSJSup 113. Leiden: Brill, 2006.

Carcopino, Jérôme. *Daily Life in Ancient Rome: The People and the City at the Height of the Empire*. Edited and annotated by H. T. Rowell. Translated by E. O. Lorimer. 2nd edn. New Haven, CT: Yale University Press, 2003.

Carson, D. A. *Exegetical Fallacies*. Grand Rapids, MI: Baker, 1984.

Christensen, Johnny. 'Equality of Man and Stoic Social Thought'. Pages 45–54 in *Equality and Inequality of Man in Ancient Thought*. Edited by I. Kajanto. Commentationes Humanarum Litterarum 75. Helsinki: Societas Scientiarum Fennica, 1984.

Coleman, Kathleen. 'Entertaining Rome'. Pages 210–58 in *Ancient Rome: The Archaeology of the Eternal City*. Edited by J. Coulston and H. Dodge. Oxford: Oxford University School of Archaeology, 2000.

Colish, Marcia L. *The Stoic Tradition from Antiquity to the Early Middle Ages*. Vol. 1. *Stoicism in Classical Latin Literature*. Studies in the History of Christian Thought 34. Leiden: Brill, 1985.

—— 'Stoicism and the New Testament: An Essay in Historiography'. *ANRW* 26.1:334–79. Part 2, *Principat*, 26.1. Edited by H. Temporini and W. Haase. Berlin: de Gruyter, 1992.

Collins, Adela Yarbro. *Mark: A Commentary*. Hermeneia. Minneapolis, MN: Fortress, 2007.

Conzelmann, Hans. *Acts of the Apostles*. Translated by J. Limburg, A. T. Kraabel, and D. H. Juel. Hermeneia. Philadelphia, PA: Fortress, 1987.

Corley, Kathleen E. '1 Peter'. Pages 349–60 in *Searching the Scriptures*. Vol. 2. *A Feminist Commentary*. Edited by E. Schüssler Fiorenza. London: SCM, 1994.

Cranfield, C. E. B. *A Critical and Exegetical Commentary on the Epistle to the Romans*. 2 vols. ICC. Edinburgh: T&T Clark, 1975–79.

Croix, G. E. M. de Ste. *The Class Struggle in the Ancient Greek World from the Archaic Age to the Arab Conquests*. London: Duckworth, 1981.

Dahlmann, Hellfried. 'Über den Lärm'. *Gymnasium* 85 (1978): 206–27.

Das, A. Andrew. *Solving the Romans Debate*. Minneapolis, MN: Fortress, 2007.

DenAdel, Raymond L. 'Seneca the Younger and the Meta Sudans'. *CB* 60 (1984): 1–4.

DeSilva, David A. 'Paul and the Stoa: A Comparison'. *JETS* 38 (1995): 549–64.

Dillon, J. T. *Musonius Rufus and Education in the Good Life: A Model of Teaching and Living Virtue*. Dallas, TX: University Press of America, 2004.

Donfried, Karl P., ed. *The Romans Debate*. Rev. and exp. edn. Peabody, MA: Hendrickson, 1991.

—— and Peter Richardson, eds. *Judaism and Christianity in First-Century Rome*. Grand Rapids, MI: Eerdmans, 1998.

Döring, Klaus. *Exemplum Socratis: Studien zur Sokratesnachwirkung in der kynisch-stoischen Popularphilosophie der frühen Kaiserzeit und im frühen Christentum*. Hermes 42. Wiesbaden: Franz Steiner Verlag, 1979.

Doty, William G. *Letters in Primitive Christianity*. Guides to Biblical Scholarship: New Testament Series. Philadelphia, PA: Fortress, 1973.

Drobner, Hubertus R. 'Christian Philosophy'. Pages 672–90 in *The Oxford Handbook of Early Christian Studies*. Edited by S. A. Harvey and D. G. Hunter. Oxford: Oxford University Press, 2008.

Dubis, Mark. 'Research on 1 Peter: A Survey of Scholarly Literature Since 1985'. *CBR* 4 (2006): 199–239.

Dunn, James D. G. *Romans*. 2 vols. WBC 38. Dallas, TX: Word Books, 1988.

Ebersohn, Michael. *Das Nächstenliebegebot in der synoptischen Tradition*. Marburger Theologische Studien 37. Marburg: Elwert, 1993.

Edelstein, Ludwig. *The Meaning of Stoicism*. Martin Classical Lectures 21. Cambridge, MA: Harvard University Press, 1968.

Edwards, Catharine. *The Politics of Immorality in Ancient Rome*. Cambridge: Cambridge University Press, 1993.

—— 'Introduction'. Pages vii–xxxvii in *Suetonius: Lives of the Caesars*. Translated by C. Edwards. OWC. Oxford: Oxford University Press, 2000.

Ehrman, Bart D. 'Introduction [to First Clement]'. Pages 18–33 in vol. 1 of *The Apostolic Fathers*. Edited and translated by B. D. Ehrman. 2 vols. LCL. Cambridge, MA: Harvard University Press, 2003.

Elliott, John H. *1 Peter: A New Translation with Introduction and Commentary*. AB 37B. New York: Doubleday, 2000.

Engberg-Pedersen, Troels. 'Discovering the Good: *Oikeiōsis* and *Kathēkonta* in Stoic Ethics'. Pages 145–83 in *The Norms of Nature: Studies in Hellenistic Ethics*. Edited by M. Schofield and G. Striker. Cambridge: Cambridge University Press, 1986.

—— *The Stoic Theory of Oikeiosis: Moral Development and Social Interaction in Early Stoic Philosophy*. Studies in Hellenistic Civilization 2. Aarhus: Aarhus University Press, 1990.

—— *Paul and the Stoics*. Edinburgh: T&T Clark, 2000.

—— 'Paul, Virtues, and Vices'. Pages 608–33 in *Paul in the Greco-Roman World: A Handbook*. Edited by J. P. Sampley. Harrisburg, PA: Trinity Press, 2003.

—— 'The Relationship with Others: Similarities and Differences Between Paul and Stoicism'. *ZNW* 96 (2005): 35–60.

—— 'A Stoic Understanding of *Pneuma* in Paul'. Pages 101–23 in *Philosophy at the Roots of Christianity*. Edited by T. Engberg-Pedersen and H. Tronier. Copenhagen: University of Copenhagen, 2006.

—— 'Paul's Stoicizing Politics in Romans 12–13: The Role of 13.1–10 in the Argument'. *JSNT* 29 (2006): 163–72.

—— 'Self-sufficiency and Power: Divine and Human Agency in Epictetus and Paul'. Pages 117–39 in *Divine and Human Agency in Paul and His Cultural Environment*. Edited by J. M. G. Barclay and S. J. Gathercole. LNTS 335. London: T&T Clark, 2007.

—— 'Gift-Giving and Friendship: Seneca and Paul in Romans 1–8 on the Logic of God's Χάρις and Its Human Response'. *HTR* 101 (2008): 15–44.

—— 'The Material Spirit: Cosmology and Ethics in Paul'. *NTS* 55 (2009): 179–97.

Engel, David M. 'The Gender Egalitarianism of Musonius Rufus'. *AncPhil* 20 (2000): 377–91.

Esler, Philip F. *Conflict and Identity in Romans: The Social Setting of Paul's Letter*. Minneapolis, MN: Fortress, 2003.

—— 'Paul and Stoicism: Romans 12 as a Test Case'. *NTS* 50 (2004): 106–24.

Fitzgerald, John T. 'Paul and Friendship'. Pages 319–43 in *Paul in the Greco-Roman World: A Handbook*. Edited by J. P. Sampley. Harrisburg, PA: Trinity Press, 2003.

Fitzmyer, Joseph A. *Romans: A New Translation with Introduction and Commentary*. AB 33. New York: Doubleday, 1993.

Furnish, Victor P. *The Love Command in the New Testament*. Nashville, TN: Abingdon, 1972.

—— 'Inside Looking Out: Some Pauline Views of the Unbelieving Public'. Pages 104–24 in *Pauline Conversations in Context: Essays in Honor of Calvin J. Roetzel*.

Edited by J. C. Anderson, P. Sellew, and C. Setzer. JSNTSup 221. Sheffield: Sheffield Academic Press, 2002.

Garnsey, Peter. 'Introduction: The Hellenistic and Roman Periods'. Pages 401–14 in *The Cambridge History of Greek and Roman Political Thought*. Edited by C. Rowe and M. Schofield with S. Harrison and M. Lane. Cambridge: Cambridge University Press, 2000.

Gehring, Roger W. *House Church and Mission: The Importance of Household Structures in Early Christianity*. Peabody, MA: Hendrickson, 2004.

Geytenbeek, A. C. van, *Musonius Rufus and Greek Diatribe*. Wijsgerige Texten en Studies 8. Assen: Van Gorcum, 1963.

Gibson, Richard J. 'Paul and the Evangelization of the Stoics'. Pages 309–26 in *The Gospel to the Nations: Perspectives on Paul's Mission*. Edited by P. Bolt and M. Thompson. Downers Grove, IL: Intervarsity Press, 2000.

Gill, Christopher. 'Stoic Writers of the Imperial Era'. Pages 597–615 in *The Cambridge History of Greek and Roman Political Thought*. Edited by C. Rowe and M. Schofield with S. Harrison and M. Lane. Cambridge: Cambridge University Press, 2000.

—— 'The School in the Roman Imperial Period'. Pages 33–58 in *The Cambridge Companion to the Stoics*. Edited by B. Inwood. Cambridge: Cambridge University Press, 2003.

Glad, Clarence E. *Paul and Philodemus: Adaptability in Epicurean and Early Christian Psychagogy*. NovTSup 81. Leiden: Brill, 1995.

—— 'Paul and Adaptability'. Pages 17–41 in *Paul in the Greco-Roman World: A Handbook*. Edited by J. P. Sampley. Harrisburg, PA: Trinity Press, 2003.

Glancy, Jennifer A. *Slavery in Early Christianity*. New York: Oxford University Press, 2002.

Goppelt, Leonhard. *Der Erste Petrusbrief*. KEK 12. Göttingen: Vandenhoeck & Ruprecht, 1978.

Grabner-Haider, Anton. *Paraklese und Eschatologie bei Paulus: Mensch und Welt im Anspruch der Zukunft Gottes*. NTAbh 4. Münster: Aschendorff, 1968.

Gregory, Andrew. 'Disturbing Trajectories: *1 Clement*, the *Shepherd of Hermas* and the Development of Early Roman Christianity'. Pages 142–66 in *Rome in the Bible and the Early Church*. Edited by P. Oakes. Carlisle: Paternoster, 2002.

Griffin, Miriam T. *Seneca: A Philosopher in Politics*. Oxford: Clarendon Press, 1976.

—— *Nero: The End of a Dynasty*. London: Batsford, 1984.

—— 'Philosophy, Politics, and Politicians at Rome'. Pages 1–37 in *Philosophia Togata: Essays on Philosophy and Roman Society*. Edited by M. Griffin and J. Barnes. Oxford: Clarendon Press, 1989.

—— 'Seneca and Pliny'. Pages 532–58 in *The Cambridge History of Greek and Roman Political Thought*. Edited by C. Rowe and M. Schofield with S. Harrison and M. Lane. Cambridge: Cambridge University Press, 2000.

Grundmann, Walter. 'ταπεινός κτλ'. Pages 1–26 in vol. 8 of *TDNT*. Edited by G. Kittel and G. Friedrich. Translated by G. W. Bromiley. 10 vols. Grand Rapids, MI: Eerdmans, 1972.

Hagner, Donald A. *The Use of the Old and New Testaments in Clement of Rome*. NovTSup 34. Leiden: Brill, 1973.

Hahm, David E. *The Origins of Stoic Cosmology*. Columbus, OH: Ohio State University Press, 1977.

Hands, A. R. *Charities and Social Aid in Greece and Rome*. Aspects of Greek and Roman Life. Ithaca, NY: Cornell University Press, 1968.

Hartmann, Karl. 'Arrian und Epiktet'. *NJahrb* 15 (1905): 248–75.

Hawthorne, Gerald F., and Ralph P. Martin. *Philippians*. Rev. and exp. edn. WBC 43. Nashville, TN: Nelson, 2004.

Hermansen, Gustav. *Ostia: Aspects of Roman City Life*. Edmonton: University of Alberta, 1981.

Hershbell, Jackson. 'The Stoicism of Epictetus: Twentieth Century Perspectives'. *ANRW* 36.3:2148–63. Part 2, *Principat*, 36.3. Edited by H. Temporini and W. Haase. New York: de Gruyter, 1989.

Hicks, Ruth I. 'The Body Political and the Body Ecclesiastical'. *JBR* 31 (1963): 29–35.

Hijmans, Benjamin L., Jr., *ΑΣΚΗΣΙΣ: Notes on Epictetus' Educational System*. Assen: Van Gorcum, 1959.

Hope, Valerie. 'Status and Identity in the Roman World'. Pages 125–52 in *Experiencing Rome: Culture, Identity and Power in the Roman Empire*. Edited by J. Huskinson. London: Routledge, 2000.

Horrell, David G. 'The Product of a Petrine Circle? A Reassessment of the Origin and Character of 1 Peter'. *JSNT* 86 (2002): 29–60.

—— *Solidarity and Difference: A Contemporary Reading of Paul's Ethics*. London: T&T Clark, 2005.

Huskinson, Janet. 'Élite Culture and the Identity of Empire'. Pages 95–123 in *Experiencing Rome: Culture, Identity and Power in the Roman Empire*. Edited by J. Huskinson. London: Routledge, 2000.

Inwood, Brad. 'Comments on Professor Görgemann's Paper: The Two Forms of *Oikeiōsis* in Arius and the Stoa'. Pages 190–201 in *On Stoic and Peripatetic Ethics: The Work of Arius Didymus*. Edited by W. W. Fortenbaugh. New Brunswick, NJ: Transaction Books, 1983.

—— *Ethics and Human Action in Early Stoicism*. Oxford: Clarendon Press, 1985.

—— 'Rules and Reasoning in Stoic Ethics'. Pages 95–127 in *Topics in Stoic Philosophy*. Edited by K. Ierodiakonou. Oxford: Clarendon Press, 1999.

—— 'Seneca in his Philosophical Milieu'. Pages 7–22 in *Reading Seneca: Stoic Philosophy at Rome*. Oxford: Clarendon Press, 2005 [originally in *HSCP* 97 (1995): 63–76].

Jaeger, Werner. *Early Christianity and Greek Paideia*. Cambridge, MA: Belknap, 1961.

Jeffers, James S. *Conflict at Rome: Social Order and Hierarchy in Early Christianity*. Minneapolis, MN: Fortress, 1991.

—— 'Jewish and Christian Families in First-Century Rome'. Pages 128–50 in *Judaism and Christianity in First-Century Rome*. Edited by K. P. Donfried and P. Richardson. Grand Rapids, MI: Eerdmans, 1998.

Jewett, Robert. *Romans: A Commentary*. Hermeneia. Minneapolis, MN: Fortress, 2007.

Johnson, Luke Timothy. 'Transformation of the Mind and Moral Discernment in Paul'. Pages 215–36 in *Early Christianity and Classical Culture: Comparative Studies in Honor of Abraham J. Malherbe*. Edited by J. T. Fitzgerald, T. H. Olbricht, and L. M. White. NovTSup 110. Leiden: Brill, 2003.

Joly, Robert. *Le vocabulaire chrétien de l'amour, est-il original?* Brussels: Presses Universitaires de Bruxelles, 1968.

Käsemann, Ernst. *An die Römer*. 3rd edn. HNT 8a. Tübingen: Mohr (Siebeck), 1974.

Klassen, William. 'Musonius Rufus, Jesus, and Paul: Three First-Century Feminists'. Pages 185–206 in *From Jesus to Paul: Studies in Honour of Francis Wright Beare*. Edited by P. Richardson and J. C. Hurd. Waterloo, ON: Wilfrid Laurier University Press, 1984.

Klauck, Hans-Josef. *The Religious Context of Early Christianity: A Guide to Graeco-Roman Religions*. Translated by B. McNeil. Minneapolis, MN: Fortress, 2003.

Klein, Günter. 'Paul's Purpose in Writing the Epistle to the Romans'. Pages 29–43 in *The Romans Debate*. Rev. and exp. edn. Edited by K. P. Donfried. Peabody, MA: Hendrickson, 1991.

Konstan, David. *Friendship in the Classical World*. Key Themes in Ancient History. Cambridge: Cambridge University Press, 1997.

—— 'Clemency as a Virtue'. *CP* 100 (2005): 337–46.

Kunst, Christiane. 'Wohnen in der antiken Grosstadt: Zur sozialen Topographie Roms in der frühen Kaiserzeit'. Pages 2–19 in *Christians as a Religious Minority in a Multicultural City: Modes of Interaction and Identity Formation in Early Imperial Rome*. Edited by J. Zangenberg and M. Labahn. JSNTSup 243. London: T&T Clark, 2004.

La Piana, George. 'Foreign Groups in Rome during the First Centuries of the Empire'. *HTR* 20 (1927): 183–403.

Lake, Kirsopp. '[Introduction to] The First Epistle of Clement to the Corinthians'. Pages 3–7 in vol. 1 of *The Apostolic Fathers*. Translated by K. Lake. 2 vols. LCL. Cambridge, MA: Harvard University Press, 1912.

Lampe, Peter. 'The Roman Christians of Romans 16'. Pages 216–30 in *The Romans Debate*. Rev. and exp. edn. Edited by K. P. Donfried. Peabody, MA: Hendrickson, 1991.

—— *From Paul to Valentinus: Christians at Rome in the First Two Centuries*. Translated by M. Steinhauser. Minneapolis, MN: Fortress, 2003.

—— 'Paul, Patrons, and Clients'. Pages 488–523 in *Paul in the Greco-Roman World: A Handbook*. Edited by J. P. Sampley. Harrisburg, PA: Trinity Press, 2003.

—— 'Early Christians in the City of Rome: Topographical and Social Historical Aspects of the First Three Centuries'. Pages 20–32 in *Christians as a Religious Minority in a Multicultural City: Modes of Interaction and Identity Formation in Early Imperial Rome*. Edited by J. Zangenberg and M. Labahn. JSNTSup 243. London: T&T Clark, 2004.

Lane, William L. 'Social Perspectives on Roman Christianity during the Formative Years from Nero to Nerva: Romans, Hebrews, *1 Clement*'. Pages 196–244 in *Judaism and Christianity in First-Century Rome*. Edited by K. P. Donfried and P. Richardson. Grand Rapids, MI: Eerdmans, 1998.

Lapidge, Michael. 'Stoic Cosmology and Roman Literature, First to Third Centuries A.D.' *ANRW* 36.3:1379–1429. Part 2, *Principat*, 36.3. Edited by H. Temporini and W. Haase. New York: de Gruyter, 1989.

Lee, Michelle V. *Paul, the Stoics, and the Body of Christ.* SNTSMS 137. Cambridge: Cambridge University Press, 2006.

Leon, Harry J. *The Jews of Ancient Rome.* Updated edn. Peabody, MA: Hendrickson, 1995.

Levinskaya, Irina. *The Book of Acts in Its Diaspora Setting.* Vol. 5 of *The Book of Acts in Its First Century Setting.* Edited by Bruce W. Winter. Grand Rapids, MI: Eerdmans, 1996.

Lietzmann, Hans. *Einführung in die Textgeschichte der Paulusbriefe: An die Römer.* 5th edn. HNT 8. Tübingen: Mohr (Siebeck), 1971.

Lindemann, Andreas. *Die Clemensbriefe.* HNT 17. Tübingen: Mohr (Siebeck), 1992.

Lona, Horacio E. *Der erste Clemensbrief.* Kommentar zu den Apostolischen Vätern 2. Göttingen: Vandenhoeck & Ruprecht, 1998.

Long, A. A. 'Socrates in Hellenistic Philosophy'. *CQ* 38 (1988): 150–71.

—— 'Arius Didymus and the Exposition of Stoic Ethics'. Pages 107–33 in *Stoic Studies.* Berkeley, CA: University of California Press, 1996.

—— *Epictetus: A Stoic and Socratic Guide to Life.* Oxford: Oxford University Press, 2002.

—— and D. N. Sedley. *The Hellenistic Philosophers.* 2 vols. Cambridge: Cambridge University Press, 1987.

Lutz, Cora E. 'Musonius Rufus: "The Roman Socrates"'. Yale Classical Studies 10 (1947): 1–147.

MacMullen, Ramsay. *Enemies of the Roman Order: Treason, Unrest, and Alienation in the Empire.* Cambridge, MA: Harvard University Press, 1966.

—— *Roman Social Relations: 50 B.C. to A.D. 284.* New Haven, CT: Yale University Press, 1974.

—— 'What Difference did Christianity Make?' Pages 142–55 in *Changes in the Roman Empire: Essays in the Ordinary.* Princeton, NJ: Princeton University Press, 1990.

—— 'The Unromanized in Rome'. Pages 47–64 in *Diasporas in Antiquity.* Edited by S. J. D. Cohen and E. S. Frerichs. Brown Judaic Studies 288. Atlanta, GA: Scholars Press, 1993.

Malherbe, Abraham J. *Moral Exhortation: A Greco-Roman Sourcebook.* LEC 4. Philadelphia, PA: Westminster, 1986.

—— '"Seneca" on Paul as Letter Writer'. Pages 414–21 in *The Future of Early Christianity: Essays in Honor of Helmut Koester.* Edited by B. A. Pearson. Philadelphia, PA: Fortress, 1991.

—— 'Hellenistic Moralists and the New Testament'. *ANRW* 26.1:267–333. Part 2, *Principat*, 26.1. Edited by H. Temporini and W. Haase. New York: de Gruyter, 1992.

—— *The Letters to the Thessalonians: A New Translation with Introduction and Commentary.* AB 32B. New York: Doubleday, 2000.

Malitz, Jürgen. 'Philosophie und Politik im frühen Prinzipat'. Pages 151–79 in *Antikens Denken—Moderne Schule. Beiträge zu den antiken Grundlagen unseres Denkens.*

Edited by H. W. Schmidt and P. Wülfing. Gymnasium Beiheft 9. Heidelberg: Carl Winter Universitätsverlag, 1988.

Manning, C. E. 'Stoicism and Slavery in the Roman Empire'. *ANRW* 36.3:1518–43. Part 2, *Principat*, 36.3. Edited by H. Temporini and W. Haase. New York: de Gruyter, 1989.

Martin, J. M. K. 'Persius—Poet of the Stoics'. *GR* 8 (1939): 172–82.

Martin, Troy W. *Metaphor and Composition in 1 Peter*. SBLDS 131. Atlanta, GA: Scholars, 1992.

Matthews, Shelly. *First Converts: Rich Pagan Women and the Rhetoric of Mission in Early Judaism and Christianity*. Stanford, CA: Stanford University Press, 2001.

May, James M. 'Seneca's Neighbour, the Organ Tuner'. *CQ* 37 (1987): 240–3.

McVay, John K. 'The Human Body as Social and Political Metaphor in Stoic Literature and Early Christian Writers'. *BASP* 37 (2000): 135–47.

Meeks, Wayne A. 'Judgment and the Brother: Romans 14:1–15:13'. Pages 290–300 in *Tradition and Interpretation in the New Testament: Essays in Honor of E. Earle Ellis for His 60th Birthday*. Edited by G. F. Hawthorne with O. Betz. Grand Rapids, MI: Eerdmans, 1987.

—— *The Origins of Christian Morality: The First Two Centuries*. New Haven, CT: Yale University Press, 1993.

—— *The First Urban Christians: The Social World of the Apostle Paul*. 2nd edn. New Haven, CT: Yale University Press, 2003.

Meiser, Martin. 'Das Christentum in Rom im Spiegel des ersten Clemensbriefes'. Pages 139–56 in *Christians as a Religious Minority in a Multicultural City: Modes of Interaction and Identity Formation in Early Imperial Rome*. Edited by J. Zangenberg and M. Labahn. JSNTSup 243. London: T&T Clark, 2004.

Meisinger, Hubert. 'Christian Love and Biological Altruism'. *Zygon* 35 (2000): 745–82.

Millar, Fergus. 'Epictetus and the Imperial Court'. *JRS* 55 (1965): 141–8.

Miller, James C. 'The Romans Debate: 1991–2001'. *CurBS* 9 (2001): 306–49.

Mitchell, Margaret M. *Paul and the Rhetoric of Reconciliation: An Exegetical Investigation of the Language and Composition of 1 Corinthians*. Hermeneutische Untersuchungen zur Theologie 28. Tübingen: Mohr (Siebeck), 1991.

Morford, Mark. *The Roman Philosophers: From the Time of Cato the Censor to the Death of Marcus Aurelius*. London: Routledge, 2002.

Moxnes, Halvor. 'The Quest for Honor and the Unity of the Community in Romans 12 and in the Orations of Dio Chrysostom'. Pages 203–30 in *Paul in His Hellenistic Context*. Edited by T. Engberg-Pedersen. Edinburgh: T&T Clark, 1994.

Murray, Michele. *Playing a Jewish Game: Gentile Christian Judaizing in the First and Second Centuries CE*. ESCJ 13. Waterloo, ON: Wilfrid Laurier University Press, 2004.

Nanos, Mark D. *The Mystery of Romans: The Jewish Context of Paul's Letter*. Minneapolis, MN: Fortress, 1996.

—— 'The Jewish Context of the Gentile Audience Addressed in Paul's Letter to the Romans'. *CBQ* 61 (1999): 283–304.

Nestle, Wilhelm. 'Die Fabel des Menenius Agrippa'. *Klio* 21 (1927): 350–60.

North, Helen. *Sophrosyne: Self-Knowledge and Self-Restraint in Greek Literature.* Ithaca, NY: Cornell University Press, 1966.

Noy, David. *Foreigners at Rome: Citizens and Strangers.* London: Duckworth, 2000.

Nussbaum, Martha C. 'The Incomplete Feminism of Musonius Rufus, Platonist, Stoic, and Roman'. Pages 283–326 in *The Sleep of Reason: Erotic Experience and Sexual Ethics in Ancient Greece and Rome.* Edited by M. C. Nussbaum and J. Sihvola. Chicago, IL: University of Chicago Press, 2002.

—— 'The Worth of Human Dignity: Two Tensions in Stoic Cosmopolitanism'. Pages 31–49 in *Philosophy and Power in the Graeco-Roman World: Essays in Honour of Miriam Griffin.* Edited by G. Clark and T. Rajak. Oxford: Oxford University Press, 2002.

Oden, Amy G., ed. *And You Welcomed Me: A Sourcebook on Hospitality in Early Christianity.* Nashville, TN: Abingdon, 2001.

Oldfather, W. A. 'Introduction'. Pages vii–xxxi in vol. 1 of *Epictetus.* Translated by W. A. Oldfather. 2 vols. LCL. Cambridge, MA: Harvard University Press, 1925.

—— 'The *Encheiridion,* or *Manual*'. Pages 479–81 in vol. 2 of *Epictetus.* Translated by W. A. Oldfather. 2 vols. LCL. Cambridge, MA: Harvard University Press, 1928.

Olson, Stanley N. 'Pauline Expressions of Confidence in His Addressees'. *CBQ* 47 (1985): 282–95.

Olsson, Birger. *Första Petrusbrevet.* Kommentar till Nya testamentet 17. Stockholm: EFS-förlaget, 1982.

Ortkemper, Franz-Josef. *Leben aus dem Glauben: Christliche Grundhaltungen nach Römer 12–13.* NTAbh 14. Münster: Aschendorff, 1980.

Penna, Romano. 'Les Juifs à Rome au temps de l'apôtre Paul'. *NTS* 28 (1982): 321–47.

Piper, John. *'Love Your Enemies': Jesus' Love Command in the Synoptic Gospels and in the Early Christian Paraenesis. A History of the Tradition and Interpretation of Its Uses.* Grand Rapids, MI: Baker, 1980.

Pohlenz, Max. *Die Stoa: Geschichte einer geistigen Bewegung.* 2nd edn. Göttingen: Vandenhoeck & Ruprecht, 1948.

Pomeroy, Arthur J., ed. *Arius Didymus: Epitome of Stoic Ethics.* Atlanta, GA: Society of Biblical Literature, 1999.

Rackham, H. 'Introduction'. Pages xi–xxxi in *Cicero: De finibus bonorum et malorum.* Translated by H. Rackham. 2nd edn. LCL. Cambridge, MA: Harvard University Press, 1931.

Rawson, Beryl. 'Family Life among the Lower Classes at Rome in the First Two Centuries of the Empire'. *CP* 61 (1966): 71–83.

Reasoner, Mark. *The Strong and the Weak: Romans 14.1–15.13 in Context.* SNTSMS 103. Cambridge: Cambridge University Press, 1999.

Reichert, Angelika. *Der Römerbrief als Gratwanderung: Eine Untersuchung zur Abfassungsproblematik.* FRLANT 194. Göttingen: Vandenhoeck & Ruprecht, 2001.

Reiser, Marius. 'Love of Enemies in the Context of Antiquity'. *NTS* 47 (2001): 411–27.

Reydams-Schils, Gretchen. 'Human Bonding and *Oikeiōsis* in Roman Stoicism'. *OSAP* 22 (2002): 221–51.

—— *The Roman Stoics: Self, Responsibility, and Affection.* Chicago, IL: University of Chicago Press, 2005.

Richardson, Peter. 'Augustan-Era Synagogues in Rome'. Pages 17–29 in *Judaism and Christianity in First-Century Rome*. Edited by K. P. Donfried and P. Richardson. Grand Rapids, MI: Eerdmans, 1998.

Rist, J. M. *Stoic Philosophy*. Cambridge: Cambridge University Press, 1969.

Robinson, O. F. *Ancient Rome: City Planning and Administration*. London: Routledge, 1992.

Ronnick, Michele Valerie. 'Epictetus'. Pages 134–9 in *Ancient Greek Authors*. Edited by W. W. Briggs. Dictionary of Literary Biography 176. Detroit, MI: Gale, 1997.

Russell, Bertrand. *A History of Western Philosophy*. 2nd edn. London: Unwin, 1979.

Saller, Richard P. *Personal Patronage under the Early Empire*. Cambridge: Cambridge University Press, 1982.

Sandbach, F. H. *The Stoics*. 2nd edn. Indianapolis, IN: Hackett, 1989.

Sandnes, Karl Olav. 'Revised Conventions in Early Christian Paraenesis: "Working Good" in 1 Peter as an Example'. Pages 373–403 in *Early Christian Paraenesis in Context*. Edited by J. Starr and T. Engberg-Pedersen. BZNW 125. Berlin: de Gruyter, 2004.

Scheidel, Walter. 'Germs for Rome'. Pages 158–76 in *Rome the Cosmopolis*. Edited by C. Edwards and G. Woolf. Cambridge: Cambridge University Press, 2003.

Schnackenburg, Rudolf. *The Moral Teaching of the New Testament*. Translated by J. Holland-Smith and W. J. O'Hara. Tunbridge Wells: Burns & Oates, 1965.

Schofield, Malcolm. 'Stoic Ethics'. Pages 233–56 in *The Cambridge Companion to the Stoics*. Edited by B. Inwood. Cambridge: Cambridge University Press, 2003.

Schrage, Wolfgang. *Die konkreten Einzelgebote in der paulinischen Paränese: Ein Beitrag zur neutestamentlichen Ethik*. Gütersloh: Mohn, 1961.

Scobie, Alex. 'Slums, Sanitation, and Mortality in the Roman World'. *Klio* 68 (1986): 399–433.

Sedley, David. 'The Origins of Stoic God'. Pages 41–83 in *Traditions of Theology: Studies in Hellenistic Theology, Its Background and Aftermath*. Edited by D. Frede and A. Laks. Philosophia Antiqua 89. Leiden: Brill, 2002.

—— 'The School, from Zeno to Arius Didymus'. Pages 7–32 in *The Cambridge Companion to the Stoics*. Edited by B. Inwood. Cambridge: Cambridge University Press, 2003.

Sellars, John. 'Stoic Practical Philosophy in the Imperial Period'. Pages 115–40 in vol. 1 of *Greek and Roman Philosophy 100 BC–200 AD*. Edited by R. Sorabji and R. W. Sharples. 2 vols. Bulletin of the Institute of Classical Studies Supplement 94. London: Institute of Classical Studies, University of London, 2007.

Sevenster, J. N. *Paul and Seneca*. NovTSup 4. Leiden: Brill, 1961.

Shelton, Jo-Ann. *As the Romans Did: A Sourcebook in Roman Social History*. 2nd edn. New York: Oxford University Press, 1998.

Sherwin-White, A. N. 'Pliny's Praetorship Again'. *JRS* 47 (1957): 126–30.

Smith, Jonathan Z. *Drudgery Divine: On the Comparison of Early Christianities and the Religions of Late Antiquity*. Chicago, IL: The University of Chicago Press, 1990.

Snyder, Scot. '1 Peter 2:17: A Reconsideration'. *FN* 4 (1991): 211–15.

Söding, Thomas. *Das Liebesgebot bei Paulus: Die Mahnung zur Agape im Rahmen der paulinischen Ethik*. NTAbh 26. Münster: Aschendorff, 1995.

Solin, Heikki. 'Juden und Syrer im westlichen Teil der römischen Welt: Eine ethnisch-demographische Studie mit besonderer Berücksichtigung der sprachlichen Zustände'. *ANRW* 29.2:587–789. Part 2, *Principat*, 29.2. Edited by H. Temporini and W. Haase. New York: Gruyter, 1983.

Sørensen, Villy. *Seneca: The Humanist at the Court of Nero*. Translated by W. G. Jones. Edinburgh: Canongate, 1984.

Spicq, Ceslas. *Agapè dans le nouveau testament*. 3 vols. Paris: Gabalda, 1958–9.

—— *Theological Lexicon of the New Testament*. Edited and translated by J. D. Ernest. 3 vols. Peabody, MA: Hendrickson, 1994.

Stambaugh, John E. *The Ancient Roman City*. Baltimore, MD: Johns Hopkins University Press, 1988.

Stark, Rodney. *The Rise of Christianity: How the Obscure, Marginal Jesus Movement Became the Dominant Religious Force in the Western World in a Few Centuries*. San Francisco, CA: HarperSanFrancisco, 1996.

Starr, Chester G., Jr. 'Epictetus and the Tyrant'. *CP* 44 (1949): 20–9.

Starr, James, and Troels Engberg-Pedersen, eds. *Early Christian Paraenesis in Context*. BZNW 125. Berlin: de Gruyter, 2004.

Stauffer, Ethelbert. 'ἀγαπάω κτλ'. Pages 35–55 in vol. 1 of *TDNT*. Edited by G. Kittel and G. Friedrich. Translated by G. W. Bromiley. 10 vols. Grand Rapids, MI: Eerdmans, 1964.

Stephens, William O. 'Epictetus on How the Stoic Sage Loves'. *OSAP* 14 (1996): 193–210.

Stirewalt, M. Luther, Jr. *Paul, the Letter Writer*. Grand Rapids, MI: Eerdmans, 2003.

Stowers, Stanley K. *Letter Writing in Greco-Roman Antiquity*. LEC 5. Philadelphia, PA: Westminster, 1986.

—— 'Paul on the Use and Abuse of Reason'. Pages 253–86 in *Greeks, Romans, and Christians: Essays in Honor of Abraham J. Malherbe*. Edited by D. L. Balch, E. Ferguson, and W. A. Meeks. Minneapolis, MN: Fortress, 1990.

—— *A Rereading of Romans: Justice, Jews, and Gentiles*. New Haven, CT: Yale University Press, 1994.

Striker, Gisela. 'The Role of *Oikeiosis* in Stoic Ethics'. *OSAP* 1 (1983): 145–67.

—— 'Following Nature: A Study in Stoic Ethics'. *OSAP* 9 (1991): 1–73.

Theissen, Gerd. *The Religion of the Earliest Churches: Creating a Symbolic World*. Translated by J. Bowden. Minneapolis, MN: Fortress, 1999.

Thom, Johan C. 'Cleanthes' *Hymn to Zeus* and Early Christian Literature'. Pages 477–99 in *Antiquity and Humanity: Essays on Ancient Religion and Philosophy. Presented to Hans Dieter Betz on His 70th Birthday*. Edited by A. Y. Collins and M. M. Mitchell. Tübingen: Mohr Siebeck, 2001.

Thompson, Michael. *Clothed with Christ: The Example and Teaching of Jesus in Romans 12.1–15.13*. JSNTSup 59. Sheffield: JSOT Press, 1991.

Thorsteinsson, Runar M. 'Paul's Missionary Duty Towards Gentiles in Rome: A Note on the Punctuation and Syntax of Rom 1.13–15'. *NTS* 48 (2002): 531–47.

—— *Paul's Interlocutor in Romans 2: Function and Identity in the Context of Ancient Epistolography*. ConBNT 40. Stockholm: Almqvist & Wiksell, 2003.

Thorsteinsson, Runar M. 'Paul and Roman Stoicism: Romans 12 and Contemporary Stoic Ethics'. *JSNT* 29 (2006): 139–61.

—— 'The Role of Morality in the Rise of Roman Christianity'. Pages 139–57 in *Exploring Early Christian Identity*. Edited by B. Holmberg. WUNT 226. Tübingen: Mohr Siebeck, 2008.

—— 'Stoicism as a Key to Pauline Ethics in Romans'. Forthcoming in *Stoicism in Early Christianity*. Edited by T. Rasimus, I. Dunderberg, and T. Engberg-Pedersen. Peabody, MA: Hendrickson.

Trapp, Michael. *Philosophy in the Roman Empire: Ethics, Politics and Society*. Aldershot: Ashgate, 2007.

Unnik, W. C. van. 'Is 1 Clement 20 Purely Stoic?' *VC* 4 (1950): 181–9.

Van Rensburg, J. J. Janse. 'The Use of Intersentence Relational Particles and Asyndeton in First Peter'. *Neot* 24 (1990): 283–300.

Veyne, Paul. *Seneca: The Life of a Stoic*. Translated by D. Sullivan. New York: Routledge, 2003.

Walker, Susan. 'The Moral Museum: Augustus and the City of Rome'. Pages 61–75 in *Ancient Rome: The Archaeology of the Eternal City*. Edited by J. Coulston and H. Dodge. Oxford: Oxford University School of Archaeology, 2000.

Wallace-Hadrill, Andrew, ed. *Patronage in Ancient Society*. London: Routledge, 1989.

—— '*Domus* and *Insulae* in Rome: Families and Housefuls'. Pages 3–18 in *Early Christian Families in Context: An Interdisciplinary Dialogue*. Edited by D. L. Balch and C. Osiek. Grand Rapids, MI: Eerdmans, 2003.

Walters, James C. 'Romans, Jews, and Christians: The Impact of the Romans on Jewish/Christian Relations in First-Century Rome'. Pages 175–95 in *Judaism and Christianity in First-Century Rome*. Edited by K. P. Donfried and P. Richardson. Grand Rapids, MI: Eerdmans, 1998.

Weaver, P. R. C. *Familia Caesaris: A Social Study of the Emperor's Freedmen and Slaves*. Cambridge: Cambridge University Press, 1972.

—— 'Epaphroditus, Josephus, and Epictetus'. *CQ* 44 (1994): 468–79.

White, Michael J. 'Stoic Natural Philosophy (Physics and Cosmology)'. Pages 124–52 in *The Cambridge Companion to the Stoics*. Edited by B. Inwood. Cambridge: Cambridge University Press, 2003.

White, Nicholas P. 'The Basis of Stoic Ethics'. *HSCP* 83 (1979): 143–78.

Whittaker, C. R. 'The Poor'. Pages 272–99 in *The Romans*. Edited by A. Giardina. Translated by L. G. Cochrane. Chicago, IL: University of Chicago Press, 1993.

Whittaker, John. 'Christianity and Morality in the Roman Empire'. *VC* 33 (1979): 209–25.

Wiefel, Wolfgang. 'The Jewish Community in Ancient Rome and the Origins of Roman Christianity'. Pages 85–101 in *The Romans Debate*. Rev. and exp. edn. Edited by K. P. Donfried. Peabody, MA: Hendrickson, 1991.

Wilken, Robert Louis. *The Christians as the Romans Saw Them*. 2nd edn. New Haven, CT: Yale University Press, 2003.

Williams, Margaret H. 'The Structure of Roman Jewry Re-Considered: Were the Synagogues of Ancient Rome Entirely Homogenous?' *ZPE* 104 (1994): 129–41.

——'The Shaping of the Identity of the Jewish Community in Rome in Antiquity'. Pages 33–46 in *Christians as a Religious Minority in a Multicultural City: Modes of Interaction and Identity Formation in Early Imperial Rome*. Edited by J. Zangenberg and M. Labahn. JSNTSup 243. London: T&T Clark, 2004.

Wilson, Walter T. *Love without Pretense: Romans 12.9–21 and Hellenistic–Jewish Wisdom Literature*. WUNT 2.46. Tübingen: Mohr (Siebeck), 1991.

Winter, Bruce W. *Seek the Welfare of the City: Christians as Benefactors and Citizens*. First Century Christians in the Graeco-Roman World. Grand Rapids, MI: Eerdmans, 1994.

Wischmeyer, Oda. 'Vorkommen und Bedeutung von Agape in der außerchristlichen Antike'. *ZNW* 69 (1978): 212–38.

Witherington, Ben, with Darlene Hyatt. *Paul's Letter to the Romans: A Socio-Rhetorical Commentary*. Grand Rapids, MI: Eerdmans, 2004.

Zerbe, Gordon M. *Non-Retaliation in Early Jewish and New Testament Texts: Ethical Themes in Social Contexts*. JSPSup 13. Sheffield: JSOT Press, 1993.

Copyright Acknowledgements

I am grateful for permission to reprint selections from the following works:

Apostolic Fathers: Volume I, Loeb Classical Library Volume 24, translated by Kirsopp Lake, Cambridge, MA: Harvard University Press, Copyright © 1912, by the President and Fellows of Harvard College.

Apostolic Fathers: Volume I, Loeb Classical Library Volume 24, translated by Bart D. Ehrman, Cambridge, MA: Harvard University Press, Copyright © 2003, by the President and Fellows of Harvard College.

Epictetus: Volume I, Loeb Classical Library Volume 131, translated by W. A. Oldfather, Cambridge, MA: Harvard University Press, Copyright © 1925, by the President and Fellows of Harvard College.

Epictetus: Volume II, Loeb Classical Library Volume 218, translated by W. A. Oldfather, Cambridge, MA: Harvard University Press, Copyright © 1928, by the President and Fellows of Harvard College.

Musonius Rufus: from Cora E. Lutz, 'Musonius Rufus: "The Roman Socrates"', Yale Classical Studies Volume 10 (1947). Copyright Cambridge University Press, reproduced with permission.

Seneca: Moral Essays, Volume I, Loeb Classical Library Volume 214, translated by John W. Basore, Cambridge, MA: Harvard University Press, Copyright © 1928, by the President and Fellows of Harvard College.

Seneca: Moral Essays, Volume II, Loeb Classical Library Volume 254, translated by John W. Basore, Cambridge, MA: Harvard University Press, Copyright © 1932, by the President and Fellows of Harvard College.

Seneca: Moral Essays, Volume III, Loeb Classical Library Volume 310, translated by John W. Basore, Cambridge, MA: Harvard University Press, Copyright © 1935, by the President and Fellows of Harvard College.

Seneca: Epistles 1–65, Volume IV, Loeb Classical Library Volume 75, translated by Richard M. Gummere, Cambridge, MA: Harvard University Press, Copyright © 1917, by the President and Fellows of Harvard College.

Seneca: Epistles 66–92, Volume V, Loeb Classical Library Volume 76, translated by Richard M. Gummere, Cambridge, MA: Harvard University Press, Copyright © 1920, by the President and Fellows of Harvard College.

Index of Modern Authors

Index of Ancient References

Index of Names

FOOD FOR FRIENDS

UPPARK: *Hampshire*

Food
for Friends

A Book of Country House
Recipes

Compiled by Maxine Meade

COUNTESS OF CLANWILLIAM

with contributions by friends and relations
and here presented in her memory by

GRAHAM RUST

SOMERTON

MMVII

Published by SOMERTON BOOKS
The Old Rectory
Somerton, Bury St Edmunds
IP29 4ND

Publication and illustrations
© *Graham Redgrave-Rust 2007*

ISBN 978-0-9556448-0-1

Contents

✿

✿

Introduction

A FTER many years of cooking and filling my kitchen shelves with every type of recipe – from the Bosphorus to the Caribbean – I have come to the conclusion that the simpler dishes, well cooked and with prime ingredients are the ones which most people prefer.

Recipes which take up days in preparation and half the wine cellar and which leave the kitchen looking as if major surgery has just been performed are often a great disappointment.

With this in mind, I decided to compile a book of mainly Country House recipes. It would contain not only old favourites of mine, but those of friends and relations equally interested in good food.

I felt it was important that the recipes should be easy to follow and not have the pages strewn with conversion tables and heraldic achievements of shallots and saucepans. Nevertheless, the presentation should be eye-catching.

So it was natural that I should think of Graham Rust, whose work I greatly admire and who is also an old friend. Not only has his work taken him all over the world, but also to many of the lovely houses in our own country. His flair for depicting such houses highlights the recipes in the following pages in the most entrancing way.

Parting with favourite recipes is not something one does lightly, and I have been greatly encouraged by the generous kindness and co-operation of my many contributors.

I hope that this is a book you will return to again and again ...

MAXINE CLANWILLIAM
London

Foreword

THIS BOOK is a marvellous tribute to Maxine by one of her greatest admirers. It was she who arranged for Graham to paint his first mural – in the hall of our house in Aubrey Road – when he was a very young man, and he has been a friend ever since. Many years later Maxine proposed that he should add illustrations to the collection of recipes, her own and those that she had contrived to extract from friends. The project fell foul of events and the menus lay in folders until now, when Graham suggested that it should be revived and published as a lasting tribute to her memory.

The recipes were mostly offered by friends in the 1950's and 60's when we made regular visits to Uppark. They bear the imprint of those days – and none the worse for that. My parents inherited Uppark in 1931 and my mother had been waiting twenty years of her married life with the prospect of reviving that marvellous house from its slumbers. She set about it with great vigour and created a wonderful home, often full of visitors expert in their various fields who came crowding round to admire the fabulous contents emerging from their time warp.

Some of the visitors had known the house at the end of the nineteenth century, among them H.G.Wells, who had lived there in his early teens in the 1880's when his mother was housekeeper. He would slip upstairs to the Saloon where he would feed his enormous appetite for knowledge from the library of 18th-century leather-bound Folios of science, botany, astronomy and history. His mother arranged the meals for the spinster chatelaine, Miss Fetherstonhaugh, who finally looked kindly on his ambitions, and some of the Uppark recipes in this book may bear his mother's imprint. Uppark was also the model of Blakesover House in Wells' novel of 1909, *Tono Bungay.*

Many years later Wells came to lunch to see his old haunts and I well remember the difficulty my father had in suffering the propositions of dialectical materialism which poured forth in a *milieu* ironically waited-on by a butler and two footmen. Nevertheless, he was back where he had been brought up and his presence provided a notably different episode in the long, continuous history of Uppark, where some of the large number of grandchildren and great-grandchildren still live.

Maxine brought our brood down to Uppark on all high days and holidays, and in between times gave wonderful lunches and dinners from the ever expanding collection of menus which form the basis of this book. Its pages will, I hope, recall good times for those who were there to enjoy them, and provide entertainment and encouragment for those who weren't.

Sadly, some of the contributors are no longer with us, and Maxine herself died on her seventy-seventh birthday in 2004. So this is very much a retrospective view of the enjoyment of good food in the last century – supported at that time by a bulk purchase of a much admired '61 *Chateau Citran* funded from the sale of our first house, in Brook Green – the first of a trail of homes all remodelled by Maxine in her own inimitable way. She would have loved this book and I cannot thank Graham enough for his generosity in bringing it to print.

CLANWILLIAM
March 2007

⁂

The sepia and wash drawings in the following pages are of homes of contributors to Maxine's book and were painted in situ by Graham Rust during May and June 2007

⁂

The Contributors

with an index of their contributions

Unattributed recipes are by Maxine herself

EDITORIAL NOTE

The recipes which follow were contributed over many years by many hands and, naturally, in different and often engaging styles. No attempt has been made to reduce them to uniformity. The retention of the use of both British and Metric measures is similarly in deference to the form in which the contributions were provided. Conversion tables at the end of the book should help users not old enough to remember the days when bananas were sold by the pound.

GIFFORDS HALL: *Suffolk*

Soups

Celeriac and Parsnip Soup

Cheese and Celery Soup

Cold Summer Soup

Iced Cucumber Soup

Gazpacho

Iced Smoked Haddock and Prawn Soup

Josephine's Fish Soup

Lettuce Soup

Cold Leek Soup

Hot Leek Soup

Nettle Soup

Yoghurt Soup

Crême Bordelaise

Sorrell Soup

Fish Soup

CELERIAC AND PARSNIP SOUP
for 8 people

1 lb celeriac root
1 lb parsnips
1 pint milk
½ pint double cream
2 onions
Seasoning and nutmeg
A little chopped parsley

Peel vegetables and cut roughly into pieces. Cover with good chicken stock and simmer gently until soft. Allow to cool a little, blend or sieve until smooth. Return to saucepan and add 1 pint of milk and the cream. Season with salt, black pepper and a little grated nutmeg.

Serve hot or cold, sprinkled with a little chopped parsley.

LADY OWEN: *Warwickshire*

CHEESE AND CELERY SOUP
for 4-6 people

3-4 ozs Stilton (or other blue-veined cheese)
2 onions
1 head of celery
1 14 oz can of tomatoes
3 ozs butter
3 tablespoons flour
1¼ pint chicken stock
salt, pepper, celery salt

Wash and scrape celery sticks and cut into thin crescents. Melt the butter and add celery and finely chopped onions. Cover saucepan and leave to sweat gently for 10 minutes. Stir in the flour, then pour on stock and tomatoes; add salt and pepper and celery salt. Bring to the boil and simmer until the vegetables are tender.

Mash up the cheese and add a few spoonfuls of the hot liquid to make a thin paste. When the vegetables are cooked, liquidise and strain. Now add the cheese mixture and heat through in order to melt the cheese. Garnish with some chopped celery leaves.

THE HON MRS RICHARD BEAUMONT: *London*

COLD SUMMER SOUP
for 4 people

½ lb sorrel or spinach
7 ozs cream
2 small pots natural yoghourt
¾ pint cold consommé
½ lb cucumber, seeded and chopped
Chopped chives
Chopped fennel leaves or tarragon if available
Salt, black pepper, lemon juice to taste

Wash and chop sorrel or spinach. Stir over moderate heat – no liquid – until reduced to a purée. When cold add other ingredients in given order. Serve chilled with chopped chives.

MRS JULIAN BYNG: *Hertfordshire*

ICED CUCUMBER SOUP
for 4 people

5 fl.ozs yoghourt	1 large cucumber
2 tablespoons cream	1 tablespoon chopped mint
1 tablespoon chopped parsley	2 tablespoons tarragon vinegar
2 cloves of garlic	Salt and pepper

Peel cucumber and grate through Magimix or Moulinex. Crush garlic and mix all ingredients. Place in the coldest part of the fridge and serve ice-cold, with Paprika.

GAZPACHO
for 6 people

2 tablespoons olive oil	1 clove of garlic, crushed
4 large green peppers, chopped	4 large spring onions, chopped
½ unpeeled cucumber, chopped	2 large peeled tomatoes, chopped
1½ cups celery, diced	1½ teaspoons salt, or more
1 teaspoon freshly ground pepper	¼ cup wine vinegar
¼ cup tarragon vinegar	5 drops Tabasco
6 cups tomato juice	

Coat the bottom of the serving bowl with oil. Add the crushed garlic and then the other vegetables, mixing well and ending with the tomato juice. Refrigerate for at least three hours and serve.

MRS CHARLES BROCKLEBANK: *Suffolk*

ICED SMOKED HADDOCK AND PRAWN SOUP
for 4-6 people

4 ozs cooked flaked smoked haddock
3 ozs defrosted frozen prawns
½ a cucumber, peeled, de-seeded and diced
½ pint of the milk in which fish was cooked
½ pint milk   1 oz butter   1 oz flour
Small carton natural yoghourt   Small carton soured cream
Chopped chives or parsley   Squeeze of lemon juice
Squeeze of onion juice, seasoning

Scald fillets of smoked haddock with boiling water and drain immediately. Poach fillets in milk. Pick over very carefully, discarding any hard bits of skin, and flake.

Make a thin sauce with the plain and fishy milk, then whizz in blender with the yoghourt and soured cream. After blending add prawns, haddock, seasoning and finely chopped chives. Leave to mature in the fridge for several hours and before serving, add the cucumber which should have been allowed to drain for an hour.

If the soup is made a day in advance, on no account add the cucumber, as it can give a metallic flavour if put in more than an hour before serving.

MRS CHARLES SHEEPSHANKS: *West Yorkshire*

JOSEPHINE'S FISH SOUP
for 6 people

2lbs solid white fish, preferably whiting (head, tail and bones if possible)

2 cloves of garlic	2 pints fish stock or water
1 large onion, finely sliced	1 medium potato, cut in pieces
½ large bay leaf, fresh or dry, pulled to pieces	
1 small green pimento	2 tomatoes
Plenty of chopped parsley	½ glass of white wine
1 dessertspoon paprika	4 dessertspoons olive oil
½ thimble saffron	Salt and pepper

One hour before cooking, squeeze half a lemon over the fish. Add stock/ water to the bones &c and bring to the boil and simmer for 20 minutes. Strain over fish in a large saucepan and add tomatoes, onion, pimento (finely chopped), potato, bay leaf, garlic, oil, paprika and parsley. After 10 minutes, before potato is soft, add ½ glass of white wine and the saffron. Season to taste. Liquidise if necessary and strain. Serve with croutons or rounds of a small French loaf and a bowl of mayonnaise or aioli.

MRS ANDREW ROLLO: *Wiltshire*

LETTUCE SOUP
for 8 people

8 ozs lettuce leaves	1 small onion
1½ ozs butter	¾ pint chicken stock
Salt and black pepper	Caster sugar
Grated nutmeg	¾ pint milk
2 egg yolks	2 tablespoons single cream

Blanch lettuce leaves for 5 minutes in boiling salted water. Drain and rinse under cold water and then chop the leaves finely. Peel and finely chop onion. Melt butter in saucepan and fry onion until soft, then add shredded lettuce, leaving a little aside. Pour stock over onions and lettuce and bring to the boil. Season to taste with salt, pepper, nutmeg and sugar.

Allow soup to cool slightly before liquidising. Add milk to soup and reheat gently for 5 minutes. Lightly beat together the egg yolks and cream. Spoon a little of the hot soup into this and blend thoroughly. Pour this into the soup and stir until it thickens. On no account should it reach boiling point, as eggs will curdle.

LADY DELVES BROUGHTON: *Cheshire*

COLD LEEK SOUP
for 8 people

6 large leeks	3 medium potatoes
2 ozs butter	salt and pepper
2 pints chicken stock	½ pint thick cream
chopped chives	

Melt the butter in a heavy saucepan and add cleaned and shredded leeks and peeled and finely chopped potatoes. Cover and cook gently for about 15 minutes, making certain that the vegetables do not stick or become brown. Now add stock and seasoning and bring to the boil and simmer for about 20 minutes or until the vegetables are cooked. Put in liquidiser and blend until very smooth. Allow to cool before adding cream. Taste for seasoning and place in the coldest part of the refrigerator. As this soup must be very cold indeed it can be helped by surrounding the bowl with crushed ice.

Serve with the chopped chives sprinkled on top.

HOT LEEK SOUP
for 6 people

6 leeks	2 potatoes
2 ozs butter	1 pint of creamy milk
½ pint of water	salt and pepper
2 egg yolks	¼ pint single cream

Melt the butter in a heavy saucepan and add peeled and sliced potatoes and cleaned and shredded leeks, keeping 1 leek aside for later. Cook gently for a few minutes, stirring occasionally with a wooden spoon, until the vegetables are almost soft. Add the milk and water and seasoning and bring to the boil and simmer gently for 20 minutes. Put through a fine Mouli, or liquidise. Beat egg yolks and cream together and very gradually add to the soup. Stir over a low heat but do not allow to boil or soup will curdle.

In the meantime blanch, drain and shred finely the leek which has been kept aside. Serve soup with this sprinkled on the top.

NETTLE SOUP
for 6-8 people

40 nettle tops	2 medium onions
2 medium potatoes	2 pints chicken stock
Juice of half a lemon	½ gill cream
Salt and pepper	

This is a soup for the Spring and it goes without saying that the young nettles should be picked wearing gloves. Remove the shoots from the top of the nettles, taking off about 2 inches including stalk and leaves.

Into a large heavy saucepan put the peeled and chopped onion, peeled and chopped potato, chicken stock, lemon juice and seasoning. Bring to the boil and simmer for about 20 minutes. Now add the washed nettle tops and bring again to the boil and simmer for a couple of minutes. Blend until very smooth, reheat and add cream. Sprinkle with chopped parsley and serve with croutons. This soup can also be served well chilled with strips of crispy bacon.

YOGHURT SOUP
for 4 people

1 pint yoghourt	¼ pint double cream
1 large cucumber	½ pint shrimps
Fresh mint	Salt, pepper and garlic

Mix half the cream with the yoghourt. Peel a very cold cucumber and shred into very thin slivers, before adding to the yoghourt. Add prawns and ¾ teaspoon finely chopped mint, salt and pepper. Leave to chill.

Just before serving work a clove of garlic into the remainder of the cream, add and adjust seasoning.

THE HON MRS NEEDHAM *Yorkshire*

CRÈME BORDELAISE
for 8 people

½ lb young carrots
2 pints chicken stock
1 cup cooked rise
⅓ pint of double cream

3 ozs butter
Salt and pepper
3 egg yolks

Melt the butter in a heavy saucepan. Into this put the young carrots, chopped up. Cover and simmer gently until the carrots are soft, stirring quite often to make certain they do not stick. Add to this the chicken stock which should have been heated separately and a cup of cooked rice.

Cook gently for 5-10 minutes, pass through a fine Mouli or electric blender. Pour back into saucepan and thicken with 3 egg yolks mixed with the cream. This should be done very carefully to avoid the soup curdling and therefore the soup should not be allowed to boil.

SORRELL SOUP
for 6 people

2 bunches of sorrell
Knob of butter
Seasoning
1½ milk/vegetable stock

Take 2 large bunches of sorrell and cut off the stalks. Sauté in butter until soft and season. Add a little cornflower to thicken, then add a mixture of 1½ pints of milk/vegetable stock or one Knorr cube. Bring to the boil then cool and liquidise. Before serving add cream and serve either hot or cold. A good summer soup.

ANGUS WARRE ESQ: *Hampshire*

FISH SOUP
for 8 people

12 prawns
12 mussels
2 pints of fish stock
¼ clove of garlic
10 lime leaves
Coriander

12 squid
12 queen scallops
4 sticks of lemon grass
3 tablespoons of chopped ginger
3 chillies

Cut up the lemon grass, garlic, ginger and chillies leaving the lime leaves whole. Divide into half. Add half the mixture to 2 pints of fish stock and simmer for 20 minutes then strain.

Prepare seafood. Before serving bring the stock to the boil, add remaining seasoning mixture and the fish. When the mussels are open the soup is ready. Serve with chopped coriander.

ANGUS WARRE ESQ: *Hampshire*

ST MICHAEL'S MOUNT: *Cornwall*

First Course or Luncheon Dishes

❧

Cheese Custards

Smoked Salmon Dreams

Melon, Prawn & Avocado Salad

Sunday Supper Soufflé

Avocado Angelique

Eggs Homefield

Crab and Grapefruit Cocktail

Deep fried Mushroom

Cornish Pasty

Jerusalem Artichokes, Scallop & Watercress Salad

Egg Mousse

A Coarse Paté

Marinated Herrings

Avocado Caviar

Oeufs Volé and Tomato Sauce

Cold Cheese Soufflé

Fresh Country Omelette

Aubergine Salad

Eggs à la Madras

Prawn Pancakes

Prawns and Rice Salad

Oeufs en Meurette

Tuna Fish Mousse

Smoked Salmon Mousse

Stuffed Yellow Peppers

Mushroom & Oregano Soufflé

Broccoli à la Polonaise

❧

CHEESE CUSTARDS
for 4 people

4 eggs plus 1 yolk	½ cup of double cream
3 ozs diced ham (optional)	2 cups milk
6 ozs grated cheddar cheese	Salt and pepper

Beat the eggs, milk and seasoning together, add the cheese and ham. Mix well and fold in the cream. Grease 8 pots (this is sufficient to fill pots of the size used for eggs *en cocotte*). Fill the pots almost to the top with the mixture. Stand the pots in a baking dish with cold water two-thirds of the way up. Bake in a fairly slow oven until the custard is set.

This mixture may be used for Quiche Lorraine.

LADY BEIT: *Co. Wicklow, Ireland*

SMOKED SALMON DREAMS
for 4 people

4 ozs thin slices ssmoked salmon	4 ozs cottage cheese
½ teaspoon Lemon juice	2 ozs chopped walnuts
Ground black pepper	Pinch paprika
Few drops of Tabasco	

Blend cream cheese with lemon juice and season with pepper, paprika, and Tabasco. Mix in the chopped walnuts. Spread a quarter of the mixture on a slice of smoked salmon and roll up neatly. Serve smoked salmon rolls on a bed of lettuce and garnish with lemon quarters.

MRS PHILIP BRIANT: *Oxfordshire*

MELON, PRAWN & AVOCADO SALAD
for 4 people

Remove the skin from a ripe melon, cut off the top and scoop out the seeds. Slice the melon into 1/2 inch thick slices. Lay the slices on plates and fill the centre space with a handful of prawns or crabmeat together with the diced avocado. Cover one side of the 'salad' with sour cream and the other side with cocktail sauce (see below) and sprinkle a little chopped parsley on top.

Serve chilled and garnished with lettuce.

Cocktail Sauce

Prepare your own mayonnaise and add a little tomato paste, tabasco, Worcester Sauce and drop of brandy.

MADELEINE GRÄFIN DOUGLAS: *London*

SUNDAY SUPPER SOUFFLÉ
for 4 people

10 slices of white bread with crusts removed
½ lb grated sharp cheese
1 pint milk
3 eggs
1 clove of garlic
½ teaspoon salt
Cayenne pepper

Crush garlic in butter. Tear bread into small squares and spread on butter. Arrange cheese and bread on alternate layers in soufflé dish. Beat eggs and mix with milk, salt and pepper. Pour mixture over bread and bake at 3¼ for 45/50 minutes.

This soufflé can be prepared in the morning, and the milk poured on at the last minute.

LADY MARK FITZALAN HOWARD: *London*

AVOCADO ANGELIQUE
for 4 people

2 ripe avocados
¼ pint of double cream
1 tablespoon caster sugar

2 limes
2 kiwi fruit

Blend the avocado flesh, lime juice and caster sugar. Beat cream until it peaks and fold into avocado purée. Serve in glass dish, decorated with peeled and thinly sliced Kiwi fruit.

THE COUNTESS OF HAREWOOD: *Yorkshire*

EGGS HOMEFIELD
2 eggs per person

Sauce
½ pint double cream
1 small tin of peeled tomatoes, chopped and seeded
1 finely chopped onion
1 finely chopped tablespoon Tiptree's mango chutney
1 finely chopped tablespoon ham or bacon
1 dessertspoon curry powder
1 nut butter
1 clove garlic
Worcester sauce
Seasoning

Fry chopped onion in butter and a little oil to prevent burning. Add garlic, curry powder and chopped tomatoes, then the chutney, parsley, French mustard and salt and pepper. Whip cream with a drop of Worcester sauce; fold into the sauce. Poach the eggs, put on the buttered toast, pour over the sauce and serve immediately.

MRS MICHAEL DORMER: *Berkshire*

CRAB AND GRAPEFRUIT COCKTAIL
for 4 people

Make a bowl of mayonnaise, with one yolk only, and ensure that the mayonnaise is as thick and as stiff as possible. Add a dash of Worcester sauce, a dash of cayenne pepper and a teaspoon or two of brandy and of sherry and a small amount of lemon juice and tomato ketchup (mainly for colouring). Now take some cooked crab claws, remove shells and sinews, but do not break up the meat too finely. Skin the segment of one or two grapefruit (about an equal amount to the crab meat),

26

removing not only the outer skin but also the skin of each segment. Remove pips and cut each segment into two or three pieces and mix with the crab meat. Then pour some of the sauce over each helping, which is best served in a glass dish.

The sauce is extremely rich but the sharp astringent taste of the grapefruit somewhat neutralises this.

GILBERT MCNEILL-MOSS ESQ: *London*

DEEP FRIED MUSHROOMS

Choose medium-sized domed mushrooms, four or five to each person. Wash, roll in well seasoned flour, then egg and breadcrumb them and deep fry in oil. Serve immediately with Tartare sauce or mayonnaise into which is added some finely chopped watercress.

THE LADY ROCKLEY: *London*

CORNISH PASTY

8 ozs flour	1 teaspoon baking powder
4 ozs lard and margarine, mixed	Salt, pepper and water to mix
8 ozs trimmed chuck steak	2 medium potatoes
1 small swede	1 medium onion
Herbs	

Cut meat, potatoes and swede into small dice. Chop onion. Mix flour, baking powder and salt together. Rub in the fat lightly, add a little water, but not enough to make the paste too moist. Roll out the paste and cut each individual pasty round a tea plate.

Place potatoes, swede and some herbs in the centre of pastry. Add pepper and salt. Put meat on top of vegetables and add chopped onion. Add a knob of butter and a little more freshly ground pepper to each pasty.

Damp the edges of the pastry and join them together to form a crimped frill. Prick 3 times with a fork to allow the steam to escape. Brush with egg and milk.

Bake at 375°F (Gas Mark 5) for 20 minutes, then reduce heat to 300°F (Gas Mark 2) for a further 40 minutes.

A heavy pastry is traditionally used in Cornwall. The wives of the tin miners used to throw the hot pasties down the mining shaft to their husbands and the pastry had to sustain a catch or bump at the bottom.

THE LADY ST LEVAN: *Cornwall*

JERUSALEM ARTICHOKES, SCALLOP & WATERCRESS SALAD
for 4 people

2 lbs Jerusalem artichokes
12 Scallops (and prepared court-bouillon)
2 bunches watercress
Walnut oil vinaigrette

Peel the artichokes. Cook gently in salted water for 8 to 10 minutes. While still warm, divide and put into the dressing. Poach the scallops in a court-bouillon for 5 minutes or until barely cooked. Drain and divide each scallop into 3 or 4 pieces.

Pick over the watercress, using only the small and tender leaves. Wash and dry well.

Combine the artichokes, scallops and watercress together in a salad bowl. Dress with the vinaigrette and sprinkle with parsley.

Peeled prawns may be substituted should scallops not be available. This salad is particularly good served with a granary French stick spread with anchovy butter, baked for 10 minutes and served piping hot.

LADY ELIZABETH SHAKERLY: *London*

EGG MOUSSE
for 6 people

5 hard boiled eggs
Paprika
Anchovy sauce
Tabasco
½ pint double or whipping cream

Salt and pepper
Worcester sauce
Harvey sauce
Aspic

Separate whites and yolks of boiled eggs and sieve yolks. Chop up whites but not too finely. Put sieved yolks into a dish and add pepper and salt, 1 tablespoon Worcester sauce, 2 tablespoons Harvey sauce, 1 good teaspoon Anchovy sauce, 4 drops Tabasco sauce and 4 tablespoons melted Aspic. Mix well (except whites), put in refrigerator until half set. Whip ½ pint of cream well. Pour into dish and put in the refrigerator to set.

For decoration:
¼ pint of aspic
1¼ teaspoons gelatine
Squeeze of lemon juice

Stir all together over low heat until gelatine is dissolved. Refrigerate and when set, chop and decorate top of mousse.

A COARSE PÂTÉ

½ lb chicken livers
¾ lb pig's liver
1 clove garlic
1 lb pork fat
½ lb unsalted butter
Salt and black pepper

Mix all the ingredients, keeping a few finely sliced strips of pork fat to cover the paté. Put in a heavy casserole, cover with the strips of pork fat and cook in a slow oven for about 1 - 1½ hours.

MARINATED HERRINGS

Marinate the herrings which have been cleaned, boned and opened up, overnight in red wine, chopped onion and salt and pepper. Turn over from time to time. Serve with whipped cream, with chopped chives and parsley and a dust of paprika.

AVOCADO CAVIAR

Half or one ripe avocado per person, depending on the size
2 jars of mock Black Caviar   1 carton sour cream
1 small onion   Lemon juice
Pepper

Mash flesh of avocado with whisk or put in blender. Add sour cream. Add onion juice by putting it through a garlic press, or grate some finely if preferred. Add generous squeeze of lemon and season with freshly ground black pepper. At the last moment fold in the mock caviar and return to empty shells.

MRS MICHAEL DORMER: *Berkshire*

ŒUFS VOLÉ
for 4 people

8 eggs   ½ teacup of creamy milk
Salt and pepper   ½ oz butter
Tomato Sauce
½ lb fresh tomatoes or tin of peeled tomatoes
1 crushed clove of garlic   2 ozs butter
Salt and pepper   Basil – chopped

Beat the eggs and add milk and seasoning. Butter 4 largish ramekin dishes and pour in the egg mixture. Place dishes in a bain-marie and cook in a moderate oven for about 30 minutes (until egg mixture is just firm).

To make tomato sauce, peel, de-seed and chop the tomatoes. Put them in a small saucepan with crushed garlic and salt and pepper and simmer for 10 minutes. Pass through fine sieve or liquidise. Blend in the butter, a little at a time, check seasoning, add finely chopped basil leaves and reheat. Serve the eggs unmoulded with the sauce poured over.

THE EARL OF CLANWILLIAM: *London*

COLD CHEESE SOUFFLÉ
for 6 people

6 slices white bread (without crusts)
1½ large cups of milk
5 eggs and one extra egg white
1 large cup of grated Cheddar cheese
Dash of Worcester sauce
Pinch of mustard powder, cayenne and nutmeg
Salt and pepper

Butter a soufflé dish. Make breadcrumbs with slices of white bread and put into soufflé dish. Break the eggs into the milk, and add all the seasonings and spices. Stir, do not beat. Now pour this over the breadcrumbs and again do not stir. Leave in the refrigerator for at least 12 hours, but preferably 3 or 4 days. Bake in a medium oven (350°F) for 1 hour.

FRENCH COUNTRY OMELETTE
for 2 people

2 tablespoons diced salt pork or green bacon
2 tablespoons butter   1 diced boiled potato
4 eggs, lightly beaten   Salt and pepper
Chopped parsley   Chopped chives

Blanch bacon for a couple of minutes, having already diced it; drain and sauté in butter. Remove and keep warm. Sauté diced potato. Combine lightly beaten eggs with the bacon, parsley, chives, salt and pepper. Pour over potatoes and cook quickly.

AUBERGINE SALAD
for 6 people

4 large aubergines	3 tablespoons olive oil
1 medium onion	1 clove garlic
Salt and pepper	3 tablespoons tomato purée
Juice of half a lemon	1 teaspoon sugar

Smear the skins of the aubergines with olive oil and put in the oven (400°F/Gas Mark 6) for 40 to 45 minutes (until soft). When cool, split skins and scoop out flesh and chop.

Sauté onion in remaining oil until soft and transparent, add aubergine flesh, garlic (which has been smashed with a little salt), pepper, tomato puree, lemon juice and sugar.

Continue cooking gently until mixture is thick and all juices absorbed, cooking with the pan uncovered. Check seasoning and chill well. Serve with chopped parsley and black olives.

THE HON MRS CHRISTOPHER SHARPLES: *Berkshire*

EGGS à la MADRAS
for 4 people

4 hard boiled eggs	2 onions
Garlic	½ pint cream
Brown breadcrumbs	1 dessertspoon curry powder
4 tablespoons chicken stock	1 tablespoon chutney

Cook onions, crushed garlic and curry powder in butter until tender. Add stock and chutney. Simmer 20 minutes to half an hour. Add chopped eggs and breadcrumbs and cream. Mix well, put in a greased fireproof dish and bake in a moderate oven for half an hour.

THE LADY MOWBRAY AND STOURTON: *Angus*

PRAWN PANCAKES
for 5-6 people

1 lb unpeeled prawns	1 pint milk
2 ozs butter	2 ozs flour
Nutmeg	Bay leaf
Peppercorns	Gruyère cheese
Brandy	¼ pint soured cream
Batter:	
4 oz plain flour	pinch of salt
1 egg	½ pint milk

Make the batter by sifting flour into a large bowl. Using a wooden spoon, make a hollow in the centre of the flour and gently drop in a beaten egg. Gradually mix in half the milk, beating continuously, until the mixture becomes smooth. Allow to stand for a few minutes, then add remainder of the milk. Mixture should be consistency of single cream. Put to one side and make filling.

Peel prawns and put to one side. Simmer shells in milk, bay leaf, salt and peppercorns, then sieve. Discard shells. Make thick white sauce using prawn flavoured milk. Add salt, pepper and nutmeg. Mix half of the Béchamel with prawns.

Make 8–10 pancakes, fill with prawn sauce. Add sour cream to remaining Béchamel sauce, then add brandy. Make quite runny and pour over filled pancakes. Sprinkle grated Gruyère cheese over top and brown under grill. Keep hot in oven until ready to serve.

MRS ROSS HANBURY: *Rutland*

PRAWN AND RICE SALAD

Packet of frozen prawns	½ lb long grained rice
1 cucumber	Salt and white pepper
Hard boiled eggs	½ pint mayonnaise
French dressing	

De-freeze and drain prawns. Cook rice and let it get cold. Not on any account to be overcooked.

Peel and cut cucumber lengthways 3 times, then, holding lengths together, chop into cubes. Sprinkle with salt and press between two plates for an hour or so. Rinse well, drain and dry. Cut in half, one hard boiled egg per person.

Add prawns to a well mixed French dressing and arrange in a mound along the centre of a large flat plate. Reserve a few prawns for decoration. Divide the cucumber cubes in two and place at each end of prawn mound. Arrange egg halves down either side and spoon mayonnaise over the top of them. Arrange spare prawns down the centre of the dish.

Equally good as first course or as a luncheon dish.

MRS MARK WINN: *Yorkshire*

ŒUFS EN MEURETTE
for 6 people

6 eggs	6 slices of French bread, fried in butter
½ clove garlic	¾ cup diced lean bacon
1 tablespoon butter	1 onion, chopped
1½ tablespoons of flour	1 cup bouillon
1 cup red wine	Bouquet garni (bay leaf, parsley and thyme)
Salt and pepper	

Sauté ¾ cup diced lean bacon in 1 tablespoon melted butter. Remove the bacon and add to the fat 1 onion, chopped, and ½ clove of crushed garlic. Stir over a low flame until pale gold. Sprinkle with 1½ tablespoons of flour and blend. Add 1 cup hot bouillon and 1 cup of red wine, salt and pepper to taste, and a bouquet garni of 1 bay leaf and one sprig each of parsley and thyme. Simmer over a low flame for 20 minutes.

Strain the sauce, which should be smooth and creamy, and replace the bits of bacon. Bring the sauce to the boil and in it poach carefully 6 eggs, one by one.

On a hot platter arrange 6 slices of French bread fried in butter and rubbed with garlic and place one poached egg on each slice. Pour the sauce over all and serve.

THE LADY CARRINGTON: *Buckinghamshire*

TUNA FISH MOUSSE
for 6 – 8 people
Makes an ideal 'light dish' for the Summer, either as a starter or a main dish.

> 1½ lbs of tinned tuna fish
> Juice of 1 lemon
> 1 oz gelatine
> ½ pint of homemade mayonnaise to which is added 2 cloves
> of crushed garlic
> 2 tablespoons freshly chopped parsley, garden mint and summer
> savory
> 1 tablespoon of fresh tarragon
> Chilli sauce

Put the tuna in a mixer or food processor. When minced, put in the mayonnaise mixture with the juice of 1 lemon. Dissolve the gelatine in hot water. When dissolved, add to the mixture and blend thoroughly.

Put the mixture into an oiled fish mould or oiled round ring. Chill in a refrigerator for a couple of hours at least to set.

To serve, turn out the mousse and garnish with watercress and prawns.

MRS IAN THOMAS: *Essex*

SMOKED SALMON MOUSSE
for 6 people

> 1 large cup of chopped smoked salmon
> 1 dessertspoon lemon juice
> ¼ teaspoon paprika
> 1 cup lightly whipped cream
> Aspic

Reduce smoked salmon to a fine purée in electric mixer. Now add lemon juice, paprika and lightly whipped cream. When all is mixed, add 3 tablespoons of liquid aspic jelly. Pour into dish or dishes to set. When set, pour over thin layer of aspic.

THE PRINCESS OF PLESS: *London*

STUFFED YELLOW PEPPERS

Cut peppers in half lengthwise and prepare in the usual way. Stuff with the following mixture and place in a medium oven for 20 minutes or half an hour.

Stuffing
1 cupful of fresh breadcrumbs per half pepper. Add enough olive oil to saturate the crumbs. Season to taste with salt and pepper and add a liberal sprinkling of capers. Mix all together and then place in peppers and bake. They should be crisp on top when cooked.

MARCHESA D'VANZO: *Italy*

MUSHROOM AND OREGANO SOUFFLÉ
for 6 people

½ lb mushrooms washed and chopped
2 eggs
½ pint double cream
6 tablespoons strong grated Cheddar cheese
2 teaspoons dried oregano
1 large clove of garlic finely chopped
1 oz butter

Fry mushrooms in butter with the garlic and oregano in a pan with a lid on so that the juices do not evaporate for about five minutes or until cooked. Put the cream, eggs, 2 tablespoons of the grated cheese and the juices from the fried mushroom mixture into a liquidiser and blend well together. Add salt and pepper and the chopped mushrooms. Butter 6 ramekin dishes and cover the bottoms with another 2 tablespoons of the cheese. Pour in the mixture and top with the remaining cheese. Cook at 370°F for about 35 minutes, when they should be well risen. Serve immediately.

COUNTESS CHARLES DE SALIS: *Somerset*

BROCCOLI à la POLONAISE

Small broccoli shoots
Butter
Fine breadcrumbs
Lemon juice
1 egg - hard boiled
Parsley or Dill, chopped

Simmer broccoli shoots in salted water or, better still, steam them. When cooked but still 'al dente', pack them into a warmed soufflé dish, trying to keep the flowers on the stalks at the centre. Keep warm at the bottom of the oven.

Now fry the breadcrumbs till they are golden; add freshly milled pepper and a little lemon juice.

Turn the broccoli out on to a hot plate and sprinkle with the breadcrumbs and if possible a coarsely chopped hard boiled egg.

Good as a first course or as an accompaniment to grilled chops or cutlets.

DAVID CARRITT ESQ: *Kent*

ARTHINGTON HALL: *Yorkshire*

Fish

Russian Fish Pie
Swiss Cheese Puff with Crab Sauce
Risotto al Vino e Salmone
Sole au Vermouth
Lobster Cutlets
Stuffed Sole with Cucumber Sauce
Lobster in Cream
Quick Lobster Thermidor
Saumon Gratinée à la Crème
Turbot Steaks à la Crème
Fillets of Sole with Almonds
Sole au Vin Blanc
Mediterranean Fish Casserole
Fish with Curry Sauce
Seviche
Lansdowne Smoked Fish Loaf
Marinated Salmon or Salmon Trout
Sea Bass with White Butter Sauce
Fish Mousse
Welsh Cod Bake
Baked Scallops
Ginger Salmon

RUSSIAN FISH PIE
for 4 people

1lb cooked smoked haddock
½ lb flaky or puff pastry
1 teaspoon chopped parsley
1 level dessertspoon finely chopped onion
Grated rind of a lemon
1 hard boiled egg
½ cup cooked white sauce
Salt and black pepper

Flake the fish and mix with the parsley, the sauce, the onion, lemon rind and seasoning. Roll the pastry fairly thin into an oblong, about 12 by 8 inches. Pile the fish mixture down the middle of the pastry, leaving a space on both sides. Fold these pieces to the middle so as to overlap, press and pinch down and do the same thing at both ends. Place on greased baking tin, brush with a beaten egg containing a little salt. Bake until pastry is golden.

LADY BEIT: *County Wicklow, Ireland*

SWISS CHEESE PUFF WITH CRAB SAUCE
for 4 – 6 people

9 inch pastry shell, uncooked
1½ cups top of the milk
Little ground nutmeg
Pinch of rosemary
1½ cups Swiss cheese, grated

4 egg yolks, lightly beaten
½ teaspoon salt
A little allspice
4 egg whites

Sauce

8 ozs lobster, flaked
2 tablespoons melted butter
Salt and white pepper
¼ cup white wine
1 tablespoon chopped parsley

Crab or shrimps
1 tablespoon plain flour
¾ cup top of the milk
1 tablespoon chopped chives

Bake the pastry shell at 450°F for 6 to 8 minutes. Reduce oven to 350°F Combine egg yolks, top of the milk, salt, nutmeg, allspice and rosemary. Beat egg whites until stiff; fold into mixture, then fold in cheese. Pour into pastry shell; bake at 350°F for 40 minutes or until knife comes out clean from the mixture. Leave to stand for 5 minutes and serve sauce separately.

Sauce

Heat the shell fish in butter, stir in the flour, salt and pepper, add the wine and top of the milk and cook thoroughly; top with the chives and parsley.

MRS CHARLES BROCKLEBANK: *Suffolk*

RISOTTO al VINO e SALMONE
for 6 people

2 full teacups of rice (Soho brown rice is best)
2 full teacups of chicken stock
2 full teacups of white wine
½ lb smoked salmon (this one can get in bits from the fishmonger)
1 good sized onion
3 ozs butter

Chop the onion fine and cook in butter until soft. Add the rice, a little salt and pepper and let it fry for a moment. Add the 4 cups of liquid (hot). Bring to the boil, then cover and let it simmer gently over a low heat for 15 minutes without stirring. Add the pieces of salmon (mouthful sized pieces) and cook for another 10 minutes.

If at the end the risotto is a little dry, add a little more stock and wine.

MRS JOHN ELTON: *London*

SOLE au VERMOUTH
for 4 people

8 fillets of Sole (or Plaice)	¼ lb unsalted butter
4 egg yolks	Salt and pepper
Dry Vermouth	Chopped parsley

Lay fillets of sole in wide fireproof dish, just cover with dry vermouth and poach. When cooked, take out fillets and keep hot. Reduce vermouth to a jelly on top of the stove, turn flame very low and add ¼ lb butter slowly and then 4 beaten egg yolks. Stir until creamy but not scrambled. Pour over fish. Garnish with chopped parsley and serve at once.

MISS ANNE MASSINGBERD-MUNDY: *London*

LOBSTER CUTLETS

1 medium to small lobster	1½ ozs flour
1 oz butter	Squeeze lemon juice
Salt, pepper, cayenne	2 tablespoons cream
Egg and breadcrumbs	

Chop the lobster finely. Melt butter and add flour, stir in enough milk to make a thick sauce. Add cream, lobster, season well. Add spawn (if any), rubbed through a sieve. Spread on a plate to cool. On a floured board and with floured hands, make mixture into small cutlet shapes. Egg and breadcrumb the cutlets and fry in smoking hot fat until brown.

This can also be made with dressed crab – in which case a dash of Worcester sauce and a little curry powder is a good addition. It works to do this in a Magimix.

This amount makes about 16 small cutlets and is good as a starter or savoury. It can be served with a lobster or prawn sauce if liked.

MRS CHARLES SHEEPSHANKS: *Yorkshire*

STUFFED SOLE WITH CUCUMBER SAUCE
for 2 people

4 fillets of sole	1 cucumber
1 small onion	2 eggs
2 ozs breadcrumbs	1 tablespoon tarragon vinegar
5 ozs butter	1 lemon
Chopped parsley	Salt and pepper

Make the stuffing by finely chopping or grating the onion. Peel and very finely dice half the cucumber. Sauté both in 1 oz butter for 5 minutes without colouring. Remove from the heat and add the fresh breadcrumbs, the grated rind of the lemon and a handful of chopped parsley. Bind with lightly beaten egg and season with salt and freshly ground pepper. Spread mixture on the fillets, roll up from the tail end and secure with cocktail stick. Place in shallow ovenproof dish which has been well buttered. Dot with small knobs of butter, cover and bake for about 20 minutes or until fish is cooked, in a moderate oven.

Cucumber Sauce

Reduce vinegar to half in a small saucepan. In a bain-marie gently melt 1 oz butter, add the egg and stir with whisk. Gradually add reduced vinegar, whisking all the time. Add remaining 2 ozs of butter, bit by bit, in small pieces. Season to taste. Now add 3 tablespoons finely diced and drained cucumber. Pour over fish and serve.

LOBSTER IN CREAM
for 2 people

1 x 2 lb boiled lobster
2 tablespoons butter
Salt and pepper
2 egg yolks
Brandy
A little paprika
Sherry
¾ cup of cream

Slice the meat of the boiled lobster and heat the pieces in 2 tablespoons melted butter for one or two minutes. Add salt, pepper and a little paprika. Pour in 1 tablespoon of warmed brandy, set it alight and shake pan backwards and forwards, until the flame dies. Beat 2 egg yolks with ¾ cup of thick cream, add 2 tablespoons of sherry and pour this sauce over the lobster. Heat over a low flame, stirring constantly.

QUICK LOBSTER THERMIDOR
for 4 people

4 small cooked lobsters	¾ pint rich cream sauce
Dry sherry	Butter
Salt and pepper	A pinch of cayenne
1 level teaspoon dry mustard	4 tablespoons grated Parmesan
Worcester sauce	Paprika

Cut lobsters in half, crack claws, remove all flesh and cut in large cubes. Reserve shells. Heat cream sauce and season to taste with sherry, dry mustard, cayenne etc. Simmer for a couple of minutes, add lobster meat and heat thoroughly. Fill lobster shells with the mixture, sprinkle with Parmesan cheese, dust with paprika, dot with butter and brown under pre-heated grill.

SAUMON GRATINÉE à la CRÈME
for 6 people

6 Salmon or cod steaks about ¾" thick	
3 tablespoons tomato purée	3½ ozs butter
8 ozs white wine	8 ozs double cream
Salt and pepper	½ oz grated cheese
1 tomato	1 lemon
½ lb mushrooms	

Clean fish, dry and season. Put 2 ozs of butter in frying pan and when foaming, sauté fish until golden. Remove and keep warm in ovenproof dish.

Mix together tomato purée and white wine, add cheese and mix. Whip cream lightly and add to sauce. Pour mixture over fish and cook in oven at 475°F for 15 minutes. In the meantime, fry mushrooms and tomatoes.

Arrange these around the fish and serve immediately.

TURBOT STEAKS à la CRÈME
for 4 people

Turbot steaks	Cooked mussels
Cooked prawns	Thick cream
Brandy	Salt and pepper

Cut turbot into thick steaks and cook for 2 or 3 minutes on each side under a pre-heated grill. Place in a well buttered fireproof dish, garnish with cooked mussels and prawns and cover everything with the cream, flavoured with salt and pepper and brandy. Bake in oven until bubbling. Sprinkle with chopped parsley and serve.

FILLETS OF SOLE WITH SALTED ALMONDS
for 2 people

4 fillets of sole	¼ lb salted almonds, chopped
¼ lb sliced mushrooms	Sherry
¼ lb butter	2 tablespoons chopped parsley
2 tablespoons lemon juice	Salt and pepper

Salt and pepper fillets and place in flat ovenproof dish which has been buttered. Cream butter, add almonds, mushrooms, parsley and lemon juice. Spread over fish and bake in moderate oven for 10 to 15 minutes. Pour over a very little sherry before serving.

SOLE au VIN BLANC
for 4 people

8 fillets of sole	4 ozs cream
1 oz flour	1 oz butter
¼ bottle white wine (not too dry)	Tarragon
Salt and pepper	

Salt and pepper the fillets, roll up and place them in a buttered dish. Put a sprig of tarragon on top and pour over the wine. Cover the dish and cook in cool to moderate oven for 15 minutes.

In the meantime, make a roux with butter and flour and while this is cooking, put the cream into a saucepan and simmer for 3 to 4 minutes until it has reduced and thickened. Add slowly to the flour and butter. Pour off wine from fish into a small pan and reduce by half; add slowly to the sauce and cook slowly for 3 to 4 minutes. Pour over the fish. Sprinkle with breadcrumbs and put under grill until brown.

MEDITERRANEAN FISH CASSEROLE
for 4 people

1 lb white fish, boned (halibut, sole, cod)	4 rashers streaky bacon
1 large onion	2 cloves garlic
1 small green pepper	6 medium tomatoes
Salt and pepper	1 tablespoon flour
Scant ½ pint dry white wine	6 basil leaves (or ½
Fried slivered almonds	teaspoon dried)

Cut fish into 1 inch pieces. Fry streaky bacon, which has been cut into small pieces, in a large heavy frying pan. Add tablespoon oil and chopped onion and blanched and finely chopped green pepper and crushed cloves of garlic. Cover and simmer for about 5 minutes until the onion is soft. Stir in 1 tablespoon flour and stir over heat for 1 minute. Take away from heat and stirring constantly, gradually pour in the wine and ¼ pint of water. Add the skinned, de-seeded and chopped tomatoes, chopped basil leaves and salt and pepper. Raise the heat and still stirring with wooden spoon, boil the sauce until it thickens. Add the fish. Cover the pan, reduce the heat and cook for about 15 minutes or until fish is cooked.

Garnish with chopped parsley, fried slivered almonds and serve.

FISH WITH CURRY SAUCE
(Very quick and easy)

White fish (sole, plaice, fresh haddock or whiting)
Flour
Oil/Butter for frying

Sauce
Spring onions
1 dessertspoon curry powder
1 carton plain yoghourt
Oil

Use any white fish you like – sole, plaice, fresh haddock or whiting. Dust the skinned fillets in flour, fry till golden in oil, or half oil/half butter.

Meanwhile, to make the sauce, chop a bunch of spring onions and fry them in oil with a dessertspoonful of curry powder. When onions are soft, add carton of plain yoghourt. Heat but do not boil. Serve with boiled potatoes.

MRS ANTHONY HOBSON: *Hampshire*

SEVICHE
This dish is typically Peruvian and is recommended as a diet dish

White fish	Fresh lime juice
Onions	Salt and pepper
Fresh Chillies	Lettuce
Corn on the cob	Sweet potatoes

Cut white fish (eg sole or queen fish) into 1 inch squares, removing all bones and skin. Marinate in pure fresh lime juice for 2 to 5 hours, depending on the quantity you are providing. Turn fish from time to time so that the fish becomes totally white as though it was cooked. When marinating is complete, strain fish and rinse slightly under cold running water and strain. Slice onions very finely, rinse in cold water and mix with the fish. Add salt, pepper and finely chopped fresh chillies.

Serve on a bed of lettuce surrounded with sliced corn on the cob and slices of boiled sweet potatoes.

MRS GERARD DE LISLE: *Leicestershire*

LANSDOWNE SMOKED FISH LOAF
for 12 people

1¼ lb smoked haddock, when skinned and boned
10 ozs kipper, when skinned and boned
1 lb cream cheese
6 ozs butter
4 ozs chopped parsley and springs of fennel if possible
Juice of 1½ lemons
Black pepper

Line bottom of 2 lb loaf tin with greaseproof paper. Mix finely chopped parsley and fennel with 1 oz of melted butter. Place a thick layer in bottom of tin. Cook haddock and kipper separately gently in water. Drain very well. Skin and bone.

Put smoked haddock in food processor or blender if possible and blend or beat until smooth. Add lemon juice, 3 ozs of melted butter and plenty of ground black pepper. Meanwhile mash cream cheese in a large bowl, add smoked haddock mixture when cool and mix very well. Now blend skinned and boned kipper with lemon juice and the remaining 2 ozs of melted butter. Season with pepper.

Make very even layer of smoked haddock mixture, then a layer of parsley and fennel, then kipper and then top up with the second half of smoked haddock mixture. Cover with cling film and allow to set overnight. Turn out carefully by releasing with a knife around the tin.

This is equally good as a first course, a lunch dish or for a buffet table.

LADY OWEN: *Warwickshire*

MARINADED SALMON OR SALMON TROUT
A very good way of treating fish not large enough to smoke.

Cut fish in half lengthwise and remove bones. (A fishmonger might be safer doing this). Weigh, and for each 2 lbs of fish, mix:
2 tablespoons coarse salt
1 tablespoon soft light brown sugar

1 teaspoon ground black pepper
Bunch of fresh dill or dried dill-weed

Place half the fish, skin side down, in a deep dish. Cover with the mixture and plenty of dill and cover the other side with remaining mixture and place on top, skin side up.

Put a dish and weights or foil and bricks on the fish and refrigerate for 36 hours, turning once and basting with the oil that appears from the fish.

Remove from liquid, cut and eat as smoked salmon. Freezes well.

MRS BRIAN BELL: *Gloucestershire*

SEA BASS WITH WHITE WINE SAUCE
for 2-3 people

To one quart of water, add 1 cup of white wine, ½ cup of vinegar, 1 carrot and 1 onion, both sliced, salt, peppercorns, a pinch of thyme, a bay leaf and a sprig of parsley. Simmer the court bouillon for 30 minutes and then poach a 2 lb sea bass in the aromatic stock.

Simmer 4 or 5 shallots, chopped with ¼ cup each of vinegar and white wine until the liquid is almost evaporated. Add, bit by bit, ½ lb creamed sweet butter over low heat so the butter will not boil, stirring continuously with a sauce whisk to achieve a creamy unctuous result. Season with a little salt, some freshly ground pepper and a pinch of cayenne. Spread this beurre blanc on the fish at the moment of serving.

THE LADY CARRINGTON: *Buckinghamshire*

FISH MOUSSE
for 5-6 people
1 lb fish for 5-6 people, 1½ lbs for up to 8 or 9 people

Simmer any white fish (cod, hake etc) very slowly until it comes easily off the bone. Put a little salt and a bouquet of herbs in the water.

Keep a cup of the water it is cooked in and add about four leaves of gelatine (which has been softened in cold water for a minute or two). Heat the gelatine and stock and strain it into the mashed up fish.

Mix very well and carefully add a cup of whipped cream and stiffly beaten whites of 3 eggs. Mix all together carefully – gently but thoroughly – with some chopped up dill. Put into a souflée dish and decorate with large prawns, 2 for each person.

NB: If for 8 people, use 2 cups of whipped cream. If made with salmon, no prawns are needed.

THE HON LADY MOSLEY: *Orsay, France*

WELSH COD BAKE
for 3-4 people

1–1½ lbs cod on the bone	1½ ozs butter
Lemon juice	Chopped parsley
2 or 3 leeks	Salt and pepper
2 oz chopped walnuts	

Cut the white and pale green parts of the leeks into thin slices and cook very gently in butter in a fireproof casserole, lay the cod on top, season with salt and pepper, sprinkle with lemon juice, walnuts and chopped parsley. Cover with buttered paper and bake at Gas Mark 5 until the fish is just tender and the walnuts brown.

LADY MARK FITZALAN HOWARD: *London*

BAKED SCALLOPS
for 4 people

6 large scallops	1 oz melted butter
Salt and pepper	Lemon juice
6 tablespoons double cream	Fresh breadcrumbs
4 bacon rashers to garnish	

Wash and dry scallops. Put 1 teaspoonful of melted butter in bottom of four of the scallop shells or remekin dishes. Quarter the scallops and arrange in shells; season and add a squeeze of lemon juice. Spoon over the cream, sprinkle with the bread crumbs and add the rest of the melted butter.

Bake in a moderate oven for 8-10 minutes. Garnish the tops with a curl of well grilled bacon.

GINGER SALMON
for 6 people

6 pieces of salmon tail	Bunch of spring onions
Approx 3" piece of root ginger	Teaspoon of plain flour
Small pot of crème fraiche	Olive oil and butter

Peel ginger and cut into 3"strips. Trim spring onions and halve lengthways, then again into 3"strips.

Heat oil and butter in a large frying pan. Toss salmon in seasoned flour, then brown on both sides, add spring onions and ginger and shake pan gently. When salmon is almost cooked through – about 10 minutes – add the crème fraiche and stir pan to incorporat pan juices.

Serve with new potatoes.

MRS CHARLES HELMORE: *Hampshire*

WROTHAM PARK; *Hertfordshire*

Poultry and Game

❧

Poussin with Cherry Sauce
Chaudfroid of Chicken
Pulled Turkey and Grilled
Frances' Chicken Casserole
Guinea Fowl à la Poste
Coriander Chicken
Duck Puffs
Parsley Chicken
Devilled Fowl
Roast Quail
Chicken Crêpes
Partridge with Olives
Rook or Pigeon Parcels
Recipe for old Grouse
Pheasant with Celery and Walnuts
Timbale de Riz au Cailles
Chicken breasts with Florentine sauce
Wild Duck with Cherries
Chicken Fricassee and Champagne
Pheasant Casserole
Chicken Dish

❧

POUSSIN WITH CHERRY SAUCE
for 6 people

3 large poussin
2 tablespoons butter
1 tablespoon oil
Cherry sauce (see recipe below)
½ teaspoon each salt, ground ginger, paprika

Combine fats and spices, brush over birds and roast in oven at 350°F for about an hour or until tender, basting several times. Meanwhile prepare Cherry sauce and keep warm over low heat. When birds are ready, remove from roasting dish and cut in half along breast bone. Arrange on serving dish and keep warm. Cover with sauce just before serving.

Cherry Sauce

Drain 1 can of black pitted cherries and reserve syrup. Combine syrup with ⅔ pint water, 1 chicken bouillon cube, 1 small chopped onion, 8 whole cloves and ¼ teaspoon ground cinnamon. Bring to the boil and simmer for 10 minutes. Strain. Return sauce to saucepan. Mix 1 tablespoon corn starch with a little cold water, add to sauce and stir over heat until it thickens. Add cherries, grated lemon peel, 1 tablespoon lemon juice and (if desired) 2 tablespoons brandy.

LADY ASHE: *Hampshire*

CHAUDFROID OF CHICKEN
for 8 people

1 large chicken or small turkey	1 tin of mock foie gras (large)
¼ pint single cream	Garlic
Seasoning	1 pkt gelatine
1 pint aspic	1 onion
2 bay leaves	
Sauce	
1½ pints of milk	2 heaped tablespoons flour
3-4 cloves	1 small onion
Seasoning	

Boil chicken for one hour or until tender, with bay leaf and onion. Reserve liquid and bones of chicken to make soup if wished. Slice the white and brown meat. Mash the fois gras with garlic, cream and black pepper. Spread on bottom of large oval dish. Arrange slices of chicken on top. Make white sauce with milk which has been infused gently for 20 minutes with bay leaf, onion and cloves. Add gelatine which has been melted with a little cold water in double boiler. Cover chicken with white sauce. When set cover gently with aspic and decorate.

MRS MICHAEL DORMER: *Berkshire*

PULLED TURKEY AND GRILLED

Left-over turkey
Olive oil
Dry mustard
Worcester sauce
Béchamel sauce

This is the best use for left-over turkey that I know. Pull the dark meat off the legs of a cooked turkey and marinate for a few hours in a mixture of olive oil, dry mustard and Worcester sauce. Dice the white meat and put aside.

Remove the dark meat from marinade, pat dry, and grill. Make a Béchamel sauce and heat the diced white meat in it. Serve with the white meat in the middle and the dark meat around it. The contrast between the bland taste of the white meat and the sharpness of the dark meat is delicious. Almost a reason for having turkey in the first place.

THE COUNTESS OF HAREWOOD: *Yorkshire*

FRANCES' CHICKEN CASSEROLE
(My Grandmother's cook's recipe circa 1900)

Line fireproof casserole with cooked spaghetti, or lasagne. Put in a layer of cooked chicken, a layer of ham, a layer of tongue, until three parts full. Make a good sauce with the chicken stock, liquid enough to run off the spoon. Flavour with shallots, finely diced and softened in butter, cream sherry and a little lemon juice.

Pour over the meat, grated cheese on top and place in oven to heat and brown.

THE LADY HOWARD DE WALDEN: *Berkshire*

GUINEA FOWL à la POSTE
for 6 persons

2 guinea fowl	½ pint red Burgundy
Grated rind of 1 lemon	4-6 tablespoons cognac
Dijon mustard	4 ozs butter
4 ozs mousse de foie gras	Lemon juice
Salt and freshly ground pepper	

Roast guinea fowl in a moderately hot oven (400°F) for 25 to 30 minutes, or until almost cooked. Cut birds into serving pieces. Reduce wine with grated lemon rind to a third of its original quantity. Add birds to pan and heat through. Flame with warmed cognac. Stir in mustard to taste and continue to simmer for a few minutes, turning the birds from time to time. Mix butter and mousse de foie gras to a smooth paste and add to pan, stirring in all the juices. Add lemon juice. Stir pieces of guinea fowl into the sauce, making sure that they are all well covered. Season to taste with salt and freshly ground pepper. Serve immediately.

MRS GERALD HOHLER: *Dorset*

CORIANDER CHICKEN
for 6 people

Take a reasonably sized chicken and cut into small joints. Salt and pepper them and fry gently in oil and butter in a thick iron stewpot. Remove chicken. In the same butter, fry a fair quantity of finely chopped onion until it starts to go golden.

Make a paste of a whole cup of coriander (can be bought ground), a small amount of turmeric and a small amount of chilli (depending on how hot you want the sauce to be). Fry this paste with the onion, stirring continuously and making sure it does not stick to the pan. Replace the chicken and add a small tin of tomato juice and several fresh, peeled tomatoes. Simmer gently until the chicken is cooked.

Serve with boiled rice, preferably with a packet of saffron.

GILBERT MCNEILL-MOSS ESQ: *London*

DUCK PUFFS
for 6 people

This recipe varies with the season. Below is a red Puff for winter and a green one for summer

1 good sized Duck (5lbs) with its liver. Unfrozen is best.
13 ozs puff pastry
1 egg
Splash of milk, pepper and salt

For Red:
½ cup thick marmalade
½ cup red jam or jelly, say black cherry conserve
12 chopped up black olives
2 well-crushed stars of aniseed, some grated root ginger
1 lb lightly boiled potatoes (new if possible)

For Green:
15 medium sized mushrooms
6 large artichoke hearts
Lots of herbs (parsley, basil, tarragon)
¼ pint of double cream

Preparatory Work: Roast the duck (but not its liver). When it's a bit less done than you normally have it, remove from oven, take off skin and remaining fat, cut flesh into strips and put to one side. Simmer the carcass and giblets and skin (not liver) with onions, carrots, herbs or anything handy in 4 pints of water for two hours, to make a good stock.

Pour through sieve, skim off fat and keep. Defreeze the pastry by leaving it around. Roll it very thin and as square as possible. You will need a big surface. Cut into two equal pieces. Superimpose one on the other, square off with a knife, throw remainder away. The two bits should be about 11 by 7½ inches each. Dust very lightly with flour and put them in the fridge. You have now got the main components. The pie will contain roast duck in a thick sauce and this sauce varies with the season.

To make the Pie: Take the pastry out of the fridge (it must stay there at least two hours). It will have shrunk – don't worry. If it has shrunk more than an inch all round, roll it out a bit. Cut a window from one of the two bits, leaving as a frame, about an inch round the side. You now have three bits of pastry, a window, a window frame and the untouched bit (call it 'the wall'). Superimpose the window on the wall, leaving the frame nearby. Break the egg into a cup; add a splash of milk and whisk. Get a pastry brush. Glaze thickly, the whole top exposed surface and the wall (try not to glaze the sides of the window). Fit the frame on to it (it will be a tight fit). Glaze the whole top surface thickly (ie the frame and the window). The result of all this is that all top surfaces are glazed, except the area of the wall under the window.

Fold a piece of foil to the same size as the pie, making edges about 1½ inches high to contain it. You are unlikely to have a baking tin of the exact size, so don't bother with one. Put the pie into the Baco-foil container and place on a shelf in the oven at 400°F. Leave for about 35 minutes. When done it should be darkish brown in places and lightish yellow in others. Remove pie from the oven. Use a small sharp knife to cut the window out. This will not be difficult. It will leave a hole into which the duck is to be poured.

Pour the rest of the dish into the hole. Replace the window. Serve, cutting cross-wise like a loaf. It ought to be enough for 6 people (which is a miracle for a duck!)

To make the rest: Lightly sauté the duck's liver. Slice finely and keep it somewhere.

Reduce the stock by boiling very hard in a saucepan. For *red* Puff, put the marmalade, jam and ginger etc into it as it boils. For the *green* Puff, add the rest of the herbs and the cream. Stir over low heat to mix it all up and warm the bits that have been lying around and getting cold. Add salt and pepper of course.

Note: The only problem is the timing. The important thing to remember is that once the pie is done, it should be eaten, so have the contents ready before cooking the pie. Some people like coriander instead of aniseed.

THE LORD PARMOOR: *Wiltshire*

PARSLEY CHICKEN

6 chicken breasts	6 oz fresh white breadcrumbs
1 medium bunch of parsley	Garlic or two shallots
Salt and pepper	Butter

Skin chicken breasts and place in a shallow ovenproof casserole. In a blender, mix bread and parsley, onion or shallots. Sprinkle over meat, dot generously with butter and bake in a moderate to hot oven for 30/40 minutes. Noisettes of lamb or boneless pork chops can be substituted for the chicken.

THE LADY ROCKLEY: *London*

DEVILLED FOWL

Cooked turkey, pheasant or chicken (trimmed)	
Lemon juice	Paprika
Cayenne pepper	Butter
Breadcrumbs	Mixed herbs

Cut cooked or left over fowl into good sized pieces and place on a shallow dish, laid out so that the pieces don't overlap. Pour over lemon juice, sprinkle liberally with paprika and cayenne and leave for a few hours. Melt butter in a saucepan and fry breadcrumbs until golden and crisp. Coat each piece of fowl with melted butter and then roll in breadcrumbs.

Place in an ovenproof dish and place in medium oven to heat thoroughly. A sprinkling of mixed herbs in the breadcrumbs as they cook adds to the to the flavour.

THE LADY ST LEVAN: *Cornwall*

ROAST QUAIL
Allow 2 per person

This recipe is very quick and easy. Quail need to be flown through a hot oven and must not be over-cooked.

Pre-heat oven to Gas Mark 7. Place quail in roasting tin with butter on their breasts and a nut of butter, salt and pepper inside. Sprinkle birds with thyme, salt and pepper and a squeeze of lemon juice. Add half a glass of wine to the roasting tin and baste two or three times. They will take 15-20 minutes or a little longer depending on the size. If juices run clear when pricked, they are ready.

Serve in a dish with watercress and the juices poured over them or on to fried bread with juices served separately in gravy boat.

Toast for Savouries:
Cut slices of bread to shape, butter both sides and bake in moderate oven till top side is golden. Made this way the toast will not become soggy.

MRS TIM RATHBONE: *London*

CHICKEN CRÊPES
for 6 people

1 boiled chicken, meat finely chopped
1 onion, finely chopped and gently fried
2 tablespoons finely chopped parsley
4 ozs finely chopped mushrooms
4 ozs finely chopped water chestnuts
Salt and pepper

Make about 12 crêpes with wholemeal flour. Then make a white sauce with the chicken stock to bind the ingredients together. Cool.

Stuff crêpes generously and put in a gratin dish. Cover them with a Béchamel sauce to which egg yolks and cream have been added. Sprinkle with Parmesan cheese, dot with butter and brown under the grill, having heated crêpes in cool oven to avoid curdling of the sauce with egg yolks.

MRS RICHARD STICKNEY: *London*

PARTRIDGE

In season from September - February. A young bird should be hung for 3-4 days and is best roasted. An older bird should be hung for 6-7 days and needs extra time and care with cooking.

PARTRIDGE WITH OLIVES
for 2 people

2 small birds	4 oz black olives
½ pint stock	1 tablespoon flour
2 ozs butter	1 glass red wine
8 slices streaky bacon	Bay leaf
4 shallots	1 teaspoon tomato puree
Parsley	Seasoning

Cover the birds with 6 slices of the bacon, roast in oven at 400 - 425°F for 20-25 minutes in two thirds of the butter, plus bay leaf, basting twice. Cut the remaining bacon into fingers and blanch. Soften the very finely chopped shallots in the remainder of the butter, adding the bacon and the olives. Cook for 2 minutes and stir in flour, stock and wine. Reduce by half. Simmer, adding puree and seasoning. Split the birds and arrange on serving dish, trimming away any rough edges. Check for seasoning. Coat birds with the sauce. It must be a coating sauce, with bacon and olives on top of the partridges.

Sprinkle with chopped parsley before serving.

DAVID TELFER SMOLLETT ESQ: *Cambridgeshire*

ROOK OR PIGEON PARCELS
for 4 people

12 rooks' or pigeon breasts
12 rashers of bacon
1 egg
Breadcrumbs
Fat for frying
1 dessertspoon chopped parsley

Cut the breasts out and skin them. It is not necessary to pluck the whole bird. Wrap each breast in a rasher of bacon, dip in the beaten egg, roll in the breadcrumbs and fry in deep fat until golden (about 7 minutes). Sprinkle with chopped parsley and serve with mushrooms and grilled tomatoes.

MRS CARLETON TUFNELL: *Gloucestershire*

RECIPE FOR OLD GROUSE

2 old grouse
2 ozs butter
1 oz flour
1 small wine glass sherry
½ pint of double cream
Salt and pepper

Cook the old grouse in the butter in a very slow oven until tender, basting from time to time. This may take anything up to 4 hours, depending on age. When virtually falling apart, take off the bone and cut into reasonable sized pieces. Put to one side. Meanwhile heat up the butter and all the juices in the roasting tin and add the flour, then milk and sherry, enough to make a fairly thick sauce.

Lastly pour in the cream, season and pour over the grouse. Serve in a ring of plain boiled rice, or savoury rice if preferred.

MRS CARLETON TUFNELL: *Gloucestershire*

PHEASANT WITH CELERY AND WALNUTS
for 3-4 people

1 pheasant	4 rashers of bacon
3 tablespoons butter	Juice and rind of 2 oranges
3 oz Madeira or Port	3 oz walnuts
1 head of celery	Salt and pepper

Cover pheasant with bacon and brown in 2 tablespoons butter in casserole. Add orange juice, Madeira, salt and pepper. Cover and simmer gently on top of stove or in a moderate oven.

Trim celery and cut crossway slices. Heat rest of butter in frying pan and add celery and walnuts. Shred orange rinds and simmer in boiling water until tender, drain and rinse.

When pheasants are cooked, remove, carve and keep hot on serving dish. Boil up the sauce, thicken if necessary with a little cornflour and water. Serve with the celery and walnuts scattered over the top, with orange rind.

THE VISCOUNTESS WHITELAW: *Cumbria*

TIMBALE de RIZ au CAILLES
for 4 people

1½ cups Patna rice
3 cups chicken stock
1 oz butter and drop of oil
Salt and pepper
8 quail

Heat butter and oil in thick casserole. Heat stock in separate saucepan. Add rice to butter and oil and stir well until well heated. Then add stock, season and cover. Reduce heat and cook gently for 14 minutes. Rice must remain moist. Remove from stove. Place quail in middle of rice and see that it is completely covered by the rice.

Place in pre-heated oven (Gas Mark 2/3) for 30/40 minutes, without casserole lid, so that the top is browned while the birds stay juicy and tender.

MADAME GERTRUDE WISSA: *London*

CHICKEN BREASTS WITH SAUCE FLORENTINE
for 6 people

6 plump chicken breasts	5 oz butter
Lemon juice	Parsley
Salt and pepper	1 tablespoon meat glaze
3 shallots	1 clove garlic
2 anchovy fillet	1 wine glass of Marsala
1 gill tomato purée	

Butter casserole dish and put chicken breasts - which have had skin removed - into it. Season with salt and pepper, sprinkle with chopped parsley and dot with butter (about 3 ozs). Over this pour two tablespoons of lemon juice and bake in a moderate oven for about 35 minutes.

In the meantime prepare a sauce by frying the peeled and finely chopped shallots and garlic in remaining butter. When soft but not brown, add the anchovy fillet, also finely chopped, plus a glass of Marsala and a gill of tomato purée. Allow to cook for 10 minutes and pass through a sieve. Re-heat and taste for seasoning.

Remove cooked chicken breasts from the casserole dish, place on a heated serving dish, pour over the sauce and serve immediately.

WILD DUCK WITH CHERRIES
for 6 people

1 large tin of cherries (preferably stoned)	1 brace of wild duck
½ lb button onions	½ bottle red wine
2 ozs butter	½ lb mushrooms
Salt and pepper	1 orange
2 carrots	Bouquet garni
2 ozs flour	

Wipe ducks, clean and put into a casserole. Add sliced carrot, 2 or 3 of the onions, the bouquet garni and the orange cut into quarters. Season and cover with red wine. Place in a slow oven and cook for several hours, until the meat almost falls from the bone. Cool slightly and then remove all the meat and put into a fireproof dish. Strain the liquid and keep, discarding the vegetables and orange. Sauté the remaining onions and mushrooms which should be finely chopped and add to the meat. Melt butter in a saucepan and stir in the flour. Gradually add the liquid the ducks were cooked in until you have a smooth sauce. Bring to the boil and add the cherries, strained from their sauce. Pour over the meat etc. Cover tightly and re-heat when required. Serve with rice or plain boiled potatoes and green salad.

LADY DELVES BROUGHTON: *Cheshire*

CHICKEN FRICASSÉE WITH CHAMPAGNE
for 4 people

3½ - 4½ lb chicken	2½ ozs butter
6 shallots	2 tablespoons flour
2½ tablespoons *Marc de champagne*	1 bottle champagne
½ lb mushrooms	3 egg yolks
½ pint double cream	Salt and pepper

Cut the chicken into 8 pieces. Melt 2 ozs of the butter in a large fireproof casserole and add finely chopped shallots. Cook slowly for 5 minutes. Push to one side of the pan, raise heat a little and add the pieces of chicken. Sauté until the flesh is golden on both sides, then turn down the heat and cook very gently for 10 minutes. Season. Sprinkle flour on both sides and cook for 10 minutes more. Flame with the *Marc de champagne* and gradually add the champagne. Bring to the boil and cook rapidly, uncovered, for 15 minutes. Meanwhile slice the mushrooms (not too finely) and sauté them in the rest of the butter. Add to the pan 5 minutes before the chicken is ready. When the chicken is tender, transfer to a serving dish.

Strain the cooking liquid and arrange the mushrooms on the dish, keep warm. Return the liquid to the pan and reduce as rapidly as possible until it will coat the spoon. Beat together the egg yolks and the cream and slowly stir in the liquid. Return to the pan and re-heat but do not allow to boil. The sauce should be smooth and fairly thick. Serve the chicken with a little of the sauce poured over the top and the rest in a sauceboat.

The French say of *marcs* that they are "fiery enough to make a goat dance" but a good *marc de champagne* is an excellent *digestif* and it gives this dish a special flavour. The only possible substitute would be Calvados.

PATRICK FORBES ESQ: *London*

PHEASANT CASSEROLE
for 6-8 people

2 pheasants	8 ozs fairly lean bacon, chopped
3 finely chopped onions	4 sticks celery, finely chopped
2 tablespoons oil	1 pint stock
½ pint sparkling rosé wine,	1 bay leaf
1 sprig parsley	1 teaspoon dried thyme
6 crushed juniper berries	Rind of half an orange
Seasoning	2 tablespoons flour
¼ lb mushrooms	

Heat the oil in a large frying pan and gently fry the bacon. Place in casserole. Now fry the pheasants quickly until brown on all sides. Place in casserole with bacon. Add the onions and celery to the remaining fat and fry gently for about five minutes. Add stock and wine, herbs, orange rind and juniper berries. Pour over the pheasants in the casserole, season with salt and pepper. Cover casserole and cook in moderate oven for 2 hours or until tender.

Remove from oven and allow to cool. Put pheasants on a plate and the vegetables and liquid into a bowl and leave overnight in fridge.On the following day, skim off any fat from the liquid and place it in a saucepan with a little dripping, stir in the flour and cook over a gentle heat until it is a rich brown colour. Gradually stir in the strained liquid and bring to the boil, stirring all the time. Skin and carve the pheasants and place in a serving dish, add the vegetables and then pour over the sauce. Add the mushrooms, cover and re-heat in a moderate oven for about 45 minutes. Serve with a sprinkling of chopped parsley.

THE HON MRS RICHARD BEAUMONT: *London*

CHICKEN DISH
for 4 people

1 Chicken	1 onion
1 carrot	Paprika
Double cream	Bouquet garni
Seasoning	Ham
Mushrooms	

Boil chicken with an onion, carrot and a bouquet garni (parsley, thyme, bay leaves, all tied together). When cooked let the chicken get cold.

Cover the bottom of a soufflé dish with pieces of cut up ham, then pieces of chicken (breast only), then cut up mushrooms and a little paprika. Repeat again in the same order, until the dish is nearly full. Pour over double cream until the dish is full. The cream must take the flavour of the chicken.

Place the dish in the oven at 200°F for an hour.

As an alternative, this dish can be made with turkey breasts.

LADY ALEXANDRA METCALFE: *London*

INVERARY CASTLE: *Argyll*

Meat

❧

Venison Stew

Haggis

Dick's Lasagne

Roast Venison with Cranbury Sauce

Braised Venison

Braised Pork with Prunes

Green Steaks

Kidneys with Cream

Easy Goulash

Butterfly of Lamb

Fresh Tongue with Blackberry & Raisin Sauce

Baked Ham

Petit Panna

Kidney Ragout

Stuffed Shoulder of Lamb

Rognons Liègeoise

Savoury Meat Loaf

Fried Calves Liver

Rich Stew

Sweet and sour Pork in Pancakes

Veal à la Crème

Pork Fillet with Cream

Mutton Curry

Aubergine & Mince Pie

Stuffed Leg of Lamb

Beef & Mushroom Stew

❧

VENISON STEW
for 4-6 people

1½ lbs stewing venison	½ lb streaky bacon
1 tablespoon fat for frying	Zest of 2 oranges
Seasoning	1 tablespoon tomato purée
¼ bottle of red wine	¼ pint of water
2 tablespoons of red currant jelly	

Take any fat off the venison. Cut venison and streaky bacon into 1 inch pieces. Brown in fat over high heat, add orange zest, wine, red currant jelly, tomato purée, water and seasoning and simmer very slowly for 1½ hours or until tender. Check for seasoning.

THE DUCHESS OF ARGYLL: *Inveraray, Scotland*

HAGGIS
for 4-6 people

½ lb ox liver	4 ozs shredded suet
4 ozs pinhead oatmeal	1 onion
Freshly ground black pepper	Salt

Place liver and onion in saucepan and add one cup of water. Simmer for 15 minutes. Meanwhile toast the oatmeal for a few minutes in the oven until light brown. Mince liver and onion and make the liquid up to a cup with water. Mix all together and season well.

Use about ¾ level dessertspoon of salt and black pepper. Turn into a greased bowl and steam for two hours.

THE DUCHESS OF ARGYLL: *Inveraray, Scotland*

DICK'S LASAGNE
for 6 people

1 small onion, peeled and finely chopped
¼ lb mushrooms, washed, trimmed and sliced
1 clove garlic, peeled and chopped
2 tablespoons oil

1½ lb lean minced beef
1 15 oz tin tomatoes
1-2 tablespoons tomato purée
Salt and freshly milled pepper
¼ teaspoon each of oregano, rosemary, thyme, basil
Dash of cayenne
½ lb lasagne
½ lb mozzarella cheese, thinly sliced
¾ lb ricotta cheese
1 egg
4 ozs grated Parmesan cheese

Heat the oil in a large pan. Add the onion and cook gently for 5 minutes to soften. Add the mushrooms and cook for two minutes, until the juices run out. Stir in the garlic. Then add the beef and brown. Drain off fat and return to heat. Stir in the tomatoes, purée, herbs and seasoning. Simmer for 20 minutes. Cook lasagne, then drain and rinse. Mix the ricotta cheese and egg together.

Grease 13 x 9½ x 2 inch baking dish and fill with layers of noodles, ricotta cheese, meat sauce and lastly, Parmesan cheese. Bake at 375°F (190°C or Gas Mark 5) for 30 minutes.

MRS RICHARD ALEXANDER: *London*

ROAST VENISON WITH CRANBERRY SAUCE
for 6-8 people

4 lb piece saddle of venison   ½ lb streaky bacon rashers
Colman's mustard   Salt
(Time taken - 1½ hours)

Cuts for roasting can be taken from the fore-quarter of saddle, which is very sweet, or from the hind-quarter which is considered to be more tender. Venison is very lean meat and should be well protected during roasting.

Rub the piece of venison with salt and mustard and cover with the trimmed rashers of bacon.

Place the joint in a covered roasting tin. Place in a very hot oven (220°C/425°F or Gas Mark 8) for about 15 minutes. Lower the heat to moderately hot for the remaining cooking time. Allow 20 minutes per 1lb plus 20 minutes extra time. When ready, serve the venison on very hot plates. Venison congeals and sets very quickly and the roast should not be taken out of the oven more than 3 minutes before serving.

Serve with gravy made of cream, mustard, red wine and a tiny bit of flour and also cranberry sauce.

MADELEINE, GRÄFIN DOUGLAS: *London*

BRAISED VENISON
for Shooting Lunches

1 haunch of venison	2 carrots
2 onions	2 sticks of celery
Bouquet garni	1 pint red wine
Bay leaves	Parsley stalks
A few pieces of celeriac	About ½ pint of stock
5-6 Juniper berries	Pepper and salt

Cut venison into reasonable sized chunks. Lay in a deep fireproof dish, pour over red wine, having rubbed a little oil into the meat. Brown vegetables in a little oil, then lay over meat with herbs and bouquet garni. Leave to marinade for a day or two, turning once or twice, then take up meat, dry on a kitchen cloth, fry quickly in pan until brown, and place in casserole. Add the wine and vegetables with stock to cover, together with crushed Juniper berries and seasoning. Cook for 1½ - 2 hours at a low temperature until meat is tender.

THE LADY EGREMONT: *Sussex*

BRAISED PORK WITH PRUNES
for 6 people

3 lbs loin of pork	¼ pint wine or cider
2 cloves of garlic	4-5 twigs of thyme

20 prunes (soaked overnight in tea)   Salt and pepper
4 slices of white bread with crusts removed.

Remove rind from pork, ease meat away from bone. Rub the meat well with salt and pepper. Chop the garlic roughly and insert between meat and bone. Put pork into braising pan, brown and add wine and thyme. Cover with foil and cook in the oven at 400°F for 50 minutes, then remove foil and reduce the oven to 310°F and cook for a further hour.

Meanwhile dice bread into small cubes and fry lightly. When browned, place on paper to absorb fat. Prunes should then be stewed in the juice they have been soaking in until only three tablespoons of liquid remain.

Arrange the loin of pork on a serving dish surrounded by the prunes and croutons.

MRS ROSS HANBURY: *Rutland*

GREEN STEAKS
Allow 3 slices of meat person

Sirloin steak   Fresh parsley
Butter   Sauces (own preference)
Green Salad

Choose lean sirloin steaks, remove all fat leaving only red meat. Cut into very thin slices, maximum ¼ inch thick. Place meat between lettuce leaves to keep steaks looking fresh. Finely chop fresh parsley – enough to cover each steak on both sides.

Have ready a burner with a shallow heavy pan. Place a small piece of butter in pan, just enough to grease it. Cover each steak with parsley (same method as using breadcrumbs) and fry slightly on both sides.

Serve with different sauces of your choice on the table, *eg* mayonnaise, sauce Bernaise, whipped cream with chives. Serve with green salad.

This dish should be served at the table and the steaks should be 'parsleyed' as they are fried.

MRS GERARD DE LISLE: *Leicestershire*

KIDNEYS WITH CREAM
for 4 people

8 sheep's kidneys
¼ lb open mushrooms
8 tablespoons double cream
Salt and freshly ground black pepper

Skin the kidneys, cut them into fairly thin slices, discarding the cores. If the mushrooms are cultivated, do not peel them, but wipe them clean, cut away the base of the stems and slice. Melt a large knob of butter in a frying pan and when it is really hot, but not brown, add the slices of kidneys and stir them round and over until they are slightly browned. Lift the kidneys out of the pan and set aside. Add the mushrooms to the pan, sprinkle them with a little salt and sauté them gently for about three minutes, stirring and turning them over from time to time. Now stir the cream into the pan, add the kidney, grid pepper over it and stir to mix everything thoroughly, then lower the heat until the kidney is thoroughly heated. Check for seasoning. Tip everything out of the pan into a heated serving dish and keep warm. Put two tablespoons of hot water into the pan, bring quickly to the boil, scrape round the base and sides of the pan to release any residue, then boil until reduced by half. Pour over the kidneys and stir in. Serve with boiled rice and a green vegetable.

THE LADY HOLDERNESS: *Yorkshire*

EASY GOULASH
for 10 people

3 lbs stewing steak	1 lb onions
4 ozs fat	½ teaspoon marjoram
2 crushed cloves of garlic	2 tablespoons paprika
1 gill tomato ketchup	Salt and freshly milled pepper

Sauté the chopped onion in the fat for 5 minutes. Add beef, marjoram, garlic and a scant pint of water or half water/half red wine andseasoning.

Bring to the boil and simmer gently in a covered casserole until tender. Combine the paprika and ketchup with two tablespoons of water and add to the ste. Cook for a further 10 minutes and serve garnished with parsley and cream.

THE HON MRS NEEDHAM: *Yorkshire*

BUTTERFLY OF LAMB
for 8 people

1 leg of lamb, boned by your butcher
Lemon juice and oil
Pepper and salt
Any fresh herbs - rosemary, thyme, parsley etc

Slit open the smallest bit of lamb that remains joined and flatten and trim fat to shape. The leg will then resemble a kite or butterfly. Pound with a rolling pin to reduce the thicker parts of the meat to an even thickness. Rub over with oil and lemon juice, salt and pepper and herbs and marinade for at least 6 hours. Pre-heat grill until very hot and grill meat for approximately 17 minutes each side. I put whole sprigs of rosemary and thyme which light up and give a lovely smell and taste of herbs. Place on heated serving dish and slice from left to right.

Serve with red currant jelly and mint sauce. Puréed potatoes are best with this as there is no gravy.

MRS ANDREW ROLLO: *Wiltshire*

FRESH TONGUE WITH BLACKBERRY & RAISIN SAUCE
for 12 people

4-5 lbs fresh tongue	3 celery stalks
1 onion	3 cloves
6 sprigs of parsley	6 peppercorns
3 teaspoons Salt	

Put washed tongue in large kettle. Add celery, onion stuck with cloves, parsley, salt and peppercorns. Cover tongue with water and bring to the boil. Simmer, cover with lid and continue to cook until tender, about 3½ hours. The skin should peel off easily when the tongue is cooked. Leave to cool in stock, then remove, peel and trim. Cut into slices and re-heat slowly in blackberry and raisin Sauce. Garnish with parsley.

Blackberry & Raisin Sauce

1 coffee cup of raisins
10 ozs blackberry jelly
Juice of half a lemon

Simmer raisins in water for several minutes, until plump. Drain and stir in blackberry jelly and lemon juice. Heat sauce slowly, stirring constantly, until jelly melts and sauce is well blended. Do not let it boil. Half a glass of Madeira or Port can be added to the sauce as a variation and if sauce should not be thick enough, add a little arrowroot (1 teaspoon to 2 tablespoons cold water).

MADAME SARACHI: *London*

BAKED HAM
for 10-12 people

1 whole ham	1 lb jar red currant jelly
2 dessertspoons Bisto	⅓ bottle red wine
1 cup cider	Garlic, salt and pepper
Split blanched almonds	Cloves
1 sliced orange	

Soak ham for at least two hours in cold water. Wrap completely in foil with cloves, 1 sliced orange and 1 cup of cider. Cook in over at 400°F for 15 minutes, then turn down to 310°F and continue to bake for half an hour to the pound.

To make sauce:
Melt jelly and boil to reduce. Mix Bisto to a paste with water and

add to jelly. Add wine and seasonings. Simmer gently and lastly, add almonds.

MRS JULIAN SPICER: *Suffolk*

PETIT PANNA
for 4 people

4 ozs rump steak	4 ozs Frankfurter sausages
4 ozs bacon	4 ozs potato
4 ozs onion	4 hard boiled eggs
Cheese sauce	1 level teaspoon curry powder

Cut the steak, sausages, bacon, potato and onion into small squares and fry them all, separately in oil and butter. After they are cooked, mix them all together in a dish.

Cut the eggs in half and put in a separate dish, cover with the cheese sauce to which the curry powder has been added. Put under the grill to brown. Serve the two dishes together.

MRS JULIAN SPICER: *Suffolk*

KIDNEY RAGOUT
for 6-8 people

20 lambs' kidneys	4 medium onions
2 large cloves garlic	1 medium tin of tomatoes
1 glass of sherry	1 teaspoon tomato paste
½ teaspoon sugar	½ teaspoon thyme
Salt and pepper	Dash of tobasco
A little flour	Cooking oil (sunflower best)

Core kidneys and cut each one into 4 pieces. Coat with flour and fry gently in oil. Add fried onions and all other ingredients. Cook in casserole in medium oven until tender - about 2 hours. A little stock or water can be added if the sauce thickens too much.

MRS PATRICK TELFER-SMOLLETT: *Scotland*

STUFFED SHOULDER OF LAMB
for 6 people

6 lb (before boning) shoulder of lamb

2 onions	2 ozs butter
8 ozs breadcrumbs	1 small head of celery
2 eating apples	4 ozs chopped walnuts
½ teaspoon mixed herbs	1 tablespoon chopped parsley
3 tablespoons cream	Seasoning

Ask your butcher to de-bone the shoulder. Remove the outside tough skin and any fat inside the shoulder. As this is a fatty piece of meat, it must be cooked at a high temperature. Cook finely chopped onions in butter till soft, but not coloured. Mix bread, chopped celery, chopped apple, walnuts and herbs together, taste for seasoning and bind with cream.

Carefully sew up the shoulder with the stuffing inside. Rub with salt and oil on outside. Cook at 400-425°F for 20 minutes per pound, plus a little longer if needed. Baste every quarter of an hour. Keep joint covered during this time, removing cover for the last half to three quarters of an hour of cooking. Make gravy from roasting juices. Lamb gravy mush be thinnish.

DAVID TELFER-SMOLLETT ESQ: *Cambridgeshire*

ROGNONS LIÈGEOISE

1 lb veal kidneys	¼ lb butter
½ pint cream	8 juniper berries
1 soup spoon Brandy	Salt and pepper

Cook kidneys gently in melted butter over very low heat. Add seasoning and the Juniper berries. When ready add heated brandy. Set alight. Add cream and stir gently. Serve immediately.

MADAME GERTRUDE WISSA: *London*

SAVOURY MEAT LOAF

for 8 people

1 lb best minced beef	1 lb pork sausage meat
2 medium sized onions	½ green pepper
6 sliced stuffed olives	Salt and pepper
6 ozs fresh white breadcrumbs	3 eggs
3 tablespoons chopped parsley	½ teaspoon tarragon
⅓ pint of milk	

Mix in a large bowl the minced beef, sausage meat, finely chopped onions, breadcrumbs, green pepper or olives, yolks of the three eggs, chopped parsley, tarragon and seasoning. Stiffly beat the egg whites and fold into the above mixture. Form a loaf with the mixture and place in long ovenproof dish with milk surrounding it, to be used for basting. Bake in moderate oven for 50-60 minutes, remembering to baste occasionally.

This dish can be served either hot or cold.

LADY ROWENA CRICHTON-STUART: *London*

FRIED CALVES LIVER

Slices of Calves' liver
Flour
Unsalted butter
Lemon juice
Salt and pepper

Cover slices of liver with lemon juice. Sprinkle with salt and freshly ground pepper. Leave for two or three hours, turning occasionally. Dust with flour and fry gently in foaming butter for the shortest possible time, otherwise the liver becomes tough.

THE LADY KEITH: *London*

RICH STEW
for 8 people

2½ lbs lean stewing steak
¼ lb streaky bacon, in cubes
Salt and pepper
Brandy
Stock or water

½ lb chopped onions
¼ lb mushrooms
3 tablespoons tomato purée
Orange peel

Dust chopped steak with seasoned flour. Fry onions and bacon. Fry steak. Add mushrooms, small piece of orange peel and tomato purée. Cover with stock or water. Add 2 tablespoons of brandy. Cook in earthenware casserole (if you have one, the flavour is much better), in oven at 350°F or Gas Mark 4, until sauce is dark red and shining and meat is tender – about 3 hours.

MRS ANTHONY HOBSON: *Hampshire*

SWEET AND SOUR PORK IN PANCAKES

1 lb fillet of pork, cut into small pieces
1½ tablespoons oil
2 tablespoons syrup
¾ pint stock
1 tablespoon cornflour
Juice of half a lemon

1 chopped onion
3 tablespoons wine vinegar
1 teaspoon Worcester sauce
Salt and pepper

Heat the oil and add chopped onion and fry gently until tender. Add syrup, vinegar, stock, Worcester sauce and lemon juice and bring to the boil. Add chopped pork and season to taste. Cook until the pork is tender (about 20 minutes) then mix cornflour with a little cold water until smooth and stir it in to thicken.

Prepare pancakes and fill with meat from saucepan and fold over. Pour remaining sauce over pancakes.

LADY CLARISSA EGLESTON: *London*

VEAL à la CRÈME

Veal or Pork fillets can be used.

Beat the fillets flat, season, egg and bread crumb and sauté in butter and oil.

Take enough double cream to just cover the number of fillets used, and bring to the boil. Add as many capers as you wish to the cream. Baste well and bake slowly in oven until tender.

Can all be prepared in advance and keeps well in the oven for tardy guests.

MRS MICHAEL GRAZEBROOK: *Dorset*

PORK FILLET IN CREAM
for 6-8 people

2 Pork fillets	½ pint double cream
1 or 2 cloves of garlic	½ lb mushrooms
Juice of 1 lemon	Salt and pepper

Cut the pork fillets into medallions and beat well. Marinate the medallions for as long as possible in lemon juice, garlic, olive oil and salt and pepper. Fry in butter until golden brown on both sides. Remove from the pan. Fry the mushrooms. Remove from fire and add the double cream. Season to taste.

MICHAEL INCHBALD ESQ: *London*

MUTTON CURRY
for 6 people

4-5 lbs mutton (I use the neck), cut up and trimmed of fat

2 medium onions, chopped	3 cloves of garlic, crushed
2 Bay leaves	8-10 cloves
8-10 peppercorns	8-10 coriander seeds
1 teaspoon ground ginger	1½ - 2 tablespoons flour
3 dessertspoons curry powder	

Cook onion and garlic gently until soft. Add curry powder and other spices. Cook gently for 3 or 4 minutes. Mix the meat into the curry mixture and brown slightly. Dredge with flour and continue cooking gently for a minute or two.

If you have no stock, dissolve 1 chicken or beef stock cube in 1 pint of boiling water. Add to meat and stir. Simmer for 15-30 minutes and then place at the bottom of oven of the AGA to cook overnight at the lowest temperature. If you have no AGA, cook slowly for 2½ - 3 hours.

Serve with boiled rice and a dish of sliced bananas in a plain French dressing. Small dishes of cucumber and tomato, if liked, but the rice and banana is essential.

THE HON LADY MOSLEY: *Orsay, France*

AUBERGINE & MINCE PIE
for 6 people

3 lbs aubergine, peeled, sliced and salted
Flour   Olive oil
1 pint homemade tomato sauce   8 ozs mozzarella cheese
3 ozs grated Parmesan cheese   ¾ lb mince
Salt and pepper

Flour and fry the aubergine without colouring them and when tender, remove from the pan and drain. Cook mince in pan with a little oil. In wide shallow dish put layers of aubergine, tomato sauce, mince, mozzarella, Parmesan and black pepper and salt. Repeat until dish is full, finishing with the cheese and a few drops of cream. Bake for at least one hour, covered in foil, in oven at Gas Mark 3. Leave uncovered for the last quarter of an hour until bubbling and golden.

Tomato Sauce
Soften finely chopped onion and garlic in oil. Add skinned tomatoes, herbs, salt and pepper, a little sugar and Basil if you have any. Simmer all together until it reaches the right consistency.

MRS JAMES WEST: *Warwickshire*

STUFFED LEG OF LAMB OR MUTTON
WITH CORIANDER
for 8 people

1 large leg of lamb or mutton	4-5 ozs stale wholewheat bread
1 tablespoon fresh parsley	1 tablespoon summer savory
1 tablespoon thyme	Juice of 1 orange
1 raw egg	1 lb sausage meat
Sea salt	Coarse ground black pepper
¾ pint stock	Cloves of garlic
Coriander seeds	

Put all the stuffing ingredients in a mixer or food processor to blend. Make an incision in the lamb or mutton. Insert at various places cloves of garlic and crushed coriander seeds. Rub the meat with salt and pepper. Brush the meat with a small amount of olive oil and lemon juice. Roast in the usual way. Serve with new potatoes, courgettes with mint and a green salad.

Nutmeg jelly complements this dish wonderfully.

MRS IAN THOMAS: *Essex*

BEEF & MUSHROOM STEW
for 4 people

1½ lbs Braising Steak	½ lb onions
½ lb mushrooms	1 clove garlic
¾ pint of stock	1 tablespoon lemon juice
1 teaspoon dried thyme, oregano	1 tablespoonful of flour

Cut the steak into cubes and brown in dripping in a flameproof casserole, add chopped onions and cook for a few minutes, then add the flour. Stir it well and add the stock, lemon juice, garlic, thyme, oregano and salt and pepper. Cover and cook in the oven at 300°F, Gas Mark 2, for 1½ hours. Take out and add the sliced mushrooms and cook for a further three quarters of an hour. Sprinkle with parsley and serve.

THE HON MRS RICHARD BEAUMONT: *London*

ALSCOTT PARK: *Warwickshire*

Hot Puddings

❧

Pecan Pie

Hot Orange Soufflé

Pommes Saint Christophe

Red Leg

Banana Fritters

Pears with Rum and Cream

Pears in Red Wine

Grand Marnier Soufflé

Prune Soufflé

Almond Puffs

Pineapple Pudding

Lemon Soufflé

Guards Pudding

Mrs Plum's Lemon Pudding

❧

PECAN PIE
for 6 people

Pastry for 1 crust pie	2½ tablespoons flour
6 ozs granulated sugar	4 eggs, lightly beaten
Pinch of salt	2 ozs softened butter
10½ ozs corn syrup	3 ozs shelled pecans

Pre-heat oven to 375°F (190°C or Gas Mark 5). Line a 10 inch flan tin with pastry. Combine flour and sugar. Combine eggs and butter. Stir in flour mixture, salt, corn syrup and pecans. Pour into pastry and bake for 10 minutes. Then reduce temperature to 350F (180°C or Gas Mark 4) and bake for a further 50 minutes. Serve warm or cool with either whipped cream or vanilla ice cream.

MRS RICHARD ALEXANDER: *London*

HOT ORANGE SOUFFLÉ
for 4 people

4 Oranges	1½ ozs unsalted butter
1½ ozs flour	Icing sugar to taste
1 tablespoon Grand Marnier	3 egg yolks
4 egg whites	¾ pint orange juice
1 extra orange	

Cut off flower end of 4 oranges, scoop out inside and leave quite dry. Butter the insides with unsalted butter and put aside. Sieve orange pieces for required amount of juice, add grated rind of the extra orange. Melt butter in saucepan, add flour, blend and add orange juice and stir until sauce is very thick and bubbling. Stir in the Grand Marnier and icing sugar. Cool and add egg yolks. Fold in the stiffly beaten egg whites and refill the orange cases with the mixture. Sprinkle tops with icing sugar and bake in a moderate oven at 350°F for 20-25 minutes.

MRS PHILIP BRIANT: *London*

POMMES SAINT CHRISTOPHE
for 6 people

1½ kg apples
125 g caster sugar
3 lumps of sugar for caramel
Apricot jam

Peel the apples and cut into small strips. Caramelise a pudding basin. Put in alternate helpings of apple and caster sugar until basin is full. Press well. Cook in a bain-marie for about three hours. Remove gently, turning out carefully on to a dish and cover with hot apricot jam.

MRS GERALD HOHLER: *Dorset*

RED LEG
an Albanian dish
for 6 people

1 vegetable marrow, grated and sprinkled with salt, avoiding seeded part. Leave in bowl to dehydrate for a couple of hours.

Make a sweet custard, add strained marrow and put in a buttered gratin dish. Cook in a bain marie in moderate oven until brownish on top. Sprinkle with brown sugar and serve with cream.

MADAME SARACHI: *London*

BANANA FRITTERS

1 egg white
Bananas
Caster sugar

Batter:
2 tablespoons flour
2 tablespoons warm water
1 dessertspoon of oil
Pinch of salt

Beat the batter ingredients well together, then add 1 stiffly beaten egg white and mix well. Cut each banana into quarters. Coat each portion with the batter. Deep fry in clean oil until golden and crisp. Roll in caster sugar and serve hot with thick cream.

THE LADY ST LEVAN: *Cornwall*

PEARS WITH RUM AND CREAM
for 6 people

6 Pears (not too ripe)
¼ lb brown sugar
3 ozs butter
¼ pint of cream
¾ tablespoons of rum
Sprinkling of orange juice

Peel and core pears and cut into quarters. Butter a fireproof dish and lay pears in it. Dot with butter cut in small pieces, sprinkle on sugar, rum and orange juice and bake in a moderate oven until tender and until the sugar has caramelised. Baste now and then. When pears are tender, remove with a perforated spoon to a clean serving dish and keep warm. Allow sauce to cool slightly, then mix in cream and pour over pears.

LORD GILLFORD: *London*

PEARS IN RED WINE
for 6 people

6 Pears
¼ pint of red wine
Strip of lemon rind
1 oz almonds, blanched and
shredded (optional)

¼ pint of water
1 teaspoon arrowroot
Small piece of cinnamon stick
5 ozs sugar lumps

Make syrup by dissolving sugar, water, wine and flavouring. Bring to the boil slowly and simmer for 2 or 3 minutes. Keeping stalks on pears, remove peel and eye from base and place in prepared syrup. Poach, covered, until tender for about 20 to 30 minutes. Remove pears and strain syrup. Mix arrowroot with a little water, mix with syrup and bring to the boil. Cook until liquid is clear. Pour over pears and finish with scattered almonds.

GRAND MARNIER SOUFFLÉ
for 8-10 people

10 eggs
Grand Marnier
5 tablespoons granulated sugar
Butter

Separate the whites and yolks of 10 eggs. Put 2 of the yolks to one side. In the top of a double boiler, beat the remaining 8 yolks until lemon coloured and end up by gradually beating in the granulated sugar. Cook the mixture over barely simmering water, stirring constantly with a whisk. As soon as the yolks have thickened, remove the top of the double boiler to a bowl of cracked ice and stir in 6 to 7 tablespoons of Grand Marnier.

Beat the 10 egg whites until stiff but not dry.

Fold in a third of the whites to the yolk mixture and mix thoroughly; then fold in the rest very lightly.

Pour this mixture into a pre-buttered 2 quart mould which has been sprinkled with caster sugar. Tie a strip of waxed paper round soufflé dish, leaving a band of paper above rim to allow for the rising soufflé. Butter the inside of this paper, the bit standing above the rim. Bake in a pre-heated oven at 450°F for 15 minutes. Sprinkle top lightly with icing sugar, remove waxed paper and serve immediately.

PRUNE SOUFFLÉ
for 4 people

½ lb prunes
4 eggs
3 ozs caster sugar

Beat the yolks of the eggs to a cream with 3 ozs of caster sugar and mix

89

them with ½ lb of prunes which have been previously stewed, drained, stones removed and fruit pulped with a fork. Add to this the stiffly whipped whites of the eggs and turn into a greased soufflé dish and bake in a moderate oven for 20 minutes. Serve at once with whipped cream.

ALMOND PUFFS
for 4 people

Beat 26 almonds very finely in a mortar or process in a Magimix with a spoonful of orange-flower water to prevent them oiling. Then add ¼ lb warmed butter, 1 gill of cream, a tablespoonful of flour, 1 egg white and 2 egg yolks. Mix well and sugar to taste. Butter some ramekin dishes for this mixture and bake in a moderate oven for half an hour. Serve with cream floured with a liqueur.

LEMON SOUFFLÉ
for 4 people

4 Eggs
3 tablespoons caster sugar
Juice and rind of 1 lemon

Beat the yolks of the eggs with the sugar, the grated rind and juice of the lemon for several minutes. Whip the egg whites and fold them in. Pour into a buttered soufflé dish and cook for 10-12 minutes in a medium to hot oven.

MADELEINE, GRÄFIN DOUGLAS: *London*

PINEAPPLE PUDDING

2 tins pineapple (10 slices each)	10½ ozs caster sugar
6 eggs	1 dessertspoon cornflour
A small glass of rum	Juice of 1 lemon

Liquidise 12 slices of pineapple and cut three slices into pieces. Put it all with 7 ozs sugar and the liquid from the tin into a saucepan and cook for ten minutes. Beat the eggs with a dessert spoon of cornflour. Add small glass of rum and the lemon juice. Pour on to the cooled, liquidised fruit. Caramelise a mould with a hole in the middle, using the remaining sugar (3½ ozs). Pour in mixture and place in bain-marie. Bake for 1 hour then test with needle to see if it is cooked. Turn out. Serve with thick cream.

MARCHESA D'VANZO: *Italy*

GUARDS PUDDING

3 ozs stale breadcrumbs   3 ozs butter
2 tablespoons caster sugar   1 tablespoon strawberry jam
1 egg   A very little milk
½ teaspoon of bicarbonate of soda

Melt the butter in a saucepan, put breadcrumbs in a basin with sugar, jam and beaten egg. Add melted butter and lastly the bicarbonate of soda, dissolved in a little milk. Stir well. Put in a greased basin and steam for 2 hours.

When serving, pour more hot jam over the pudding and serve with thick cream.

LADY ALEXANDRA METCALFE: *London*

MRS PLUM'S LEMON PUDDING
for 6 people

8 ozs sugar   2 eggs
2 ozs margarine   Grated rind and juice of 1 lemon
2 tablespoons flour   ½ pint milk

Heat the lemon juice and put into a basin with grated rind, sugar and margarine. Mix thoroughly. (The hot lemon juice will dissolve other ingredients). Stir in the flour and just a pinch of salt. Add the egg yolks and beat the mixture well, then gradually mix in ½ pint of milk. Beat egg whites stiffly and fold in. Put into straight sided dish and bake in oven for about ½ to ¾ hour at 350°F. Serve with cream.

MRS JAMES WEST: *Warwickshire*

ALNWICK CASTLE: *Northumberland*

Cold Puddings

Fruit and Cream Brulée
Raspberry Galette
Casata Pugliese
Italian Lemon Pie
Coffee Mousse
Chocolate Mousse
Mulberry Ice Cream
Chocolate Pudding
Victorian Brown Bread Ice Cream
Oranges and Sultanas
Fresh Mint Ice Cream
Floating Island
Crunchy Apricot & Orange Ice Cream
Hungarian Soufflé
Apple Brulée
Prune Mousse
Melon with Cherries
La Galette de Dordogne
Rich Apricot Cream
Crême de la Crême
Peach Syllabub
Black Currant Leaf Sorbet
Rose Petal Sorbet
Honey Mousse
St Barnabas Prune Cream
Gabriel Pudding
Elderflower Sorbet
Somerton Pudding

FRUIT AND CREAM BRULÉE

Everyone must surely have had success with the well tried formula of placing sliced fresh fruits (peaches, raspberries, grapes) in the bottom of a soufflé dish, with a layer of whipped cream on top, followed hours later by a layer of caster sugar and caramelized under a very hot grill.

A delicious winter pudding can be made by substituting a well flavoured, slightly tangy apple purée. Allow to cool, then cover with ½ pint whipped cream. When set (overnight is best), sprinkle with a thick layer of caster sugar and place under a hot grill to caramelize. Leave to get cold.

MRS JULIAN BYNG: *Hertfordshire*

RASPBERRY GALETTE
for 6 people

For Almond pastry:

6 ozs plain flour	3 ozs butter
1 oz shortening	1½ ozs ground almonds
1½ ozs caster sugar1	egg yolk
1-2 tablespoons cold water	8 inch flan ring1
1½ lb raspberries	

For glaze:

¼ lb red currant jelly	¼ pint water
3 level tablespoons arrowroot	A little melted red currant jelly

Rub fats into flour, add almonds and sugar. Mix egg yolk with water and add to dry ingredients. Work to firm dough, chill then roll out. Line flan ring and bake blind for 10-15 minutes in a medium oven. Allow to cool.

Brush base with melted red currant jelly, arrange raspberries in case and coat with glaze.

Glaze: Heat ¼ lb red currant jelly with ¼ pint water. Bring gently to the boil, blend with 3 level tablespoons arrowroot. Return to the pan and cook until clear plus another two minutes.

THE LADY EGREMONT: *Sussex*

CASATA PUGLIESE

for 10 people

Italian Savoiardi or plain Madeira cake

8½ ozs caster sugar

3 ozs mixed lemon and orange candied peel

Marsala - rum - glacé cherries

10 ozs butter

5 ozs plain chocolate

4 egg yolks

3 ozs peeled almonds

Put the almonds in a baking tin with a little butter and sugar and bake in the oven until golden brown, shaking from time to time. Chop them and add to mixed peel. Cut cherries in half and also add to peel. (Leave some cherries whole for decoration).

Whip the egg yolks well with the sugar, add the butter (made soft) in pieces and continue to whip. Add 4 tablespoons of rum and whip again. Divide this cream in two. In one part add the grated chocolate and in the other the mixture of chopped almonds etc.

Wet a mould and line with polythene paper. Line the bottom and the sides of the mould with the sponge cake cut in slices. Sprinkle with Marsala. Pour in first the chocolate mixture and then the other one. Finish with more slices of sponge cake.

Put in the freezer overnight. Half an hour before serving, take the cake out of the freezer and leave in the refrigerator. Just before serving, un-mould on to a serving dish. Peel off the paper, sprinkle with a little Marsala and put some whole cherries on top for decoration.

MRS JOHN ELTON: *London*

ITALIAN LEMON PIE

for 4 people

2 lemons (juice and grated rind)

2 ozs butter   1 oz brown sugar

2 rounded tablespoons caster sugar

Grated chocolate for decoration

4 ozs digestive biscuits

1 medium frozen lemon mousse

¼ pint double cream

Crush biscuits with rolling pin. Melt butter, add brown sugar and biscuit and mix well. Press mixture into bottom and sides of a dish and leave to set.

Mash mousse to a cream with fork, add lemon rind, juice and caster sugar. Whip cream until thick but not stiff and fold into mixture. Turn lemon cream into crumb dish and sprinkle top with grated chocolate.

Put into refrigerator for 4-5 hours and serve as a pudding.

THE LADY HOWARD DE WALDEN: *Berkshire*

COFFEE MOUSSE
for 6 people

2 large eggs	2 ozs caster sugar
2 dessertspoons instant coffee	4 tablespoons water
½ oz gelatine	½ pint double cream

Beat eggs and sugar together until thick and creamy. Dissolve gelatine in water and add coffee powder; mix thoroughly and add to beaten egg mixture. Fold in whipped cream. Place in refrigerator to set.

THE DUCHESS OF NORTHUMBERLAND

CREAMY CHOCOLATE MOUSSE
for 6 people

4 ozs dark chocolate	4 eggs
½ pint cream	1 tablespoon brandy

Separate the eggs. Chop chocolate roughly and put into top of double saucepan. Stir over hot water until melted. Remove from the heat, cool a little and then blend in egg yolks one at a time. Beat until the mixture is smooth and thick. Foldd in whipped cream, brandy and then stiffly beaten egg whites.

Spoon into individual serving dishes and refrigerate until firm. Decorate as desired.

THE DUCHESS OF NORTHUMBERLAND

MULBERRY ICE CREAM
for 8 people

2 lbs mulberries
1 pint full cream milk
Sugar

1 pint double cream
8 egg yolks

Stew mulberries well in a very little water and sugar to taste. Sieve.

Make a custard with the egg yolks and milk. Cool. Add lightly beaten double cream, then the mulberry juice. Freeze. Serve with extra mulberry syrup poured on top and dentelles or thin sponge fingers.

MRS RICHARD STICKNEY: *London*

CHOCOLATE PUDDING
for 8 people

½ cup very strong coffee
16 oz bar plain chocolate
10 eggs (separated)

Melt chocolate bar in warm coffee. Stir well, adding a little more water if necessary. When cool, add egg yolks and fold mixture into beaten whites of eggs. Refrigerate for at least 12 hours.

MRS PATRICK TELFER-SMOLLETT: *Scotland*

VICTORIAN BROWN BREAD ICE CREAM

3 ozs wholemeal bread (without crusts)
¼ pint single cream
½ teaspoon vanilla essence

½ pint double cream
3 ozs icing sugar

For syrup:
2 ozs granulated sugar

3 tablespoons water

Dry bread in oven until crisp and crush with rolling pin. Whisk double and single cream until it leaves a slight trail. Fold in sieved icing sugar and vanilla essence. Put into freezer, covered for one hour.

97

Dissolve granulated sugar in water and boil for 1 minute. Stir in brown breadcrumbs. When mixture has cooled slightly, mix with a fork so it is crumbly and leave until cold. Turn ice cream into basin and beat until smooth. Fold in crumb mixture and freeze for at least 2 hours.

THE VISCOUNTESS WHITELAW: *Cumbria*

ORANGES AND SULTANAS
for 4 people

4 oranges	¼ lb granulated sugar
2½ fluid ozs water	Handful of sultanas
Pine nuts	Cointreau

Remove peel, pith and pips from the oranges. Slice oranges into thin slices and place in glass bowl. Take peel and slice in very thin strips, add a little water and boil until tender, strain under cold water and add to the sliced oranges. Make a syrup with the sugar and water, to which you add a large soup spoon of Cointreau and also a large spoonful of pine nuts. Pour this on to the fruit while still hot and leave to cool.

MADAME GERTRUDE WISSA: *London*

FRESH MINT ICE CREAM

4 ozs caster sugar
¼ pint water
1 teacup of mint leaves, stripped from stems
Extra leaves for decorating
Juice of ½ lemon
½ pint double cream

Dissolve sugar in water over low heat, then bring to the boil. Wash mint leaves and squeeze dry. Finely chop in blender and add to hot syrup. Leave until mixture is cold and then strain into basin. Add strained juice of lemon and double cream. Lightly whisk all liquids together. Add a little green food colouring. Put into a container, cover and place in freezer. When the mixture becomes icy, fork the edges into the centre. When the ice cream is nearly frozen transfer to basin and give a good beating. I find it is best frozen in a loaf tin and cut into slices, decorated with sugared mint leaves, (leaves brushed lightly with egg whites and dredged thoroughly with caster sugar).

Allow 30 minutes for ice cream to soften before serving.

MRS ROSS HANBURY: *Rutland*

FLOATING ISLAND
for 6 people

6 eggs
16 sugar lumps
6 level tablespoons caster sugar
2 oz packet of gelatine

Dissolve gelatine in a little water. Make syrup with sugar lumps and half a cup of water. Whisk the whites of the eggs very stiffly and add caster sugar towards the end of the beating, adding a little at a time. To this mixture gently add the gelatine and then syrup. Have ready an oiled jelly mould. Pour mixture into it to set. Make a cold Sabayon sauce, adding Curaçao instead of sherry. When the pudding is set, it can be upturned on a large dish, preferably round, with the sauce poured over it.

CRUNCHY APRICOT & ORANGE ICE CREAM
for 4 people

½ lb dried apricots	1 orange
2 ozs flaked almonds	1 egg white
Caramel made with 4 oz caster sugar and a nut of butter	
1 oz sugar	Cinnamon stick
½ pint of cream	

Cover apricots with water and soak overnight. Cook apricots in a covered pan in the water they soaked in with the sugar, the rind of the orange (which has been removed with a potato peeler), the fruit of the orange and a stick of cinnamon. Blend and allow to cool.

Make caramel by melting sugar with butter and when just turning golden, add flaked almonds and let them toast in caramel until deep brown but not burned. Turn on to greaseproof paper and spread to a thin layer. When cold, break into small pieces.

Whip cream with egg white until just holding shape. Mix in apricot mixture and add two-thirds of nutty caramel. Put in freezer and allow to freeze.

Serve in scoops in a bowl with the remainder of caramel sprinkled on top.

LADY OWEN: *Warwickshire*

HUNGARIAN SOUFFLÉ
for 4 people

3 tablespoons of golden syrup
1½ teaspoons powdered gelatine
3 eggs
½ pint double cream
2 tablespoons of Cointreau

Dissolve gelatine in as little water as possible. Heat the golden syrup but do not boil. Pour into dissolved gelatine and leave to cool. Divide eggs and whisk whites until stiff. When gelatine is not quite set, pour into whites, put into a wet mould and allow to set.

Put egg yolks, 1 tablespoon of golden syrup, cream and Cointreau in a bowl and whisk until it thickens. When mould has set, turn out and pour sauce over the top. Serve with plain biscuits or sponge fingers.

MRS MARK WINN: *Yorkshire*

APPLE BRULÉE
for 8 people

Cooking apples	Sugar
Water	1½ ozs granulated sugar
4 (size 5 standard) egg yolks	¾ pint double cream (boiling)

First stew the fruit in 1 tablespoon of water. When ready, put into a soufflé dish, leaving 2 inches space at the top. Meanwhile boil sugar and water together until they caramelise. As it turns brown, pour into the apples. Stir well and allow to cool.

Make a crème anglaise with sugar, egg yolks and cream. Gradually beat the sugar into the egg yolks in a mixing bowl and continue beating for two or three minutes, until the mixture is pale yellow. Still beating, very gradually pour in the boiling cream, in a slow stream of drops so that the egg yolks are slowly warmed. Pour the mixture into a saucepan and place over a moderate heat, stirring slowly and continuously with a wooden spoon, until the crème thickens. Do not let the custard come anywhere near simmering. Then take the mixture away from the heat and beat for one or two minutes. Strain through a fine sieve on to the top of the apples. Put dish into fridge. When mixture is very cold, make another caramel and pour on top of the crème and let it harden.

MISS NINA CAMPBELL: *London*

PRUNE MOUSSE
for 6 people

½ lb prunes, soaked overnight in tea
Sugar to taste
Rind of half a lemon and a squeeze of lemon juice
¼ pint prune juice
½ oz gelatine
3 tablespoons lightly whipped cream
1 egg white, whisked to a firm snow

Simmer prunes till tender in the tea in which they have soaked, add sugar, lemon rind. When tender, drain and sieve, add lemon juice. Add gelatine to prune juice and dissolve over gentle heat. Stir into purée and test for sweetness. When cold, fold in cream and lastly egg white.

PRINCESS ALPHONSE DE CHIMAY: *Warwickshire*

MELON WITH CHERRIES
for 4 people

2 medium canteloup, cavaillon or ogen melons
About 5 ozs caster sugar or 2 tablespoons maple syrup
4 ozs stoned cherries
Squeeze of lemon juice
⅓ bottle of champagne

Cut the melons in half and remove the seeds. Scoop out the flesh, being careful not to cut through the skin (a grapefruit knife is useful for this).

Cut the flesh into small cubes and place in a bowl. Add the sugar (or maple syrup), cherries and the champagne and chill for several hours or better still, overnight. Also chill the half shells of the melons.

When you are ready to serve, test the fruit for sweetness and, if necessary, stir in a little more sugar or maple syrup. Divide the fruit between the melon shells. They may need to have a little piece cut off the bottom so that they stand upright but be careful not to cut through to the flesh or the juice will run out.

PATRICK FORBES ESQ: *London*

LA GALLETTE de DORDOGNE
for 6-8 people

Sweet Short Pastry

8 ozs plain flour	Pinch of salt
4 ozs butter	2 ozs caster sugar
1 egg yolk	1 or 2 tablespoons water
1 loose based 9 inch flan dish	

Filling

4 ozs broken walnuts	2 level tablespoons honey
¼ pint single cream	Dusting caster sugar

Make pastry, roll out and fit in base of tin. Fill tin with chopped walnuts, mixed with honey and 1 tablespoon of cream. Cover with the rest of the pastry and make 3 slashes on top. Brush surface with the rest of the cream and dust with sugar. Bake tart in moderate oven for about 25 minutes. To be eaten cold or warm.

MRS MICHAEL GRAZEBROOK: *Dorset*

RICH APRICOT CREAM
for 6 people

8 ozs dried apricot soaked in water overnight   Juice of half a lemon
4 tablespoons apricot brandy   2 medium eggs
10 fluid ozs thick cream   1 oz chocolate curls
6-12 Langue de Chat biscuits

Cook apricots, add extra water if necessary to just over fruit. Bring to the boil and simmer for about 25 minutes. Cool slightly. Purée the apricots, adding the lemon juice and apricot brandy. Cool completely.
Separate the egg whites from the yolks and whisk whites until stiff and they form peaks. Whip cream until thick. Fold the whipped cream into the purée, then fold in egg whites. Pour the mixture into a serving dish and chill. Arrange the chocolate curls on top of the chilled dessert. Serve with langue de chat biscuits.

THE MARQUESS OF HERTFORD: *Warwickshire*

CRÈME de la CRÈME
for 7 people

Beat the whites of 5 eggs until stiff but not dry, beating in ¼ of a teaspoonful of cream of tartar and one cup of granulated sugar, a little at a time. Butter a 9 inch pie plate (this allows servings for 7 with no need to stint helpings). Pour the meringue mixture over the plate, spreading evenly. Bake for 1 hour in an oven heated to 200F. Remove from the oven and cool.

Beat the yolks of the 5 eggs until thick and place in a double boiler with 4 tablespoons of lemon juice and the grated rind of 1 lemon and ½ a cup of sugar. Cook for about 10 minutes or until thick.

Beat half a pint of heavy cream with a few drops of vanilla essence.

Spread a thin layer of this cream over the meringue, then spread the lemon mixture and top off with the remaining cream. Place in a refrigerator for at least 2 hours and serve very cold.

THE LADY MOWBRAY AND STOURTON: *Angus*

PEACH SYLLABUB
for 6-8 people

¾ pint dry white wine
2 tablespoons lemon juice
6 ripe peaches

3 ozs caster sugar
2 level teaspoons grated lemon rind
½ pint double cream

Mix wine, sugar, lemon juice and rind in a large basin. Skin the peaches by pouring boiling water over them and leaving them for 2 or 3 seconds. Drain and remove stones. Slice thickly and add to above. Leave for several hours. Drain peaches and reserve juices. Divide slices into individual glasses.

Add wine mixture to cream and whisk until stiff. Spoon over slices and chill. Serve on day of making.

THE HON MRS CHRISTOPHER SHARPLES: *Berkshire*

BLACK CURRANT LEAF SORBET
for 6-8 people

1 pint water
Pared rind of 2 lemons
4 handfuls of black currant leaves
1 lb black currants

6 ozs sugar
Juice of 3 lemons
Green colouring

Make a syrup by putting rind of lemons, sugar and water in saucepan. Dissolve slowly then boil rapidly for 6 minutes. Add black currant leaves, cover and let it get cool. Allow it to infuse until well flavoured, then drain, squeezing the leaves. Strain through fine sieve and add lemon juice and few drops of colouring to produce a very pale green. Freeze in bowl or individual pots until firm.

Cook black currants in just enough water to cover with 2 tablespoons of sugar. Take three quarters of this mixture and liquidise it. Add to the rest of the cooked black currants and serve hot in sauceboat with sorbet.

MRS JAMES WEST: *Warwickshire*

ROSE PETAL SORBET

You don't need a large rose garden, just a friendly chemist who will let you have a small bottle of concentrated rose water. They undilute ordinary rose water 3 to 1 to make the concentrate so this mixture is very strong and a shaky hand or over-enthusiastic tip of the bottle will produce a really filthy taste.

Make a syrup with 1 pint of water and 8 ozs sugar. Stir until sugar melts and then boil for about 10 minutes. Add juice of one large or two small lemons and cool. Add 2 teaspoons of rose concentrate to taste and one or two drops of red colouring to make it a very pale pink, then freeze.

When it has frozen, put it in a food processor or electric mixer and beat well, adding about half a well beaten egg white and re-freeze. Remove about half an hour before serving.

MRS CHARLES SHEEPSHANKS: *Yorkshire*

HONEY MOUSSE
for 6 people

8 eggs   10 ozs honey
Slightly less than ½ pint cream

Separate the yolks from the whites of the eggs and beat whites until very stiff. Heat 10 ozs honey until very hot in bain marie and then pour slowly over beaten egg yolks, letting the honey pour from some height. Whip until mixture thickens, then pour in the egg white first and then the beaten cream.

Chill well. Chopped almonds can be sprinkled on top.

105

ST BARNABAS' PRUNE CREAM
for 6 people

1 8oz tin of prunes or 8 ozs of prunes, soaked overnight and stewed
in sugar
½ pint of double cream   Chopped almonds
Sugar   Juice of 1 lemon

Stone and mush prunes, add lemon juice and sugar. Add whipped cream
and garnish with lightly roasted chopped almonds.

MADAME SARACHI: *London*

GABRIEL PUDDING
for 4 people

¼ pint double cream   ¼ pint yoghourt
2 large ripe bananas   Small jar of stem ginger
1 dessertspoon browned, chopped nuts

Beat cream until thick. Add yoghourt and chopped bananas plus two
teaspoons of the syrup from the ginger and one heaped dessertspoon of
finely chopped ginger. Put into a glass bowl and sprinkle with the nuts.
Leave in the fridge for a couple of hours before serving. Serve with some
firm biscuits.

COUNTESS CHARLES DE SALIS: *Somerset*

SOMERTON PUDDING
Serves 6 people

1¾ lbs fruit (raspberries, strawberries, blueberries, blackberries,
redcurrants, blackcurrants, cherries and the odd grape)
5 ozs caster sugar
Juice of half a lemon
1 small farmhouse white loaf, 1-2 days old
Butter and thick cream

This is a variation of the classic summer pudding, using what one has in
the larder. Make up the bulk of the 1¾ lbs of fruit with raspberries and red

106

currants. The remainder can be a variety of the above, according to taste.

Remove the stalks from the currants and stone any cherries. Rinse the fruit taking out any mouldy raspberries. Cut the larger fruit into small pieces.

Place the sugar, fruit and lemon juice in a large saucepan and cook over a medium heat until the sugar has melted – about 3-4 minutes. Do not over-cook. Remove from heat.

Lightly butter a 1½ pint pudding basin. Slice the bread and remove the crusts, then line the basin, slightly overlapping the slices and pressing them together to seal the joins. I find scissors helpful to cut the bread to size.

Reserve a cupful of the juice and pour the fruit into the lined basin. Place a layer of bread on top and cover with a loose sheet of cling-film. Then put a small plate or saucer on top and add a 2 lb wieght to compress the pudding. Refrigerate overnight.

Before serving, slip a knife around the inside edge and turn out on to a dish, pouring over the reserved juice. Decorate with a few berries and a sprig of mint. Serve sliced with cream on top.

GRAHAM REDGRAVE-RUST ESQ: *Suffolk*

ELDERFLOWER SORBET
serves 6 people

Zest of one orange	Juice of one lemon
3 large handfuls of elderflowers	9 ozs caster sugar

Put orange zest, lemon juice and elderflowers in a large bowl. Boil sugar with 1 pint of water for about seven minutes to make a syrup. Pour hot syrup over fruit and flowers and leave to steep for about an hour. Strain liquid through a fine sieve lined with muslin. Transfer to a container to freeze.
Once the mixture is half frozen, break up with a fork, then re-freeze. Do this twice.

Serve with homemade shortbread biscuits.

MRS CHARLES HELMORE: *Hampshire*

RAGLEY HALL: *Warwickshire*

Savouries

Tomato Ice
Iced Brie
Dominicans
Welsh Rarebit
Parmesan Wafers
Cheese Cushions
Saighton Savoury
Mushrooms au Gratin

TOMATO ICE
Either as a first course or a savoury

Equal proportions of mayonnaise (I always make my own with olive oil, but you can perfectly well use good bought mayonnaise), tinned tomato purée and sour cream.

Mix all three with plenty of salt and ground pepper, a few small specks of crushed garlic and the juice of half a small onion.

Freeze, preferably in the dish in which it is to be served. Place foil on the top. Take out of the freezer and put in the fridge at least an hour before serving.

Decorate with thin slices of cucumber or peeled prawns and serve with hot cheese biscuits.

THE LADY HOLDERNESS: *Yorkshire*

ICED BRIE
for 4 people

8 ozs Brie cheese (preferably without skin)
6 tablespoons dry white wine
6 ozs double cream
1¼ teaspoons salt
Pinch of cayenne pepper
3 tablespoons fresh white breadcrumbs
1 oz freshly grated Parmesan cheese

Force Brie through a fine sieve, leaving skin on if too ripe. Add wine and cream until the mixture is almost liquid. Add seasonings and breadcrumbs. Pour mixture into an ice tray. Set firm (approximately 2 hours) in freezing compartment.

To serve, cut into 1½ inch squares and sprinkle with Parmesan cheese
Serve very cold but not frozen.

MISS ANNE MASSINGBERD-MUNDY: *London*

DOMINICANS

makes 11 or 12

2ozs Butter	2 ozs plain flour
6 Eggs (separated)	6 ozs Parmesan cheese
Milk	

Make a thick Béchamel sauce with butter, flour and milk. Mix well and allow to cool slightly. Add beaten egg yolks and grated parmesan cheese.

Whip whites until very stiff and then fold into mixture. Pour into greased castle pudding tins and fill three quarters full. Cover each tin with greased paper or foil, tied down with string.

Steam for 20 minutes in a covered saucepan, filled halfway up the tins with boiling water. Turn out on to greased fireproof dish and pour over a small bowl full of cream mixed with the remainder of the Parmesan cheese. Bake 10 minutes in a moderate oven. Once the Dominicans are turned out they can wait 30 minutes or so before baking.

LADY ELIZABETH SHAKERLEY: *London*

CHEESE CUSHIONS

Pasta pastry:

8 ozs plain flour	Pinch of salt
2 ozs butter	Lukewarm water to mix

Filling:

6 ozs cheese	2 ozs butter
1 egg	Seasoning

Make filling by creaming butter, beating in cheese then egg and seasoning. Roll out dough thinly on a lightly floured board. Make rounds 2½ inches in diameter. Damp edges, put a good ½ teaspoonful in each round, fold over and press edges together. Fry cushions in deep fat until nicely browned. Drain and serve hot, sprinkled with some grated cheese.

THE MARCHIONESS OF HERTFORD: *Warwickshire*

WELSH RAREBIT

A war-time recipe from Yorkshire
for 4 people

1 oz margarine
1 oz plain flour
Pinch of salt
1 good teaspoonful of mustard powder
2 ozs grated cheese
½ pint of milk

Make an ordinary Béchamel sauce with the margarine and flour and enough milk so it is fairly thick. Add mustard and salt and then grated cheese. Put in a saucepan on a very low flame to cook gently for about a quarter of an hour, stirring from time to time. Bring sharply to the boil just before eating. Pour into a sauceboat and spoon over crisp hot toast. Eat immdediately.

THE LADY HOWARD DE WALDEN: *Berkshire*

PARMESAN WAFERS

Quickly dip some think ice cream wafer biscuits in melted clarified melted butter, sprinkle liberally with Parmesan cheese and brown in a hot oven. Serve immediately.

SAIGHTON SAVOURY

for 4 people

1 tablespoon butter	1 tablespoon milk
1 large egg, separated	5 ozs Cheshire cheese
Dash of Worcester sauce	½ teaspoon mustard
Pinch of cayenne pepper	4 slices (medium cut) from small white loaf

First melt the butter, then add grated cheese, milk, mustard, Worcester sauce and seasoning. Stir constantly over low heat until the cheese has melted. Remove pan to cool for a minute the add egg yolk and stir in until smooth.

Whisk egg white until stiff and fork into mixture.

Have hot buttered toast to hand (crusts removed). Spoon the mixture on to each slice and place under hot grill until golden brown. Serve immediately.

SALLY, DUCHESS OF WESTMINSTER: *Gloucestershire*

MUSHROOMS au GRATIN
for 4 people

Preheat oven to Gas Mark 7 (220° c).

Wash and peel mushrooms and arrange, skin side down, in a lightly buttered fire proof dish, interspersed with the stalks.

Sprinkle lightly with salt, pepper, chopped shallot, parsley and cheese, then cover thickly with the breadcrumbs. Place a knob of butter on each mushroom.

Place on the top shelf of pre-heated oven for 12-15 minutes.

Serve in the dish.

GEORGE DENISTOUN WEBSTER ESQ: *London*

CAMERON HOME FARM: *Loch Lomond*

Sauces, Cordials, Cakes
Sweetmeats & Garnishes

Sauce Hollandaise
A Blender Hollandaise
Bernaise Sauce
Sauce Soubise
Greek Lemon Sauce
Spaghetti Sauce
Tomato Sauce for Fish
Cumberland Sauce
Dandelion Bud Sauce
Hot Chocolate Sauce
Lemonade
Elderflower Water
Rum Punch
Pain Perdu
Cameron House Cake
Chocolate Curd Cake
Highland Gingerbread
Cheese Biscuits
Crispy Orange Biscuits
Chocolate Rum Truffles
Seville Orange Marmalade
Christmas Fruit Salad
Rowan Jelly
Homemade Mustard
Sara's Red Tomato Chutney

SAUCE HOLLANDAISE

3 tablespoons of wine vinegar	6 peppercorns
Half a bayleaf	A blade of mace
3 ozs butter	3 egg yolks
Salt and pepper	

Put the wine vinegar, peppercorns, bay leaf, mace and seasoning into a small saucepan and reduce to a dessert spoonful. Break yolks of eggs into a bowl and add vinegar and a small nut of butter. Beat well. Place the bowl in a bain-marie (on no account let the water of this boil) and, with a wooden spoon, stir until yolks thicken, then add the remainder of the butter a little at a time (the butter should be soft). Try not to thicken too quickly.

This sauce should be served warm rather than hot.

A BLENDER HOLLANDAISE SAUCE

Put 3 egg yolks into a liquidiser, add a few drops of lemon juice and 1 tablespoon of water. Blend for a minute then pour in slow but steady stream of 6 ozs boiling hot butter. When mixed, pour into warmed bowl and beat with wire whisk.

BERNAISE SAUCE

4 tablespoons white wine vinegar	6 peppercorns
Half a bayleaf	Pinch of tarragon and chervil
1 small chopped shallot	2 egg yolks
3 ozs softened butter	A teaspoonful of meat glaze
1 scant teaspoon tarragon	1 scant teaspoon chervil
Salt and pepper	

Proceed as for Hollandaise, adding shallot this time to the wine vinegar. When the sauce begins to thicken in the bain-marie, pour on the reduced vinegar and add the softened butter, nob by nob as the sauce thickens, stirring constantly. When finished adding the butter, stir in the meat glaze, tarragon and chervil. Taste for seasoning.

116

SAUCE SOUBISE

½ lb onions, blanched and finely chopped
½ pint of thick Béchamel
1 oz cutter

¼ pint cream
Salt and pepper

Simmer onions in the melted butter until tender but not coloured. Add onions to béchamel and simmer for 5 minutes. Put through sieve or liquidiser. Add cream.

GREEK LEMON SAUCE (Good with chicken)

1 oz butter
½ pint hot chicken stock
2 eggs
2 tablespoons cold water

2 level tablespoons flour
Salt and pepper
Juice of 1 or 2 lemons

Make a roux with the butter and flour and cook gently for 10 minutes. Then add hot stock very slowly, stirring all the time. Beat the eggs until light and frothy and while still beating, add the lemon juice and then the cold water. Now add the stock mixture gradually and return to the heat, taking care that once the hot stock has been added to the egg and lemon juice, the sauce does not boil, otherwise it will curdle.

SPAGHETTI SAUCE

1 16oz tin of peeled tomatoes
6 rashers of streaky bacon
1 teaspoon oregano or dried basil
1 tablespoon butter
6 cloves

1 small tin tomato purée
2 medium sized onions
1 tablespoon oil
2 large bay leaves
Salt and pepper

Melt the oil and butter in a fireproof casserole. Fry the bacon, cut in small strips. Add finely chopped onion and cover; cook until onion is soft but not coloured. Now add all the other ingredients. The tomatoes can be broken up with a knife or fork. Cover and simmer for about 15 minutes. Garlic can also be added and cooked with the onions.

TOMATO SAUCE FOR FISH

3 tablespoons tomato purée	8 ozs white wine
8 ozs double cream	1½ ozs grated cheese
1 oz butter	Salt and pepper

Mix together tomato purée and white wine, add cheese and butter. Whip cream lightly. Cook sauce gently and add whipped cream. Pour over fish.

CUMBERLAND SAUCE

4 oranges	2 lemons
1 gill of Port	½ gill of vinegar
1 dessertspoon French mustard	2 tablespoons caster sugar
1 lb red currant jelly	Salt and pepper

Finely shred the peel of the oranges and lemons. Boil for 5 minutes, or until tender, in water and drain. Return to the saucepan and add the port, vinegar, mustard, sugar, seasoning and juice of oranges and lemons.

Add the red currant jelly and cook slowly for about 20 minutes. A teaspoon of arrowroot slaked in a dessert spoon of water or Grand Marnier can be added. Strain, bottle and keep in the refrigerator.

DANDELION BUD SAUCE
for 4 people

A creamy white sauce
A teacupful of tightly furled dandelion buds, or rather less
4 triangles of crisp fried bread

The dandelions must be gathered before any of the petal appears. To impart their own distinct, slightly sharp flavour to whatever dish they grace, they should be added to a rich Béchamel sauce about 10 minutes before serving. Simmer with an occasional stir. Some of the buds will open and shed their petals which will then fleck the sauce like tiny streaks of egg yolk.

This dandelion sauce is excellent poured over poached or hard boiled eggs or with pieces of lamb or chicken (leftovers, in fact). The edge of the fireproof dish in which it is served should be garnished with triangles of fried bread, pointing upwards like battlements.

DAVID CARRITT ESQ: *Kent*

HOT CHOCOLATE SAUCE
for 6 people

3 ozs dark chocolate, broken into small pices   5 ozs icing sugar
5 ozs brown sugar   4 ozs cream
2 ozs butter   ½ teaspoon vanilla

Combine chocolate, sugar and cream in a saucepan. Melt and stir well and bring to the boil. Boil until it thickens. Add butter and vanilla. Remove from heat and beat until proper consistency for either sauce, fudge or frosting.

To be served hot with ice cream. It can be kept in the refrigerator and re-heated over hot water as needed.

MRS RICHARD ALEXANDER: *London*

LEMONADE

Put the thinly peeled rind of 3 large lemons (no white pith), the juice of the lemons, ½ lb lump sugar and a quart of boiling water into a large crock. Stir until sugar is dissolved and let it infuse for a few hours.

Strain and chill, adding, if you like, a sprig of mint and a few slices of lemon.

ELDERFLOWER WATER

This is a refreshing drink for the Summer and can be kept in bottles in a cool place for several weeks. Cut enough heads to make about a pint of well compressed flowers. Place in a large crock with the grated rind and juice of 2 lemons plus ½ lb lump sugar. Pour over this 3 pints of boiling water and stir until the water dissolves. Leave for 24 hours. Strain and pour into bottles. Leave in a dark, cool spot. Chill before serving.

CARIBBEAN RUM PUNCH

The basic recipe for a rum punch is: 1 part sour, 2 parts sweet, 3 parts strong, 4 parts weak.

Lime juice is the sour part. Not a sweetened lime cordial but the undiluted, unsweetened juice of limes. If lime juice is not available, use unsweetened lemon juice.

Sugar syrup is the sweet. Make your own sugar syrup earlier in the day by dissolving demarara sugar in an equal bulk of water. Using warm water will help to dissolve the sugar quicker but you will need time to let it cool before using it in the punch. Make as much as you like since it will keep and is always useful in other ways.

Rum is the strong part. Use either the light rums or the more traditional dark or Navy rums. The latter give a more traditional flavour.

Add 4 parts of water and mix well. Pour over ice and grate whole cinnamon and nutmeg on the top of the drink.

NB: Always grind your own whole spices. Whole spices freshly ground are better in flavour. They are certainly of better quality. For example, when the nutmegs are graded, they are floated in water. The ones with worm holes, thence with air inside, float on the top and the sound ones sink to the bottom. The 'floats' end up in the grinder.....

IAN THOMAS ESQ: *Essex*

PAIN PERDU

Cut a few slices from a slightly stale white loaf, not too thin and with crusts removed. Damp with a little milk, previously boiled with a tablespoonful of caster sugar and a teaspoon of vanilla essence and cooled off. Be careful not to get the bread sodden or it will fall apart. Dip the bread in 2 egg yolks which have been well beaten, coating evenly on both sides.

Fry to a golden brown in hot foaming butter. Dust with sugar while frying. Serve with thick cream, clotted cream if possible.

THE HON MRS SEYMOUR BARNES: *Malta*

CAMERON HOUSE CAKE
(Disaster proof for non-bakers)

1 lb self raising flour	1 lb mixed fruit (including peel)
½ lb soft brown sugar	1 lb solf margarine
2 ozs almonds (keep some for decoration)	
3 eggs	Cup of strong tea
½ teaspoon mixed spice	Pinch of cinnamon or nutmeg

Boil fruit, nuts, margarine, sugar and tea in saucepan for one minute. Cool. Blend cooled ingredients with flour and spices and lightly beaten eggs. Put in baking tin lined with greaseproof paper and bake in moderate oven, about 300°F for 2½ - 3 hours. Cool in tin.

MRS PATRICK TELFER-SMOLLETT: *Scotland*

CHOCOLATE CURD CAKE

6 ozs chocolate digestive biscuits	3 ozs butter, melted
½ lb Philidelphia cream cheese	4 ozs granulated sugar
6 oz plain chocolate, melted	2 large eggs, separated
A few drops of vanilla essence	½ pint double cream

Crush the digestive biscuits and mix into the melted butter. Spread on to the bottom of a spring-sided cake tine and cook in the oven for 10 minutes. Take out and allow to cool.

Mix the cream cheese, 2 ozs of sugar, egg yolks and essence together and add the melted chocolate.

Whisk the egg whites until stiff and fold in the remaining 2 ozs of sugar. Whisk the cream to the soft peak stage. Add the whisked cream to the chocolate mixture and mix thoroughly, then fold in the whisked egg whites. Turn the mixture on to the biscuit base and put into the fridge until required.

To serve, unclip the spring and remove the ring. Place curd cake on a serving plate, removing the bottom of the cake tin if you can, grate plain chocolate on to the top and enjoy.

MRS ADRIAN LEVIEN: *Northumberland*

HIGHLAND GINGERBREAD

½ lb butter	½ lb soft brown sugar
½ lb self raising flour	½ - ¾ lb black treacle
1 teaspoon bicarbonate of soda in ¼ cup of warm milk	
2 eggs	Juice of ½ lemon
2 tablespoons ground ginger	¼ lb crystallized ginger, chopped
1 tablespoon ground cinnamon	1 teaspoon ground cloves

Melt butter, sugar, beat in eggs and fold in all the other ingredients: warm treacle first. Add bicarbonate in milk last. Spread this thinly in two well greased tins and bake in a moderate oven for 1½ hours. If put in one tin it is liable to come over the top.

CHEESE BISCUITS
Makes about 20 biscuits

2 ozs grated Parmesan cheese	2 ozs grated Cheshire cheese
2 ozs soft butter	2 ozs plain flour, sifted
Pinch of cayenne pepper	

Mix all the ingredients together – the fat in the cheese will form the dough with the butter and flour. Roll out and cut with 2 inch cutter.

Bake for 10 minutes in oven at 190-195°C. This dough can be used for quiches, using savoury or fish fillings.

CRISPY ORANGE BISCUITS

Grated rind of 1 orange	2½ ozs butter
1 egg	4 ozs self raising flour
2½ ozs sugar	Sugar for sprinkling

Sieve flour and rub in fat. Add sugar and orange rind. Mix to stiff dough with egg yolk. Knead dough and roll out to ¼ inch thickness. Cut out with a 1½ inch cutter. Brush over with white of egg and sprinkle with sugar. Bake in a moderate oven for 10-15 minutes. Take care as they burn easily.

CHOCOLATE RUM TRUFFLES

9 ozs plain chocolate	4 ozs unsalted butter
2 ozs caster sugar	2 tablespoons thick cream
2 egg yolks	3 tablespoons rum

Melt the chocolate and butter in a saucepan over a low heat, stirring fairly constantly. Allow to cool. Put the egg yolks and sugar in a bowl and beat until pale, creamy and foaming. When the chocolate is cool, add slowly to the mixture. Now add the cream and rum.

Put the mixture in refrigerator until right texture to roll. The simplest way to do this is to scrape the surface of the mixture with two teaspoons, shaping the chocolate to the size of large marbles. Now roll in cocoa, making sure your hands are sufficiently covered in cocoa, otherwise the chocolate will melt.

Store at once in deep freeze or refrigerator.

LADY TANIA COMPTON: *London*

SEVILLE ORANGE MARMALADE (1)
Makes about 6 lbs

1 lb Seville oranges
3 pints of cold water
Strained juice of 2 large lemons
3 lbs Preserving sugar - or cube sugar can be used

Wash, halve and squeeze the juice from the oranges. Keep all pips. Wash, halve, and squeeze lemons. Add juice and pips to those of the oranges. Tie all pips in a piece of muslin. Mince or shred the orange halves (I put mine in the Magimix). Put peel, water and bundle of pips into a preserving pan and stand for 24 hours.

Remove pip bag and squeeze out all jelly like substance. Place pan over medium heat and bring to the boil. Simmer until peel is thoroughly soft. Now stir in orange and lemon juice and sugar. Stir until sugar is completely melted. Raise heat to keep at a rapid boil and when it takes on a slightly darker colour, in little over half an hour, drop some on to a saucer to see if it jellifies. Stir at the very end to mix peel in the liquid. Leave for half an hour, stir once more, before pouring into pre-heated jam jars. Cover, seal and label.

SEVILLE ORANGE MARMALADE (2)
Makes about 20 lbs

Wash 4 lbs Seville oranges, halve and squeeze them, keeping pips in one bowl and juice in another. Slice peel finely or coarsely, according to preference, and put in a preserving pan. Add the orange juice and 12 pints of cold water. To the pips add 2 pints of boiling water and put aside. Leave all to stand for 24 hours.

Next Day: To each measured pint of the pulp, add 1 lb of preserving sugar. Heat gently until all the sugar is dissolved, stirring occasionally with a wooden spoon. Now raise the heat and cook fast until ready to set (test). When ready, remove from heat, stand for 5 minutes and pour into pre-heated hot jars. Cover, seal and label.

CHRISTMAS FRUIT SALAD
for 10 people

16 oz can red cherries	16 oz can peach slices
16 oz can pineapple pieces	½ cup granulated sugar
½ cup raisins	½ cup sultanas
½ cup prunes	½ cup chopped dried apricots
¾ cup Brandy	

Drain syrup from fruit. Remove stones. Put syrup in saucepan and add sugar and bring to boil. Add raisins, sultanas, prunes and apricots. Leave until cold and then add brandy.

Store in refrigerator at least 2 weeks before eating either in a bowl covered with cling film or store in jars. Will keep for months as long as it is in the fridge.

LADY ASHE: *Hampshire*

ROWANBERRY JELLY

Rowanberries, the fruit of the Mountain Ash, have a most attractive sweet, sour flavour and the jelly is especially good with hare and venison.

Gather the berries when quite ripe, quite sound and quite dry. Pull from the stalks and put in a deep pan. Cover them completely with water and boil until they appear to be soft (10-15 minutes). Mash slightly and strain through a jelly bag, giving the bag a squeeze now and then, to get part of the pulp through.

Allow 1 lb of sugar to 1 pint of juice. Put in a preserving pan and bring to the boil. Simmer steadily until it sets when tested on a cold saucer. Skim very carefully before pouring into pre-heated pots. It usually takes from 30-45 minutes to boil. It mellows and improves when 1 or 2 years old.

HOME-MADE MUSTARD

½ lb Colman's dry mustard
½ pint wine vinegar
6 peppercorns
1 dessertspoon olive oil

½ lb caster sugar
4 dry bay leaves
6 cloves

Mix mustard powder and sugar. Boil vinegar with the spices, pass through a sieve and pour boiling over mustard and sugar. Mix until smooth. Add olive oil, re-mix and put in jars.

SARA'S RED TOMATO CHUTNEY

3 lb skinned red tomatoes   2 lbs dark brown sugar
1 oz dry chillies (or about 6 fresh, chopped and seeded)
2 cloves of garlic, chopped
2 ozs root ginger, peeled and chopped
½ pint of red or white wine vinegar

Put all ingredients in a large saucepan and boil until thick. This takes about an hour. Bottle.

MRS MARY LUZ ARBUTHNOT-LESLIE: *Aberdeenshire*

Measures

LIQUID
British

1 quart - 2 pints - 40 fl ozs   1 pint - 4 gills - 20 fl ozs
1 gill - ¼ pint -5 fl ozs   1 tablespoon - just over ½ fl oz

Approximate Equivalents

British	*Metric*
1 quart	1.1 litre
35 fl ozs	1 litre
18 fl ozs	½ litre

American

1 quart - 2 pints - 32 fl ozs
1 pint - 2 cups - 16 fl ozs
1 cup - 8 fl ozs
1 tablespoon - ⅓ fl oz

Approximate equivalents

British	*American*
1 quart	2½ pints
1 pint	1¼ pints
½ pint	10 fl ozs
1 tablespoon	1½ tablespoons
1 dessertspoon	1 tablespoon

SOLID

British 16 ozs - 1 lb   *Metric* 1,000 g - 1 kilogramme

British	*Metric*
1 lb (16 ozs)	450 grammes
1 oz	25 grammes
2 lbs 3 ozs	1 kilo (1,000g)
1 lb 2 oz	½ kilo (500g)
9 ozs	¼ kilo (250g)
3½ ozs	100g

OVEN TEMPERATURES

Slow	150°C / 300°F	Gas Mark 1-2
Moderate	180°C / 350°F	4
Hot	220°C / 425°F	7
Very Hot	230°C / 450°F	8

The Housekeeper's Room
UPPARK: *Hampshire*

Recipes transcribed and edited by
CAROLINE PARKER

Typography, design and production by
JOHN COMMANDER

Reproduction and printing by
TITUS WILSON, KENDAL, CUMBRIA

Bound by
SMITH SETTLE, GUISLEY, WEST YORKSHIRE